developing digital short films

P9-EJT-734

Contents at a Glance

developing
digital short films

sherri sheridan

New Riders

800 East 96th Street, 3rd Floor, Indianapolis, Indiana 46240
Boston • Indianapolis • London • Munich • New York • San Francisco

Developing Digital Short Films

International Standard Book Number: 0-7357-1231-X

Library of Congress Catalog Card Number: 2001096477

Printed in the United States of America

First printing: April, 2004

09 08 07 06 05 04   7 6 5 4 3 2 1

Interpretation of the printing code: The rightmost double-digit number is the year of the book's printing; the rightmost single-digit number is the number of the book's printing. For example, the printing code 04-1 shows that the first printing of the book occurred in 2004.

Trademarks

Warning and Disclaimer

Publisher
Stephanie Wall

Production Manager
Gina Kanouse

Development Editor
Kathy Murray

Project Editor
Michael Thurston

Copy Editor
Keith Cline

Senior Indexer
Cheryl Lenser

Proofreader
Beth Trudell

Compositior
Kim Scott

Manufacturing Coordinator
Dan Uhrig

Interior Designer
Kim Scott

Cover Designers
Aren Howell
Sherri Sheridan

Cover Art Designer
Nathan Vogel

Media Developer
Jay Payne

Marketing
Scott Cowlin
Tammy Detrich

Publicity Manager
Susan Nixon

Table of Contents

Part I   Digital Storytelling

1 **Generating Ideas for Digital Short Films**   17

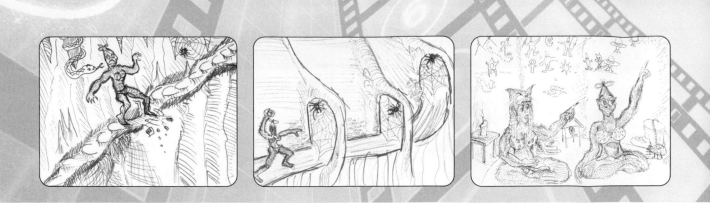

This book is dedicated to Nathan Vogel (a.k.a. DJ Dr. Spook), for all of his unwavering positivity, late-night drawing sessions, boundless enthusiasm, unconditional love, and 24/7 tech support over the last eleven years. Nate has inspired thousands of digital filmmakers and animators around the world through his art, music, friendship, technical assistance, films, classes, and events. Thank you, Nate, for being such a bright light in the world, and teaching me most of the digital stuff I know.

2 Creating Original Characters, Themes, and Visual Metaphors   55

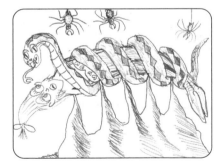

Part II Visualizing Your Script

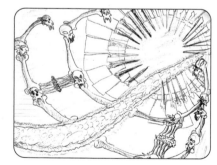

8 Preproduction Story-Editing Choices   273

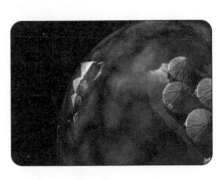

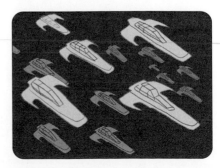

About the Author

Sherri Sheridan is the Creative Director at Minds Eye Media (**www.mindseyemedia.com**) in San Francisco, where she spends her time creating all sorts of digital projects. Over the years she has directed, produced, animated, written, and designed projects for a wide range of clients, including Fortune 500 companies, major record labels, TV/cable stations, feature-film studios, advertising agencies, and video game companies. She is the co-author of *Maya 2 Character Animation* (New Riders, 1999).

Currently, Sherri is creating a series of international Developing Digital Short Films Workshops based on the ideas in this book. She is also writing, developing, and directing several original scripts for digitally enhanced shorts and feature films.

Over the years, Sherri has helped inspire thousands of graduate computer animation students from around the world, helping them to tell their own stories using their favorite digital tools, at the Academy of Art College in San Francisco. While teaching these students, she started developing the foundation for a unique step-by-step digital visual storytelling process, which has grown into this wonderful book.

Before founding Minds Eye Media in 1995, she helped develop Shockwave Technology at Macromedia, and created the first Shockwave movies on the web. Sherri has a BA in English from U.C. Berkeley and went to San Francisco State to study interactive design and computer animation for her graduate work.

About the Contributors

Developing technically accurate books is a priority at New Riders Publishing. We rely on the skills and advice of technical experts to guide the authors in the creation and development of their manuscripts. The following reviewers have provided their input—and we offer our thanks for their hard work and dedication.

Illustrator/Technical Editor Part Three

Nathan Vogel (a.k.a. DJ/VJ Dr. Spook) is the 3D Special Effects Director at Minds Eye Media. He spends most of his time creating a wide variety of cutting-edge digital projects, music videos, dance party projection graphics, 3D interactive games, motion graphics, feature-film special effects shots, and original computer-animated shows. Nate is a certified Maya Trainer for Alias and has taught thousands of students around the world to realize their visions using all sorts of software. He is the co-author of *Maya 2 Character Animation* (New Riders, 1999).

Dr. Spook has a new trance record company called GeoMagnetic (**www.geomagnetic.tv**), featuring DVDs full of original digitally enhanced music videos and fresh electronic music from around the globe. One of his latest music videos, "Deep Step," is a featured case study in this book. Dr. Spook is an internationally renowned psychedelic trance DJ/VJ, who has recently begun writing his own trance music and is gearing up to release his first musical DVD in 2004.

Honorary Co-Writer Part One/Technical Editor Part One

Michael Feit Dougan is a USC graduate and scholarship winner. His screenwriting credits began with Public Access, which earned the Grand Jury Prize for "Best Picture" at Sundance. He went on to write, direct, and produce the short subjects "I/O Error" and "In This Corner." Michael produced and edited "Making Metamorphosis," which premiered at the 2001 Mill Valley Film Festival. As a professor, he won both the Presidential and ASB Teacher of the Year Award as well as being awarded "Teacher of the Week" by the *San Jose Mercury News*. Michael also regularly lectures at San Francisco's Film Arts Foundation and works as a freelance consultant. He can be reached through his company web site, **www.ArchimedesEntertainment.com**.

Acknowledgments

I would like to thank Nate for being there every step of the way to hold my hand throughout this very lengthy project. He drew hundreds of illustrations for this book, tech edited Part Three, and made sure my production files did not contain any sloppy software techniques. Thank you Nate for contributing so much of your creative magic to this book, and staying up with me deep into the night on so many deadlines to get this thing to print. *Developing Digital Short Films* is as much yours as it is mine in so many ways, and I thank you for always being there and teaching me so much along the way.

A very special thank you to Michael Feit Dougan for contributing so much of the brilliance to Part One of this book, and being such a tireless tech editor. I thought I knew how to tell a story and write a script, until I started taking his screenwriting classes at Film Arts Foundation in San Francisco. Thank you Michael for making writing fun again and for being the best writing teacher and script reader I have ever encountered. Although Michael did not write any sections of this book, a great deal of the information in Part One was gathered from his classes. I folded much of his knowledge into my step-by-step process to make it even better. Specific sections in Part One that are based on his ideas alone and deserve extra special credit include: The Goldman Five Character Trait System, 40 Plot Points for Feature Films, Play Let's Make It Worse, Setting the Pace of Your Scenes (Scene Shapes), and the screenwriting exercises at the end of Chapter 4.

I would also like to thank all of my family and friends, who I have not seen much of over the last three years while writing this book. My late mother, Mary Jane (MJ) Sheridan, for instilling in me a great love of the English language, literature, reading, poetry, writing, and fine arts at such an early age. My father, Thomas (TJ) Sheridan, for always being there and giving me such wise warrior advice all along the way. Scott Jenkins for the technical assistance and dog wrangling. Shaffer and Aslan for being such patient and hard-working canine models. Mary-Ann Mullen, for helping with typing and always brightening my day with her cheerful thoughts and phone calls. Monika Imagika Magana, for being my other set of hands on Part Three and a fabulous digital effects model.

A very special thank you to all of my teachers over the years, including those from Film Arts Foundation in San Francisco. Special thanks to Daven Gee, Greg Harrison, Vivian Hillgrove, Daniel Olmstead, David Lynch, Mitchell Block, David Freeman, Brooke Hinton, Michael Schneider, T. Harv Eker, Walter Murch, William Goldman, and Francis Coppola. Thanks to Brennan Doyle for the digital camera shot feedback, Peter Moody for the local location shot tips, and Kent at Fatbox Films for the talking cow images. Thanks to Robert McKee for writing *Story*, Michael Hauge for *Writing Screenplays That Sell*, Christopher Vogeler for *The Writer's Journey*, and Linda Seger for all of her great books. Joseph Campbell for being a visionary ahead of his time. Kevin Cain for asking me to teach my first 3D story concept class at the Academy of Art College many years ago. Michael Dougan, John Gibson, Brook Hinton, and Nathan Vogel for tech editing this book. And a big thank you to all of my students over the years, who have taught me so much by testing out all of my wacky homework assignments, and providing such valuable feedback.

A higher level of cosmic thank yous and boundless appreciation for the constant guidance, love, light, good energy, information, ideas, synchronicities, and inspiration on this project from the Supreme Being (a.k.a. God). Thank you for presenting me with this magnificent opportunity to inspire others to be creative and tell their own stories. Another set of higher frequency thank yous to The Ray Lords of the Great Bear, Space Cowboy, and all of my guides. Sanaya Roman, Duane Packer, Orin, and Da Ben for all of their amazing books, tapes, and seminars. Michael Gosney for the Arcosanti trip that inspired the direction of the material in these pages, and The Hopi Elders for the sacred cornfield.

Many thanks to all the artists and filmmakers who contributed to this book. Torsten Klimmer, for being such a visionary and showing us how we can all change the world through digital filmmaking (**www.liquidcrystalvision.com**). Greg Scanavino (a.k.a. Young American Primitive) for allowing me to use images from the "Beyond" music video. Lori Froling and Rhonda Malmlund at Universal/Geffen Records for granting me the use of images from the "Beyond" music video. Julie Hill at Artbeats for providing such beautiful stock footage. Glenn Grillo for being one of my bluescreen actors and contributing some of his digital images. Xenomorph (**www.xeno-morph.de**) for being such an enthusiastic bluescreen actor. Nate, Irina Mikailova, and Kenji Williams for the "Deep Step" music video images (**www.abastructure.net**). Neesa Griffith, lead singer of the soon to be really famous band Foxgluv (**www.foxgluv.net**), and all the other Foxglove music video dancers for the bluescreen shoot. The Goddess Temple in Santa Cruz for the use of the bluescreen. Patrick Flanagan and Stephanie Sutton for the super Megahydrin that kept me going during this long project. Maya Sanders, Sam Micelli, Donnie Bruce, Chris Hatala, Jeff Vacanti, Ivan Wachter, and all the other artists who contributed their work as inspiring examples in these pages.

Special thanks to all the folks at Adobe for making software that has changed the way we communicate visually. Steve Kilisky, and the entire After Effects team, for keeping my favorite software cutting edge. Tam Winston and Christopher Huntley, for the Movie Magic Screenwriter fully enabled (for shorts), non-timed-out demo version on the CD. Lee Harrison and Richard Manfredi at Sonic Fire Pro for the great soundtrack software. Frank Colin at Final Draft for keeping me up to date with my favorite screenwriting software and for being such cool guy.

This book would have never been written were it not for the constant and gentle encouragement of Chris Nelson from New Riders to "just do an outline." Thank you, Chris, for knowing that there was a book in this idea, and not giving up in your continued quest for me to write it over all those insightful lunches and dinners. Stephanie Wall for being such a fantastic person to work with and always listening to my wild ideas, while understanding my unique, funky, comic-book vision of the material. Thank you also, Stephanie, for having so much integrity, patience, and passion for this roller coaster project. A big super goddess thank you to Kathy Murray, for being such a wonderful editor, and adding such great energy and enthusiasm every step of the way. Jody Kennen, for overseeing the first version of the book. Steve Weiss, for getting this book back on track when it looked like it wasn't going to happen. The Pearson Legal Department for doing such a thorough and complete job on every issue that came up. Aren Howell for the fine tuning of our cover design. A very special thanks to all of the super talented editors and layout people at New Riders, including Michael Thurston and Kim Scott. And many more thanks to all of the other wonderful people at New Riders and Peachpit, who I never got to know, that helped make this such a groundbreaking and innovative book.

Tell Us What You Think

As the reader of this book, you are the most important critic and commentator. We value your opinion and want to know what we're doing right, what we could do better, what areas you'd like to see us publish in, and any other words of wisdom you're willing to pass our way.

As the Publisher for New Riders Publishing, I welcome your comments. You can fax, email, or write me directly to let me know what you did or didn't like about this book—as well as what we can do to make our books stronger. When you write, please be sure to include this book's title, ISBN, and author, as well as your name and phone or fax number. I will carefully review your comments and share them with the author and editors who worked on the book.

Please note that I cannot help you with technical problems related to the topic of this book, and that due to the high volume of email I receive, I might not be able to reply to every message.

Fax: 317-428-3382
Email: **stephanie.wall@peachpit.com**
Mail: Stephanie Wall
           Publisher
           New Riders Publishing/Peachpit Press
           800 East 96th Street, 3rd Floor
           Indianapolis, IN 46240 USA

Introduction

"The important thing is to create. Nothing else matters; creation is all."
—Pablo Picasso

Movies are the dominant art form of our time and of the past century. Each generation of filmmakers has a new set of tools available with which to communicate visually. At the dawn of the 21st century, this generation has an almost mind-boggling array of digital plasticity to stretch and bend into just about anything the artist can imagine. For the first time in history, creative people have been freed from the big Hollywood-type moviemaking system where it takes lots of people and huge amounts of equipment, time, and money to create a film. Now with some clever thinking and free time, an individual can craft a fine film with little expense. The trick today seems to be coming up with fresh ideas to cast in the digital forge of independent desktop moviemaking.

In our music video "Beyond" for Geffen's Young American Primitive, we created a 3D organic spaceship that blasts out of a 2D photo-collage temple. The musician was blue screened, then duplicated three times to become a new set of characters. Special effects and filters were layered on top of the clothes to create unique-looking alien creatures. This book will help you find original ways to present your story ideas using all the power of your digital tools.

In this shot from *Liquid Crystal Vision*, a dancer was blue screened wearing a blue top to make her upper body transparent. Special software techniques were used to make everything that was blue become transparent. The set was dropped in behind the dancing girl, using Tortsten's vacation footage from the Ankor Wat. This gives the impression that the girl is dancing like a spirit across the temple walls and saves the time and expense of having to shoot actors on location. What new ways can you use blue-screen techniques to show us something we have not seen before while taking full advantage of footage you have already shot?

Without a good story idea developed into a carefully crafted script, it is almost impossible to create a compelling film. There are no formulas for how to tell a guaranteed successful story in a film, but there are some tools screenwriters and storytellers have used for years to create compelling tales. Archetypal stories seek to re-create slices of the universal experience with unique individual and cultural expressions. This book focuses on creating short films that portray original film worlds and unique characters in the heat of good solid archetypical conflict utilizing all sorts of digital powers.

This book is written for the no-budget, independent digital filmmaker or student. The ideas presented will help you think of stories you can do all by yourself, or with a small group of friends, using a DV camera and some basic software. If you are working on a film with a multimillion-dollar budget, you usually specialize in doing one thing. If you are creating your own film with no money, you get to do a little bit of everything! The no-budget filmmaking techniques explored in this book are not supposed to look like

definition

Bluescreen Shooting an actor or subject against a bright blue or green background, and then using special software to make those colors transparent in post. Other images, backgrounds, or sets can then be layered behind and in front of characters to create unique shots and storytelling styles.

big Hollywood movies. These independent short films have their own unique visual style and rely heavily on great storytelling, clever ideas, and the use of digital tools to tell stories in new ways.

The techniques in these pages are geared for digital video "filmmakers," 2D animators, 3D animators, documentary filmmakers, game designers, music video artists, and interactive storytellers. Game designers and interactive storytellers need to create the same types of compelling characters and interesting worlds as in the movies. All of these groups of digital creatives are referred to as "filmmakers" from here on out to simplify things—unless it is necessary to split the groups. The lines between these different production styles are starting to blur, and will continue to blur even more in the coming years as modern digital filmmakers stretch their tools to communicate in new ways. I predict that within the next 10 years, most big Hollywood "films" will be made all digitally, too. Although real film is beautiful to shoot, the average cost of around $100 a minute just for stock and processing places it out of range for most people's creative budgets. Learning to make films with digital video and animation software makes more sense these days.

George Lucas thinks the next *Star Wars* is going to be made on a desktop computer. The first 10 years of this century will be the decade of the digitally enhanced film for both shorts and features. What types of new stories do you have to tell that might be considered the next big thing?

Getting the Most Out of This Book

The goal of this book is to help you learn to think in new ways about telling visual stories and creating digital films from initial ideas to final renders. You learn narrative conceptual design techniques as well as a few software tips. This book follows a tutorial format designed to be completed in a 10-to-15 week course, with 10 hours of homework per week. The goal of these exercises is to produce a final script, storyboards, and Animatic ready to go into production. I invite you to follow along to create your own award-winning digital short films based on the ideas presented in this book.

If you are in a class, you may want to do one chapter a week, depending on how much time you have to create. If you are an individual living in a remote region (or state of mind), think of this book as a class you are taking where you may want to set aside a few hours a week to complete the exercises, or you could take a year to finish the book if that feels more comfortable. You will not get much out of this information unless you follow along with the exercises to some extent. If possible, small study groups are encouraged to have others to bounce ideas off of for feedback. If you do not read much, you may just randomly open the book to a page and read about a technique, and then practice applying it to your film idea.

The following elements help you learn about the various aspects of digital filmmaking and give you tips and suggestions for individual and group projects:

- **Step in the Process Project**. These projects are essential to complete in order to follow the step-by-step preproduction process for creating a digital film in this book. All of these projects are designed to be put in a black, hardbound drawing book about 9×12 inches in size unless otherwise noted. For some chapters, you need a pack of 3×5- or 5×8-inch index cards. Many of these project exercises build on the preceding ones. These projects were designed to help spark highly original and creative ideas when developing your digital film. I will assume you know how to use your DV camera and edit together some clips using basic software to complete the exercises in this book.

- **Superfreak Projects.** These projects are for people who want to go the extra mile, have lots of free time, and think creatively fast. You should at least read over these, even if you do not want to do them, to get an idea of new ways to think about things. Most of these exercises are challenging. Think of them as extra credit. Do the ones that sound fun or helpful if you have time. You may want to just think about how you would do each of them for a moment before reading on.

- **Sketch Projects.** One way to go the extra mile and generate lots of fresh visual storytelling approaches is to do rough sketches of the ideas you generate. If a project exercise suggests listing possible

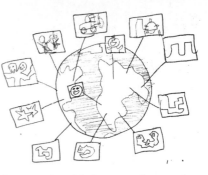

Our emerging global community cannot evolve without honest, compelling, and powerful storytelling from new voices. Films are snapshots of our modern cultures and individual insights into life. A person's drive to create a film these days is much the same as that of the ancients, who passed down their knowledge and wisdom orally, with stories told over campfires.

"One learns by doing a thing; for though you think you know it, you have no certainty until you try."
—*Sophocles*

definition
Animatic Slideshow test of a film idea, created by scanning storyboards and adding a rough soundtrack.

time-saving

Do Some Shorts Before Attempting a Feature. You may want to start your filmmaking career by making a few short films before attempting a feature-length one. There are lots of horror stories of beginner filmmakers taking their life savings (or advances on credit cards) to shoot their first feature film and learning some very hard lessons. It is much easier to fine-tune your visual storytelling style and technical problems with shorts, especially for digital filmmaking, where one person may be wearing lots of unfamiliar hats. You do not want to shoot hundreds of hours of blown light, bad sound, or shots that just do not work. Build up your visual storytelling skills slowly. The longer your film, the more it will challenge you in every way.

"This is the practice school of writing. Like running, the more you do it, the better you get at it."
—Natalie Goldberg

"It is by sitting down to write every morning that one becomes a writer. Those who do not do this remain amateurs."
—Gerald Brenan

ways to use your favorite software to design a unique character, you may want to do rough sketches of your favorite ideas in your drawing book.

- **Group Projects.** If you are working in a class or small group, these projects help break up the assignments between several people. Be creative with these ideas. If your group comes up with a better way to collectively think of any of these exercises, feel free to improvise. You may see a Superfreak project that you all want to try by coming up with one idea each.

- **Writing Exercises.** These *optional* sidebar projects are designed to help you start writing *something* before you embark on writing a short script at the end of Chapter 4 "Writing Scenes, Conflict, and a Short Script." If you feel you are becoming overwhelmed with too many new ideas and techniques, I strongly recommend that you do these writing exercises. Most of them are found in the first four chapters. These are not supposed to be award-winning short stories, but exercises designed to help you wrap your mind around new storytelling techniques one at a time. They should take around 30 minutes and be about two to five handwritten pages, depending on your writing experience. Writing one rough short story a day while you go through the first four chapters is a great way to build up your storytelling muscles, while strengthening your own unique storytelling voice. You will also gather many new ideas from doing these exercises to use in your film. Writing for 30 minutes first thing in the morning works great for many people.

- **Time-Saving Tips.** These ideas may save you time or help you plan your preproduction schedule better.

- **Money-Saving Tips.** These tips are designed to save you money and suggest ideas for shamelessly self-promoting your films on a tight budget.

- **Creativity Tips.** The creative process for developing a film takes many forms. A few of these tips are included to help you stay enthusiastic about your project and find new ways to tailor the steps for your own individual creative process.

- **Movie Box.** This box suggests films you may want to check out that illustrate specific techniques discussed in the book.

- **Inspiring Quotes.** These quotes from famous people are placed strategically to add time-tested wisdom and help keep you motivated and enthusiastic about developing your film idea.

The other suggested activities or questions found in the text are of a more optional sort. Ponder these suggestions if you have time, or do them if they seem especially helpful to your particular project. You will not be able to use all the ideas you generate in these projects in one short film. The goal is to learn the techniques to add to your visual storytelling toolbox. After you learn some of these basic techniques, you should think of them automatically when approaching future projects.

There are as many ways to create a film as there are people who make films. You will not agree with everything I say in this book, and that is fine. Use what works as you refine and develop your own creative process. The step-by-step techniques that I have included are in no way complete for making a film from start to finish. The information in these pages covers the types of things I wish I would have known when I started making digital short films back in 1993. Many of the exercises in this book are a result of teaching thousands of students how to make digital short films for their final thesis projects at animation schools. My goal is to present enough interesting and simple techniques to inspire you to make your own original digital short films.

If you have read my story development chapters in the book *Maya 2 Character Animation*, please be advised that the ideas in these pages are a little different and much deeper.

A sample story is developed throughout the book. The illustrations show examples of the specific storytelling techniques visually. I wrote the book first, and then went back and developed an example story using the step-by-step process. This digital short film example idea was specifically designed to use as many of the techniques as possible throughout the entire book.

The rough illustrations in this book are examples of ways to generate visual storytelling ideas by sketching out characters, sets, shots, and objects. I could have hired professional illustrators to do the sketches, but then you would have all been very intimidated about your own ability to draw well. The rough sketches in this book are the types we use in preproduction and are about the level you should shoot for in your own work. You do not want to create detailed, beautiful sketches

"Why should we all use our creative power...? Because there is nothing that makes people so generous, joyful, lively, bold, and compassionate, so indifferent to fighting and the accumulation of objects and money."
—Brenda Ueland

of rough ideas that will probably change later. Do not worry about how well you can draw. Just do your best to sketch out ideas in your drawing book as you go along to see what images communicate the best visually. Drawing possible shots is good practice for storyboarding and will often generate visual story ideas you would not think of by simply writing things down. Practice copying some of the drawings in this book to get a feel for how to do rough sketches if you are still at the stick figure level.

It proved impossible to find short film examples that everyone could easily view, because many of the DVDs, VHS tapes, and Internet sites that show them are hard to find and often change locations. Many of the techniques that make a great feature film also make a great short. I had to make the choice to use some feature film examples to illustrate key points, so that you could find them and study them in-depth on your own. The short films I do use as examples are generally well known by the Spike and Mike Animation Festival and Resfest crowds.

superfreak!

Do You Want to Make Big Feature Films? A good way to break into the big moviemaking money machine is to create an independent short film that wins some awards on the festival circuit. The first question a studio person will ask you is, "Do you have a script?" If you have a great original feature screenplay with an engaging pitch ready to go, you might get a budget to do your first feature. If you do not have a good feature script ready to go, you get to keep making short films for free! *Or* you could ask to direct someone else's script that has already gotten a "go" for production, if you just want to direct and break into the industry. You need to decide for yourself what direction you want to go and how much time you want to devote to screenwriting. You may be able to turn the short film idea you develop in this book into a feature script if your characters and film world are interesting enough. Another smart approach is to take a great visual story and write a successful novel, sell the screen rights, and then have the studio pay you to write the script.

"What's important is finding out what works for you."
—Henry Moore

Becoming a Better Digital Filmmaker

"Believe in your success. Picture yourself having what you want."
—*Sanaya Roman*

"The big gap between the ability of actors is confidence."
—*Kathleen Turner*

To become a better digital filmmaker, you need to spend some time studying some other areas between your renderings. If you want to be a really good visual storyteller, you should be taking classes, reading books, and learning all the time. The remainder of this introduction covers some subject areas you will want to explore and presents some ideas to help you realize your digital filmmaking goals.

Screenwriting

If you want to make your own films, you need to know how to tell a story visually in a format you can communicate to other people. Screenwriting is a *required skill* for any serious independent filmmaker. A director without a script is merely a hired gun for someone else's ideas. Write your dream feature screenplay after reading some books on the subject; or take a screenwriting class to learn how to write a good screenplay, while getting feedback on your ideas and writing style.

The same ideas that make a great short film make a great feature, but the scope and plot points are a little different. Much of the information in the first four chapters of this book will also help you write a good feature-length script. Chapter 3, "Developing Plot Points," lists 40 basic plot points for writing a feature. Creating short films is a good way to get a feel for what it would be like to make a much longer one.

Acting

Screenwriters are like actors, acting out or improvising the entire film in their heads as they write. You may want to take a method acting class for the following reasons:

- To learn about dramatic tension, beats, and three-act structure.
- To appreciate what actors go through on the set. After you have had to crawl back into the most embarrassing moment of your childhood and then recite a monologue from that space, you will gain a new respect for what actors do.

Good Screenwriting Books

- *Writing Screenplays That Sell* by Michael Hauge (Harper Perennial, 1991)
- *Story* by Robert McKee (Regan Books/Harper Collins, 1997)
- *The Writer's Journey* by Christopher Vogler (Michael Wiese Productions, 1998)
- *Creating Unforgettable Characters* by Linda Seger (Henry Holt, 1990)
- *Making a Good Script Great* by Linda Seger (Samuel French, 1994).

creativity tip

Write a Short Story Every Day. A good way to keep your storytelling muscles in shape is to write one short story each day. Lots of good ideas for both shorts and features come from short story ideas. Feel free to write these in a more relaxed structure than the process presented in this book, just to see where the ideas and characters take you. You can always go back and add twists and plot points later, if the main idea is interesting in some way. Practicing one specific technique in this book at a time, for each short story, is a good way to learn them. Remember, your ideas make your films, so do what you can to generate lots of possibilities. You could write these short stories instead of completing the writing exercises, if you already feel comfortable generating lots of short stories.

- To understand how to talk to actors better and motivate each individual one for what the scene needs.
- To understand how many different ways an actor can interpret or approach a scene.
- To understand how important acting it is to give characters clear motivations.
- To feel more comfortable acting out your animated characters in front of a mirror to get the motion right.
- To feel more comfortable acting out your story, and the voices of your characters, while pitching your ideas in front of a group of potential investors or cast and crew members.
- To get a better sense of how to make your characters really come alive emotionally in a scene.

The History of Filmmaking, Cinematography, and Animation

Study the great directors behind the cameras of the best films ever made. It's all been done before in one visual form or another. You don't have to reinvent the wheel with every storyboard panel. Visually creative people have been setting up shots, constructing interesting characters, and designing sets ever since the first story was told. Find the "Top 10 Favorite Film" lists from directors you like and see whether you can tell where they borrowed ideas. Storyboard, shot by shot, films or scenes from films that you think worked really well or are similar to current projects you are developing. Try to figure out what the director

was thinking when he composed each shot. There are literally hundreds of people behind every shot in a big-budget film controlling every aspect of what ends up on the screen. Ask yourself why all these particular choices were made and how they impact your enjoyment of each scene, how they make you feel, and what each shot makes you think is happening as the film moves forward.

Photography

Experiment with taking pictures of weird places, strange pets, graffiti, interesting looking people, funky architecture, postcard sunsets, or any other compelling visual elements. Start your own clip media library of reference shots for brainstorming, bluescreen layers, or textures. Commercial clip media is often overused and is easy to spot.

"Every artist joins a conversation that's been going on for generations, even millennia, before he or she joins the scene."
—John Barth

During a trip to Paris, I took a bunch of photographs at Jim Morrison's grave. These images later ended up as a 2D photo collage set for an After Effects animation called *Goth Grrls*. What types of photos or video footage do you already have that might be useful for creating a digital short film?

Storyboard your favorite shots from great films to learn more about how to tell a visual story.
Shown here are the first few minutes of *Citizen Kane*. Notice how beautifully composed and
balanced each shot appears and how each shot tells a very dramatic story visually.
Illustrations by Maia Sanders

As you get more comfortable composing still frames in photography, your eye will be better developed to compose moving camera shots. Hang out in artsy bookstores going through the coffee table photography books. Ask yourself, "What makes this a good photograph?" or, "What does this image make me feel or think?" as you look at each picture. The photographer may have shot a hundred rolls of film for that subject and chosen the one in the book as the best. If you are working on a specific project, you may get some ideas about visual styles to use in your film based on a particular photographer's look.

Fine Arts and Performing Arts

Studying any area of the arts will help you become a better filmmaker. Obviously, you can't master painting, sculpture, music, illustration, dance, and theater; if you already have an interest in one area, however, you may want to develop it further.

Painting and illustration are particularly good backgrounds for both

"Learn to see, and then you'll know that there is no end to the new worlds for our vision."
—Carlos Castaneda

future filmmakers and animators. The same things that make a great painting or picture make a great shot. Computer artists lacking fine-art skills have a more difficult time making their projects look good.

Drawing

If you don't know how to create basic drawings or sketches, you will have a more difficult time communicating your visual ideas to other people working on your film and planning out your shots. Animators need to know how to draw more than filmmakers. Practice doing rough sketches of locations, camera shots, and characters in your spare time. Tracing copies of your favorite comic books is a good way to learn how to storyboard, while developing an eye for framing shots and creating good compositions.

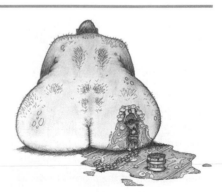

Liquid Crystal Vision is a feature-length DV documentary created by Torsten Klimmer (**www.liquidcrystalvision.com**). This project is an example of a first-time filmmaker, trained as a traditional painter/illustrator, who made an absolutely beautiful first film. Torsten had a good artistic eye developed before he even picked up a DV camera, which helped make his shot compositions so visually appealing. This film was shot using a Sony TRV-900. Notice how well the DV camera handles this low-light situation—even in a smoky fire! What types of low-light night shooting could you do with your DV camera to capture some original-looking shots?

Being good at figure drawing will help you design anatomically correct exaggerated characters such as this giant, 3D, carnival fat man, or anyplace else your imagination may take you.
Illustration by Chris Hatala

"All things are full of signs, and it is a wise man who can learn about one thing from another."
—*Plotinus*

Gesture-type drawings focus on getting the energy of the pose or shot with rough line sketches. This style of drawing works great for quick and rough storyboards or for people who find drawing challenging. Use this type of quick drawing style to create some rough sketches of your story ideas and characters as you go through this book.

superfreak!

Life Drawing. Take a figure-drawing class or attend life-drawing open studios for three hours a week to keep your eye in shape.

superfreak!

Take a Graphic Design Course or practice copying designs in Photoshop, Illustrator, or Flash that appeal to your sense of style from books, magazines, or the Internet. You will gain a greater understanding of the process involved if you re-create a nice layout with pictures and professional type. An increased awareness of design will make the credit sequences of your films look more professional, too.

Life drawing off of a live model keeps your eye finely tuned to the nuances of how to really see things such as shadows, shapes, and light. Check local art schools for life-drawing classes and open studios. If you can draw a twisted-up humanoid, you can sketch just about anything. Most large animation studios consider life drawing important enough to offer life-drawing studios for their animators during lunchtime. Burne Hogarth's books *Dynamic Figure Drawing* (Watson-Guptill, 1996) and *Dynamic Light and Shade* (Watson-Guptill, 1991) are great to study. You may want to practice copying the sketches from these books, if drawing classes are not offered in your area.

Graphic Design and Sacred Geometry

Great filmmaking and animation requires a good design sense. Understanding how colors work together, type, layout, and visual communication will improve the way you design your shots, sets, and characters.

Sacred geometry will give you an understanding how we relate to shapes and mathematical constructs in our visual world, and thereby help you design better shots, sets, and characters. *A Beginner's Guide to Constructing the Universe* by Michael Schneider (Thames and Hudson Inc., 1995) and *Sacred Geometry* by Robert Lawlor (Thames and Hudson Inc., 1989) are great books to get you started in this fascinating and useful subject.

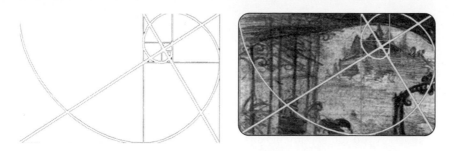 

If we lay a golden rectangle over the first few shots of *Citizen Kane*, we find that the light in the window matches perfectly with the birth of the golden spiral. This magical spot serves as a match cut for a series of shots leading up to the room with the light on where Kane is about to die. A 720×480 Photoshop golden rectangle file (goldenspiral.psd) is on the CD if you want to play with finding this spot in your frame. Import the Photoshop file layer into your DV editor for a transparent guide. You may want to experiment with flipping the image around horizontally and vertically to find different geometric sweet spots in the frame for possible story focal points.

Become a visual cultural detective. It helps to have a visual theme when taking pictures on the road. This Thai dog is one of 100s of dog pictures I have taken all over the world. In every country, I noticed the dogs looked different. The same things that make a good dog photo make a good shot. When designing 3D characters, I often refer to my dog photo collection to get ideas for variations. And I always remember to give my models treats! What visual themes might you be interested in exploring with still shots or DV when you travel for a possible future short film?

Become a More Interesting Person

Interesting people do unusual things and have more fascinating stories to tell. There is no substitute for life experience. If you spend your time in front of a computer or TV, you may have a smaller scope of life experiences to cannibalize for story ideas. Take a few weeks off and backpack through India (or any country) to open your eyes to some new ways to see life. Become a black belt in karate. Study in depth some esoteric field that has always inter-ested you, such as petroglyphs of the American Southwest or Feng Shui. Climb a mountain in Africa. Join a local mime troupe. Be in a band. Kayak the Amazon. Try out different forms of yoga and meditation. Go to events you would not normally attend, such as Celtic Fairs or vintage-clothing shows. Take a road trip across your own country and visit sacred sites or do a photo essay on truck stops. Notice how the light changes completely depending on where you are in the world, the weather, and the time of year.

superfreak

Write a List of 50 Things You Want to Do in This Lifetime. List them, no matter how far out, and try to do one each year! These types of experiences often spark great ideas for original films. Bring your DV camera with you and make a short film about your adventure. How could you create one of these ideas vicariously using your digital tools? If one of the things on your list is to take a space journey to Mars, you could create a digital short film about the experience using photocollage or 3D sets and blue-screen characters.

"The real mystery of life is not a problem to be solved, it is a reality to be experienced."
—*J.J. Van der Leeuw*

definition

Phenomenology The study of the development of human consciousness and self-awareness.

This colorful guy was taking a motorcycle trip through India when Torsten caught a shot of him with his DV camera. *Liquid Crystal Vision* contains lots of footage from Torsten's traveling experiences. What new people and places could you show us in your film? What new film ideas could you create to take full advantage of your existing vacation DV footage?

"People say that what we're all seeking is a meaning for life. I don't think that's what we're really seeking. I think that what we're seeking is an experience of being alive, so that our life experiences on the purely physical plane will have resonances within our own innermost being and reality, so that we actually feel the rapture of being alive."
—Joseph Campbell

Become a Phenomenologist

Screenwriting is a glorified form of phenomenology. You re-create slices of real life on the screen. You cannot do this truthfully unless you understand to some degree how you relate to the world and other people. Learn as much as you can about yourself, your motivations, beliefs, reactions, reality constructs, and values. Develop your own philosophy of life to showcase in your films. What are the plot and theme goals of your own life? These will show up on the screen to some degree. Do you behave in your own life like a character you would like in a film?

Meet new people. Talk to them about their lives and gather stories. Think of every place you go and every person you meet as an opportunity to gain new insight into the human psyche, what makes it tick, what makes a person interesting, what people care about, and how life affects each person differently. Storytelling really tests writers' limits as to their knowledge of humanity, history, society, spirituality, cosmology, and nature.

You may be wondering how you are going to have time to do any filmmaking or animation at all if you have to know all of these other things. This is why you need to start *now*. The best filmmakers usually have some training in several of the fields previously mentioned. Being an independent filmmaker or animator is one of the most challenging careers around, but at least you will never have to worry about being bored!

"Know the true value of time; snatch, seize, and enjoy every moment of it. No idleness, no laziness, no procrastination, never put off till tomorrow what you can do today."
—Lord Chesterfield

Do Not Let Anything Stop You From Making Your Film

We live in a very fast world these days. Setting aside the time and energy to make a digital short film may seem very challenging to some of you reading this book. Below are some common reasons people use when they get stuck and some possible solutions to help keep you on the right track.

1. **Lack of film ideas.** Do the project exercises in this book. All of the visual storytelling techniques presented in these pages are designed to inspire a multitude of ideas.
2. **Lack of time or organization.** When you look back over your life at some point, having

created your own original short film will probably stand out in your mind as one of your most treasured personal achievements. Have you ever heard the expression that if you want something done you should give it to a busy person? Why do you think people say this? How many filmmakers do you know that spend years making a short film or talk about making a film that never seems to get done? The right time to start making your film is *now*.

The best way to get any project completed is to set realistic creative deadlines using a simple calendar system. Keep a preproduction calendar on your wall, computer, or PDA, to write down your creative goals for each week. There is something magical about writing down specific creative deadlines that make the ideas flow much faster. If you know you want to go into production on your short film in three months, put that goal on your calendar and then work backwards each week to see what needs to happen. A Final Animatic may need to be completed two weeks before production begins, to allow time to organize shots, actors, or crews. A rough set of storyboards may need to be sketched one month before the Animatic, to allow time for the soundtrack or voice actors. A final script may need to be completed one month before the rough storyboards are due, to allow time for shot visualization.

Each day may have specific goals, such as, "Think of final story idea or plot points."

I used to resist using calendars and daily goals, until I tried it, and found that all my projects took off much faster. Set goals that are easy to accomplish so that you do not become overwhelmed or discouraged. You are usually the producer and boss of your own independent short film. If you do not stay organized and focused to make your project happen, who will?

3. **Lack of the "right" equipment.** Make the film you can afford to make today. Start making films now with whatever you have and you will become a magnet to better equipment and software when you start producing results. Any film you make will be a wonderful learning experience, and most short film festivals are not that picky about what kind of camera or software you are using if the idea is good. You almost never need to make a 35mm short film, because most people will usually see it on VHS or television.

4. **Lack of motivation.** The only reasons to make a digital short film are to get work, win awards, or make money. Be clear on this when you start thinking of film ideas. Visualize how good you are going to feel when you watch your final film. Or visualize yourself working at your dream film job, accepting an Academy Award, or being a very successful filmmaker/animator living a life you love.

5. **Thinking you are just not a very creative person or feeling creatively blocked at any point.** Read *The Artist's Way* by Julia Cameron (J. P. Tarcher, 2002) and do the nine-week course in the book. This book presents a great philosophy of how essential it is to just show up at the page each day to let new ideas flow. The importance of creating something—anything—each day, instead of getting stuck worrying about the quality of the art, is explored. Several of the inspirational quotes in these pages were pulled from this wonderful book.

Do the writing projects in Part I, "Digital Storytelling," or write a short story every day based on the project exercises if you start feeling overloaded with too many new ideas.

"We are traditionally rather proud of ourselves for having slipped creative work in there between the domestic chores and obligations. I'm not sure we deserve such big A-pluses for that."
—Toni Morrison

Why You Should Spend Time Doing Preproduction

The most effective way to learn a new software package, or get familiar with your desktop DV system, is to come up with an idea and create it using the same type of preproduction process most film and animation studios follow. It is much wiser to take the extra time to develop a good idea for a short film than to just sit down and start clicking away doing what the computer wants to do, instead of what you may want to see as an end result of all those hours. The best design tool is a *pencil*. This is where we will begin generating ideas. We have all seen films that were technically perfect or had great characters, but left us feeling like the story was not really there and that a great deal of time had been wasted.

Remember: Flawed stories cannot be saved by special effects.

Part I of this book helps you think of an original story idea and write a script ideal for a digital short film. Part II, "Visualizing Your Script," helps you take your script and turn it into a visual story, developing each shot on the screen for maximum impact. Part III, "Creating Digital Short Films for Different Production Styles," explores new ways to tell stories using the strengths of digital tools such as DV, 2D, and 3D animation.

Digital Storytelling

chapter 1

Generating Ideas for Digital Short Films

"Imagination is more important than knowledge."
—Albert Einstein

You are about to embark on a storytelling journey. The ideas presented in these first four chapters were developed to help you tell an original and emotionally compelling visual story.

time-saving

A Short Film Means Short. The official length for short films in the United States is less than 30 minutes; in Europe, however, a "short film" can be up to an hour long. If you have never made a film before and are shooting it in DV, you may want to keep the total length less than 10 minutes. If this is your first animated short film, keep the film to less than 5 minutes. The big film festivals have a very hard time programming short films that are longer than 20 minutes, and usually prefer funny short films around the 5-minute mark.

Original Visual Ideas. This 3D Maya character was created by Nathan Vogel, based on what it might be like to see a being energetically with an aura and chakras. Many modern filmmakers use digital software to explore the unconscious, unseen realms, or inner workings of the human mind and heart to tell stories in fresh ways. This image is a good example of using digital tools to show us something we may not have seen before in a visually interesting way. What are some original visual ideas or new point of views you could include in your film idea that would be easy to do with your favorite digital techniques or software capabilities? This idea of seeing spiritual energy is combined with the book's example story later.

Beginning the Story Concept Process

Screenwriting is more like architecture than it is a whoosh of sudden creative inspiration that magically pours out over the pages. Your script is the blueprint for constructing every aspect of your film. Great screenplays have lots of depth and are built up in layers, using the types of techniques presented in these first four chapters.

The first step to making a short film involves finding a great original idea to develop into a script. If you do not have the story for your film down before shooting, you do not have anything. By the end of this chapter, you should know the following:

1. Who is the main character in your short film?
2. What does your main character want to achieve?
3. What types of themes are you interested in exploring?
4. What makes your idea original?
5. Are you sure this is a film idea you would love to see?

"For a creative writer posses-sion of the 'truth' is less important than emotional sincerity."
—*George Orwell*

The Most Important Thing

What is the goal of telling a good story? What is the primary goal of any film, play, novel, song, TV show, video game, or animation? Think about this for a moment before you read on; it is a very important point. Most people say that their primary goal is to entertain or make money. These things are important, but may not happen unless you approach it this way:

The first and primary goal of a filmmaker is to evoke a series of strong emotional responses from the audience throughout the entire story.

People also like to be entertained by amusement and surprise, inspired by the character's noble actions, informed about new relevant ideas, and explore fresh perspectives and insights on life. Above all else, however, you need to get the audience emotionally engaged in the story, to stimulate their curiosity about the characters and events. This does not happen by showing characters crying or screaming at each other.

You engage the audience when you tell the truth emo-tionally based on your own experiences and original insights about life in your film.

Review the emotional impacts of your favorite films. What did you feel when you were watching them? When you go to the movies, keep an eye on the audience. See whether you can get an emotional read on how involved they are in the story. Films that don't do well usually fail to evoke any emotion at all.

Basic Story Structure

There are four types of film: narrative, documentary, experimental, and postmodern. Although this book focuses more on creating classic narrative films, you can use the ideas presented in any form of visual storytelling. Here's the basic structure of a story that you will want to wrap your short film around to practice applying the techniques in this book:

> It is a story about a *protagonist* (lead character) who *wants* something (goal) that forces him to take *action*. He meets with an escalating array of *conflict*s (obstacles) leading to a final *climax* and *resolution*.

Do not freak out at this point if you think this classic story structure is dated and boring. Almost all films use this structure, and the trick is finding an original approach. You learn plenty of techniques in this book to create other types of films, but we need a basic structure to apply to all the different exercises.

Beware of people who offer you formulas, rather than tools, for writing a script. That said, I'm about to throw a bunch of techniques at you. You will not be able to use all the techniques presented in this book during a single short film. Use what works and get familiar with the concept behind each idea. You need to understand the rules first to break them effectively later.

Compare learning to create films with learning to play the guitar. Most people start by learning a few basic chords and simple songs. A whole new world opens up each time you add a new chord or instrument to your repertoire. Short films are like songs. Creating a feature film is more like composing an opera. Lots of compacted information is headed your way in these pages. Think of each concept as a new chord you are learning, which you can use to create more intricate stories. You may not like each new chord or technique, but at least you will be aware of it if you ever want to use it again.

Even if you want to do a funky abstract digital art film, choose a main character with a goal by the end of this chapter. You need to follow the basic story structure to do the exercises in this first part of the book. When you feel more comfortable with the techniques, you will feel more confident to delve into more experimental approaches to storytelling. Let's start with some definitions:

- **Character.** The actions and reactions of your characters drive the plot forward. Characters create their own realities as externalizations of their inner worlds in a sense.
- **Plot.** The series of events that happen in the story to the characters.
- **Theme.** Invisible underlying universal–controlling idea, moral message, concept, emotion, issue, essence, or soul of a story.
- **Conflict.** Obstacles that stand in the way of the protagonist in achieving his or her goals.
- **Interaction.** Characters interacting, connecting, and disconnecting from other characters, ideas, or things. Not all stories are based solely on conflict. Many times in a short film, an interaction or connection occurs that results in a conflict, discovery, or decision. This initial connection often leads to a disconnection and possible reconnection later.

Ideally, you want your audience to be laughing out loud, crying out in surprise, biting their fingernails, worrying about the characters, jumping out of their seats with joy, recoiling in fear, screaming out in terror, feeling at one with the universe, or exhausted from all the activity. These reactions are harder to achieve than you might think. How can you wrap your film idea around strong universal emotional charges?

"Making art is a journey."
—*Meinrad Craighead*

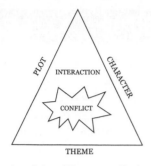

Character, plot, and theme are the basic building blocks used to weave together films. These three concepts can be viewed as a pyramid. Theme is the base for the story. Conflict sits in the middle, generating friction to keep the three sides moving. Interaction happens as we watch characters connect and disconnect from other people, ideas, and things.

A driving metaphor is useful for understanding the way these three ideas work together. The car is the plot that carries the driver (or character) through the story, fueled by the invisible theme (or gas). Conflicts are the obstacles on the road that keep the driver from reaching his or her destination (goal). Characters interact with the people, ideas, and things they encounter, which may help them to change and grow.

"What you accept as true will create your reality."
—*Sanaya Roman*

definition

Protagonist Lead character and focus of the plot. A vessel through which the story flows. Usually one of the first characters you see in a film.

Antagonist The character or thing that stands in the way of the protagonist accomplishing his or her goals.

superfreak!

List the Plot Goals of Your Favorite Film. Carefully watch one of your favorite films and list the plot goals of the main character, and then list what obstacles stand in the character's way. Pay attention to this idea when you read scripts or watch films, to see how many different ways goals and obstacles can be layered into a story.

Character

You need to get the audience to identify and care about your characters. Viewers are supposed to become attached to the characters in your story, and then you make them suffer. Your film becomes a vicarious emotional experience for the audience members. They feel what the characters feel. They see their own lives and struggles on the screen and look for answers on how to live better. "That which does not kill me makes me stronger," Nietzsche once stated, and this famous statement serves as a good lesson for piling up the obstacles between your characters and their goals in your story.

Great characters are original. Everyone relates to them, but they come in forms we have never seen before. Are your lead characters good enough to inspire a doll? How do you create really compelling original characters that leap off the screen visually? How can you use some of your digital tools to create new forms of characters? Audiences might have trouble relating to a deaf mute aborigine who lives in a cave and spends his days rubbing rocks together, but they have no problem crawling into the skins of Luke Skywalker, Hannibal Lector, Woody the cowboy doll in *Toy Story*, or Nemo the little clownfish in *Finding Nemo*. The wants and needs of this second group of characters are in some ways similar to universal human needs.

Short films are often about fast changes in characters. People like to see characters transform before their eyes after going through intense life-altering situations.

Short films tend to have big emotional switches and few locations, which means that you really have to work the character angle. Some characters do not change, but cause the audience to undergo a change by watching what the characters experience onscreen. When characters do not change and fail to meet their goals, it is called a *tragedy*.

Plot

Plot is defined as a series of events that happen in a story unfolding in a linear fashion. Narrative films feature life with all the boring parts cut out, presented in a three-act structure.

In short films, Acts One and Three each tend to take up about 1/6 of the total screen time, with Act Two comprising 2/3. Quick setups and fast resolutions work better when you have less time to tell a story. Feature films have more time to develop Acts One and Three.

Shown here are the basic plot points for a short film using a three-act structure. These plot points do not have to be in this order. How would you tell a story if you started with a scene from the resolution and then went backward, such as having a character confess to a crime by going over the details? Some basic plot points to keep in mind while generating initial ideas are as follows:

Three-Act Structure	Concepts Covered	Short Films*	Feature Films*
Act One	Beginning/establishment	1/6	1/4
Act Two	Middle/development	2/3	1/2
Act Three	End/resolution	1/6	1/4

*As percentage of film per act

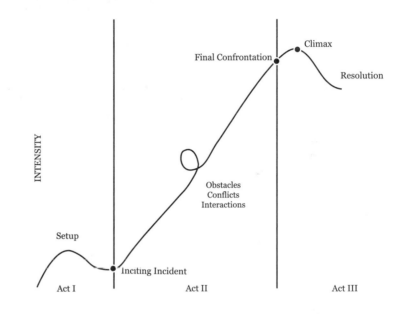

1. **Setup.** How will you introduce us to your characters, film world, and story? How will you show your character in his or her normal life? The audience needs a chance to get to know your main character, along with the limits and possibilities of the film world.
2. **Inciting incident.** What event happens that forces your character to act by choosing a goal and committing to making it happen?

3. **Obstacles/conflict/ interaction.** What are some obstacles or conflicts your characters might face while attempting to accomplish their goals? What types of interactions might they have with other characters, ideas, or experiences?
4. **Final confrontation.** Confrontation between two characters that has been building up.

5. **Climax.** Highest point of audience interest where the plot reaches a crescendo. What is the big climatic event at the end where we see whether the characters succeed in accomplishing their goals?
6. **Resolution.** Ties up the loose ends in the story, such as who lives, who dies, who gets the girl, and who lives happily ever after.

Theme

writing exercise 1.1

Write a few pages or a rough short story that answers the six plot points. If you have never written a story before, just answer the questions for each basic plot point as it relates to your story idea. If you do write, see how much of your own personal storytelling style can come through in the telling of the story. It is fine when doing these optional writing exercises to be very flexible with yourself. You may write for three pages and still be in the setup, then not feel like finishing the story, which is fine. The important thing is to just write *something* for one to five pages to build up your storytelling muscles.

Theme is the unspoken and invisible moral message, deeper meaning, underlying idea, or essence of the film. What idea is controlling how and why life changes throughout the film from one condition to the next?

Some common themes are love conquers all, good triumphs over evil, greed destroys, loyalty, balancing compromise, redemption, the downside of runaway ambition, or finding meaning in life. Many themes can be narrowed down to one word such as love, greed, forgiveness, loyalty, or desire. Theme is what makes a movie memorable, and without it you will craft a soulless film that people forget right after they see it. The theme of most Hollywood "summer" action movies is "let's make money." (They are ultra theme light.) The theme of most commercials is "buy our product." The difference between the latest Hong Kong action thriller and *Crouching Tiger Hidden Dragon* is the

latter's strong theme. Powerful themes tend to linger in our minds long after the film has ended.

Not all movies have themes. It is your choice whether to develop one in your film. Usually a theme naturally surfaces while you are writing a first draft. You may then choose to carefully layer the controlling idea more deeply into every aspect of the film. The more I explore working with themes, the more I try to nail them down as soon as possible to add more depth to my stories.

Themes involve a very soft touch and subtle delivery. The most effective themes gently suggest the idea to the audience, in such a way that they think it is their own idea by the end of the film. You need strong opinions to be a good filmmaker. Great filmmakers care enough about their subjects to take a tenacious *point of view* (POV). You must really believe in what your film is about, while showing us what you find to be beautiful, important, and moving. The best themes will come from your own emotions, experiences, and insights about how life works. If you do not really believe in the theme you choose for your film, neither will your audience.

You may not always know the theme you are exploring when you start thinking of ideas, but you do need to nail it down by your final script. Sometimes the theme you choose will change as you write different versions of your script. Develop only one theme per film; otherwise, the meaning will start to unravel.

Look! No theme above the water in our iceberg motif! Theme is the invisible foundation of a film. Ninety percent of the iceberg is submerged, and so is the theme in your films. For a theme to be successful, it must be unique, distinct, and invisible. The tricky part with theme is that the audience will hate it if you bring it to the level of plot and try to spoon-feed it to them or shove it down their throats.

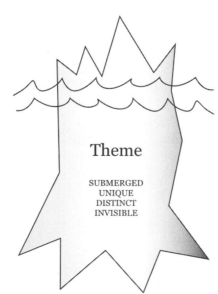

Theme

SUBMERGED
UNIQUE
DISTINCT
INVISIBLE

Exploring Themes in Existing Films

Sometimes it is easier to understand how themes work in film by looking at how other filmmakers have used them in the past. Defining film themes can spur lots of heated debate. Know that you may not agree with the themes chosen. The tables on the following pages lists films with their corresponding themes to give you an idea of how transparent, yet powerful, themes can be. You may want to watch some of these films while just thinking about the themes and see how much they show up in each scene through the characters, metaphors, action, framing, dialogue, and sets.

note

Please email me if you have a different idea about any of the themes in the following table. Include some specific examples from the film supporting your opinion of the theme. I will update this list on the site that is supporting this book at **www.mindseyemedia.com**, and will add new digital films and themes as they come out. You may also email me at **sherri@mindseyemedia.com** with any questions or input regarding this book. Make sure to place the title of the book or the abbreviation DDSF in the Subject line so that I know your email is not junk mail.

Exploring the Theme of Synchronicity

If you want to create a short film based on the theme of how synchronicity (meaningful coincidence) controls the outcome of life events perfectly, you may want to first list visual ways to show this theme as it relates to events happening in the general plot. Possible plot: A character trying to get to work on time. Theme: Synchronicity. Ways to show theme in plot: Character meets, in unusual ways, other people on the way to work. Character finds things and overhears strangely relevant information. Character misses a bus only to get a ride from a new stranger who turns into a mentor. Character and mentor get lost, but find out that they are in the perfect spot to find new jobs they like even better at the end. All of these plot situations are influenced and controlled by the prevailing theme of synchronicity, which is almost invisible in the actual story.

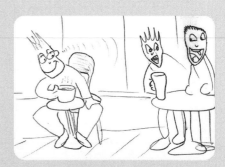

Themes in Feature Films

Feature Films	Themes
African Queen	Organized religious spirituality into a direct experience of spirituality.
Alien	Fear of the unknown.
Alien 2	The strength of motherhood.
American Beauty	Desire leads to suffering.
Antz	Think for yourself.
Apocalypse Now	There is a fine line between insanity and sanity.
The Bad and the Beautiful	Creativity and corruption.
Bad Lieutenant	Redemption of a lost corrupt man.
The Big Chill	Warmth of friendship against cold world.
The Blair Witch Project	Arrogance of youth lacking respect for themselves, surroundings, and subject.
Brazil	Consequences of individuality in a totalitarian dictatorship.
Boogie Nights	Self-delusion.
Buckaroo Bonzai	Superhero with a pure heart can see evil.
Casablanca	Loss of love for some greater cause.
The Celebration (DV)	Dark secrets destroy families.
Citizen Kane	Exploration of personality; who was Kane?
Clockwork Orange	Violence is a cost of individuality and nonindividuals have a loss of soul.
Cold Mountain	The futility of war and how war changes people.
The Cruise (DV)	The beauty of Manhattan.
Dangerous Liaisons	Courtship as combat.
Dr. Strangelove	Exploration of systems and their crushing of individuals.
Fargo	Treasure the little things in life.
Fatal Attraction	Cost of deception.
Finding Nemo	Don't give up. "Keep swimming."
The Graduate	Alienation of '60s youth.
Lord of the Rings (1)	Even the smallest person can change the world. Pure heart needed to wield great power.
Magnolia	Forgiveness in Los Angeles.
The Matrix	Rise of a superman against the system of the future.
The Matrix Reloaded	Choice verses destiny.
Memento	How humans construct and deconstruct reality.
The Piano	The need for creative expression.
Princess Mononoke (2D)	Everything is alive and connected in our environment.

Themes in Feature Films (continued)

Feature Films	Themes
Pulp Fiction	Seeking out redemption in underworld with emphasis on loyalty.
The Remains of the Day	Individual versus place within class society. Class society destroying individual.
Requiem for a Dream	Addiction to dreams.
Run Lola Run	Exploration of how the power of love can change fate.
Shrek (3D)	Seeing inner beauty. When you can love someone else, you can love yourself.
Star Wars	A hero coming of age, taking on lost father's path.
Terminator	Humans being destroyed by their own machines.
There's Something About Mary	Love is more important than beauty. Struggles with perfection.
Things to Do in Denver When You're Dead	Honor among thieves.
Trainspotting	Conflict between life and death urges.
Toy Story (3D)	Being the most favorite toy.
The Usual Suspects	Construction and reconstruction of memory and identity.
Waking Life (DV)	Exploration of lucid dreaming state. What is real verses what is illusion.
Wall Street	Greed leads to corruption.
Wizard of Oz	The importance of home and family.
You Can Count on Me	Loves evokes love.

Themes in Short Films

Short Films	Themes
Ah L'Amore	How money affects dating for men.
Balance	Working as a group to maintain status quo versus individual want.
Delusions in Modern Primitivism	Pushing the limits of self-expression in society.
I/O Error	Personality in conflict with itself cannot survive.
The Last Supper	Money changes relationships.
Le Processus	Perils of conformity and ostracism.
Life Lessons	Cost of creative process.
Lily & Jim	Communication problems between sexes.
Some Folks Call It a Sling Blade	Empathy and tolerance.
The Terminal Bar	Exploration of a place (bar) over time.
Transit	Seduction of innocent.
Zen & the Art of Landscaping	American dysfunctional families.

Developing Themes in Your Films

How do you show something like theme when it's supposed to be invisible? One way is to use metaphors. Aesop's fables are classic tales with themes that have lasted thousands of years. They are full of animal characters who get into all sorts of situations with strong moral messages. These types of stories often work great for animation and digital effects (FX).

"Getting an idea should be like sitting down on a pin; it should make you jump up and do something."
—E.L. Simpson

The Themes of Aesop's Fables

Fables	Themes
The Hare and the Tortoise—Race between a fast rabbit and a slow turtle.	Slow and steady wins the race.
The Boy Who Cried Wolf—Shepherd boy has fun yelling "Wolf!," then laughs at villagers when they come to help. Real wolf shows up one day and no one comes to help. Sheep and boy get eaten.	Habitual liars are not to be believed even when they tell the truth.
The Lion and the Mouse—A lion lets go of a sleeping mouse he caught. Later the lion is caught in a net and the same mouse chews him loose.	If you help someone, that person will help you.
The Goose That Laid the Golden Eggs—Farmer finds a goose that starts laying golden eggs. He gets greedy and cuts the goose open to find source of gold. He finds nothing, and the goose is dead.	Don't try to push your luck too far.
The Donkey in the Lion's Skin—A donkey dresses himself in a lion's skin and chases animals for fun. Then he makes a donkey sound and is discovered to be a fake.	A fool may deceive others by his appearance or dress, but his words will soon give him away.
The Fox and the Grapes—A fox goes to a vineyard to eat grapes. The grapes are just out of his reach. He gives up, saying they are probably sour anyhow.	It's easy to despise what you cannot attain. Sour grapes.

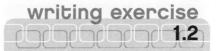

project
1.1

Repurpose an Old Fable. How could you take an old fable with a good solid theme such as *The Goose That Laid the Golden Eggs* and update it for a modern digital short film? What if you turn the goose into a strange lizard-type animated creature that emits blue ooze whenever you feed it chocolate-chip cookies? This ooze transports you to other dimensions when you lick it. Maybe the kid who figures this out starts charging to lick his pet, but gets greedy in the end, killing the lizard. You could justify lots of special effects with an animated lizard creature and dimensional travel effects. Go through the fables listed in the chart and see whether you can think up modern versions with good digital visual twists in the stories.

writing exercise
1.2

Write a rough short story based on your favorite Repurpose an Old Fable idea.

creativity tip

Allow Your Creative Ideas Time to Percolate. Stories often need time to roll around in your imagination until you find the right approach. Pay attention to where and when you get new ideas and write them down as you go through the processes in this book. You should find yourself thinking about your film while doing other activities and experimenting with new ideas, shots, and scenes in your head. Trying to force yourself to think up a film concept really fast from start to finish, and then going into production, may not give the idea enough time to evolve. Sometimes you may find you write better on a tight deadline; usually, however, creative ideas become tighter and deeper after lots of fine-tuning and time to grow. Be careful also of overworking ideas, because stories do not always get better with too much tinkering.

The Responsibility of Being a Filmmaker

It's a great responsibility to be a filmmaker. How do you want people to feel when they see your film? What emotional responses are you trying to evoke? What are the new themes for the 21st century that you are passionate about developing in your own stories?

When you think about it, being a filmmaker gives you the power to influence a greater number of people, in a more direct way, than any other art form does today. Plato suggested exiling all storytellers and poets in Athens back in 388 B.C., because he said they were dangerous to society. Writers and filmmakers hide their ideas inside their stories, and can change what people believe, if the highly charged emotions, insights, and experiences ring true to the audience.

To avoid organizing actors and location shoots, I opted for hand drawing my characters and using photo collage and hand-drawn sets for my animation *Goth Grrls*. Even if you cannot draw really well, you can learn to do simple 2D animations to express your film idea, using software such as After Effects or Flash. Film festivals are rapidly embracing new styles of digital storytelling, over straight shooting styles, to show what is new on the horizon.

superfreak!

Think Up Original Digitally Enhanced Story Ideas. As you go through the screenwriting steps in Part I, concentrate on thinking up easy-to-do digital characters, sets, special effects, and visual ideas. If you are new to digital filmmaking, flip through Part III first.

definition

Original Idea Fresh idea, never before seen or explored on the screen in a film, animation, TV show, or game. What is new, different, and original about your short film idea? These new ideas could include an original POV, character type, film world, idea, subject, or visual storytelling style.

Using Digital Tools to Create Original Films

Originality is the cornerstone of a great short film. Stories are not only about what you have to say but also how you say it. Using all the power of digital wonders, a modern film-maker can tell stories in ways never seen before. "Show, don't tell" is the cardinal rule, and showing us things in fresh ways helps make a film highly original. The story underneath all the digital magic needs to have a strong foundation; otherwise, the film will seem like a gimmick. You do not want to appear to have graduated from the digital Toys R Us Special FX School of Film. On the other hand, you may only have a cheap DV camera, no budget, and some very powerful software for your storytelling tools, in comparison to films that have millions of dollars and hundreds of people. Use every strength in your arsenal as a digital independent filmmaker to tell the best and most original story possible.

In which types of highly original ways can you tell stories using some of your digital tools? The obvious answer is to add some whiz-bang special effects or to create some 3D monsters, because this is what we have become accustomed to when we go to see movies. This book, especially in Part III, explores some more creative and subtle uses for digital storytelling that will help you express your ideas in new ways.

If you know you want to create a modern 2D or 3D animated film, you should do a quick read about creating characters and sets for those styles in Chapters 10 and 11. Do not perform the project exercises in Part III; just get an idea of ways to create unique characters and sets using DV, 2D, or 3D. If you want to create a film in which you mix production styles, you may want to flip through Part III just to get a sense of some production-oriented story ideas. Alternatively, you may just keep reading and develop a script, and then add production-oriented story ideas later during rewrites.

project
1.2

Choosing Between DV-, 2D- or 3D-Oriented Story Ideas. The following brainstorming exercises in this chapter are designed to help you get a visual story idea to develop for the rest of this book. What types of digital tools or software do you want to use for your short film? If you are new to digital filmmaking, you may want to flip through Part III of this book to get an idea of narrative uses for easy special effects, set designs, and anima- tion techniques. If you are not sure, or know you want to do a straight DV film (without any special effects), you do not need to read ahead. If you are interested in using things such as bluescreen characters in your DV film, you may want to read the sections "DV Character Design Ideas" and "200 Narrative Bluescreen Ideas" in Chapter 9, "Digitally Enhanced Storytelling Techniques."

money-saving

Don't Even Try to Make a Hollywood-Looking Film. If you are an independent digital filmmaker, odds are your first short is not going to look much like *Lord of the Rings*, *Star Wars*, *The Matrix*, or *Harry Potter* (unless you are a 3D wizard!). Let this idea go now. Even if you have a $20,000 budget, your film will not look much like a mainstream one. It will look thin in regards to the number of extras, acting abilities, scene locations, lighting, camera work, and production values. There is a reason big feature films now easily cost upward of $50 million to make with professional cast, crew, set design, special effects, equipment, permits, makeup people, costumes, and multiple location budgets. A new 21st-century independent digital film aesthetic is taking hold, one that looks quite different and leans heavily on nonprofessional actors, handheld cameras, available sets, digital manipulation, and animation software to tell stories in new and original, no-budget ways. Writing a great script is therefore an essential ingredient for low-budget digital films, to make up for the obvious thinner production values seen on the screen.

In *Liquid Crystal Vision*, Torsten Klimmer interviewed people and then applied video effects filters that went with their "energy." The theme of this DV documentary explores the spiritual experiences, community, and personalities in the worldwide trance music scene, which fits nicely with the trippy visual effects. This is a great technique for making boring old video footage look original—if you have a good reason to do it.

Generating Original Ideas for Digital Short Films

Ideas for short films can come from just about anywhere. You need to observe how you work creatively and remember to write down any possible ideas in your notebook when you think of one or type them into your PDA. You may want to carry a small tape recorder to catch ideas while driving or during other activities. The initial concept for a film usually starts with a main character, visual shot idea, subject, or conflict. Ordinarily, any idea you think up has already been thought of by someone else. Therefore, you will find it helpful to create an inventory of your interests to help stimulate original story ideas and then combine them in ways you may not have connected before.

Try combining two completely different favorite ideas to get something unique.

Your own favorite character types, settings, subjects, ideas, and genres should become quite apparent as you go through the exercises in this chapter. Narrow down the focus of your storytelling style to concentrate exclusively on those particular subjects that hold the most fascination for you.

Brainstorming Techniques

You now need a 9×12-inch, black, bound drawing book to organize the upcoming exercises. The bigger the drawing book, the better, so that you have room to sketch and put random thoughts together. Just make sure that you can carry it around comfortably to catch any sudden inspiration surges. Ideas are plentiful until you really need one, so make sure to write down all of yours as you think of them; otherwise, you will probably forget them later.

"A creative writer can do his best only with what lies within the range and character of his deepest sympathies."
—Willa Cather

"A hunch is creativity trying to tell you something."
—Anonymous

Putting Your Pets to Work. How could you use your pets, convenient people, or old photos to create original films? These gothic detective characters with the heads of German shepherds were inspired by my sister's dogs. I blue screened the dogs sitting down (to keep their necks still), and then placed their heads on the blue-screened body of German rock star Xenomorph (**www.xenomorph.com**). This is an example of an original character created using the power of digital manipulation. The set was constructed using my travel photos of Prague.

Allow a couple pages of space for each of the following lists. Add to them as you go through your week and think of new ideas. I keep a separate drawing book for each of the following brainstorming categories and add to them accordingly. You may want to clip out pictures from magazines showing characters, sets, or shots that you may want to try and work into one of your films someday. Drawing books work great for pasting in magazine pictures or Photoshop printouts alongside sketches and notes.

If you already have some ideas you want to use for a short film, fill them into the exercises that follow. In the character list, for example, place your main character for your idea. Be open to changing your initial concept if you think of something even more original while going through the following brainstorming exercises.

Brainstorming for Characters

A fascinating and original lead protagonist is usually an essential main ingredient to creating a great short film. What types of characters would you absolutely love to see on the screen? Push your imagination to see where you may be able to use some of your digital tools to construct characters with special powers, body parts, or abilities that audiences have never seen before.

Begin by making a list of 20 possible main characters. Focus on creating original ones, not characters you have seen in other movies. These could come from stories

you've written, sketched, animated, or thought about creating. Some of these characters may be from famous films or animations that you combine with parts of other characters or actors to create new versions. These 20 characters could also be based on real people you know or animals, as long as you change them enough to create original screen versions. If you do not have any original characters ready to go, follow the sidebar tips on creating new characters from famous existing ones. If you are creating an animated film, make sure your characters are visually original and fun to animate. Experiment, using digital tools, by combining parts of real people and other well-known movie or animated characters in new ways. The goal of this exercise is to be able to see and feel what each original character is about, using as few descriptive words as possible.

1. Create three columns on a page and label them as shown in the following chart.
2. List 10 original main characters or protagonists to be the possible focus of your short film. You can change the age of an actor, the sex of a well-known character, or combine two different characters or people to create an original one as the chart shows. Add a few descriptive adjectives to help us really *see* the character.
3. State where the character might currently live to get a regional flavor of their environment.
4. Specify age range, such as teenager, early 20s, late 30s, or middle 40s.

5. Attach an actor to dream cast your original character. Use the chart in the section "The Essence of the Actor" that follows if you get stuck thinking up possibilities. Feel free to combine actors with people you know if it seems to make a more interesting or original character. I have taken my friend Katie and combined her with a teenage Parker Posey, preserving Katie's essence but getting more of a sassy version. Animated characters still need a famous voice actor attached to get the essence.

6. Assign each character a visually interesting occupation that fits with the character. It could be a past or futuristic job. Use the list in the "Occupational Ideas" section that follows if you need help thinking of ideas. You may want to just list 10 occupations that you think sound fun visually, and then match them to each character. If a character is too young for an actual occupation, write down what that character likes to do for fun that may turn into an occupation later, such as one who loves to climb trees at night and wants to be a spy.

7. Pick one brilliant thing the character can do better than almost anyone else in the film world and one big character flaw. Just guess what these things might be at this point.

The Essence of the Actor

Sometimes it helps to get a better feel for an emerging character by dream casting the character with an actual actor. The following list gives you some ideas and provides a few spaces to fill in names for your own favorite actors. A 9-year-old butterfly witch played by Drew Barrymore has a much different feel from one played by Whoopie Goldberg. Adjust the ages of the actors to fit your own original character essences.

Creating Original Characters Chart

Character	Possible Occupation	Best Talent / Worst Flaw
Christopher Walken (early 30s); worldly, hip, brilliant, techie, lives in bohemian Paris apartment	High-tech archeologist who uses underground 3D scanner to find lost cities	Great intuition/Too spaced out
A detective with the head of a German shepherd (bluescreen dog head/human body; voice by mid-20s Jack Nicholson; lives in old church basement in Prague	Rogue detective who investigates supernatural occurrences in dog world	Can smell "things" from very far away/ Bites other characters uncontrollably sometimes
Reese Witherspoon in early 20s; goth, femme fatal; lives in wild London squat	Shock performance artist	Great fire spinner/Clumsy when nervous
Katie (my friend) in mid-20s played by Parker Posey; new age, artsy; lives in Brooklyn loft	Animal telepath	Master telepath/Possessed

Female Actors		Male Actors	
Drew Barrymore	Cameron Diaz	Jack Nicholson	Samuel L. Jackson
Sissy Spacek	Katharine Hepburn	Jeff Goldblum	Ben Affleck
Reese Witherspoon	Angelica Huston	Val Kilmer	Anthony Hopkins
Kate Winslet	Juliette Binoche	Christopher Walken	Harrison Ford
Rene Zellweger	Diane Lane	Bruce Lee	Sean Penn
Gwyneth Paltrow	Catherine Zeta-Jones	Jackie Chan	Billy Bob Thornton
Jodie Foster	Julia Roberts	Nicholas Cage	Richard Gere
Shirley MacLaine	Sandra Bullock	Clint Eastwood	Ed Harris
Uma Thurman	Claire Danes	Robin Williams	Kevin Costner
Whoopie Goldberg	Oprah Winfrey	Keanu Reeves	Tom Cruise
Meryl Streep	Lucille Ball	Bruce Willis	Billy Crystal
Elizabeth Taylor	Angela Lansbury	Arnold Schwarzenegger	Michael Douglas
Marilyn Monroe	Bette Davis	Leonardo DeCaprio	Matthew McConaughey
Nicole Kidman	Kathy Bates	Tom Hanks	Denzel Washington
Goldie Hawn	Sigourney Weaver	James Woods	Edward Norton
Kate Hudson	Parker Posey	Brad Pitt	John Travolta

Using Existing Characters to Create Original Ones

You may want to list your favorite characters from films, animations, TV shows, comic books, novels, games, people you know, relatives, pets, or celebrities, and then turn them into other original versions. If you really love Spiderman, try taking the most interesting parts and developing highly original versions. Spiderman's cool thing is that he is part bug and part human. In the following chart, I list different bugs in one column and different human types in the other to create a new character, such as a little-girl butterfly witch. Create characters *you* would love to see in a film or animation. What ways could you use some of your digital tools to create new characters? The little-girl butterfly witch could be a bluescreen actor with a pair of 2D animated butterfly photograph wings that pop out when she gets scared. Attach an actor and an age range to the character to get a better feel for the character's essence, such as a 9-year-old Drew Barrymore butterfly witch.

Bugs	Human Character Types	Combinations
Butterfly	Businessman	Butterfly witch
Bumblebee	Little girl witch	Mosquito vampire
Dragonfly	Elderly vampire	Bumble bee businessman
Mosquito	Young fairy-tale princess	Fairy-tale princess dragonfly

Occupational Ideas

People are what they do in a sense. What types of careers or occupations might fit in nicely with your original characters?

Astronaut	Musician	Professional soccer player	Computer programmer	Game designer
Butler	Astrologer	Advertising executive	Astronomer	Accountant
Car thief	Knight	King/Queen	Retiree	Archeologist
Cartoonist	Veterinarian	Model	Fireman	Hit man
Chemist	Clerk	Mailman	Congressman	Priest
Clown	Comedian	Wrestler	Witch	Detective
Dentist	Doctor	Lawyer	Artist	Plumber
DJ/VJ	Student	Mortician	Vagabond	Warrior
Editor	Explorer	Fisherman	Fortune teller	Politician
Engineer	Landscaper	Actor	Racecar driver	Painter
Hands-on healer	Lifeguard	Policeman	Pirate	Novelist
Investment banker	Government employee	Stockbroker	Burglar	Construction worker
Magician	Witchdoctor	Hairdresser	Guru	Gangster
Poet	Spaceship commander	Psychiatrist	Teacher	Reporter
Soldier	Sheriff	Belly dancer	Slave	Shaman
Tour guide	Researcher	Wizard	Matchmaker	Cook
Circus clown	Professional surfer	Dictator	Cowboy	Talk-show host
Student	Bum	Fashion designer	Housewife	Hunter

project 1.3

Top 10 Characters. In your drawing book, list your 10 favorite original characters in an abbreviated form as seen here:

1. Christopher Walken as a high-tech archeologist who has great intuition but is really spaced out.
2. Supernatural detective with a German shepherd head who is really good at smelling clues but sometimes bites other characters uncontrollably.
3. Reese Witherspoon as a goth, shock performance artist who is a really good fire spinner but clumsy when nervous.

writing exercise 1.3

Write a few pages on a day in the life of your favorite character you brainstormed.

Brainstorming for Film-World Settings

The world you create in your film should be interesting enough to support a whole cast of compelling characters. What unique approaches can you take to create the places inside your film? Settings are like background characters that help tell the story in their own way. The originality of films often comes across in the choice of settings. In *Harry Potter*, we see what life would be like inside a wizard school. *Lord of the Rings* shows us a magical land full of interesting creatures such as talking trees. *Star Wars* takes us into the future of space battles. *Finding Nemo* shows us what it would be like to be a little fish living in a big ocean. What unique settings could you create using your favorite software that we have not seen before in a visual story? How could you show us a different perspective of a place we have seen before, in a fresh way, using some of your digital tools?

Film-World Settings and Emotional Moods

Film-World Setting	Emotional/Visual Moods
Stalactite cavern made of crystals	Magical, powerful
Tunnel crypts beneath Paris	Creepy, spooky, scary
Bigfoot clan cave in lost underground city	Otherworldly, native, ancient
Arcosanti—futuristic archeology in Arizona	Futuristic, geometric, creative, community, desert

project 1.4

Make a List of 10 Film-World Settings You Have Always Thought Would Look and Feel Great on the Screen. Add dates and adjectives if it helps you to see the setting better in your mind. Don't sweat the logistics just now. For instance, if you think a great set would be inside the tomb of some pyramid, list it; don't worry that authorities may not let you shoot inside a pyramid tomb. Anything goes! Just put it down. The sky is truly the limit as far as digital goes, which is why it's so much fun! It is always easier to pull ideas back than to push them out further later. Beside each set location, list the emotion you associate with it. The table on this page provides a few examples to get you started.

Arcosanti, a futuristic city in the Arizona desert about an hour north of Phoenix, combines architecture with ecology. This place was designed by the visionary architect Paolo Soleri, and would be a great set for an independent film dealing with environmental issues or futuristic themes. What other types of architecturally interesting places that we have not seen before would look good in your film?

This beach in Thailand with an after-party spider web in the background might make an ideal location for a scene where two people discuss traveling between worlds like spiders do in mythology. What types of vacation DV footage or photos do you already have that you could use to create symbolic virtual sets or backgrounds?

Wow! Shots

Sometimes you will think of a great single shot that turns into a film world or specific scene location. Occasionally, you will see a shot that takes your breath away because it is so visually powerful. Perhaps the composition is superb or the match cut from one scene to the next works perfectly. Maybe it's just a beautiful scene that looks like a stirring series of award-winning photographs set in motion. You want to include as many Wow! shots in your film as you can imagine.

definition

Wow! Shot Everyone who sees it should go, "Wow! What a great shot!"

Local Sets

What unique locations do you have in your area that might make an interesting film world or setting? Every square inch of Los Angeles and New York City has appeared on film somewhere. Are there any haunted, creepy places in your town? What about historical sites, strange-looking power plants, beautiful gardens, magnificent rock formations, cinematic cemeteries, national landmarks, lookout points, hip nightclubs, abandoned buildings, strange museums, weird stores, or wacky houses? Where is the best spot in your town to see a sunset? What's the scariest, happiest, most romantic, most scenic, most diabolical, or most futuristic place within a 100-mile radius of your home? How could you take existing locations

near your home and make them seem like they are in a different time or place? You usually do not need a film permit for a monopod DV shoot, and may be able to shoot the scene fast if your actors have been well rehearsed. You may also be able to shoot the set without the actors and drop them in later using a blue screen, or use animated characters, if you plan your shots carefully.

- **San Francisco water-treatment plant.** This location would make a great set for a low-budget futuristic film.

- **Japanese Tea Garden in Golden Gate Park.** A picture of Tokyo on the screen with a cut to characters in this garden scene would make it look as if this shot had been taken in Japan.
- **Muir Woods.** Local grove of old redwood trees for fantasy forest setting.

project
1.5

List 10 Wow! Shots. Make a List of 10 Wow! shots you have always wanted to see in a movie. Don't think plot, character, or theme yet. Don't think about whether you can create the shot yourself or can afford to shoot on location. Indulge completely in your fantasy of having every available resource to plan 10 of the best visual shots you have ever wanted to see on a screen. Create a setting after each shot to show the type of world it encompasses, if it is not obvious.

superfreak!

Draw Little Thumbnails (Small Rough Sketches) of Wow! Shots. Create a section in the back of your drawing book to sketch some of your favorite Wow! shots from films you love. After each great film you see, pick one shot you thought worked really well and sketch it in this back section.

I always thought it would be fun to see two characters having a conversation while falling down a bottomless stalactite pit. This Wow! shot idea became the setting for a short script taking place in a cavern.

Brainstorming for Favorite Story Flavors

Audiences are like tourists who embark on a trip through a film. If you feel like gunfights, horses, or going on a vacation to a dude ranch, you may want to pick up a western at the video store. If you feel like being scared or going to Romania, get a Dracula film. People often choose films based on what type of emotional ride or world they are craving to experience. What are your favorite types of stories, destinations, moods, or genres (story tones)?

Story Flavors: 37 Varieties

This following list is designed to help you narrow down the types of stories you are most interested in developing. If you had to pick just one story flavor from the following list as your absolute favorite, which one would you choose? Pay attention to what story flavors you are most interested in exploring with your films so that you can study other similar films for visual ideas. Experiment by combining different flavors to create new ones, such as a science-fiction, obsession-reality

show or a postmodern historical fantasy. Have fun with this exercise. Add any categories that you are interested in exploring and that I may have missed.

1. **Action/adventure.** Big adventures, hero journeys, disaster, survival, daring stunts, and action sequences.
2. **Animation.** Far-out or surreal visual elements with objects that can turn into other things. These stories usually show us something real actors or sets cannot do as easily, such as talking animals or living toys.
3. **Ensemble.** Stories about groups of characters unified by a common theme.
4. **Experimental.** Avant-garde rule breakers. Creating films that audiences may not even understand.
5. **Biography.** Find meaning of the person's life (theme), and make the person the hero (or anti-hero) in his or her own tale.
6. **Buddy.** Friendship or nonromantic close relationships developed over a series of events.

project 1.6

Local Settings. Make a list of 10 original local settings that might work well for a film. State what type of scene or shot the setting would be perfect for in a film.

project 1.7

Top 10 Sets. Create a Top 10 list of favorite sets, Wow! shots, or local locations you could possibly use in your short film. Choose your favorite settings from the lists you created in this section.

Plugging Into Ideas and Inspiration

Writer's block often occurs when we do not feel plugged into the "artistic flow." If you ask creative people where their ideas come from, they will often answer that they just "pull them out of thin air." Creative ideas seem to be floating around above our heads in an invisible cosmic soup that we dip into with sudden flashes of new thoughts. Julie Cameron talks about this process in her wonderful book *The Artist's Way* (J. P. Tarcher, 2002). Many artists approach creativity as an almost spiritual process, where you need to make yourself available to catching these new ideas. Develop your own original creative rituals: Wear a special hat. Use a lucky pen. Pray for ideas. Meditate on story directions. Sit at your paper or laptop for an hour each day waiting for the muse to show up. Take a walk and ask for ideas to come into your head. Every artist has his or her own way of plugging into inspiration, so experiment with finding ones that work best for you!

7. **City symphony.** Films about a single location with different perspectives, characters, events, and time frames.

8. **Comedy.** Show how characters in the best situations still manage to mess up, or create "fish out of water" tales. These stories are often used to showcase the brutality of social life.

9. **Crime.** Murder mystery, detectives solving cases, reporters investigating crimes, prison stories, heists, spy stories, criminals/victims getting revenge, courtroom dramas, organized crime.

10. **Disillusionment.** Protagonist's view of life changes from positive to negative.

11. **Documentary.** True story about event, people, or place.

12. **Drama.** Passion, madness, dreams of human heart.

13. **Education.** Protagonist changes worldview from negative to positive by learning something new.

14. **Fantasy.** New-world rules playing with time, space, and laws of nature.

15. **Historical.** Stories from the past often work great to show us some themes of our present situations at comfortable distances.

16. **Horror.** Bad, evil, scary, creepy things.

17. **Journey.** Trip, road trip, or travel tale.

18. **Love story.** What gets in the way of romantic love?

19. **Maturation.** Coming-of-age story.

20. **Mockumentary.** Fiction that looks like a real documentary.

21. **Music video.** Short film for a song and hopefully with some story, theme, or context.

22. **Musical.** Songs used to tell stories from any genre. What are the new digitally enhanced musicals going to look like?

23. **Myth.** Hero journeys, ancestral memories, prehistory, moral conduct, or urban legends.

24. **Obsession/addiction/temptation.** Willpower versus obsessions/addictions/temptations.

25. **Personal anthology.** Video diaries, personal events.

26. **Postmodern.** No single lead protagonist with distortion of time and space.

27. **Punishment.** Good protagonist turns bad and is punished.

28. **Psychodrama.** Madmen, serial killers, crazy people, nuthouses.

29. **Reality shows.** Real-life, voyeuristic-style stories. TV shows such as "The Osbournes" or "Survivor."

30. **Redemption.** Protagonist goes from morally bad to good.

31. **Science fiction.** Possible future, unknown past.

32. **Societal problems.** Political, racial, medical, educational, business, environmental, family.

33. **Sports.** Big character change in relationship to sporting event.

34. **Supernatural.** Spiritual or freaky occurrence in unseen realms.

35. **Tragedy.** Cautionary tales, somber themes, catastrophic characters.

36. **War.** Combat, prowar/antiwar.

37. **Western.** Wild West. Good versus evil. Gun fights, cowboys, bank robberies, cattle drives, Indians, ranches, horses, and saloons.

Four Basic Types of Films

Classic narrative. Single protagonist with linear time (time frame of events obvious to viewer). Everything you need to know about story presented clearly. Cause and effect clearly observed. Objective viewing experience (viewer conclusions about story similar). Focus on making viewers *feel*.

Postmodernism. May not have a single lead protagonist. A distortion of time with jumps in time and space (nonlinear time), where audience may not know where in time events are taking place. May ignore cause and effect completely. Mixing other forms or styles of films together. Strong awareness of unusual camera techniques to tell story. Subjective viewing experience with lots of space for each viewer to decide meaning and story. Focus is on making viewers *think* more about the story, less focus on feelings. Classic postmodernism film: *Citizen Kane*.

Documentary. Organizing information that already exists.

Experimental. No characters even necessary. Nonlinear time. No cause and effect. Viewer understanding unnecessary; experience of film enough.

Glenn Grillo created *The Godegg*, an experimental supernatural film, in 3ds max and After Effects (**www.arcanerealities.com**). He uses ancient spiritual symbols throughout the piece as the viewer flies along through 3D spaces with aliens, angels, temples, and eggs. What types of experimental films might you be interested in making using digital tools to show us things we have not seen before?

What do films in your favorite story flavors or genres always do? Study a few of your favorite films that are similar to the one you are about to create and see what works and what does not. How can you do a love story in a style no one has seen before? How can you use some of your digital powers to update an old story style? How can you mix genres to come up with a fresh combination for your short film?

Please do not choose experimental, documentary, or reality shows to take through the step-by-step process in this book. If you really want to do one of these forms, create a mock script of what you think the film might be like to complete the exercises in these chapters. Although this book is geared more for classic narrative films, you can apply many of the techniques to other types of films.

"When we write from experience, we harvest our lives."
—Bonnie Goldberg

writing exercise 1.4

Write a few pages on a film idea for a favorite story flavor or genre. Concentrate on including unique genre elements.

project 1.8

Top 10 Story Flavors. Choose one of the preceding 37 flavors, or a combination, as your absolute favorite story flavor, and then pick 9 more for your Top 10 list. Try mixing flavors that sound fun and original to watch. A crime fantasy, sports horror, war musical, supernatural crime thriller, animated mockumentary, action experimental, or science-fiction biography might spark some new ideas for short film approaches.

Creating Unique Genre Elements

All stories have been told before in one way or another. The originality of your characters, plot events, activities, interactions, dialogue, theme, and settings will give your film a unique genre color. This original color you add to your story ideas will make your film into either a regurgitated amateur Hollywood knock-off or a wholly stunning never-before-seen masterpiece of clever originality. Got spaceships? Do them differently than we have ever seen before. *Star Wars* showed us a new version of the future unlike anything we had seen before in a science-fiction movie. *Harry Potter* took us into the world of wizards and magic. *Lord of the Rings* presented us with elves, hobbits, orcs, and humans having battles in supernatural places. *Spiderman* let us peek into what it would be like to shoot webs from our wrists and have amazing superhero abilities. *Toy Story* let us feel what it would be like to be a toy. *Antz* took us into the mentality of an ant colony. What types of new genre styles could you create using some of your digital storytelling tools?

Doing a gangster film? Make sure it does not look anything like *The Godfather*, *Pulp Fiction*, *Goodfellas*, *The Sopranos*, or any other crime film we have already seen. What unique elements or color could you add to your criminals to make them more interesting? A great gangster film, *Things to Do*

Brainstorming for Favorite Subjects

Sometimes just figuring out what you are interested in helps you think of story ideas. The more you know about a subject, the better you will be able to use it in a film.

"Creativity is the power to connect the seemingly unconnected."
—William Plomer

writing exercise 1.5

Write a rough short story based on a magazine, Internet, or newspaper article from a favorite publication.

I have been scribbling sketches of the Egyptian god Thoth in my notebooks. His silhouette and unique design makes him a prime candidate for an original animated character. What types of historical or mythological figures hold the most fascination for you that might pop up in a film somewhere? Why do you like them and how can you develop the most interesting parts of the idea into an original digital short film?

I have always been fascinated by the idea of Bigfoots, Native American beliefs, and white-trash stereotypes. I combined these three ideas and wrote a series of short scripts and a feature about a group of 3D Native American white-trash Bigfoots, which I believe are pretty unique. The spirituality of the Native American beliefs fit nicely with the resourceful white-trash aesthetic to show the Bigfoots as mystical redwood forest scavengers living on the fringes of human existence. Remember to think of combining ideas you would love to see in a film.

---

in Denver When You're Dead, has a very scary hit man called Mr. Shhhh, played by Steve Buscemi, who looks pretty harmless until you see him in action. If you can master unique genre elements, you can take almost any story and make it worth watching. How can you update your favorite story flavor combinations or genres for the 21st century using your digital tools?

In Goth Grrls, when the main character Violet gets a new idea, a blinking skull appears above her head. The skull replaces the usual blinking light bulb above traditional 2D animated characters who suddenly get bright ideas. This animation pokes fun at the goth scene, and the blinking skull is a unique genre element, along with monster skeleton bones on the walls and other creepy things. What ways can you take the style of your genre and incorporate visually unique things?

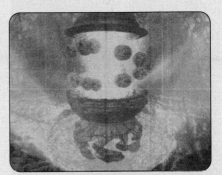

In our music video Beyond, we created a temple that turned into an organic spaceship. This metaball warp core powers the spaceship, and turns the archeologist musician into triplet aliens wearing LCD clothing. These are unique science-fiction genre elements used to tell a journey story in a new way.

Brainstorming for Favorite Subjects. What areas of interest fascinate you the most? Answer the following questions to help you come up with a Top 10 list of subjects:

1. **What are your Top 3 favorite magazines right now?** *Outside, National Geographic, Vogue, Maxim,* or *Popular Science*? These are all clues about what subjects might show up on your final list. List your top three favorite magazines and what about the subject matter interests you the most. How could you take a story out of one of these magazines and turn it into an original short film idea?

2. **What are your Top 3 favorite books?** Create a brief sentence or two about the plot using the story concept sentence discussed earlier. See whether you can find the theme of each story and sum up the unique subject matter or genre element.

3. **What are your Top 3 favorite hobbies or areas of study?** These activities may include adventure travel, sports, arts, collecting, gardening, yoga, watching TV, playing video games, or anything else you love to do in your free time. How can you work these interests into a film? If you are into building rock sculptures in your garden, perhaps you could build an interesting miniature set for a scene.

4. **What Top 3 historical events, time periods, or people interest you the most?** Explain specifically why each subject fascinates you if possible.

5. **Do you have any favorite myths?** Myths work great for digital films because you can use effects and animation to create some of the more fantastic elements. These types of stories explore events that happened before written history, show patterns and beliefs that give meaning to life, develop shared ancestral memories, fill the gaps between the unconscious and conscious, examine moral behaviors, and help give groups of people identities. What types of myths are particular to your location or culture? If you are a little fuzzy on the various myths out there, you may want to pick up Joseph Campbell's *Power of Myth* (Anchor, 1991) book or DVD with interviews. What are the new myths for the 21st century? Use the adaptation techniques later in this chapter to create original stories from existing myths. You may just want to list the types of myths you like, such as Hindu or Native American, and read some books on those subjects if you are really into doing a mythic tale.

6. **What are your Top 3 favorite urban legends?** These types of stories also make particularly good digital films because you can justify the special effects and have lots of fun playing with reality. Are you interested in local regional legends, Bigfoots,

UFOs, ghost stories, lost cities, monsters in the sewer, conspiracy theories, or weird alternative dimensions? For a great catalog on urban legend books and magazines, check out The World Explorer's Club at **www.wexclub.com**. This site was started by David Hatcher Childress, a cutting-edge archeologist, who writes the fascinating *Lost Cities* series. These books have some great story ideas for creating original sets, creatures, and film worlds. List your Top 3 favorite urban myths and what aspect about the myth is the coolest part. Add any film ideas for adapting the cool part of the myth, or combining it with another idea to create an original one.

I adapted the most fascinating part of an American Indian story to explain how my characters disappeared into thin air. This dimensional vortex gate idea came from the book Haunted Mesa *by Louis L'Amour, about an American Indian legend that tells of this happening in certain spots. How can you take the best parts of your favorite stories and create new original ones?*

Combine Ideas to Create Five New Ones. Using your Top 10 Subject list, try combining two ideas from other subjects or Top 10 lists in this chapter to create an original idea. You could take one of your characters and ask yourself how that character might change when combined with a favorite subject.

Brainstorming for Software Capabilities

What types of software are you using? Many experienced digital filmmakers use a wide variety of software. Hollywood or mainstream films have multimillion-dollar budgets and hundreds of specialized professional people working on every aspect of each shot. You might only have a DV camera and some very powerful software. Use your strengths to your advantage when planning small independent films to tell stories in new ways.

List digital story ideas for using some of your favorite software. You can be as general or specific as you like. If you are new to digital filmmaking or animation, you may want to thumb through Part III of this book for ideas. Write down digital techniques that you think look really interesting or that you want to try, such as using a bluescreen pet for a character.

When it came time to think up an idea for a 3D IMAX film sequence, our company, Minds Eye Media, looked at its favorite software of the moment first. Arete, from Digital Nature Tools, does 3D water effects, waterfalls, water fountains, oceans, waves, and anything else with water you can imagine. The idea of a water roller coaster ride began to emerge. We listed all of our ideas, drew a map, and planned out the shots. This is an example where the software took precedence over everything else.

Digital Filmmaking Software Capabilities

Digital Video	2D Animation	3D Animation
Photo collage virtual sets	2D *South Park*-style hand-drawn characters.	3D sets such as fantasy settings, prehistoric places, or anything else
Film-look filters	Flash-style motion graphic sets.	Hairy 3D mythical creatures
Lightning bolts effects	Scan and pan photo backgrounds.	3D weather effects such as tornado swarms
Bluescreen characters	300-foot-tall metaphorical or surreal animated photograph characters.	3D water fountains that make shapes for visual metaphors or new security devices
Prehistoric film-look with tons of damage showing cavemen	An oversized human head blue screened onto a stick-figure 2D animated body.	An alien 3D garden with talking plants
Lightning bolt special effects going between people as energy connections	Pictures of pressed butterflies animated by titling wings. Then duplicating to form hundreds on the screen, writing patterns in the air.	A 3D human aura, with chakras, energy circuits, and blobs of colors

note

Narrow Your Brainstorming Scope.
If you know what subject you want to use or you are doing a series of short films on the same subject, narrow your scope with this exercise. I could narrow my whole chart to ideas only about Native American Bigfoots. I would then create a column of 10 Bigfoot characters (based on the actors or interesting people I know), 10 Bigfoot settings, 10 Bigfoot subjects (could be anything they deal with), and 10 software capabilities that I could use in their Bigfoot world. You should get enough ideas to do a whole series of short films using this technique.

project 1.11

Fill in a Brainstorming Chart with Top 10 List of Ideas. Open your drawing book to two new (and blank) facing pages. Draw five columns with the headings listed here and fill in the ideas you have already gathered. The obvious trick is to start with the first character and then go across the rows and pick the most appropriate film world or set, story flavor, subjects, and software capabilities that might go together. The five columns should have the following headings:

1. Top 10 Characters
2. Top 10 Film World/Settings
3. Top 10 Story Flavors
4. Top 10 Subjects
5. Top 10 Software Capabilities

Fill in these columns with the lists you created.

"If you do what you've always done, you'll get what you've always gotten."
—Anonomyous

project 1.12

Top 5 Sentences. Create five story concept sentences for short film ideas using the preceding chart. The goal is to think up good, original ideas you would love to see in a short film. Everyone's chart is going to be different depending on subjective interests. You should see patterns in characters, subjects, settings, and story flavors if you have strong likes and dislikes. Construct your five best story concept sentences in this form:

It is a story about a Top 10 character who lives in a Top 10 film world/setting. This story explores the subject of Top 10 subject in a Top 10 story flavor using Top 10 software ability.

Do whatever you have to at this point to combine ideas or think of new ones to get a story idea that excites you. Plot and theme goals, along with conflict, will be added to these sentences soon. The following examples show you how the story sentences look with the information from the chart plugged in:

It is a story about a young Reese Witherspoon Native American whitetrash Bigfoot girl who lives in a Bigfoot clan cave. This story explores the subject of mystical creatures in an animated supernatural maturation story, using 3D Bigfoots, DV footage of forest and campers, 2D animated cave paintings, and 3D/DV/2D photo sets.

writing exercise 1.6

Write a rough short story based on one of your favorite story concept sentences.

Brainstorming Chart For Story ideas

Top 10 Characters	Top 10 Film Worlds/Settings	Top 10 Story Flavors	Top 10 Subjects	Top 10 Software Capabilities
Christopher Walken as a high-tech archeologist	Bigfoot clan cave	Animated supernatural comedy	Lost cities	Lightning bolts/ 3D sets
Supernatural detective with a German shepherd head	Tunnel crypts beneath Paris	Historical horror	Supernatural occurrences	Bluescreen characters
Reese Witherspoon as a goth shock performance artist	Arcosanti, futuristic city in desert	Modern love redemption	Mystical creatures/ Bigfoots	3D characters

Discovering Your Own Creative Process

Every storyteller or artist has his or her own way of generating ideas. You never know when a creative spark will just hit you with a great story idea that may pour out in a burst of inspiration. The step-by-step process in this book is designed to help fire off these idea surges, and it's your responsibility to write all of them down as they surface. I often try out multiple script ideas by writing short stories, listing interesting characters, key story points, scene ideas, cool shots, events, or dialogue. I do not think in this step-by-step process when making a film, but I do think about most of these things at some point while writing ideas down. The more visual storytelling techniques you learn, the more you will automatically think of them while trying out different approaches to making films.

I created a main character for my short film example by combining several different ideas. I took my Reese Witherspoon shock performance artist and made her a Bigfoot to fit with my Bigfoot cave setting. I then changed the character's style from gothic to Native American white-trash to better fit the Bigfoot world. How could you combine different favorite ideas from your lists? This was my first rough sketch of the main bigfoot character. She is ideal for 3D animation, because it would be hard to find a real Bigfoot or use costumes. The mythical supernatural abilities of Bigfoots, such as their incredible strength and ability to dematerialize at will, work great for using digital special effects. To pick her out from other characters in shots and silhouettes, I have put her in a bikini and tied a big bow on her head.

"If you wait for inspiration, you'll be standing on the corner after the parade is a mile down the street."
—Ben Nicholas

"All you need to do to receive guidance is to ask for it and then listen."
—Sanaya Roman

Plan Time to Research Story Ideas. When thinking about creating a new story, it helps to do some research on your rough ideas. Internet search engines, books, encyclopedias, magazines, films, or any other information about a particular subject will help you generate more story possibilities. When your inspiration is running low or is blocked, doing some research can help get your creative juices flowing again. For my Bigfoot story idea, I went online and printed out lots of information from different web sites.

This helped me stay true to the Bigfoot essence and generate lots of fresh story ideas I would not have thought of on my own. I read somewhere that eyewitness accounts often reported seeing Bigfoots banging rocks together. This sparked a new visual Wow! shot idea, which made me think how fun it would be to show a Bigfoot drumming circle using huge rocks. Try to always see ways to apply research ideas to stories while creating a unique visual film world.

Adaptations

If you are still having trouble coming up with an idea, try doing an adaptation. Sometimes it works great to take an existing story from a movie, animation, book, play, magazine, newspaper article, or story, and re-create the spirit of it in a short film. The best types of adaptive stories are full of visible outward events and do not happen mostly in the character's head. Remember that the majority of prose is intended for the human mind and usually does not translate well onto the screen.

note

Adapting to Rights Issues. Don't do straight adaptations unless you have the rights in writing. You *must* change the story enough that it becomes your own. A 2D student of mine liked the children's story *The Giving Tree*, but did not want to have any problems with rights issues, so she changed the tree to a pond with the same theme.

How to Adapt an Existing Story

Here are some ideas to consider when you are attempting to adapt existing story ideas into wholly new original ones:

1. Change the sex, age, race, species, or culture of characters.
2. Change the location or time period.
3. Adopt the story to your own interests. Let's say I want to loosely adapt Ayn Rand's novel *The Fountainhead*, about an architect in the mid-1900s meeting with resistance to his new modern style. I could make the main character an Asian woman and put her in the near future as a designer of utopian communities meeting with resistance. Or maybe she could be a futuristic fashion designer, junk sculpture artist, or sacred landscaper.
4. Change the genre or story flavor to a new one or a new combination.

5. Try to change the story to justify some new digital storytelling device. Maybe in my new version of *The Fountainhead*, I could have the characters bluescreened, living in a 3D-modeled utopian city. You want to show the audience something they have not seen before in a way that fits nicely into the story and uses all of your digital powers. If you do not know 3D, you could try photo collages or drawing the utopian city and dropping it in behind the characters to create a new visual cinematic style. This type of approach is covered more in Part III.

6. Keep the spirit and theme of the piece intact.

7. Change the quest object, plot goal, and obstacles.

"Just as appetite comes by eating, so work brings inspiration."
—Igor Stravinsky

8. Change the POV. Whose side of the story are we hearing? What would *Star Wars* be like from the POV of Darth Vader?

9. Ask, "What if?" What if that tragic mountain climbing accident you read about in a magazine happened in an animated world of 3D Yetis?

10. Short stories obviously work better for short films. Collecting favorite short story genre anthologies may spark some new ideas to adapt.

Bigfoot Video. I could take my Bigfoot idea and ask, "What if someone finally captured a real Bigfoot close up on video?" This could be part of my story or it could form the basis of my plot. I decided to have a shot of an unmanned video-surveillance camera capturing a Bigfoot walking by in the deep forest. During my research on the Internet, I read that scientists were installing these cameras, which sparked the shot idea.

superfreak!

Creating an Original Adaptation. Create one original adaptation short film idea using the techniques discussed. Make sure you change the ideas enough to create a wholly original concept.

Incorporating Plot Goals

Now that you have an idea for your short film, you need to give the story some structure by thinking of a plot goal for your main character. Take your Top 3 ideas and choose three possible plot goals for each story concept sentence. The three plot goals may relate as a series of goals in one story, or be separate main goals for completely different ideas. Longer films often have several plot goals that change throughout the story depending on the length. The first goal could be to sneak into the aquarium and the second one to get a picture swimming with the rare giant squid. Short films of less than 5 minutes usually only have time for one or two plot goals. Experiment with running your story concept idea down the list of goals and see which ones sound the most fun visually and fit best with your ideas. Be very specific after you choose your type of plot goal. "To not get caught" needs to be more specific, such as "to not get caught sneaking into the aquarium." Start to see the film in your head and imagine different characters and situations emerging.

writing exercise 1.7

Write a rough short story using some of the adaptation techniques.

"You must have long-range goals to keep you from being frustrated by short-range failures."
—Charles C. Noble

project 1.13

Top 10 Films. Make a list of your Top 10 favorite films with plot summaries. Or list 10 films you saw lately that you enjoyed. (Do not get stuck on picking the all-time best 10 films.) After each film, list the plot goals. Describe in a few lines why you enjoyed the film so much. Was it the main character? Did you like the places in which the story took place? Was the ending a total surprise? To start to see where your own style may be heading, you need to figure out what types of films you like. You will most likely be drawn to similar themes, too. Do not make a list of your Top 10 films to impress people with your vastly sophisticated film knowledge. Be honest with yourself. Add the theme, subject, and story flavor of each film if possible.

Plot Goal Chart

Review your favorite stories, or go to your local video store and read the backs of the boxes, to add to this list of common plot goals.

To Survive a Coming-of-Age Vision Quest. One of the plot goals I thought might be interesting to develop visually, using special effects and animation, was to survive a coming-of-age shamanic journey vision quest in a dark cave. In this shot, my character falls into a long tunnel full of sharp rocks. I got the idea for a vision quest from my Native American research.

Funky Bigfoot World. In one of my favorite films, *Buckaroo Bonzai*, a hip low-budget film world was created to show the alien characters and space technology. I want to use this type of funky aesthetic when planning my Bigfoot film-world look. Shown here is a Bigfoot cave with sleeping nests and found campground objects inspired by my research (I read Bigfoots often take things from campsites). What favorite film looks or styles would you like to use as inspiration for designing the feel of your own stories?

Plot Goal Chart

To slay a monster	To get rich	To find treasure
To win the race	To advance spiritually	To get around the system
To rule the world	To become famous	To overthrow government
To stop a bomb	To become successful	To stop a bad thing from happening
To defeat an enemy	To blackmail someone	To become a better person
To win political office	To get someone to do something	To evolve to a higher state of being
To become king/queen	To trick someone	To survive a dangerous vision quest
To get revenge	To find meaning in life	To travel to distant lands
To save the world/land	To solve a murder	To prove a theory
To cure disease	To catch a killer	To get a promotion
To stop a natural disaster	To solve/fix a problem	To get a date
To fall in love	To understand something	To explore new territory
To get the girl/guy	To learn a new skill	To fix broken transportation
To solve a crime	To become a top warrior	To invent a new device
To solve a mystery	To become a leader	To make something new
To steal something	To fight for a just cause	To have a successful art show/event
To win a war	To do what is right	To save a current relationship
To stop a war	To help people	To destroy someone

Exploring Your Own Life Plot Goals

Often the types of things we dream about doing become the plot goals for our own personal lives. You may spend lots of time fantasizing about being a gourmet cook while spending your days as a stockbroker. These desires point to some deep urge inside you that may be showing you a new direction your life is heading. If you daydream about something often, it usually means this is something you are passionate about creating on some level. These types of daydreams or wishes often form the foundation for good archetypal stories.

Universal desires sometimes come in the strangest individual packages.

If you were to make a film about the stockbroker opening his first restaurant, you might appeal to people of all walks of life pursing their own dreams in similar ways. You would think of as many obstacles as possible for obtaining this goal in a surprising way as you develop the script.

"If you are seeking creative ideas, go out walking. Angels whisper to a man when he goes for a walk."
—Raymond Inmon

project 1.14

Top 10 Life Plot Goals. List the 10 things you want to do in this lifetime, rephrased as plot goals. The important thing is to be honest about what would really be meaningful and fun if you could do anything. Decide what type of plot goal it might be from the ones listed previously. Add any life plot goals that I may have missed to the preceding list. For example, I want to walk the 500-mile spiritual Camino path across northern France and Spain. The plot goal would be to go on a trip or a vision quest.

To defeat evil	To find/rescue someone	To travel through time
To help someone die	To communicate with another	To change history
To help another group of people improve their lives	To defeat evil aliens	To maintain the status quo
To uncover a conspiracy	To right a wrong	To start a revolution
To win a bet	To sell/buy something	To explore a new reality/dimension
To rob a bank or place	To let go of someone	To find/deliver an object
To escape from prison/situation	To overcome obstacles to love	To become popular within a group
To nurse something back to life	To recover from past tragedy	To have a successful first date
To create a work of art	To murder someone	To stop a baby from crying
To break an enemy code	To avoid being killed	To heal a sick character or group
To find inspiration	To avoid being destroyed by obsession/addiction	To train a pet or dog
To start a business	To revolt against something	To find a secret place
To throw a party/event	To seduce someone	To change careers
To get a job	To prove innocence	To fix a terrible mistake
To find inner peace	To find truth	To clear possession of one's soul
To become a professional something	To be accepted	To do something
To become a champion something	To free something captured	To explore a place
To survive a deadly situation	To get through a difficult situation	To explore a character's life

Brainstorming for Themes

What's important to you? What nuggets of wisdom have you gathered to share with the world? Themes grow out of who you are and how you believe life works. The best ones come from your own emotions, experiences, and insights about people and the world. What ideas are you hooked on exploring in your creative work? As a filmmaker, you need to find your subject, story flavors, and subsequent themes. Most filmmakers play with similar themes and genres in their films. Martin Scorsese is hooked on redemption themes. Lars Von Trier deals with sexual compulsion.

superfreak!

Turning Life Goals into Film Ideas. Take your Top 10 Life Plot Goals and turn 5 of them into a brief idea about a possible digital short film. Write a short story (3–5 pages) about your favorite short film idea from this exercise.

project 1.15

Pick Plot Goals for Each of Your Top 5 Ideas. Pick 1 or 2 plot goals for each of your Top 5 ideas from the previous brainstorming chart exercise where you created 5 story concept sentences. List the specific goals in the order they occur if you have multiple ones. Short films less than five minutes in length usually only have time for one or two plot goals. You may want to do some research on story subjects to stir up fresh ideas at this point.

writing exercise 1.8

Write a few pages showing a character trying to accomplish a goal or series of plot goals, while encountering lots of unexpected conflict or obstacles.

I could turn walking the Camino path (life goal) into a sacred stalagtitie cavern (top setting), for a 3D Bigfoot (top 10 character). By researching the types of experiences and challenges people who have walked the camino path report, I could add details to my story such as parts of the trail being very dangerous. In one place on the Camino Path, there are viscious packs of wild dogs, which I could replace with poisonous snakes to fit the cave setting.

A Shamanic Journey. As a filmmaker, I'm interested in exploring themes dealing with how the unseen spiritual world connects to the physical world we see everyday. Digital tools greatly expand my palette for creating these spiritual realms with an original vision. Shown here is how the beginning of a shamanic journey might look for a Bigfoot. Using 3D animation and special effects, the character's spirit dives into a pool of water, while drumming, to show how it enters the shamanic journey world. What new visual ways can you express themes you are personally interested in developing using some of your digital tools?

David Lynch prefers to explore unseen connections—in the dark side of human reality—and how nothing is what it seems.

Your age will often determine the types of themes that are important to you. Teenagers think a lot about fitting in. Twenty-somethings think they know it all. Thirty-somethings start to figure out their place in the world. Forty-somethings are more concerned with family and relationships. Men and women focus on different types of themes. Write a list of the types of themes you think are important to communicate from the wisdom you have collected about life over the years.

I thought it would be fun to develop the theme of how every lifeform has a unique purpose to experience, accomplish, and share with one another. One way I could show this theme is to have a character discover its life purpose during a vision quest shamanic journey. Other creatures could be performing their life purpose, such as a spider that spins prophetic symbols in its web each day, foreshadowing important future story events. What visual way could you have multiple characters show us a recurring theme in one of your film ideas?

project 1.16

Top 10 Personal Themes. Create a list your Top 10 favorite themes that you may want to develop in films. Refer to the previous list of themes in films if you get stuck trying to figure out what constitutes a theme. A theme can be any truth you have discovered in your life or idea that controls why events are happening in a story. Make sure your theme is universal in some way, containing a deep truth about life that you have personally experienced.

project 1.17

Top Themes. Pick one possible theme for each of your Top 5 story ideas. This theme may change later as you develop your final story choice.

project 1.18

Top 3 Experiences and Themes. Make a list of the Top 3 experiences in your life that transformed you in some big way. Figure out the theme of the experience or what you learned if possible. These experiences may include things like losing someone or something dear to you, winning something, moving to a new town, getting really sick, experiencing a big disappointment or spiritual revelation, meeting a special person, taking a trip, getting a divorce, or facing a life or death situation or a past traumatic experience. If you will be sharing these with people, be mindful about your privacy if that is an issue.

Defining the Themes of Your Emotional Experiences

What types of themes have you adopted as your truth from high-intensity experiences in your life? People make decisions about how they relate to the world and how the world works depending on what happens to them. Keep these personal truths in mind to cannibalize ideas for developing powerful emotional stories.

Ezzie, my Bigfoot character, could be her own worst enemy and antagonist. I created one story where she has read too many women's fashion magazines, full of airbrushed, Photoshop-treated super models. This gave her a complex about not being good or pretty enough that makes her do silly things. Almost all woman feel this way at some point when looking at magazines, and would connect more to the character. I decided to create a separate character for a stronger antagonist example in the final version, but did consider this idea as a possibility.

"He that wrestles with us strengthens our nerves and sharpens our skills. Our antagonist is our helper."
—Edmund Burke

Attaching an Antagonist

You need to define your antagonist to develop conflict and include in your pitch. Refer to your list of possible plot goals, and then ask who or what could be standing in the way of your main character accomplishing each goal. The biggest challenge is to come up with an original antagonist we have not seen before in a way that fits nicely with the story or film world.

The antagonist is not necessarily an evil or bad character. It could be a tornado, organization, or even the protagonist himself if he is his own worst enemy. Truly evil characters or forces take great pleasure in hurting other people or life forms are called villains.

Antagonists do not have separate theme goals. Instead they represent the anti-theme of the protagonist. If your theme is that greed destroys, your antagonist will be the greediest person in the film who would usually get destroyed in the end. You may want to make your antagonist mysterious so that the audience wonders how he got so twisted. In *Star Wars*, this character is Darth Vader, representing the dark side, with a body so mangled he has to live in a machine-like suit. Many movies usually succeed or fail based on the originality and power of the antagonistic force.

project
1.19

List Your Top 5 Favorite Antagonists. Go through your favorite films or think of the best villains you have ever seen onscreen. Your list might range from Cruella De Vil in *101 Dalmations* to the Ring Wraiths in *Lord of the Rings*. List what you liked about them that made these particular antagonists stick out in your mind. In what ways are they original? How do they have their own personalities and desires that we can understand to some degree? How do these antagonists stand in the way of the protagonists accomplishing their plot goal? What qualities make the scariest villains?

Antagonist Idea Chart

Competitor	Commander	Social pressure	Boss
Corporation or head of corporation	Lawyer	Criminal	Organization or head of organization
Madman	Evil person	Spirit	Wealthy respected person
Pirate	Protagonist himself/ herself	Leader	Dangerous animal
Outlaw	Bad alien	The system	Thug or gang
Monster	Someone blackmailing someone	The police	Characters with different viewpoints
Natural disaster		Enemy	Disease
Family member	Robot	The government	Character seeking revenge
Authority figure	Cursed object	Local bully	
		A teacher or mentor	

Anti-Plot + Anti – Theme = Antagonists

If your antagonist is a real bad guy, keep in mind that everyone is always doing the best they know how to get through life. Not many people think of themselves as bad, because they rationalize everything they do based on who they are and their experiences. Hannibal Lector in *Silence of the Lambs* does not see himself as a monster. Bad people deserve love just like everyone else. Villains are often the most charming people in town because they have to be able to get away with their evil deeds. Cynical characters often have a confused set of values and do not understand the nature of love. Keep these things in mind when designing your antagonist.

Scary Bigfoot Witchdoctor. The antagonist idea I came up with for my Bigfoot world is a character to represent the shadow side of our subconscious. I designed a rough character based on holy men in India who worship Shiva. This Bigfoot is covered In long black dreads, smokes a pipe, and has powerful eyes with a screeching roar that scares all the other creatures. A buzzing swarm of hornets hover around him to add an extra element of fear, and would make good use of digitally enhanced particle effects.

> **note**
>
> **Glowing Crystal Bigfoot Skull.** This antagonist idea is an animated crystal skull, which guards the sacred shamanic cave where the other Bigfoots go to have vision quests. He teases the young Bigfoots to test them during their quest and shoots them lightning bolts surges when they make a mistake or lose concentration. What types of digital effects can you add to make your antagonists more original?

project 1.20

Create Antagonists. List one idea for brilliantly original antagonists that might work in each of your five short film ideas. See how you can make them a negative manifestation of your chosen theme.

Final Story Concept Sentence to Pitch

It is now time to choose the best of your five story ideas to develop into a pitch. Make sure this is a film idea that you would love to see. You will be developing this one idea for the rest of the book.

How to Pitch an Idea for a Film

Pitching is another required skill for any serious filmmaker and is an art form in itself. If you have a great original idea for a film, you should be able to communicate it to anyone in a 30-second short pitch. The "30-second elevator pitch" you will learn here is based on the possibility of being trapped in an elevator for a short amount of time with a studio head or famous actor. This quick conversation could get your film into production, based on the listener's enthusiasm about being involved in your project.

writing exercise 1.9

Write a few pages on a day in the life of one of your new original antagonists.

project 1.21

State Your Final Film Idea. Answer the following questions for your final favorite short film idea. If you are not sure which of your Top 5 ideas to choose, try running them by a few friends and see which one they think sounds the most interesting. It may also help to write a short two- to three-page story of each idea to see which one turns out best, if you are having problems choosing.

1. Protagonist?
2. Unique film-world setting?
3. Original idea/subject not seen before?
4. Story flavor?
5. Specific plot goals?
6. Antagonist?
7. Digital software capabilities being used?
8. Theme?

"Skill to do comes of doing."
—*Ralph Waldo Emerson*

note

Obtaining Free Caffeine. Approach the local espresso bar and ask them to donate caffeine and croissants to your set on the day of the shoot in exchange for a mention from you in the credits. You will need to pitch your film to the manager of the coffee shop to get him or her excited enough about the idea to want to be associated with your project. If your pitch is great, it's easy to get free treats.

Pitching is also important to independent shorts to gauge story interest and to attract talent and money. A well-known editor or actor is more inclined to work for much less on a film that sounds interesting or has a chance to garner some success on the festival circuit. When you get your pitch down, use it every time someone asks you what your film is about.

Pitching Checklist

Pitches work best if they are extremely entertaining, brief (less than 30 seconds), and surprisingly original. You need to cover five things in your pitch, using two lines or less:

1. **Start with an opening hook statement or question.** What is the most interesting and original aspect of your film idea? How can you grab the listener's attention right away with a bold opening statement?
2. **Protagonist/antagonist.** What are these characters about and what do they want that is in conflict? Keep it very simple.
3. **Plot.** Don't give away the ending, and provide no details or dialogue. Briefly explain specific plot goals.
4. **The title.** Picking a great title for your film is extremely important. People should be able to tell what your film is about simply by hearing the title. Think of your short film as a product that needs just the right name. You should include as much information about the characters, setting, theme, or genre as possible. *Star Wars* is

about a war in space. *Jaws* is about a man-eating shark. *Finding Nemo* is about finding a fish named Nemo. Keep the title short, simple, compelling, exciting, descriptive, and original. Review the titles of your favorite films to see how this works.

5. **Comparisons.** Check out two or three example films or popular books that relate to your idea in some way. All pitches need to speak the language of universal meaning, regardless of gender, race, age, or culture. The comparisons may be culturally specific. Comparisons help people get a handle on the feel of your film. "*Jaws* in outer space" is the movie *Alien*. "Cowboys and Indians in space" is *Star Wars*.
6. **Unique story flavor.** This is about atmosphere, location, POV, time, characters, or mood. What is the flavor of your film that makes it interesting? Woody Allen's New York City looks completely different than Martin Scorsese's New York City.

"In a general sense, all artists are shamans, insomuch as they are channeling images or concepts on behalf of the collective."
—*Vicki Noble*

Pitching Tips

Keep in mind the following tips while pitching your ideas:

1. **Be extremely entertaining.** Tell your listeners a story they have not heard before in a fun way. Act out the characters. Move around the room. Make your enthusiasm about your film infectious. If you are not excited about your idea, how do you expect anyone else to be?

2. **Make your pitch original.** Start with a hook-type question, the antagonist, some startling situation, or fascinating conflict. Each pitch is different. Find the most exciting element and see how you can open with that idea.

3. **Present your best pitch first.**

4. **Do not mention the theme or the ending.** Theme is supposed to be invisible in your film, so you do not want to mention it in the pitch. Giving away the ending deflates your pitch. Leave people hanging as to what happens next to gauge an audience's interest in how the story unfolds.

5. **Use visual aids if you have any.** This is easier when you are sure what your idea is, the script is finished, and some preproduction is underway. Even at this stage, a rough drawing of a character really helps people relate to an idea. I prefer pitching with storyboards and large color illustrations of the main characters if that is an option. This of course would take longer than 30 seconds, but it should still be as short as possible. You can open a longer pitch with a really good 30-second one to get people's attention.

6. **Know your pitch and idea inside and out.** Do not answer "I don't know," when asked a question. Think your ideas through a little before pitching. Make something up. You want to have the tone of authority when talking about your project.

7. **Be very respectful of people's time when pitching.** Be gracious. Do not get mad at your listeners if they do not like your ideas. It's better to find out now. If they tell you the idea sounds like a movie they already saw, do not argue with them. They are doing you a big favor by listening. Pitch to your parents, siblings, friends, strangers in a cafe, other students, or anyone else you can round up for a few minutes. Buy them coffee or lunch. You may need to approach these people again about other ideas, so you want to make sure they feel well treated.

8. **Get feedback.** Ask your listeners what part of your idea they liked best and what parts sounded a little off. Your goal is feedback, not showing people how well you can pitch. After your pitch, be quiet and *listen*. Their initial reaction is what you need to gauge. If they looked excited to the point of being speechless, you are on the right track. If they look confused, bewildered, uncomfortable, and like they want to run out the door rather than tell you what they think, you have a problem pitch or a problem idea.

9. **No disclaimers or technical information.** Do not talk about camera shots, technical considerations, why you want to do the film, or how you think the idea still needs a lot of work. If you start a pitch by apologizing in advance for how silly it is, they will hear your pitch through that "this is not important—it is half done" filter. Believe in your ideas and your pitch or do not waste people's time.

10. **Pitch into a tape recorder first.** Practice pitching over and over again in a mirror first. Get to know your pitch by heart without reading from any notes. When you think you have it down, tape record the pitch and listen to it to see how it sounds to your ears. Is it a film you would want to see?

"To whatever degree you listen and follow your intuition, you become a creative channel for the higher power of the universe."
—Shakti Gawain

superfreak!

Videotape Your Pitch. After you have your pitch down, try videotaping yourself delivering it. Maybe your eyes wander at a certain point, or the way you are acting out one of the characters looks strange rather than funny. You may want to reserve one DV tape to record all your pitches so that you can see how your pitching style evolves.

group project

Practice Pitching in Front of Each Other. Have each person do three pitches in front of the group. Make sure that one person times the pitches to help keep them under 60 seconds. 30 seconds is optimal but is hard to do sometimes, so start long and then whittle the pitch down if possible. Give each other feedback on pitching style and story ideas.

"The quieter you become, the more you can hear."
—Baba Ram Dass

"The creation of something new is not accomplished by the intellect but by the play instinct acting from inner necessity. The creative mind plays with the objects it loves."
—C.G. Jung

project 1.22

Top 3 Ideas. Pick your Top 3 story concept sentences or short film ideas. Create a 30- to 60-second pitch of each idea. Use one or two sentences to cover each of the six areas on the pitch checklist.

Sample Pitch: "What would it be like to be a young Bigfoot shaman, who secretly lives in the forests around Mt. St. Helen's? The *Bigfoot Shamans* is about a resourceful teenage bigfoot girl named Ezzie, who gets banished from her tribe for getting caught stealing chocolate bars from campers. Rugaro, the mean witchdoctor of the tribe, wants her to leave because he is secretly threatened by her growing mystical bigfoot powers. He tricks her into going on the most deadly vision quest possible, deep inside the most dangerous caves in the still active volcano.

Ezzie struggles to survive a very deadly spiritual journey in hopes of rejoining the tribe. This film features realistic 3D animated bigfoots in caves, DV actors in redwood forest settings, and 2D animated shamanic journey sequences. It feels like a cross between *Antz*, with Bigfoots instead of ants, and a spiritually flavored Native American version of Gummo meets Harry Potter inside a volcanic series of vision quest caves."

project 1.23

Pitch Your Ideas. Over the next week, pitch your top three ideas to at least five people and ask for feedback. Watch the movie *The Player* if you have never heard a pitch to get an idea of how it's done. Keep track of which ones people like the best and why. You may be in love with one of your ideas, but other people may think it sounds like something they have already seen or find the characters or story less than compelling. Pitching a few ideas now can save you loads of rewrites later and expose obvious problems in the story. You want people to react with delight at end of the pitch and tell you it sounds like a wonderful short film they would love to see.

Final Story Idea

You now need to commit to one final story idea for the remainder of this book to do the project exercises. Use the pitch idea that received the best feedback. Make sure your film idea is one that you would love to see and are you enthusiastic about creating it. All the remaining projects in this book build on the story foundation you have established in this chapter.

chapter 2

Creating Original Characters, Themes, and Visual Metaphors

"I love Mickey Mouse more than any woman I've ever known."
—Walt Disney

Character, plot, and theme are the building blocks of a great short film. This chapter focuses on creating original characters, developing themes, and ways to create a unique visual, metaphorical, and symbolic language in your film.

Creating Powerfully Original Characters

> "You cannot dream yourself into a character; you must hammer and forge one for yourself."
> —James A. Froude

> "One of the reasons why so few of us ever act, instead of react, is because we are continually stifling our deepest impulses."
> —Henry Miller

The more you know about your characters, the easier it is to write your script. Assigning original sets of goals, traits, history, and other qualities creates characters with real emotional depth and personality. In this section, you will develop the main characters you chose for your final script idea in Chapter 1, "Generating Ideas for Digital Short Films."

Creating Active Characters

The strongest protagonists are usually active. Make sure your characters are not on a "magic carpet ride" type of journey through the story, just being carried along by a series of uncanny coincidences. When planning stories, keep in mind the three states of being for characters:

1. **Passive.** Lump: no goals, no plans, no energy to do anything. Part of the scenery, like colorful statues in a garden.
2. **Reactive.** Goal, plan, *or* pursuit; two out of three: Needs a little boost to get going, but heading toward goal.
3. **Active.** Goal, plan, *and* pursuit; fully engaged in quest to achieve goal.

Have your characters make *active choices* that *make events happen*. Force your characters to deal and learn from these choices as the story develops.

Watch your favorite films and see whether you can tell which state each character is in, in each scene, and how this state affects the conflict and audience interest in the story. You will discover that the active character state is much more engaging to watch.

Defining Characters

Short films do not have time to develop complex plots, so they often depend more on character. Plot is character personified in a sense. Characters are defined through their *choices*, *actions*, and *reactions*. Recognize that every character creates his or her own situations (plot) from the externalizations of his or her inner world (character).

This reclining Bigfoot is a passive character with no plans, goals, or energy. He just lies around all day. Notice how this character is not as interesting to watch as the one with a plan, goal, and motivation to make things happen.

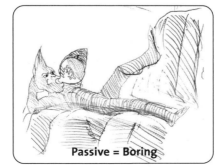

Passive = Boring

Active = Interesting

What a character does is more important than what a character says.

Characters need action and behavior to show us who they are. Guidance is good to have bestowed upon your characters, but do not have them become puppets of outside forces. They must act for themselves to show us who they are and what they think is important enough to fight for against heavy opposition.

You can define character in three ways, listed here in order of importance:

1. **Action.** Observing how they react to situations by what they do.

2. **Dialogue.** Listening to what they say.

3. **Third-party dialogue.** Listening to what other characters say about them. You could establish a whole character before he even walks on the screen by what another character says about him. The power of third-person dialogue is that you tend to believe it more if someone else says something about someone, rather than if the actual character claims to be something. How would your character's parents describe him or her? What description would a best friend, lover, or worst enemy provide?

project 2.1

List Three Active Choices. Create three active choices your main characters could make in your short film to accomplish the plot goal you chose in Chapter 1.

writing exercise 2.1

Write a few pages about one character going from a passive to a reactive to an active state of being. Or you could write about three characters in one situation, where one character is passive, one reactive, and one active.

project 2.2

Defining Characters. List at least one idea for using action, dialogue, and third-party dialogue to establish characters in your film idea.

movie note

In *Apocalypse Now*, Martin Sheen's character describes the men in his outfit with a voice over (VO) as the camera pans around the gunboat. He starts off by saying the soldiers are a "group of rock and rollers with one foot in the grave," foreshadowing upcoming events. One edgy character is described as "being wrapped too tight for Vietnam. Probably wrapped too tight for New Orleans." We learn about Martin's character by the way he describes other people in this brilliant, all-around character-defining monologue. How could you use a similar technique to quickly establish characters in your short film?

Big Granny tells her pet bobcat things about Ezzie when she's not around or is out of hearing range. How can you use third-party dialogue to help establish characters in interesting ways? What ways could you use digital tools to have characters talk to animated objects or animals, such as a conversing bobcat that gives advice?

movie note

The animated short film *Transit* tells the story of Emmy, an archetypal femme fatal, seducing Oscar the butcher, who ends up killing her oil-baron husband. The story happens in 11 minutes, is told backwards in cities all over the world through disappearing travel stickers on a suitcase, and has no dialogue. We understand everything we need to know about these characters by what they *do* in each scene, how they *react* to each other, and the *choices* they make. Pay attention to this "show, don't tell" concept when planning your visual stories.

writing exercise 2.2

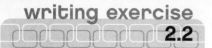

Write a few pages where you define a character or group of characters using action, dialogue, and third-party dialouge.

> *"We should know what our convictions are, and stand for them. Upon one's own philosophy, conscious or unconscious, depends one's ultimate interpretation of facts. Therefore it is wise to be as clear as possible about one's subjective principles. As the man is, so will be his ultimate truth."*
> —Carl Jung

superfreak!

List Three of Your Own Personal Plot and Theme Goals. Make a list of three personal goals for both outer (worldly) wants and inner (soul) needs. These will often surface in your characters in some way.

creativity tip

Get to Know Yourself. You need to really know yourself to build good characters and stories. The more you understand yourself, the better you understand other people. We all share similar experiences of desires, suffering, dreams, hopes, and the struggle to find value in our daily lives. Carry a notebook around with you to write down what you observe in regards to what is important to yourself and other people. Build your characters out of parts of people you know and assemble them into layered dimensions of contradictions.

What Does Your Character Want and Need?

Your protagonist should have two basic goals related to both plot (want) and theme (need).

Want is the worldly plot goal to save the princess, rob the bank, save the world, find the treasure, or win the race.

Need is usually the unconscious inner motivation that compels the character to act in irrational ways.

As characters attempt to get what they want, they often get what they need. Need may oppose want. Needs never change in a film, whereas wants often do. A character may want to die of a broken heart, when what he or she really needs is love. Need is something the audience often starts to see before the protagonist does, watching as the character learns throughout the story. Study yourself and other people. See what makes people tick underneath what they want and need to create believable characters.

Character want = Plot goal

Character need = Theme goal

Motivations = Why they made these decisions based on want/need

> *"The world stands aside to let anyone pass who knows where he is going."*
> —David Starr Jordan

My main Bigfoot character Ezzie's plot goal is to pass her vision quest, so she can stay with her tribe and not be banished to wander alone in the forest forever. What she needs to learn is to trust her intuition in order to pass her vision quest and claim her rightful spot in the Bigfoot tribe as the daughter of a long line of powerful shamans and warriors. Ezzie is afraid of her Bigfoot psychic powers at the beginning of the story and learns to use them better during the vision quest. In this shot at the beginning of the story, she trips on a log in the forest on her way to steal the chocolate that gets her into so much trouble. A voice in the wind tells her to "go back," but the smell of the chocolate is stronger and she ignores her intuition. Later in the story, a similar voice will be heard, and she will listen to it this time to show how she is learning to trust her intuition.

Creating Theme Goals for Your Characters

Take the theme you chose in Chapter 1 and turn it into a theme goal for the protagonist. Theme goals tend to be underlying unconscious needs characters have to develop, ones that will usually help them with their plot goals and character growth. If your theme is that greed leads to corruption, as in the movie *Wall Street*, your protagonist may struggle between greed and corruption while going through the story. Maybe your characters struggle to determine who they want to be in a world ruled by this theme. Work with the plot goal you picked in Chapter 1 for the following exercise.

- **Theme of film.** Controlling idea, moral message, underlying essence, or deeper meaning of film.
- **Character theme goal.** How a character needs to grow to accomplish plot goal or show the film theme.

In the film *Wall Street*, Charlie Sheen's character is the protagonist, representing the theme of how greed leads to corruption. We watch as he struggles throughout the film to find a balance between the two extremes and still become a success. Michael Douglas's character is the antagonist, representing the anti-theme personifying intense greed and corruption. Charlie Sheen's character has the following goals he attempts to achieve within the overall film theme parameters:

- **Theme of film.** Greed leads to corruption.
- **Protagonist plot goal.** To become a successful businessman.
- **Protagonist theme goal.** Needs to redefine who he wants to be and his place in the business world amid greed and corruption.

writing exercise 2.3

Write a few pages where you show a character struggling to achieve both a plot and a theme goal.

project 2.3

What Does Your Protagonist Want and Need? List three ideas for each goal type. Pick your best ones to develop.

"To grow and know what one is growing towards—that is the source of all strength and confidence in life."
—James Baillie

"He turns not back who is bound to a star."
—Leonardo da Vinci

Theme Goal Brainstorming Chart

To let go of past	To come of age	To overcome past trauma
To take responsibility for actions	To see perfection in themselves and others	To gain self-confidence
To find happiness		To redefine self in world
To find inner peace	To let go of any fears and trust that everything is happening perfectly	To reach a new level of understanding
To let go of being a victim	To learn something	To overcome a fear of something
To believe in something worthwhile	To change way of being in the world	To find purpose in life
To define new version of self	To be honest with themselves or others	To realize something that changes perspective on life
To find a balance between extremes	To resolve conflicting inner beliefs	To become a leader
To let go of self-destructive behaviors	To learn compassion for others	To create life intentionally instead of being carried along by circumstances
To fit into new world	To see the world in a new way	
To find love	To find one's own truth	To trust inner guidance rather than logic
To change inner beliefs	To make peace with the past	

Ezzie falls into a deep pit of quicksand during the climax while on her Shamanic journey and starts to drown. Her initial urge is to fight her way to the surface, but then she hears her little voice that tells her to levitate out. If she ignores the voice of her intuition, she will die and not accomplish either plot or theme goal.

project 2.4

Three Theme-Triggered Climaxes. How could your main character's theme goal decide the climax of your film? List the theme of your film, plot goal of main character, theme goal of main character, and three possible ways these ideas could all connect at the end.

project 2.5

Mutually Exclusive Goals. Create an ending that makes the plot and theme goals mutually exclusive. Your protagonist cannot have both of them and must choose between the world (worldly plot goal) and his or her soul (inner theme goal need).

"Follow your bliss. Find where it is and don't be afraid to follow it."
—Joseph Campbell

Theme Goals Determine the Climax

Another way to think of theme goals, or character need, is to ask yourself what the character is learning, or how the character is growing during their journey through the film. Some characters are always in transition until the final fade out if they grow a great deal. The more a character grows inside, the more external challenges the character can handle. The bigger the external goals, the more internal change needs to occur.

The theme goal reaches its climax with the film's plot goal climax and is usually the reason the ending goes positively or negatively.

In the short film *Last Supper*, the protagonist thinks he has won the lottery at the climax, not knowing it's a trick played on him for fun by his wife. Believing he is suddenly rich, he now feels comfortable showing a more honest side of himself, by telling her he is leaving her and has been sleeping with her sister for the past eight months. He places the keys to his Jaguar, credit cards, and house keys on the table to leave them for his wife, which symbolically states theme, too. The theme is how money changes relationships, and this decides the man's reaction at the climax. If money didn't matter in relationships for this film, he would have reacted differently to thinking he had won the lottery.

"Everything's in the mind. That's where it all starts. Knowing what you want is the first step towards getting it."
—Mae West

Creating Mutually Exclusive Plot and Theme Goals

Sometimes you may want to make the plot and theme goals mutually exclusive. In *The Maltese Falcon*, the main character wants to find the person who killed his partner and needs the perfect woman to love. When he finds out at the end that the perfect woman he now loves killed his partner, he has to decide which goal is more important to achieve. How could you create this conflict with your character to craft a great ending where the character must decide between his or her soul and the world?

Often, achieving plot goals means winning in the world. Theme goals usually involve winning on a soul level.

Ezzie has one quick chance to place her palm prints and carve her initials and sacred journey symbol on a special wall to prove her vision quest is complete at the end. Her intuition tells her to check out a sound coming from a deep hole, creating a situation with mutually exclusive plot and theme goals. As she falls into another series of caves, she finds a deeper hidden chamber where the heads of the tribe carve their symbols if they hear the special call. This elevates her standing in the tribe when she returns with a talisman from this special chamber.

Creating Character Identification

When an audience relates strongly to a film, they are identifying some aspect of themselves with the characters they see on the screen. Include as many of the following character identification techniques as possible when creating each of your characters. Don't use all of these techniques on just one character; it would be too confusing. Try to incorporate identification ideas that already fit your characters in some visual way. The trick is not to make these too obvious or sappy. Make sure they are original and artfully presented in a very subtle way. Several of the following character identification techniques are taken from Michael Hauge's wonderful book *Writing Screenplays That Sell*. Add to this list as you see qualities in characters that make you want to watch them and feel connected with them in some way.

1. **Admirable.** The character is really good at something we can admire, such as being an expert in their field, brilliant, wise, witty, beautiful, very talented, resourceful, or respected.

2. **Similar opinions/desires.** You relate to the character's view of the world and what the character wants.

3. **Flaws.** Imperfections—physical, emotional, spiritual, psychological, or personality. Give your characters lots of neurotic tendencies to make them more interesting. Characters who are in conflict with themselves are interesting to watch. Try to make flaws symbolic to theme. In *Finding Nemo*, the theme is to not give up and "to keep swimming." Nemo has one fin that is smaller than the other, and his father is afraid of everything out in the ocean. Dorie cannot remember anything for very long, which is a very funny flaw that works well to keep reviewing the same story information. Add to these lists as you see films.

writing exercise 2.4

Write a few pages where you show how a character's theme goal decides the outcome of their plot goal.

movie note

In *Life Lessons*, Lionel the painter says he wants Paulette to stay, but what he really needs to inspire his painting is passionate turmoil in his relationships. He becomes both the protagonist and the antagonist as his own worst enemy, because his plot and theme goals are in such direct conflict. Lionel wins in the world with a successful art show at the end, although he loses another relationship on a soul level.

"A man is fortunate if he encounters living examples of vice, as well as virtue, to inspire him."
—Brendan Francis

Types of Flaws

Physical	Emotional	Spiritual	Psychological	Personality
Missing limb	Mood swings	Religious/Spiritual zealot	Obsessive/compulsive	Arrogant
Scars	Cries easily	Cult fanatic	Schizophrenic	Rude
Ugly	Emotionally devoid	Evil tendencies	Manic depressive	Delusional
Bad teeth	Laughs at the wrong things	Terrified of killing anything	Narcoleptic	Dishonest
Obese	Uncontrollable anger	Believes the world is going to end soon	Multiple personalities	Self destructive
Disfigured	Insecure	Extremely superstitious	Going crazy	Mean spirited
One leg shorter than the other	Afraid of everything	Always trying to convert other characters	Memory problems	Ego-maniac
				Clumsy
				Stupid
				No Integrity

Character Flaws Add Personality. This flawed Bigfoot is missing a leg and has scars, bad teeth, torn ears, strange religious emblems on his necklace, and a crazy look in his eyes. All of these imperfections make him much more realistic and interesting than a so-called perfect Bigfoot. How many character flaws can you incorporate visually into your characters?

"Learn from the mistakes of others—you can't live long enough to make them all yourself."
—Martin Vanbee

"People never improve unless they look to some standard or example higher and better than themselves."
— Tyron Edwards

project 2.6

Add Character Flaws. Create three flaws for each of your main characters. Try to connect their main flaws with their abilities to achieve goals.

4. **Superhero qualities.** The character can do something amazing such as breathe under water and talk to fish (Aqua Man). Must balance all superhero qualities with equal vulnerabilities, such as what kryptonite does to Superman. What original visual superhero qualities could you create that are perfect for animation and digital effects?

5. **Visual appeal.** Great actors have what is known as "screen presence," meaning that you cannot take your eyes off of them in the frame. When Elizabeth Taylor walks onto the screen, you watch her above all else. Visual appeal is often thought of as sexual appeal.

Jack Nicholson may not be the most handsome man in the world, but he has great sex appeal. Animated characters need wonderfully original design, great personalities, and exaggerated movements to create strong visual appeal.

6. **Introduce the main character ASAP.** Make it clear who the main character is, and introduce him or her right away.

7. **Sympathy.** Your audience really feels where the character is at emotionally and empathizes. Your character is having a hard time, bad luck, or a bad day; is in pain; just lost everything; or is involved in an unjust situation.

movie note

In the 2D animated short *The Last Day*, the husband has a compulsive sawing problem when it comes to furniture. His wife likes to take her eyes out and shake them like dice in an irritating way. What new types of visual flaws can you give your character to enhance with animation or special effects that are metaphoric?

Superhero Qualities

Runs super fast	Has the ability to shift physical locations at will
Can see through things	
Can talk to beings on other stars for guidance	A magical scorpion tail sprouts out of body and stings people
Ability to talk to plants	Ability to tunnel underground with head
Shape shifter	
Mind reader	Can move objects with mind
Body parts turn into spaceship	Has a magical lasso only they can use
Ability to sprout wings and fly	Ability to make people do things by gently suggesting ideas
Can see 10 seconds into the future when looking into special stone	

8. **Place in jeopardy.** First you get the audience to care about and identify with your characters, and then you make them suffer by placing the characters in emotional, physical, or spiritually dangerous situations. The audience loves to worry about characters *if* they relate to them.

9. **Familiar setting/situations.** What types of places or situations can you put your characters in that are both universal and unique? A family dinner table, classroom, or job situation.

10. **Eyes of the audience.** The character goes through the story and learns surprising things at the same time the audience does.

11. **Empowered.** Active characters that make decisions to do something. Characters with no power to change their situations are hard to relate to, boring, and frustrating to watch.

"All life is a chance. So take it! The person who goes furthest Is the one who Is willing to do and dare."
—Dale Carnegie

12. **Underdogs.** Characters in ordinary lives who are called on to do great things against all odds of success. Give your characters normal boring jobs or place them in situations where they are underdogs.

13. **Good sense of humor.** The character is witty, funny, tells good jokes, is playful, does entertaining things, or is clever.

14. **Helps others.** The character goes out of the way to assist other people or animals. Avoid cliché helping actions.

15. **Loves children/family/pets/self.** Have your characters smile at kids, joke with old men in elevators, call their mothers, stop to pet dogs, and compliment themselves in the mirror.

16. **Artistic.** The character creates artwork or appreciates art.

17. **On a mission or has a special calling.** Show how your characters are completely inspired by some higher purpose, greater idea, or selfless mission. Maybe they want to accomplish something in your story for the good of others or to serve.

"Without heroes, we are all plain people, and don't know how far we can go."
—Bernard Malamud

project 2.7

Character Identification. List 10 ideas to improve character identification for each main character in your film.

This Bigfoot carves redwood stumps with chainsaws he steals from the lumberjacks. Showing his artistic side will help the audience identify more with the character. As you write your script, remember that these types of character identification techniques are good to show. This character could be carving a symbolic object out of a redwood tree while talking to another character who is playing with a beloved pet.

superfreak!

Watch *Finding Nemo* for Character Identification Techniques. Watch the first 30 minutes of this film and list as many of the previously discussed character identification techniques as you can. Notice how using these techniques helps you relate to the characters emotionally. You need to set up strong character identification in Act One, so this is a good place to study how other films do this in artful and original ways.

writing exercise 2.5

Write a few pages where you describe a day in the life of a character using as many of these character identification techniques as possible.

writing exercise 2.6

Write a few pages where you describe your main character based on their history. You could do it chronically, have a character telling their life story to someone, or have another character talking about someone else's life story.

"The soul that has no established aim loses itself."
—Michel de Montaigne

Creating a Character History

You will have a hard time creating believable characters without thinking about their personal history. Find original ways to slowly reveal important and unique information about their pasts as it relates to the story.

"There is no present or future, only the past, happening over and over again now."
—Eugene O'Neill

Developing Psychological Profiles

Everything inside a character's head will affect how they see their world and how they act and react on screen. People identify with characters who have similar emotions, opinions, attitudes, and beliefs. True emotion is the real source of our connections to other people. Make sure that your characters have powerful desires and opinions to create compelling moments and events on the screen. Answer the following questions to get a sense of how your

---

Character History. Answer the following questions for both your protagonist and antagonist:

1. **Naming your characters.** How can you create original names for your characters that relate to their role in the story or the theme of the film, or that serve as metaphors for traits? You may want to refer to baby naming, family name, or other types of dictionaries to create symbolic first and last names. A cold-hearted snippy character named Sally Davis is not nearly as unique and descriptive as Nettle Frost. "Nettle" for the stinging plant and "Frost" for cold. Refer to the character traits later in this chapter to see what types of synonyms you may be able to use for names. What types of nicknames could you give your characters that relate to their history?

2. **Physical descriptions.** Height, weight, hair color, wardrobe style, posture, eye color, scars, cultural background, imperfections, and general visual impression at first glance.

3. **Life experiences.** Write one sentence each for three major events in your character's life that define who the character is and how the character sees the world. For instance: At 5 years old, the character stole a bicycle, got caught, and then decided he or she was bad because of what the stern policemen said. At 10, the character's parents divorced, the character's mother moved away to a strange place with the character, and the character never again felt a sense of "belonging." At 21, the character had a vision of their life purpose and remains focused on achieving this at all costs. Have these life-changing events define your character's attitude and feelings toward life.

4. **Free-time activities.** Hobbies, skills, interests, collections, sports, travel, favorite band, and favorite thing to do on Sunday or day off.

This 14-year-old Bigfoot girl is named Ezmerelda Firerose, but most of her friends call her Ezzie. She comes from a long line of shamanic Bigfoot women who knew how to talk to plants and use them for healing. On the night she was born, there was a big fire where the wild roses grow near the Bigfoot clan cave, which is how she got her last name. She is 8 feet tall and weighs 267 pounds; she has sapphire blue eyes and bright red hair. One of her favorite things to do is spy on campers and steal their candy bars. She also likes to make sculptures out of junk she finds on the side of the road and natural objects such as rocks and bones. Her current most-used expression is "wicked," which she overheard an English anthropologist say while scouting for Bigfoots in the forests.

character thinks and feels about the world.

The emotional reactions of characters in a film are how we understand them visually.

1. What is the general emotional mood of your characters? Are they broken up inside or fresh and innocent? Are they cynical or positive?

2. How do your characters speak to themselves inside their own heads? Are they very critical and hard on themselves or do they think everything is wonderful and just better and better? Write three lines of inner dialogue to show general psychological character states, such as, "I never do anything right," "Nothing ever happens the way I want it to," or "I'm just not good enough." Or does the character think more along the lines of, "Oh great, another wonderful day!," "I can't wait to go to school," or "I just know something really good is going to happen."

"Our minds shape the way a thing will be because we act in accordance to our expectations."
—Federico Fellini

"When I look at the future, it's so bright, it burns my eyes."
—Oprah Winfrey

5. **Dialogue.** How the character talks. What are the character's favorite words? What kinds of special words could you add to things the character says? "That's great!" is not as interesting or revealing as, "Oh goody goody gumdrops!" Watch any films similar in genre dialogue to the one you are creating to get fresh ideas.

6. **Sociology.** Social status in film world, including education, money, friends, family background, neighborhood, city, and environment. Effect of outside world situation on characters both internally and externally. Suppose, for instance, that identical triplets were all separated at birth. One was reared with Eskimos, one in Beverly Hills, and one on the streets of Bombay. How would their social environments make them all different at age 21?

7. **Biggest heartache or disappointment.** What was the biggest heartache or disappointment that your character has ever experienced? What possible fear did the character develop around this experience? Maybe if the character lost a best friend at a young age, they become afraid of getting attached to anyone else.

8. **Most prized possession.** What is your character's most prized possession?

9. **Secret dreams.** What does your character secretly dream about becoming or achieving? What does your character daydream about in his or her spare time? How does your character view their future?

10. **What is missing in the character's life?** What one missing thing does your character think having would make his or her life perfect? What life situation is your character trying to change in your story?

11. **What relationships are most important to your character?** Is your character really close to his or her mother but has never seen his or her father? Who is his or her best friend? Think about including archetypal relationships in your story, such as father/son, teacher/student, priest/man, God/man, husband/wife, or boss/employee. Make sure you build strong, contrasting characters for important relationships to help each other grow and keep the story interesting.

Ezzie secretly dreams of jumping her motorcycle over the biggest cavern in the Bigfoot cave.

My protagonist Ezzie is very dramatic emotionally and has big mood swings. Her biggest flaw is that she is overly optimistic about things and fails to see problems until it is too late. In this shot, she is at her lowest point in the cave, having a vision of her grandmother in the lines of the rocks, who reminds her of why she is on the vision quest. The two characters joke about how things are not going too well and use humor to help get her into a more positive mental state in order to continue.

"A man is what he thinks about all day long."
—Ralph Waldo Emerson

project 2.9

Psychological Profiles. Answer the questions in this section to get a feel for how your characters think and feel about their lives.

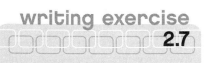

writing exercise 2.7

Get inside your main character's head and write a few pages of how they think during a possible situation in your story.

3. How do they interpret external experiences internally? Do they think everything is their fault or do they never take responsibility for their behaviors?

4. Do they have any psychological problems or flaws, such as being neurotic, delusional, depressed, slightly nutty, forgetful, or obsessive? Do they suffer from uncontrollable outbursts of rage or overwhelming panic attack-type disorders?

5. What is your character's biggest secret insecurity? Are they afraid they are not good enough, not beautiful enough, or not smart enough? What might they think is terribly wrong with them that they do not want anyone else to know?

6. What strong opinions, attitudes, or beliefs does this character possess? Do they feel they have a clear purpose in their life or higher mission to accomplish? What are they willing to fight for under pressure?

7. What is your character's biggest emotional scar or shameful past event that they repress or hide from themselves or others?

8. What types of emotional weather did your character's family have when they were growing up? Was it a happy family or a stressed out one? How does this affect your character's mindset now?

9. Are there any original ways you could show some of these psychological states on screen, using your digital tools to help the audience better understand your character's inner world? A character who has a very negative inner dialogue with a cheerful outer attitude could be shown to be in conflict by using a separate, softer soundtrack for the inner voice on top of the normal dialogue at key moments.

What Is Your Character Afraid Of?

Fear is an emotion caused by the anticipation or awareness of danger or pain. This powerful state is generated in a character's subconscious mind based on negative thinking, past experiences, or current reality beliefs. Courage is the ability to take action in spite of fear, while thinking positively about future results. The more a character is afraid, the less likely they will take any action. The less fear a character has in their perceptions of reality, the more power and excitement they will have to accomplish their goals. Emotional states are like magnets, which attract situations that match the emotion being broadcast. A character who is really afraid of something will actually attract that thing into his world in order to resolve it. Audiences love to see characters wrestle with fears, since this is a universal emotional struggle for most people.

Not all characters are even aware of their fears. Unconscious fear drives a character's reactions, and you need to know what these are. Some characters may wear masks that hide their fears and often appear to be the opposite of the fear. If a character is terrified of people finding that the character is not as good as they appear, that character may act very snotty to cover up their insecurity. In *Life Lessons*, Lionel is afraid underneath all his flurry of actions that he will not be able to paint if his lover leaves. This causes him to react with extremely fearful freak-outs whenever his girlfriend threatens to leave. In *Finding Nemo,* Nemo's overprotective father is terrified of little Nemo getting eaten by another fish, since this is what happened to his wife and other children. One way to find fear in a developing character is to ask, "What would this character do if they *knew* they could not fail?"

After you know what your character is really afraid of, you know what they need to face.

Types of Fears

Fear of losing someone or something very precious to you	Fear of not knowing how to do something
Fear of not being good enough	Fear of being wrong
Fear of being ridiculed	Fear of physical pain
Fear of not being loved or wanted	Fear of illness
Fear of failure	Fear of being rejected
Fear of being vulnerable	Fear of being poor or homeless
Fear of past trauma repeating itself	Fear of someone finding out a big secret or insecurity about you
Fear of snakes, spiders, viscious dogs, alligators, sharks, or killer bees	Fear of being caught for something you did in your past
Fear of getting hurt or injured	Fear of a particular person, thing, or situation that has been harmful in the past
Fear of things getting worse	
Fear of losing what you already have	
Fear of being alone	

Ways a Character Might Overcome a Fear

Character faces fear and succeeds, gaining confidence.	Character tries very hard to cover up fear and finally breaks down about truth or is exposed
Hits bottom and asks for help or realizes there is nothing left to lose	Character snaps from tension of fear and gets into more emotionally free state
Character becomes so paralyzed by fear they become weak and close to some form of death which causes big realization	Character realizes fear is costing them too much and lets it go
Character takes a little step out of fear and meets with success, then takes another	Character is motivated by the welfare of others to act and get out of fear
Character starts taking some form of action	Character relives past traumatic event in some way and works through fear

Ways To Show Characters Overcoming Fears

If fear stops a character from taking action, you will need to show what motivates them enough to push through their fears in order to obtain their plot and theme goals. Below is a list to help you think of ways to show characters working through their fears, old wounds, or emotional blocks.

My main character Ezzie's biggest fear is getting bit by one of the poisonous snakes or spiders that live in the vision quest caves. She flashes on this fearful image in her mind when the witchdoctor tells her she must go into Rattlesnake Cavern, the most dangerous place of them all, for her vision quest.

Ezzie is sticking her arm down the body of a this giant rattlesnake to retrieve her lightening bug friend who accidentally flew into its mouth. Ezzie is first shown reacting with extreme terror to any snake, then getting more and more comfortable around them, since they are all over the vision quest cave. I use her reactions to snakes and spiders to show her character growth in the story. The more she masters her intuition, the less afraid she is of the creatures. What unique ways can you show your characters gradually overcoming their fears in your story?

"Everything is so dangerous that nothing is really very frightening."
—Gertrude Stein

project 2.10

Worst Thing. What would be the worst thing that could happen to your protagonist? What is your character most afraid of? Are there any unconscious fears your character may have that they are unaware of or hiding from?

The most important thing to this Bigfoot is looking really good. He is especially proud of his unusually long Bigfoot hair. His biggest fear is losing his hair or going bald, which seems to be happening a little more each day, causing him great stress. His unconscious fear is not being loveable if he loses his hair. How can you create different believable layers of fear for your characters that match the concerns of people you know?

writing exercise 2.8

Write a few pages about how your main character developed their biggest fear and give some ideas on how they might overcome it by taking action.

superfreak!

Character History in Films. Study your favorite films and write character histories from what is revealed about the characters onscreen. How do they experience life through their own personal reality filter? What does your protagonist's reality filter look like? Show this unique reality construction and contrast it with the other characters' views in your film.

Bigfoot Scaredy Cat. This Bigfoot who is normally supposed to be huge and brave is instead afraid of every little critter in the forest because he got bit once on the foot as a youngster.

Adding Universal and Unique Qualities

All characters have both universal and unique qualities. How is your character a universally generic archetype? Is your protagonist a rebel, saint, madman, hero, sinner, solider, mother, cowboy, detective, gangster, fortune-teller, outlaw, drunk, shopkeeper, or businessman? Is there something going on with this character we can all grab onto?

Then you need to make that archetypal character unique and stunningly original. What about a detective who can't remember anything (*Memento*) or an ant that wants to do things differently than the other ants (*A Bug's Life*)? A cowboy living in New York City (*Midnight Cowboy*)? A poor, single, mother-of-three fortune-teller living in the deep south (*The Gift*)? An orphan boy with unusually powerful wizard skills (*Harry Potter*)?

superfreak!

Favorite Film Character Qualities. Go through your favorite films and list how the lead characters are both archetypal and unique.

project 2.11

Universal and Unique Qualities. For each main character in your film, assign a universal and unique quality combination that we have not seen before in a film. These qualities may overlap with character traits.

Incorporating Unique Qualities

What does your character do that might be described as an eccentricity, strange behavior, or unique way of doing things? Adding unique qualities to your characters make them seem more original and realistic. Do they listen to swing music while gardening in cocktail attire, drive around naked at night and shoot at mailboxes to relieve stress, put ketchup on their pizza, or have five little dogs with them at all times? Are they attracted to really fat people for relationships or blondes that drive old muscle cars? What do they do when they are sad? Do they eat chocolate chip cookies in a bubble bath? We need to see these things to feel like your characters are real. There are no vanilla people, so don't make characters without any special flavor or color.

Questions to Consider for Unique Qualities

When thinking of unique qualities, see how you can relate qualities to the plot, character history, and backstory.

1. What weird hobbies might they spend time doing? Fly fishing? Lawn bowling? What two weird hobbies could you combine for a new one?
2. Where do they like to shop? Thrift stores or Saks?
3. Strange musical tastes? Food? Movies? Entertainment?
4. Sexual quirks? Dating preferences? How do they show affection?
5. What strange thing or pet peeve really upsets your characters?
6. Do they have offbeat eating habits or order food in restaurants in an unusual way?
7. How and what do they drive?
8. Strange nonverbal mannerisms? Grind their teeth, blink uncontrollably, turn their heads around fast as if seeing something?
9. Do they have any unusual talents?
10. What types of far-out clothes do they wear?
11. How do they react to stress? Overeat? Beat up stuffed animals? Chop wood?
12. How do they practice their spirituality? Strange rituals or meditations? Do they go to an unusual church?
13. What is your character's idea of a unique dream vacation?
14. What is the weirdest thing about your character?
15. What are the strangest things people you know do that make them unique? How could you use these to spark original ideas?

Creating a Backstory

The world your characters inhabit need to be as interesting and unique as the characters themselves. The backstory consists of past events in your film world that directly affect the protagonist's emotional involvement in the plot as the story unfolds. Characters need emotions and attributes to really come alive, and these are developed through the backstory and character history. You need to define the limits of your film world in the backstory. Audiences will inspect your fictional world to find limits. These limits also help set up the conflict.

Banana Slug Cravings? This Bigfoot has an unusual taste for fresh banana slugs. What unique food quirks does your character have that might make the audience squirm?

project 2.12

Create Five Unique Qualities. Using ideas from the preceding list, create at least five possible unique qualities for each of your main characters.

writing exercise 2.9

Write a few pages of a day in the life of one of your main characters, concentrating on showing as many of their unique qualities as possible.

"You cannot dream yourself into a character; you must hammer and forge one for yourself."
—James A. Froude

writing exercise 2.10

Write a few pages about the history of your film world. You could describe it like you are doing a documentary film on some interesting aspect or like you are writing a research report.

"He might never really do what he said, but at least he had it in mind. He had somewhere to go."
—Louis L'Amour

"Education should be the process of helping everyone to discover his uniqueness."
—Leo Buscaglia

Bigfoot Boulder Tossing. This character makes decisions by tossing boulders off a cliff and seeing where they land.

Creating a Backstory. Write a one- to two-page description of your film world. Use short paragraphs or lists to answer the following types of questions. Add any questions you think are important to develop your backstory. If the characters live underwater, you are going to have to explain how they breathe.

1. How are your characters' current behaviors related to past film world events?
2. How far out of town do most people go?
3. Who runs the film world your characters inhabit?
4. What is the social pecking order?
5. Who makes the big decisions?
6. What is considered good or bad in your world?
7. What would your character give his life for to achieve in this world?
8. What makes life worth living in your world?
9. What is the best and worst thing that can happen to a character in your world?
10. What are the characters in your story most concerned with— surviving each day or having perfectly manicured nails?
11. How do your characters shop, eat, make love, work, exercise, and pray. Really imagine it in your mind to get into these characters and their worlds.
12. Draw an overhead sketch or map of the house, town, city, region, or planet that your film world encompasses.

Characters Making Tough Choices Visually

How can you place your characters in positions where they must make difficult choices? How can you show them making these choices and stretch them out over time to see them really struggle? Show how the characters may be in conflict emotionally inside themselves over the choice. What types of insights could you have your characters discover during their decision-making process? Positive interactions with the world produce positive attitudes, and negative ones produce negative characters. The best stories are about choices and commitment. The decision-making process needs to be *shown* as visual actions.

Personal Visual Decision Making. List five actions (that can be shown visually) that you undertake when trying to make important decisions. Maybe you jog, take a bath, throw darts, roll dice, consult a psychic, go bowling, surf, take a poll of all your friends, pace, pray, ask for guidance in your dreams, do a tarot reading, play hockey, meditate, shoot at tin cans, or watch for superstitious signs. What do you do differently when forced to make a big decision under pressure?

Visual Decision Making. Make a list of five ways to show the protagonist in your story making a big decision. A character who is pacing while making a decision is perceived differently than one who throws darts. How does your character make choices under extreme pressure? Exaggerate the normal decision-making behaviors in tense situations. If the character usually paces, perhaps under pressure the character paces quite frantically.

Incorporate Character Contradictions

People act differently around different people. You probably act differently around your friends than you do around your mother, lover, or boss. Create your supporting characters to bring out contradictory sides of your protagonist. Maybe you have a super-ambitious protagonist who is riddled with guilt about the extremes he goes to, to achieve his goals. With Character B, your protagonist is a sharp, angry, and ruthless competitor. With Character C, your protagonist acts like a sad, soft, guilty child. With Character D, your protagonist is happy and carefree. Use this technique to show characters that are beautiful on the outside, but who may be a complete mess on the inside.

Creating Strong and Revealing Character Reactions

The events in your story reveal the characters by how the characters *react* to them. Plot is a collection of events or actions toward a resolution. Character is the action and reaction of individuals in the story to the plot. Often the underlying theme is what *causes* characters to make the decision to react in certain ways. If you were creating a film on the theme of the destruction of greed, for instance, your characters personifying greed would always choose to react with the greed mindset to each situation as they destroy themselves.

You must remember to give screen time for the reactions of the characters to each event in your film. This allows the emotional impact to sink in with the audience members.

Ezzie meets a lightening bug mentor in the vision quest cave who offers to be her guide. The bug is half blind and bumps into things but seems helpful. Later in the story we find out that the lightening bug works for Rugaro the witchdoctor and has been reporting back to him on Ezzie's progress. When the bug talks to Ezzie he seems scatterbrained, but when he reports into Rugaro we see that he is very cunning and sharp. This character contradiction makes the story more deep and interesting than just having the bug as a helpful character.

These two Bigfoots are having very different reactions to what they just saw. One reacts with horror, whereas the other laughs; these different reactions reveal character. What ways can you have your characters react differently to events in your story to help us understand how they see the world?

project
2.16

Contradictions. How can you incorporate some form of contradiction into your main characters? What other sides of your characters can be presented in different situations? How can you use different characters to bring out different sides of your protagonist?

"The growing belief that you create your own reality is one of the most major shifts happening right now."
—Sanaya Roman

project
2.17

Character Reactions. List five ways your character could react to various events in your story. Make sure to create specific reaction shots for these moments in your script. Create one situation in which two or more characters react completely different to the same event.

"Life is the sum of all your choices."
—Albert Camus

Character Traits

To create consistent and original characters, it helps to define their basic traits. By picking one unique character-trait set for each of your main characters, you will be able to keep track of who they are when imagining them in situations, writing dialogue, and planning actions.

A character trait is anything that determines the way the character sees the world and how the character thinks, speaks, and acts.

Relate your trait sets to the character history, film world environment, backstory, social standing, occupation, emotional state, psychological profile, appearance, and other exercises you have already done.

Cliché characters have combinations of character traits we have seen before onscreen.

"The Goldman Five" Character-Trait System

Michael Dougan developed this technique to construct characters by assigning them five simple trait combinations. This idea is based on some things William Goldman said in his wonderful book *Adventures In The Screen Trade* (Warner Books, 1983).

"Choosing a goal and sticking to it changes everything."
—Scott Reed

"Nature arms each man with some faculty which enables him to do easily some feat impossible to any other."
—Ralph Waldo Emerson

One best trait. The thing this character is better at doing than anyone else in the film world.

One worst trait. The biggest negative trait that prevents the character from achieving goals and may cause the downfall of the character if it is not overcome.

Three other traits. These other three traits are ones you add to make sure your character has an original combination of traits.

The big negative trait has to be a flaw or weakness that prevents the character from obtaining his or her goals. If your character's main plot goal is to drink himself to death (*Leaving Las Vegas*), being an alcoholic may be his *best* trait to accomplish that goal. You can track growth and change in a character by monitoring that one negative trait. By changing, a protagonist may turn this negative trait into a positive one by the end of the film. Try not to duplicate positive or negative traits among character sets. If you have one kid who has the best collection of comic books hanging out with other comic book kids, have them all specialize in different types of comic books.

The antagonist usually cannot overcome his or her negative trait at the end, which results in the antagonist's ultimate downfall. Most antagonists are either ignorant of their worst trait or completely revel in it. A tragic character loses all his good traits in a downward spiral throughout the story, from the weight of the big negative trait pulling him under. Hannibal Lector is better at killing people than anyone else (main positive for his plot goal). We may not like serial killers, but we admire Hannibal's skill. He is a genius, gourmet cook, and classy guy. His big negative trait is that he is completely insane. Study your favorite films for these trait sets to see how different combinations are developed for each character.

Character-Trait Chart

The following traits are loosely divided into positive and negative. Good traits help characters accomplish their goals, whereas worst traits stop them from getting what they want and need. Do not pick two traits that are similar. Lots of traits that do not sound very much alike are, such as "warrior" and "brave." It is fine to have two character traits that are cliché, as long as you balance them with two traits that are really original to create a unique set. You can add traits later that pop up while writing your script and remove ones that are not being used.

project
2.18

List Traits. Create a unique set of traits for each main character in your film. Use the character trait chart for ideas. After you have decided on your final five unique trait sets for each main character, write the character's name and trait set on an index card and hang it up next to your script-writing area. These cards help keep your characters consistent to their main traits as you write your script.

Character Trait Chart

Possible Best Traits	Other Possible Traits			Possible Worst Traits
Champion	Intelligent	Airhead	Fake	Insane
Professional	Athletic	Aloof	Activist	Addicted
Master	Affectionate	Middle class	Moody	Dead inside
Top	Fearful	Beatnik	Corporate	Mean
Model	Worrywart	Gypsy	Homeless	Alcoholic
Warrior	Brave	Thief	Hippie	Negative
Beautiful	Positive	Intuitive	Cool	Poor
Courageous	Average	Bitchy	Dork	Annoying
Rich	Loyal	Bookish	Trashy	Depressed
Charming	Blue	Nerd	Cultivated	Crazy
Talented	Competitive	Liberal	Boring	Corrupt
Well educated	Creative	Convict	Nice	Greedy
Mentor	Conservative	Dishonest	Natural	Obsessed
Happy	Confused	Curious	Mysterious	Evil
Caregiver	Black humor	Glamorous	Nervous	Clumsy
Childlike	Delicate	Fugitive	Obnoxious	Gossip
Funny	Deluded	Forgetful	Outlaw	Hot tempered
Compassionate	Dissatisfied	Foolish	Party animal	Hypochondriac
Loving	Easy going	Freak	Peaceful	Ignorant
Artistic	Uptight	Gentleman	Young/old	Impulsive
Independent	Cowboy	Humble	Political	Jerk
Enlightened	Anal	Hood	Playboy	Irresponsible
Enthusiastic	Drifter	Holy	Perfectionist	Maniac
Heroic	Motherly	Intense	Genius	Neurotic
Imaginative	Egomaniac	Lucky	Sexy	Cruel
Inspiring	Fashionable	Logical	Perky	Cynical
Passionate	Streetwise	Loud	Responsible	Psychotic
Integrity	Heartbroken	Lonely	Small-town	Possessive
King/queen	Cheap	Musical	Shy	Violent
Leader	Mindful	Simple	Superficial	Zombie
Survivor	Stubborn	Stressed	High strung	Burned out
Wise	Storyteller	Listless	Tough	Worthless
Prodigy	Modern	Alien	Wild	Broken
Psychic	Worldly	Soft	Biker	Slothful

superfreak!

Keep Adding to Your Trait Chart. Add interesting character traits from movies you see for future reference.

"We are shaped and fashioned by what we love."
—Johann Wolfgang von Goethe

superfreak!

What Is Your Absolute Best and Worst Trait? Notice how these may pop up in your characters and usually change as we grow and learn.

writing exercise 2.11

Write a few pages about a main character where you only concentrate on showing their five main character traits in action. If their best trait is being a top-ranked mountain climber, then you could start with them climbing a mountain. You might also want to write a few pages with two main characters interacting with each other, focusing on how their different trait sets cause agreement and conflict.

This Bigfoot is better at levitating (floating) than any other one in the clan. This unusual best trait works great for animation and is something we have not seen much of before onscreen. What types of unique digitally enhanced character traits could you give your character (for instance, the ability to fly, glow, or become invisible)?

Developing Themes In Films

In Chapter 1, we already looked at several ways to develop themes in your films. The following is a list of techniques you may want to start thinking about when incorporating themes into your script. Each theme and story is different and will require a unique approach on how to integrate it carefully. Many of the following ideas use metaphors and symbols, which will be covered more in-depth in the next section. A deeper discussion of ways to show themes using different types of metaphors is continued at the end of this chapter.

1. **Controlling idea.** Show how the story events are being controlled by one idea, such as the synchronisity theme example from Chapter 1.

2. **List positive and negative manifestations of theme in plot and character.** If you are working with the theme of how love heals all, you may want to list situations where there is an abundance of love, a total lack of love, and a medium amount of love, then show how healing is affected in each situation. You could list characters the same way, then put them in strong relationships together. One character may personify great love, one may seem devoid of any love, and a few may demonstrate the middle of the emotional theme spectrum.

3. **Show main characters changing in respect to theme.** Pick a negative and positive manifestation for a thematic character. Have the character start out in the negative theme state and then change to the positive one you are showing. A film about freedom may start with a character who is very upset about the constraints of their freedom, and by the end of the story is completely free and happy, after going through a big ordeal for change. Showing characters that change will be covered more in Chapter 3.

4. **Use metaphorical characters.** Use your digital tools to show things like animal characters playing human roles, such as the ones in Aesop's fables.

5. **Assign characters metaphorical occupations that relate to theme.** What occupations best relate to the essence of your theme? A detective in a crime thriller looking for the meaning of life (theme)? A boxer throwing a fight that ruins his career or for a gangster to show struggles with loyalty (theme)?

6. **Pick a theme color.** Use a neutral or limited palette for your scenes, then pick a contrasting color, such as red, to use only for thematic symbolic objects so that they stand out. In *Transit*, red is used to show the theme seduction of an innocent, with blood stained aprons, bright sensual strawberries smeared on the characters' skin, and hot red hair for the leading man.

7. **Dialogue.** Characters can make remarks about the theme such as "No one has any values anymore" in a story about the disintegration of values in modern life.

8. **Create an original tag line in the dialogue.** "Keep swimming" is used in *Finding Nemo* to drive home the theme of don't give up.

9. **Character tells a story or fable.** What existing fables or new stories could you have characters tell each other that show theme? In *The Crying Game*, The Frog and The Scorpion fable is told over and over again to show the theme at key points.

10. **Use metaphorical locations.** In the movie *The African Queen*, the theme has to do with moving from an institutional experience of spirituality to a direct one in nature. The film opens with a church scene in the middle of the jungle and then quickly moves to a boat on the river.

11. **Character actions.** How could the characters act and react in your film to show theme? In *Finding Nemo*, the main characters never give up, which is the theme.

12. **Metaphoric scene activities.** If your theme is how people struggle to be perfect, you could list several scene activities that would illustrate this point. A character getting ready for a blind date tries a new hair gel that makes them look like a scarecrow.

13. **Symbolic nature shots.** Nature is full of metaphors and symbols that people relate to on a very deep level. If your theme is redemption, you could show shots of an old tree everyone thought was dead coming back to life in the spring as a subplot.

14. **Sound.** The way you set up your soundtracks can also communicate theme, which will be covered more in Chapter 7. The sounds of laughter might be heard in the background during positive theme moments and the sound of people wailing may be used during negative theme scenes. Characters may also sing songs or be at places where thematic songs are being played.

15. **Lightening and staging.** The way you plan your shots can communicate theme visually, and will be covered more in Chapter 6. A film dealing with trust may show two opposing characters having a tense conversation while walking between sharp objects. The lighting around the positive theme character may be brighter than the one around the negative manifestation.

16. **Use metaphors and symbols.** The following section will help you to better use different types of metaphors and symbols to explore your themes and tell your stories in deeper ways visually.

"Hold fast to dreams, for if dreams die, life is a broken-winged bird that cannot fly."
—*Langston Hughes*

"Unless you give yourself to some great cause, you haven't even begun to live."
—*William P. Merrill*

project 2.19

Think of five visual ideas on how to develop the theme of your film using some of these techniques.

When my main character accomplishes her plot goal of completing her vision quest, she tattoos herself with a symbolic brand she saw in her shamanic journey. This symbol helps us see that she has undergone a great transformation. What types of symbols or metaphors can you include in your story to show whether your characters achieve their plot and theme goals?

"The most beautiful emotion we can experience is the mystical. It is the power of all true art and science."
—Albert Einstein

Using Metaphors and Symbols to Tell Stories

Movies themselves are metaphors for how humans experience life on a deeper level. Creating a unique language of metaphors and symbols for your film is a big part of being a visual storyteller. Symbolic images help us to understand abstract concepts that cannot always be translated into words. I use the word *metaphor* to encompass metaphor, symbol, motifs, and leit motifs for the remainder of this book to simplify things.

Metaphor = Action/Sound. Visual or auditory representation of a separate action, experience, or idea. A character blows out (action) a candle in a bedroom to show death of a loved one.

Symbol = Object/Sound. Visual or auditory representation of another object. The candle (object) is in the shape of a ballerina to show grace and beauty.

Motifs = Collections. Collections of related metaphors or symbols used to represent a related concept. Lights or flames going on and off to show life or death states throughout a film.

Leit Motifs = Repetition. The repetition of identical metaphors or symbols to represent a greater concept. The color of the candle is gold (valuable color), along with other gold symbolic objects and activities in each scene to show the overall concept of what is valuable in a character's life.

Setting Up Metaphors and Symbols

You can set up metaphors and symbols in your films in two basic ways:
- **Universal** metaphors and symbols have all been used before and everyone understands them right away.
- **Personal** metaphors and symbols are those you create by first presenting them and then defining them for the audience.

I developed a leit motif using snakes and spiders to represent unknown fears in my vision quest cave story. Ezzie's biggest fear is poisionous snakes and spiders, and the cave is full of them playing various archetypal roles. At the end of the story, during her shamanic journey, she meets the King Rattle Snake and Queen Black Widow who help her to understand her fears and give her lots of valuable information. Snakes are symbolic of sacred knowledge, death, fear, and rebirth, which fit nicely with the story. Spiders are known for their ability to travel between the real world and the mystical world, which is what the character needs to do to accomplish her plot goals.

Where to Place Metaphors and Symbols in Your Story

Metaphors and symbols can be used to develop plot, theme, and character in deeper ways visually. As a filmmaker, you need to create a unique metaphorical language in your story. You may want to practice taking different storytelling techniques in this book and seeing how you could apply them in metaphorical ways. If you want to show character history, you could have the character doing a metaphorical scene activity from the past, such as a martial arts meditation. You may want to place certain symbolic objects in key scenes, like pictures from exotic travels. The following list will help you think of ideas on where to place metaphorical activities or symbolic objects in your story to help develop plot, theme, and character:

1. **Objects/props.** Household items, flags, T-shirts, games, art in room, statues, furniture style, shape of windows, magazines, pictures, weapons, wall hangings, books, instruments, pets, cars, people, houses.

2. **Music/sounds.** Background sounds, songs, atmospheric music bed, music in scenes, street noises, weather sounds, sirens, people crying/laughing/screaming in the next room, weird unexplainable sounds, heaters, equipment, natural sounds, animals, event sounds. Conceptual narrative sound design and auditory metaphors are covered in Chapter 7, "Narrative Sound Design."

3. **Color.** The color of everything in the frame may mean something. Refer to the color section in this book to explore some meanings associated with each basic color. Carefully choose colors for everything in each scene, including for costumes, sets, lights, cars, hair color, makeup, props, sky, fur, and weather. If your theme had a color, what would it be? Chapter 6, "Mise En Scène for the Twenty-First Century," covers the use of symbolic color in more detail.

4. **Words.** Heard in dialogue or appearing on sets or otherwise onscreen (pop-up bubbles to indicate thought, subtitles, and so on). Posters in the background, titles, onscreen text with background info, poems, fables, stories inside stories, signs, subtitles for slang, graffiti, product names on packages, license plates, bumper stickers, billboards, song lyrics, street names, character names, location, event lingo, speeches, slang, vocabulary, dialect, cultural misinterpretations, multiple meaning for some words, word puzzles, T-shirt sayings.

5. **Sets.** Location as character. What does the setting say about the mood of each scene? A conversation in a junkyard has a different context than one at the top of the Eiffel Tower. National monuments, natural settings (swamps, waterfalls, caves, rivers, ocean, desert), cities with different personalities, small-town local flavor, visual themes,

"Artists are channels for cultural feelings and creators of images that the culture is hungry for and doesn't even know it."
—*Vicki Nobel*

"Once you understand symbolic things, you, too, will see symbols everywhere."
—*Joseph Campbell*

project 2.20

Pick a Color for Your Theme. Choose one color to represent the theme of your film. List five ways to use this theme color, both on physical objects and as a metaphor.

I/O Error. In this short film by Michael Dougan, he uses the metaphor of twin boys to show the theme of how two opposing sides of a person cannot coexist peacefully. One boy is good, and one is evil. Triplet actors were used for the little boys, and compositing techniques in post were used to duplicate the adult actor who plays the grown men.

During the opening shots of *Citizen Kane*, we are drawn up to a point of light as we get closer and closer to the window of the room in which Kane is dying. When he dies, the light goes out. This is a good use of metaphoric lighting to represent story events. How could you use a similar technique in your story?

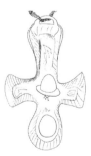

This symbol, worn around the neck of a character, was created by taking an ahnk and turning it upside down to show strange religious beliefs. The shape of a flying saucer was laid over the cross to symbolize alien creators. How can you take two symbols and combine their meanings and shapes to make a unique one for your film?

types of businesses, geographical themes, amusements parks, clubs, bars, graveyards, temples, stores, abstract interpretations of the Internet, art galleries, circus tents, fantasy places.

6. **Character types.** People who represent the theme or plot to the extreme (positive or negative, even an extreme mix of the two). Costumes, stereotypes, fashion preferences, cultural backgrounds, accents, jewelry, uniforms, piercings, tattoos, hats, clothes, masks, T-shirt sayings.

7. **Lighting.** Colored lights, light sources, brightness, lighting subjects specific to metaphor. Good characters may be in bright light, whereas evil characters may be darkly lit. Quality of light (time of day as a metaphor). Glowing around certain characters, face-lighting strategies to evoke emotion, source of light (sun, spaceship, flaming building) as metaphor, spinning ambulance lighting in room to represent emergency situation.

8. **Staging.** Placement of characters and metaphoric objects inside the frame to represent relationships. Where are your characters in relationship to each other metaphorically? You could have three characters who form a love triangle standing around a fire to represent a secret affair about to be uncovered. What metaphoric items surround the characters? Are they talking while walking

"In nature's infinite book of secrecy, a little I can read."
—*William Shakespeare*

through a field of sunflowers or in between cactuses? What metaphoric objects could you place between characters to show relationships or emotional states during a scene? Two characters on opposite sides of the frame with knives hanging on the wall between them may represent conflicting emotions. How could you use a series of staging metaphor shots to show relationships? In *Citizen Kane*, one of Kane's marriages dissolves in front of our eyes as, in a few quick match cuts, Kane and his wife sit farther and farther away from each other at bigger and bigger dinner tables.

9. **Fables.** How could you interject little stories into scenes to show plot, theme, or character? You might want to have just pictures of parable characters or allude to them visually through stuffed animals, statues, paintings, cartoons, or drawings on the set. Try to think of new ways to incorporate parables visually into your films. Perhaps you could make your own little cartoon fable to play on a TV in the background during a scene. You might make up your own original Aesop-type fable, which the characters could discuss, see in a play or on TV, read in a book, hear about in dialogue, or be relayed by a magical object. In the *Crying Game*, the theme of how you can't change your basic nature is developed by the characters talking about the frog and scorpion fable in each of the three acts. The frog agrees to give the scorpion a ride across the lake, but then gets stung.

10. **Symbol dictionaries.** You may want to start collecting resources for metaphors, such as symbol or dream dictionaries, to help you tap into universal subconscious visual metaphors.

Listed here are some examples of symbols and possible meanings. Record your own favorite symbols and what they mean to you for use in your films.

"Each thing is like a form everlasting and comes round again in its cycle."
—*Marcus Aurelius*

Animal	Symbolic Meaning
Bee	Society, industry, work, dangers of courtship, immortality, rebirth, order
Bird	Freedom, flying, between higher and lower worlds
Dragon	Money, fame, danger, myth, fire
Horse	Chivalry, spiritual carrier, supremacy, generosity, courage
Raven/crow	Death, war, supernatural, transformer, trickster, messenger, prophet
Pet	Unconditional love
Firefly	Perseverance, spirits of the living, souls of the dead, passionate love
Unicorn	Gentleness, wise rule, famous children
Wild animal	Dangerous passions and people
Woodpecker	Noisy, guardian, aggressive
Dog	Loyalty, guardian, friend
Shark	Danger that lurks out of sight, fear
Dolphin	Playful, spiritual mediator between worlds, helper
Butterfly	Metamorphosis, rebirth, false lover, transformation, soul, summer, joy, witches
Dove	Peace, messenger, holy, renewal of life, vulnerability, sensitivity, spirit
Peacock	All-seeing, pride, vanity, solar glory, royalty, immortality, love, beauty, paradise
Owl	Wisdom, scholar, occult powers, all-seeing, death, supernatural protector
Spider	Weaving, letters, ability to travel between worlds, architecture, pain
Snake	Sacred knowledge, death, afterlife, rebirth, phallic, fertility, eternity, magic, fear
Elephant	Memory, intelligence, wise nature
Bear	Creation, guardians, spirit guide, strength, transformation, healing, courage
Crocodile	Creative abilities, predator, hidden danger
Horned animal	Expanded perception
Nursing animal	Unconditional motherly love
Bull	Earth, male, physical, danger, powerful

"Creativity is harnessing universality and making it flow through your eyes."
—Peter Koestenbaum

List Possible Metaphors and Symbols for Your Film. As you go through the following example metaphor and symbol charts, list one idea for each type of chart to use in your film. For example, pick a symbolic animal that may appear somewhere in your story as a pet, in a painting, discussed in dialogue, or as a character in a fable. Practice combining metaphors and symbols and using repeating patterns to create a unique visual language.

Plant	Symbolic Meaning
Honeysuckle	True devotion, sweetness
Garlic	Protection, antiseptic, healing
Fennel	Restores lost vision
Lavender	Calming, sweet, soothing for burns and wounds
Dandelion	Troublesome, tough and persistent
Rose	Queen of flowers, love, devotion, beauty, sweetness, creative powers
Thyme	Courage, bravery
Sunflower	Sacred, gold, sun, wild, tall, attractive
Rosemary	Love, remembrance, fidelity (The wife rules the house when rosemary is planted outside.)

Weather	Metaphoric Meaning
Lightning	Unexpected changes
Tornado	Violent destructive behavior
Floods	Chaos, destruction, welled-up emotions overflowing, retribution
Hurricane	Forces beyond our control, passion
Rain	Sadness, romantic, cold, fetility, precious, life-giving
Rainbow	Wholeness, beauty, perfection, bridge between heaven and earth, unity
Hot and Sunny	Hot tempers, sensual, summer, lazy, fun
Cold and Icy	Frozen emotions, cold feelings, static, winter, sharp, harsh, survival, death

Object	Symbolic Meaning
Axe	Authority, sacrifice, punishment
Bubble	Beautiful but fragile object, nonpermanent, childlike happiness
Egg	Cosmic totality
Fig	Psychic ability, fertility
Flame	Danger, anger, speed
Honey	Pleasure, sweetness, fertility
Ice cream	Pleasurable, sensual tastes
Quartz	Becoming more powerfully expressive
Satellite	Communication
Shoes	Grounding, in touch with life (Weird shoes mean new change.)
Waves	Ups and downs of life
Anchor	Stability, grounded, sanctuary
Bell	Warning, disaster, death, alarm, religious
Fire	Passion, desire, anger, destruction
Spiral	Rebirth, learning, evolution, path
Sun	Creative energy, male, transformation, higher consciousness, light
Moon	Unconscious, intuition, female, cycles, changing
Dent	Unfortunate event
Drowning	Overcome by emotions
East	Birth, consciousness
Kissing	Acceptance, approval, respect
North	Unknown
South	Earthly passion/sensuality
Victory	Overcoming conflict between two parts of ourselves
West	Spiritual awareness, death
Coins	Wealth
Grapes	Fertility, wine, pleasure, harvest
Falling leaves	Harvest, dropping, letting go, surrender
Crystal	Clarity of perception
Fountain	Source, life-giving spring, medicinal, spiritual refreshment
Gate	Change in state, secular power, ownership, new beginnings
Well	Supernatural portal, birth, blessings, mercy, unusual events
Flag	Identity, nationhood, allegiance
Ladder	Ascent/descent, spiritual transformation, stages of work, death

Occupation	Metaphoric Meaning
Butcher	Death, rejuvenation, bloody, violent
Outlaw	Rebellious, anarchy, lawbreaker
Queen	Female authority figure, ruler, political
Artist	Inner creative force made physical
Banker	Authority, manager of resources, wealth
Doctor	Healer, authority, respect, caregiver
Guru	Wisdom, father figure, unconscious, knowledge
Priestess	Intuitive, female, moon, independence, responsibility, clarity, balance, clairvoyance
Rock Star	Superman, decadent, talent
Landscaper	Sculpting earth, connected to plants, making natural things beautiful
Lawyer	Server of justice, shark-like instincts
Solider	Brave, team player, trained for combat
Stockbroker	Risk taker, big money, fast decisions
Waitress	Server, cheerful
Secretary	Detail-oriented, office worker, assistant
Actor	Trained to pretend different feelings or personalities, hard to read

Scene Activities	Metaphoric Meaning
Kneeling	Respect, humility, sacred, spiritual, asking for guidance
Getting a tattoo	Transformation, symbolic of character change, rebel, outsider
Dancing	Ecstasy, trance, celebration, ritual, playfulness, worship, performance
Bathing	Cleansing, rebirth, purification, regaining youthfulness
Journeying	Spiritual quest, search, pilgrimage, test, new beginnings, change
Hunting	Skill, prowess, risk, death, persecution, domination

"Nature is written in symbols and signs."
—John Greenleaf Whittier

"Geometry is knowledge of the eternally existent."
—Plato

superfreak!

Combining Metaphors. How could you combine some of the previous examples of metaphors to create new ones? Create three different combinations with explanations for what they represent. How could you add specific colors and numbers to deepen the meaning? You could compose a shot of a queen figure eating a fig, with two woodpeckers on her shoulder, next to a pyramid, with lightning bolts in the background, to symbolize female authority, guardians, psychic ability, concentrating power within, and unexpected change.

11. **Numbers.** Sacred geometry is universal and will help you plan story elements using numbers as metaphors. You could have a character say he has seven (often associated with being lucky) dreams about an upcoming event. Or use the corresponding geometry and shapes when constructing your scenes, such as having seven colored stones on an altar that a character uses to pray for things.

12. **Juxtaposition.** Show the audience one metaphor or symbol, then another, and have them draw a third separate conclusion from the two. Chapter 8, "Preproduction Story-Editing Choices," covers in depth ways to use juxtaposition.

"Our biggest failure is our failure to see patterns."
—Marilyn Ferguson

According to Norse mythology, horses could understand the will of the gods. Odin rode an eight-legged stallion called Sleipnir. The eight from our number chart symbolizes the ability to go between worlds (like spiders with eight legs). This combination of number and symbol works well for this myth. How could you combine established metaphors to create original ones? How could you use your digital tools to create new visual metaphors? It would be interesting to see an eight-legged 2D or 3D animated horse.

Number	Symbolic Meaning
1	Number "1," top of group, circle, wholeness, center, unity, one-self, independence, single purpose, universe, equality, seed, stable, father, intolerance, stubbornness
2	Partnership, duality, indecision, balance, 2 sides, opposites, relationships, root, mother, indecision, indifference, making choices
3	Third time a charm, things always come in 3s, 2 failures to 1 success, triangle, harmony, freedom, completion, relationship/balance, holy divinity, power, God's halo
4	Square, strength, stability, Mother Earth, heart, 4 directions, 4 elements, grounded, clumsiness, dull
5	Human body, 5 senses, stars, leaves, communication, nature, footprints, regeneration, vortex, authority (five-star general/sheriff star) spiral/transformation (the yellow brick road in *The Wizard of Oz* begins as a golden spiral (based on 5) to symbolize transformation).
6	Structure, balance, order, function, time, weights, intuition, practical
7	Magical, God, spiritual, cycles, excellence, myth, luck, musical harmony, crystals, rainbow, chakras, religion, virgin, dreams, voices, sounds, higher self, levels
8	Renewal, death/resurrection, nourishing, resonance, cosmic breath, chessboard, moon phases, limitless growth, goddess, traveling between higher and lower worlds (spider), atom groups, natural vibration
9	Completion, spiritual awareness, pregnancy, gift, highest attainment, ocean, horizon, ultimate extension, worship, essential elements, cosmic ruler
10	New beginning, high honor, whole family, perfect, top score
11	Master number, mystical, gateway, higher dimensions, higher consciousness

This Bigfoot biting the head off of a raven (death) could be a metaphor to foreshadow a close brush with death or a metaphor for overcoming the fear of death.

"The moon lives twenty-eight days and this is our month. Each of these days represents something sacred to us.... You should know also that the buffalo has 28 ribs, and that in our war bonnets we usually wear twenty-eight feathers. You see, there is a significance for everything, and these are things that are good for men to know and to remember."
—*Black Elk*

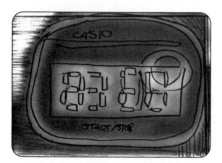

Clocks are sometimes shown going haywire when something in the film world is out of synch. What other types of ordinary symbolic objects or metaphors could you play with visually to show the state of your film world changing?

project
2.22

Use Metaphors and Symbols. Think of three ideas to show character history using metaphors and symbols somewhere in your film.

Using Visual Metaphors to Show Character History

Metaphors and symbols are a great way to develop your character history. Go through your character history questions and see how you could show the important points using metaphors.

"Honors and rewards fall to those who show their good qualities in action."
—*Aristotle*

Character History	Metaphoric/Symbolic Image Description in Script
Strange rituals in family for immortality.	Blue shrine full of glass bees in character's bedroom.
Weird hobbies for character in position of authority.	Royal sporting axes hung on walls.
Character feels trapped in old relationship.	Character eats partner's pet bird to symbolize loss of freedom.
Dangerous person.	Pet alligators and venomous snakes crawl around backyard.
Well-educated and cultured upbringing.	Has a grand piano delivered to house.
Misses lost love.	Carries a picture, gift from beloved, or ribbon from hair.
Artistic side.	Artwork displayed.
Most prized possession is an old love letter.	Letter is kept in a secret draw in a gold case.
Character is very happy and playful emotionally.	Wears rainbow suspenders, has a pinball machine in his bedroom, and has funny toys
Character needs tension to create.	Character turns on music really loud late at night to build sculpture, disturbing other people.
Character is terrified of getting sick.	Wears gloves, disinfects chairs before he sits down, wipes off phones, wears a surgical mask outside.
Character thinks the good old days were better.	Character drives a 1957 Chevy and wears vintage clothes.

Using Visual Metaphors to Show Backstory

Metaphors are great to develop the backstory for your film without having to explain everything.

Using Visual Metaphors to Show Character Traits

Metaphors are great tools to use when developing character traits.

This sacred Bigfoot cave has symbolic paintings on the walls that tell the history of the clan (to develop backstory information).

Backstory Information	Metaphoric/Symbolic Image Description in Script
Leader of film world as an outlaw	Picture of king surrounded by gun collection framed on the wall.
Social order of people in town	Rich people wear bright colors, walking poodles; poor people wear gray and are sweeping the street.
Lay of the land with edge of the known world said to be forbidden	Mural featuring a map with the edge of world full of monsters; characters call it "the edge."
Important heroes who character admires	Temple devoted to dead hero in middle of town.
Past catastrophic event	Pitch-black historical memorial site with a big flame still burning.

project 2.23

Backstory Objects. Choose 10 items to place symbolically on your sets to represent the backstory of your film using the metaphoric approaches previously described.

Character Trait	Metaphoric/Symbolic Image Description in Script
Leader	Uniform, medals on chest, ribbons, special gold scepter.
Professional wrestler	Superhero outfit, mullet, gold chains with wrestling medals around neck, apartment full of wrestling posters and trophies.
Alcoholic	Silver flask in pocket, mini liquor bars in secret spots in each location, drinking at each location.
Lover	Tattoo of girl's name on heart, carrying fresh picked flowers, digital effects slight golden glow aura.
Humble	Character hiding from recognition events, awards.
Well–educated	Carries books everywhere, uses a magnifying glass to look at things, wears glasses, hangs out at museums.
Uptight	Hair perfect, tight starched clothing, gets upset about litter on the street or slow people at stores.
Warrior/solider	Scars on body, wears hidden weapons, jumps when people touch him from behind, flips into martial arts pose when startled.

"Enthusiasm for one's goal lessens the disagreeableness of working towards it."
—*Thomas Eakins*

project 2.24

Character Trait Metaphors and Symbols. Think of three ideas to show character traits using metaphors and symbols somewhere in your film.

This Bigfoot finally snaps one day during a date and punches a hole through a tree. How could you show your characters having uncontrollable outbursts or overwhelming emotional moments that cause them to change suddenly in your film?

Using Visual Metaphors to Show Character States

Mental, emotional, physical, spiritual, and intellectual states of characters should be expressed through metaphoric and symbolic cues. An object may be present in the scene to symbolize a character's state or the character may say something that gives us a clue.

In *Transit*, the Venice hotel room has clothes all over the floor, symbolizing how messed up Emmy's life has become with Oscar. She has a black eye, too. These visual clues let us know her character state in the scene. In the Baden-Baden scene with her husband, the hotel room is perfectly neat—with separate twin beds symbolizing the state of their marriage. How can you use symbols like this to show us character states in each scene?

project 2.25

Create Character States. Think of three ideas to show character states using metaphors and symbols somewhere in your film.

"Spend time every day listening to what your muse is trying to tell you."
—Saint Bartholome

"Some days, you tame the tiger. And some days, the tiger has you for lunch."
—Tug McGraw

Character State	Metaphoric/Symbolic Image Description in Script
Someone not what he or she seems	Reflection in funhouse mirrors
Wise shaman head of tribe	Says he only "drinks out of ancient skull"
Person going crazy	Gory disturbing art project the character is making throughout film
Loss of life force	Crops in field dying
Relationship status negative	Couple fighting over the color of drapes
Lost-love memory	Pendant with old picture around neck
Revenge for death of loved one	Handmade knife from loved one's family
Midlife crisis	Character buys Harley-Davidson motorcycle
Obsessed with food	Character digging around for hidden candy bars
Scientific mindset	Has vision looking into liquid inside heated glass beaker
Losing important object	Dog floating down the river
Spiritual epiphany	Shaves head or cuts off hair to symbolize new beginning or mindset
Needs to control every little thing because of fear of chaos in world	Arranging objects in straight lines
Needs to feel clean in a dirty business	Taking very long and meticulous grooming shower with lots of special lotions and shampoos
Character hitting bottom	Character starving in a dark messy house

Using Visual Metaphors/ Symbols with Nature Shots

In the animated short *Transit*, we see subtitles of what happens to the characters at the end. When the information comes up about Emmy being missing and her body never found, an ominous shark fin glides by the floating suitcase in the water and then the suitcase sinks. This symbolizes foul play is involved in her disappearance; after all, sharks can eat people and leave no clues. A puddle of blood then forms on the surface of the water, letting us know that Oscar killed her, cut her up, and threw her body overboard in the suitcase. All of this information is conveyed with simple text on the screen and a shark fin moving around a symbolic suitcase covered with travel stickers from the places they had visited together.

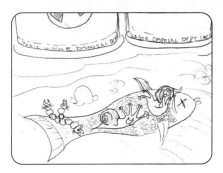

Mutant bugs and snails in a toxic waste dump cave could be used to show the dangerous effects of chemicals on living organisms.

Event Occurring in Scene or Another Area	Metaphoric/Symbolic Image Description in Script
Death	Black crows on a snow-covered black winter tree
Rebirth/resurrection	Springtime shots of flowers blooming, little birds in nests chirping, sunny skies, green grass
Losing important relationship	Dog watching a ball roll into storm drain and looking upset
Someone about to steal	Fox in henhouse stealing chickens
Catastrophic event coming	Comets (lens-flare effects) in sky
Rough emotions	Big waves crashing on rocks
Spiritual epiphany	White animal being born in a barn
Murder	Blood running into water
Lots of work to be done	An anthill or bees in background
Angry emotions boiling over	Heat waves melting up from a prickly cactus-covered desert road

"Come forth into the light of things. Let nature be your teacher."
—William Wordsworth

project 2.26

Create Nature Shots. Think of three ideas to use nature shots with metaphors and symbols to visually develop information in your story.

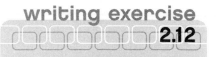
writing exercise 2.12

Write a few pages concentrating on just using different types of metaphors, symbols, and themes.

This bluescreened character is floating over a motion graphics timeline animation of his life as a dream. How could you create an original dream sequence in a film using digital tools? Maybe you could build a surreal dreamscape in a 3D or 2D photo collage, and use bluescreened characters flying or drifting over areas.

superfreak!

Write Down Your Dreams. If you have problems remembering your dreams, just tell yourself before you go to bed that you will remember them and keep a notebook with a pen nearby so that you can write them down as soon as you wake up. You may even want to tell yourself to dream that night of certain themes or questions to see what comes up. Write all dreams down even if they do not make sense, because they might reveal their meanings later. Sketch any cinematic elements of dreams next to the description if you have time.

Using Your Dreams to Help Create a Personal Visual Language

Many of us have developed a personal system of metaphors and symbols from life experiences hidden deep inside our subconscious, and these often show up in our nightly dreams. Maybe whenever you dream about playing chess, you are having to think strategically about changing some situation in your daily life. You may want to keep a dream journal and get a sense of how your mind thinks about metaphor and symbol, which you can then work into your films. The more you write down your dreams, the more you understand how you personally think in visual symbols and metaphors. Dreams can often help us find new ways to communicate visually on a deeper subconscious level, to show emotions or situations that may be hard to explain with straightforward dialogue or action.

Using Metaphors and Symbols to Show Theme

As discussed earlier, metaphors and symbols are great ways to show theme in subtle ways. You could turn your characters into animated animals or use some of your digital tools to invent new types of metaphoric characters. What other ways can you use metaphors and symbols to show themes in your film?

David Lynch is a master of cinematic metaphor. All of his films, and the TV show *Twin Peaks*, are worth studying for how they handle metaphor in bold, simple, and original ways. He is particularly good at creating personal metaphors and symbols. An opening scene in the film *Fire Walk with Me* takes place at an airport (new beginnings); this sets up the whole film. A dancing girl in a red dress comes out and does a quick pantomime, but says nothing, as the three detectives carefully watch. Later on in the car, one detective asks the more experienced one what the dancing girl meant. Below is a chart breaking down the metaphors and symbols of the

"dancing girl" scene. The audience would never understand the meaning of this symbolic language unless the characters explain them, which makes the metaphors a personal creation of the filmmaker.

The theme of the movie is that in the search for meaning, you cannot know everything and nothing is what it seems, which is wonderfully illustrated with the use of visual metaphors and symbols. Detectives as characters are metaphors for solving a mystery, such as solving life's mysteries, which is part of the theme of the film. Theme and metaphor are often tied together very closely in visual stories.

This scene is interesting because of the original use of metaphors and symbols. If the film would have started in an office with the detectives talking about the case, it would have been flat, uninteresting, cliché, and boring. The startling use of personal metaphors in this film pull us into the story, much like a puzzle we need to solve to understand what is happening.

Shot in *Fire Walk with Me*	Metaphoric/Symbolic Meaning
Someone smashes a TV set during one of the opening shots.	This film is going to be different from the TV show *Twin Peaks*.
FBI detective has a safe strapped around his body.	"He cracked the Whitman case," meaning this man is good at solving mysteries.
David Lynch makes a cameo as an FBI boss.	This is important information, so pay attention.
Dancing girl in a red dress comes out with a sour-looking face and does a quick pantomime.	Sour face means problems with the local authorities.
Dancing girl's eyes are both blinking.	Trouble higher up with sheriff and deputies.
Dancing girl has one hand in pocket, and one in a fist.	The local authorities are hiding something, and they are going to be belligerent.
Dancing girl starts walking in place.	This case will involve a lot of legwork.
Different colored thread has been used to alter the girl's dress to size.	Tailored dresses are code for drugs.
Blue rose pinned to dress.	No such thing as a blue rose. More experienced detective tells the other one, "Can't tell you about that." Hermeneutic search symbol.

definition

Hermeneutic The search for meaning. This popular philosophy comments on how humans search for meaning in films. Watch for this idea and see how each director handles it differently.

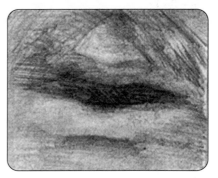

Metaphoric Puzzles. Orson Wells gives us an extreme close-up of Kane's last word, "Rosebud," which serves as the mystery puzzle to be solved in the film.

Creating Film Puzzles with Metaphors

Films are like puzzles and people like to try and figure things out in their heads. What was "Rosebud" a metaphor for in *Citizen Kane*? This is the dying Kane's last word at the start of the film, and the rest of the movie is a search to discover who or what Rosebud was about. Film geeks continue to argue about the true meaning of "Rosebud" whenever the subject comes up.

How can you put a puzzling aspect in your film to make it more engaging? Can you ask some type of visual question or create a visual puzzle? In *Memento*, the main character is trying to figure out who killed his wife, which gets pretty messy and confusing because he cannot remember anything for more than 10 minutes. Polaroid pictures serve as the metaphoric puzzle pieces this character uses to try and put his past back together. The answer to both these film puzzles are still not very clear even by the end of the films. Sometimes it is more interesting not to solve everything for the audience and let them figure it out for themselves (or continue to question).

superfreak!

Create a Puzzle in Your Film. Think of some way to twist your plot around a mystery or puzzle for the audience to solve. Review your favorite films that have puzzles and add the techniques used to this list. A good approach is to begin near the middle or end of the story and figure out some reason to go over what happened. You might use a detective interviewing someone about a crime, an old person thinking about her life, a reporter interviewing someone, a character reflecting back on his experiences through old photographs, a character telling his story in a voice-over, or present a mystery to be solved.

Film Puzzle Ideas to Get You Started

A character cannot remember something, but she is trying to find out what it is by using visually metaphoric clues.	A mystery event, crime, or situation needs to be solved.
Key character says something puzzling and then disappears.	One character is trying to find out the truth about someone/something that is not what it appears to be.
The character is displaying puzzling behavior, which is discovered to be connected to a past and forgotten trauma.	The character is trying to understand a strange situation. The character is in such a setup, alternate reality, or dream.
The character finds a strange object or information he has been tracking down.	Use multiple story lines, different character POV's, or characters intersecting at key points.

Working with Positive and Negative Theme Charges

Another way to work with metaphor and theme is to play back and forth between negative and positive manifestations throughout the film.

Different characters often represent different perspectives on the same theme. If you are doing a theme on loyalty among gangsters, you could have one super-loyal gangster, one who is playing two different crime families against each other, and some people who go back and forth between loyalty and disloyalty. What happens to these characters shows us your theme. If the super-loyal character gets rich and the two-timing one dies horribly, loyalty is a good thing. If the super-loyal gangster gets killed and the disloyal one wins the big prize, loyalty is not important or is even a bad thing in your film world.

Characters themselves can be great metaphors for themes.

The main character in Kafka's *Metamorphosis* wakes up one day as a cockroach. How can you play with transforming your character types to showcase your theme better? Digital tools and animation techniques make it easier to turn characters into bugs or other metaphoric creatures. *Harvey* is a 10-minute short film from Australia with a character that is literally sawed in half (3D effect) looking for his better half or ideal relationship (a great use of visual metaphor with digitally enhanced original character design). How could you use DV effects or 2D/3D animation to metaphorically show your characters in a new way?

What type of metaphor can each of your characters represent in your film world? What do the characters do for a living, how do they dress, what kind of cars do they drive, where do they live?

Themes sometimes represent best dreams or worst flaws. Who is

---

definition

Theme Charge Negative or positive manifestations of theme.

project 2.27

List Positive and Negative Theme Charges. How could you have different characters or situations represent positive and negative sides of your theme?

destroyed? Who grows? What special quality in the protagonist helps him achieve his goals? In *Lily and Jim*, both main characters want a relationship, but both of them have pretty ineffective communication skills (worst flaw and theme).

Using Visual Metaphors to Develop Theme

The theme, or unspoken moral message of the story, needs to be carefully handled. You must make sure the audience gets the theme on some level, but not be too preachy (a delicate balance). Metaphors provide a great way to communicate theme while telling your story visually.

You can use existing metaphors or create your own original visual metaphoric language for your film. Suppose that you are doing a film on the theme of greed. You might have all the really greedy characters wearing green, talking about money, clinging cash registers in the background, characters using greed-type slang such as "time is money," people in the background chasing blowing dollar bills, or a lead character counting his money as he delivers his lines. The best approach for developing visual metaphors and symbols is to create a list of possible ideas and then see which ones you can play with without being too obvious or preachy.

A character falling into a bottomless pit could be metaphoric for diving into the unconscious. The theme of my film is that every living being has a specific purpose. The theme goal of my protagonist is to find her purpose by learning to trust her intuition. Showing her falling into a pit is a good way to symbolize going deep inside to find her purpose and trust the hidden parts of her intuition.

Theme	Metaphoric/Symbolic Image Description in Script
Treasure the little things in life.	Character eating fresh pie, savoring every bite.
Alienation of youth.	Young character looking out of place at grownup party.
Desire leads to suffering.	Character getting beat up trying to get what he wants.
Exploration of character.	Searching for meaning of last word uttered on deathbed.
The blurry line between sanity and insanity.	Show all the characters acting crazy but functional.
Violence as cost of individuality.	Hip, artsy, unique criminal characters.
Cost of deception.	Pet cat found hanging on clothesline by antagonist.
Power of love can change fate.	Character screaming so loud that he wins game of chance to save lover.
War changes people.	Main characters all experience extreme changes as result of war. Some characters die, some become very scarred, and others get very resourceful.

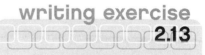
writing exercise 2.13
Write a few pages about how to show your theme using a unique set of metaphors and symbols.

project 2.28
Showing Theme. Think of five symbols or metaphors to show theme in your film.

"The privilege of a lifetime is being who you are."
—*Joseph Campbell*

The opening shot of the film *Memento* shows a fresh Polaroid picture as it develops. It takes a moment for viewers to realize that the film is rolling backward—the picture is becoming less clear the longer we watch it. This is a great visual symbol for the theme of the way we reconstruct memory and how what we remember fades and changes over time. This whole film is told backward in short memory bursts because the main character can remember things for only 10 minutes at a time. Polaroids are the way this character keeps track of who people are and what he thinks is happening. The opening shot tells us a great deal about the character, plot, and theme in a stunningly original visual metaphor that is both simple and deeply complex at the same time.

When you really understand your main characters, metaphors, and theme, it is much easier to develop the events in your story and write your script. Building up original characters is like creating new beings in the world who start to take on a life of their own inside your imagination. Creating strong metaphors and themes will make your story deeper and help you choose visual designs that fit the ideas you are presenting.

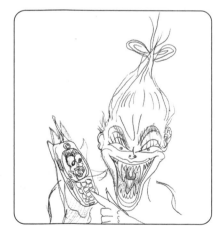

Ezzie stole a video cell phone from a camper and likes to crank call the speed dial people and scare them with her big furry face and ferocious roar. Sometimes during the film, she calls different people on the phone and asks for help or advice, or does something silly. This helps show a connection between the Bigfoot film world and the human world. A Bigfoot using a video phone could be interpreted as a metaphor for the way technology is trickling down into the masses and changing our lives in unexpected ways. This idea could be used as a subplot device in an animated series where the character steals a different phone each week and talks to a new cast of speed dial people. How could you incorporate a unique digital storytelling approach in your film as a symbol or metaphor for theme? Maybe your character could consult his PDA—playing DV video clips you create to show a higher power guiding him through the story. What other digitally enhanced gizmos could you use to tell us a story in a new way?

chapter 3

Developing Plot Points

"The goal is to live with godlike composure on the full rush of energy, like Dionysus riding the leopard, without being torn to pieces. A bit of advice given to a young Native American at the time of his initiation: 'As you go the way of life, you will see a great chasm. Jump. It is not as wide as you think.'"
—Joseph Campbell

No formulas exist for writing a good script. There are as many different ways to tell a story, write a script, or make a film as there are people who do these things. One of my favorite tools when developing script ideas is to play with plot points. Plots need to feel like they are always changing direction, while building toward a climax. The writer needs to know how the story is going to end, and then twist the plot points toward that solution in a variety of unexpected ways. By using plot points when preparing a script, you will keep your story moving, and can easily estimate page count between important events.

"A novelist must know what his last chapter is going to say and one way or another work toward that last chapter.... To me, it's utterly basic, yet it seems like it's a great secret."
—Leon Uris

This chapter covers various types of story styles and plot points. After you have a clear idea of what your film is about, it is time to choose the shape that will best communicate the ideas. Conceptually developing a film idea rarely happens in the linear step-by-step process outlined in these pages. It often feels more like being in the middle of a chaotic storm of possibilities that you try to nail down into a cohesive story. By choosing plot points, you will build a strong foundation to build up a series of individual scenes.

Aristotelian Dramas

definition

180-Degree Character Arc Change
A completely life-altering change in perspective or view of self in the world. Usually the protagonist becomes conscious of this big change right around the climax, during some sort of epiphany.

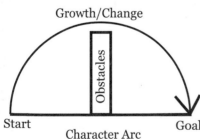

This is a diagram of the way a character arc changes 180 degrees throughout the course of a story. Notice how the size of the obstacles relates to the amount of change. At the height of the curve, the character has changed quite a bit. On the downward side of the arc, those new changes are incorporated into the way the character reacts to obstacles.

"A beautifully told story is a symphonic unity in which structure, setting, character, genre, and idea meld seamlessly. To find their harmony, the writer must study the elements of story as if they were instruments of an orchestra—first separately, then in concert."
—Robert McKee

Dramas focus on the passion, madness, dreams, epiphanies, and inner workings of the human heart in full-spectrum emotional glory. The types of choices your characters make under extreme pressure reveal who they are to the audience.

In Aristotelian dramas, the protagonist changes one character trait 180 degrees. Usually this involves overcoming the worst flaw that is blocking the character from achieving his or her main goals.

If you change, you will succeed. The protagonist changes throughout the story by learning from experiences in the plot. These dramatic changes are called *character arcs*. A character could change from being a follower to a leader, self-destructive to self-loving, ineffective communicator to clear communicator, unkind to kind, waitress to movie star, or reckless to responsible. What big inner changes have you had to make to accomplish goals in your own life? How can you cannibalize these experiences for your films?

Characters must be constantly growing and changing with traits that distinguish them from each other in this type of drama.

Audiences like to see characters change in little growth spurts. Sudden, abrupt changes in characters are not as believable as changes that result from the character learning to be a new way through trial and error over time. Some characters may suddenly change because of shocking or extreme experiences.

Aristotelian Drama Book

Story by Robert McKee is a great book to study for creating dramas, where we watch characters change and grow while they overcome a series of obstacles.

Creating Character Arcs

Dramas have main characters who must evolve, learn, change, or grow to accomplish plot and theme goals. This growth is called a character arc and is often related to the theme of the story. In the movie *Finding Nemo*, Nemo's dad is the protagonist, representing the theme of how he should never give up in his constant struggle to overcome his own fears and find his son in a very big and dangerous ocean.

Theme of film. Do not give up; "keep swimming."

Protagonist plot goal. To find his only remaining son.

Protagonist theme goal. To find a balance between being an overly protective parent and dealing with his own fears of losing his only son.

Character arc. Goes from being an over-protective parent afraid of leaving the coral reef, to swimming across the entire ocean to find his son, battling all of his worst fears along the way.

The following chart may help you think of some interesting character arcs. Most of these arcs listed could also be reversed, such as the character going from happy to sad or sad to happy. Character arc changes usually do not start to kick in until the beginning of Act Two, when the character commits to achieving a goal. You set up the initial character state in Act One. In Act Two, we watch the protagonist change slowly, as he or she learns from experiences in the film. By the end of Act Three, the character realizes the change during some epiphany-type moment.

When my protagonist falls into a quicksand pit during her shamanic journey, she experiences a big shift in learning to trust her intuition. This causes an epiphany for the character, which is shown by her calmly rising out of the quicksand covered in the strange, glowing cave fungus. How can you show your character changing and having epiphanies in visually dramatic ways?

definition

Epiphany Moment of realization for character or audience that they did not understand before.

Character Arc Chart

Character Begins as This	Character Changes into This
Innocent	Corrupt, then wisdom/balance
Thoughtless	Wise
Uptight	Easygoing
Angry with the world, unhappy, or depressed	Happy to be alive
Atheist, lacking faith	Spiritual
Prejudiced against certain person or group	Seeing the unity in all life
Being stuck/trapped in life	Becoming unstuck/free
Brutal	Compassionate
Dead inside	Fully alive
Fear of death	At peace with death
Fear of vulnerability	Embracing love and vulnerability

continues

Character Arc Chart (continued)

Character Begins as This	Character Changes into This
Afraid of everything	Couragous and fully engaged in living life
Insecure/Feeling like a nobody	Confident/Finding self-worth
Follower	Leader
Greedy	Generous
Group reality	Individual-created reality
Hating self	Accepting one's own flaws
Hating someone	Accepting people with flaws
Introvert	Extrovert
Naive	Worldly
Self-centered	Caring about others
Negative view of life	Positive outlook
No connection to others	Becoming part of group
No sense of right or wrong	Ethical
Not knowing self	Deep self-knowledge
Not feeling loveable	Becoming very lovable
Not responsible for actions or life	Taking full responsibility for his or her life working
Obsessed with _____	Letting go of _____
Out-of-control life	Back on life track
Overcome with guilt	Letting go of guilt
Self-destructive	Self-loving
Socially awkward	Socially triumphant
Waitress	Goddess
Stuck in past tragic experience	Recovering from tragedy and getting on with life
Total cynic	Learning how to make a difference and be loving
Unaware of self-defeating behaviors	Fully in control of creating happy life
Unkind/mean	Kind/sweet
Washed-up failure	New success
Addicted to _____	Free of addiction and need to shut down
Seeking revenge	Seeing the power of forgiveness
Violent	Gentle
Cultured, useless Southern Belle	Independent resourceful farmer
Insane	Sane

In *Braveheart*, Mel Gibson goes from being a follower to a leader. In *Lord of the Rings*, Frodo goes from innocent to opening his eyes to the darkside. In *Shrek*, Shrek goes from an unkind ogre to kind and loving. In *Harry Potter*, Harry goes from being a mistreated orphan to a famous wizard child. Tragedies usually have characters on a negative arc going from good to worse. In *Transit*, Emmy goes from a recklessly playful femme fatal to a fearful dead woman. The butcher in *Transit* goes from innocent family man to a worldly murderer.

Showing Small Character Changes In Steps

How do you make changes that last in your own life? Think of ways to show how your characters are changing slowly in the story using a process similar to the following:

1. Show negative condition or state that needs to change, with character unaware of the problem.
2. Show character becoming aware of problem and thinking about change, but is reluctant to change.
3. Show character committing, or trying, to change in small ways with repeated successes and failures. Show backslides into old ways of being.
4. Show character making a big change at the height of confronting big obstacles, conflict, an ordeal, or death in some form.
5. Show character integrating a new way of being into an old way of doing things, with possible backslides into the old state occurring less and less.

6. Show character finally mastering the new change with no sign of the old way of being.

Ways To Show Characters Changing

Below is a list of ways you can use to show how a character is growing and changing in your film. In *Cold Mountain*, Nicole Kidman's character arc goes from useless, cultured southern belle to resourceful, independent woman farmer. We see these changes happen very vividly in her appearance when she goes from wearing long white dresses, with complicated hair styles and frilly flowered hats, to wearing black pants, a long black coat, long braids, and a dark cowboy hat while shooting turkeys with a shotgun.

- **Changing Appearance:** Clothing choices, hair styles, posture, way a character moves, color of clothing, makeup, physical well-being, hat styles, jewelry.
- **Change In Posture/Attitude/ Demeanor:** Character could go from being really uptight and prissy with a straight back to a disheveled, slouching, happy mess.
- **Change In Reactions:** Show a character reacting one way at the beginning of the story, then reacting differently to similar events as the story unfolds. This shows the character gaining more confidence and skill.
- **Change In Environments:** Show the character in one setting or place that changes dramatically along with the character arc: a clean house becoming a messy house.

project 3.1

Character Arcs. Decide on a character arc for your protagonist. Make sure it relates to the theme of your film and the theme goal.

"Things do not change; we change."
—Henry David Thoreau

"Good stories make you feel you've been through a satisfying, complete experience. You've cried or laughed or both. You finish the story feeling you've learned something about life or about yourself. Perhaps you've picked up a new awareness, a new character, or attitude to model your life on."
—Christopher Vogler

In my Bigfoot story, Ezzie goes from being terrified of symbolic snakes and spiders to making friends with each one she meets. Her theme goal is to learn to trust her intuition, which helps her get more in tune with the animal kingdom and less afraid of the unknown.

project
3.2

Think of ten small ways to show your main character changing throughout your story.

writing exercise
3.1

Write a few pages focusing on a main character with a clear character arc, who changes in small ways.

This Bigfoot brands his girlfriend's initials onto his arm as a young man to show how much he loves her. As an older Bigfoot, he changes the letters of the brand to match his new wife's initials, symbolizing character growth in learning to let go of the past.

- **Change In Activities:** Show the character doing and learning different things. Maybe they start out wasting their free time sitting on the porch, staring off into space and looking sad, and then they have a realization and begin frantically building a symbolic boat in the backyard.

- **Change In Social Relations:** Show the character growing or changing in the way they relate to other characters. The first time we see them in a social situation they may seem uncomfortably stiff, and by the end of the film they are hugging everybody.

- **Changes In Speech:** Have the characters change the way they talk, and have the words they use reflect new growth, change, and outlook. Use the dialogue techniques from Chapter 4, "Writing Scenes, Conflict, and a Short Script."

- **Change In Priorities:** Show how different things are becoming important to the character as they grow. At the start they may think keeping up their appearance is critical, in the middle they may just be trying to survive each day, and at the end they may be content with taking each day as it comes, trusting in their new found abilities.

Using Metaphors and Symbols to Show Character Arc

A character changing can be subtly shown by attaching metaphors and symbols to the individual growth states. You should be able to tell what state of growth your character is in by tracking the condition of the visual symbol attached to it.

"Times of great calamity and confusion have ever been productive of the greatest minds. The purist ore is produced from the hottest furnace, and the brightest thunderbolt is elicited from the darkest storms."
—Charles Caleb Colton

movie note

***Braveheart* Flower Shows Character Growth and Condition.** In the movie *Braveheart*, a purple star thistle flower is given to Mel Gibson's character as a young boy at his family's funeral by his future wife. When he returns home as a man, we see that he has kept the star thistle pressed in the pages of a Bible. The woman he marries then embroiders the purple star thistle flower onto a handkerchief, which Mel then carries through the whole film as a symbol of his love for his wife and freedom (theme). He kisses this bloodied and beat-up handkerchief before he goes into battle. Notice how a purple star thistle flower is a perfect symbol for these characters, because it is beautiful (love), tough (enduring), and thorny (dangerous). A rose would have been too cliché and soft for this story.

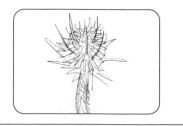

project
3.3

Attach a Metaphor or Symbol to Show Character Arc. Think of three possible ideas for using unique metaphors or symbols to show character change throughout the film. The symbol should change along with the character in some way.

writing exercise
3.2

Write a few pages about a main character with a clearly defined character arc, who changes in small ways. Focus on using metaphors and symbols to show change.

Character Arc/Growth/Change	Metaphoric/Symbolic Image Description in Script
Naive to reckless	Clean, nice hotel room with rich husband to messy, cheap motel room with poor lover.
Wealth to poverty	Crisp new clothes to old ones with holes.
Fear to love	Dark bedroom lighting to sunny, warm bedroom recently painted yellow.
Boy to man	Fighting big bear and getting claw necklace as a teen. As an adult, letting the same bear escape being shot, showing respect for the creature.
Group reality to individual reality	Generic short hair to shaved head with a new tattoo.
Brutal to compassionate	Treasured statue of famous leader gets blown up and then rebuilt in more loving pose.
Character snapping emotionally from one extreme arc to another	Throwing prized photographs of achievements out of a window to show new priorities.
Dead inside to a lust for life	Dead rose garden in backyard to a new, blooming bigger one.
Follower to leader	Gang member removing leather jacket that gang members wear, after realizing he can no longer be part of gang.
Innocent to jaded	Long blonde hair on young girl, then cut short, and then long and dyed black.
Powerless to powerful	Magic object that becomes more useful as character learns to use it with his own power.

Zen and the Art of Landscaping

In this short film, an unwitting lawn boy is lured inside a nice suburban home by a seductive housewife. All of the characters undergo a major change in perspective about life during 17 minutes in a kitchen. The events in the story are as follows:

1. Mom gets out of car with grocery bags and flirts with new young landscaper named Zen.
2. Mom seduces Zen in the kitchen.
3. Son walks in unexpectedly from college catching Mom kissing Zen.
4. Son tells Mom that Zen went to high school with him and always beat him up.
5. Mom and son fight about her kissing Zen in kitchen.
6. Dad comes home from work early and wants to know what is going on.
7. Mom accuses Dad of sleeping with bag girl at supermarket. Dad wants to know what Mom's got going on with Zen.
8. Son tells parents he came home to tell them he was gay.
9. Parents tell son he is adopted.
10. Dad says Mom never wanted to have kids because she was worried about her hips getting bigger.
11. Zen realizes that the supermarket bagger Dad is having an affair with is his wife.
12. Son hits Mom accidentally when trying to hit Zen.
13. Family turns on Zen as he escapes by holding them back with his weed whacker.

All of this revelation is pure Aristotelian drama, with each character experiencing big, life-altering changes.

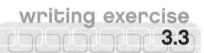

project 3.4

List three possible ways your main character could experience a death of some sort in your story. What types of possible realizations or transformations does the character experience?

"You have got to find the force inside you."

—Joseph Campbell

The Hero Journey Cycle

Hero journeys are myths that seek to re-create the universal human life experience. Characters in these stories go on journeys into the unknown and face different forms of death that cause deep transformations. Myths are powerful for telling stories with strong themes because they form patterns of meaning.

Hero journey emphasizes plot, whereas Aristotelian dramas emphasize extreme character growth.

Batman, Indiana Jones, James Bond, Buckaroo Bonzai, and Superman do not really change during their hero journey tales. They survive snakes, traps, evil villains, bomb blasts, car chases, Nazis, bullets, bad aliens, and impossible odds. Hollywood is a great cannibal of mythology, and many blockbusters are based on the steps of the hero myth.

writing exercise 3.3

Write a few pages about a main character experiencing some form of death. Focus on the character having some big realization during the worst part.

money-saving

Guaranteed Great Story Structure. Hero journeys are one of the easiest stories to execute successfully, because people seem to respond so well to this type of structure. About 80 percent of Hollywood films are types of hero journeys. The hardest part is creating an original one, which is where digital tools may help by showing things we have never seen before in a mythic structure. Special effects and supernatural myths go very well together.

Forms of Death for Your Character to Experience

When characters confront death in stories, they experience some form of irrevocable loss where the character cannot get something back in the same form again. Here is a list to help you generate ideas.

Physical death	Loss of relationship
Sickness	death of dreams
Near death experience	Surviving hard times or situation
Loss of limb	Starving, running out of water or air to the point of death.
Surviving death-defying experience	Torture
Surviving deadly situation	Loss of freedom
Loss of innocence	Losing identity
Death of possibility	Losing a close friend or relative
Emotional death	Loss of beauty
Death of planet, world, or town	Knowing for sure they are going to die and then surviving
Death of consciousness	Death of spouse
Psychological death	
Losing faith	

movie note

The movie *Shrek* cunningly combines Aristotelian drama and hero journey. He starts off as a reluctant hero, a bitter loner ogre living in a swamp wanting to get rid of all the creatures camping on his land. By the end, Shrek is transformed into a very loveable friendly guy with a beautiful girlfriend; Shrek has become a jolly hero. This is an engaging way to combine the two styles.

Big Granny is Ezzie's grandmother and mentor for learning about herbs and the history of the tribe. Ezzie flashes back to wonderful childhood memories of her grandmother throughout her journey in the cave at key moments. Big Granny is a wise old Bigfoot Shaman who is also a very respected medicine woman. Her special digitally enhanced powers include being able to shape shift into animals and fly around as a semitransparent spirit without a body to gather information. What new forms of mentors can you show us in your stories that have digitally enhanced skills or powers?

Short Hero Journeys

You will not have time to go through all 15 of the following plot points in a very short film. The ones noted with stars are the essential points to include in a short hero journey. Play with the order of the plot points, while paying attention to creating a big climax at the end. Become familiar with them and experiment with the parts that interest you the most. For example, you may have the mentor be a talking rock on the road that says one line to help the hero. Perhaps your series of tests takes place quickly at a gas station encounter. How could you use your digital tools to spice up each step of the journey in an original way? The following steps are my interpretation of Joseph Campbell and Christopher Vogler's hero journey books:

15 Hero Journey Plot Points

*1. **Ordinary world.** Protagonist in his or her drab, ordinary world that should contrast dramatically to the new one coming up. Usually fish-out-of-water main character who does not quite fit in. Drab farm, boring suburbs, dead city, dying land, slow planet. This setup can be really quick, with the problem showing up almost immediately.

*2. **Call to adventure.** A challenge is presented to the character in the form of a big problem to maintain status quo (what's normal). Fears build up inside the protagonist. Must establish stakes of success/failure. Clear hero goal that forces him to leave what is familiar and go into the unknown to retrieve something. Join war, quest to save land, solve a crime, rescue someone, get revenge, achieve a dream, right a wrong, win a race, prove something, figure something out, fix something, untangle a mystery, or remove a curse.

3. **Hero refuses call.** Fear of unknown creeps up, and protagonist does not want to go on the journey. Thinking of turning back. Reluctant hero in need of fresh, *personal* motivation. Make it too scary at home now. Hero's family gets murdered, bad prophetic dreams, house burns down, gets chosen by mistake to go, or loved ones plead for help.

"Desire and fear: These are the two emotions by which all life in the world is governed. Desire is the bait and death is the hook."
—*Joseph Campbell*

Essential Hero Journey Reading

Joseph Campbell's *The Hero with a Thousand Faces* (Princeton University Press, 1972), and Christopher Vogler's *The Writer's Journey* (Michael Wiese Productions, 1998), which summarizes Campbell's book in wonderful ways for screenwriters.

Ezzie meets a series of mentors during her vision quest. When she enters the shamanic journey part of her vision quest, she is greeted by her spirit animal, who happens to be a Loch Ness Monster named Nessy. This mentor teaches her how to navigate the spiritual realms.

"One thing that comes out in myths is that at the bottom of the abyss comes the voice of salvation. The black moment is the moment when the real message of transformation is going to come. At the darkest moment comes the light."
—Joseph Campbell

*4. **Mentor/supernatural assistance arrives.** A wise teacher or mystical force shows up. New tools, training, advice, medicine, food, weapons, or information are given. Mentor or teacher has been to the unknown side and helps hero prepare. Many stories have multiple mentors in different forms. Make sure these characters are original and avoid clichés. Wise old wizards, tough drill sergeants, bosses, teachers, parents, scientists, shamans, holy men, coaches, doctors, gods, ghosts, spirits, mystical creatures, or forces.

*5. **Hero leaves home.** Hero decides to go on journey and leaves home. Plot goal is clearly stated. Ship sails off, romance begins, train gets rolling, trek begins, trip starts.

6. **Crossing the first threshold.** Show nexus of film world where different types of characters meet on the edge of the new world. Places such as bars, parties, races, dances, festivals, shows, sporting events, or gatherings. Act Two begins.

7. **Tests on the road.** Hero meets new characters and decides who is a friend or foe. A series of new mentors may also be encountered. Information is gathered. Rules of new world established. New challenges and skill tests. Hero must muster courage, abilities, and skills inside first to show them outside. Good place to develop characters by showing how they respond under stress.

Notice how the hero journey plot points cross over into the dark, unknown, new world and then end up back in the ordinary world.

The Hero Journey

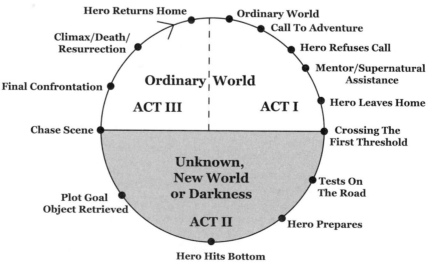

Separation → Transformation → Return

8. **Hero prepares before the most dangerous place.** Hero stops to prepare and plan at gate of enemy headquarters or underworld. Hero needs to outwit guards, break security, and consult maps (labyrinths, hell, enemy headquarters, dragon caves, bank vault, land of dead, evil castle, dangerous chambers).

*9. **Hero confronts greatest fear.** Not sure whether hero will survive. Trapped in clutches of villain, death of relationship, rites of passage, slain monster, battle to life or death situations.

10. **Hero hits bottom/death/ resurrection.** Hero hits bottom battling worst fear and appears to have died. Things look very bleak for the hero to ever accomplish the plot goal. Must be done convincingly. Does not have to be physical death. Could be death of dream, relationship, goal, spiritual, psychological or emotional death, or disaster. Hero miraculously figures out how to get out of trap, remembers some way to kill monster, live again, work it out, resurrect his spirit, or a flash of insight on how to survive and continue quest.

*11. **Plot goal object retrieved**. Hero accomplishes plot goal in unexpected way. Celebrates getting magical sword, grail, elixir, knowledge, prize, princess, plans. Act Three begins.

12. **Chase scene.** Attempt to return to ordinary world full of complications with enemy in full pursuit. Antagonistic forces descend, car chases, foot chases, spaceship chases, magical flight, or daring escapes.

13. **Final confrontation.** A confrontation between two characters over an issue that has been building since the beginning comes to a head. A sword battle, meeting, or personal conflict is confronted.

*14. **Climax/death/revelation/ resurrection.** The second brush with death, where the hero faces death or appears dead. A transformation or revelation occurs, causing a form of rebirth. Final exam to test mastery of new skills. Final plot goal accomplished. "Use the force, Luke" in *Star Wars*. We see he has mastered his new skills by using his intuition to blow up the Deathstar in one last shot.

*15. **Hero returns home.** Hero returns home with treasure, information, and transformation. Shares lessons, delivers treasure to save the world, gets a medal in a new uniform, wins over the girl, welcome-home ceremony, hero shown as new person in old world.

Creating Visual Symbols for Quest Objects

Most hero journeys revolve around a character searching for a symbolic quest object to achieve the plot goal. You may want to link quest symbols with plot or theme goals as shown in the following chart. How could you use some of your digital tools to create a new form of a symbolic quest object such as an animated talking statue or a Pandora's box that, when you open its lid, plays prophetic movies like a laptop?

"Mythology helps you to identify the mysteries of the energies pouring through you. Therein lies your eternity."
—Joseph Campbell

Creating Fresh Digital Mentors. This 500-year-old wise woman would make a great mentor and an original 3D character if you really wanted to play up her wrinkles and age.

project 3.5

Create an Original Symbolic Quest Object. If your story is a hero journey, what type of symbolic quest object could you create that relates to your plot, theme, and film world?

writing exercise 3.4

Write a short story based on your hero journey short project idea.

Quest Subject/Goal/Theme	Symbolic Quest Object
To save dying planet/world	Rare plant to stop disease
To prevent invasion by evil aliens	Technological gizmo or simple solution to stop alien technology
To find meaning in one's life	Ancient talking rosebush
To discover lost civilization to save humanity	Carving on sacred cave wall that moves
To defeat enemy	Blueprints of enemy headquarters trapped in hologram character
To gather mystic knowledge around philosophy, religion, spirituality, or magic	Powerful wand that shoots poisonous spiders or helpful fairies depending on user
To find truth, honesty, directness, purpose of life	High-tech mythical bow and arrow found in lost-city vault
To discover lost knowledge, writing, publication	Sacred scroll with words and images that animate very slowly over time
To prove bravery, intellect, logic, analysis	Magical sword that can be used only in the spirit world
To find love, goddess energy	Imprisoned miniature princess who lives in bottle
To explore relationships, emotions, sexuality	Golden cup that refills itself with different elixirs, which have images playing on the surface

project 3.6

Creating Hero Journey Mentors. Create three ideas for digitally enhanced hero journey mentors. What types of digital makeup or special powers can you add to show us some new versions we have not seen before? Maybe it could be something as simple as putting real human video lips on a talking symbolic object such as a statue.

project 3.7

Hero Journey Short. Take your short film idea and turn it into an original hero journey. Open your drawing book to two blank facing pages and make eight columns for the essential plot points, listed with stars above, and two columns for extra ones you may want to add. Brainstorm five possibilities, events, or settings for each plot point based on your short film idea. Pick the best ones and write them at the bottom of the column on the pages. Play with the order of these plot points and see what new film ideas come up.

10 Basic Flavors of Hero Journey Myths

Almost all the story flavors from Chapter 1, "Generating Ideas for Digital Short Films," could also be turned into a hero myth.

1. **The creation.** Man becoming conscious (*The Matrix*)
2. **Disaster myths.** Death/rebirth (*Twister*)
3. **Early times.** Prehistory (*Clan of the Cave Bear*)
4. **Journey to other worlds.** Heaven/hell, alternate dimensions (*What Dreams May Come*)
5. **Love story.** Hero goes to great lengths in the name of love (*Titanic*)
6. **Morality tale.** Doing what is right or fighting evil enemy (*Lord of the Rings*)
7. **Parallel stories.** Several different journeys or flavors told together (*Pulp Fiction*)
8. **The apocalypse.** End of world threat (*Armageddon*)
9. **The common man hero.** Regular person called to be a hero (*Spiderman, Finding Nemo*)
10. **Future myths.** Challenges of future and technology (*2001*)

Tragedy

Tragedies are stories to show us how we should *not* live our lives. This story structure serves as a vehicle for cautionary tales, with somber themes, full of disastrous and catastrophic conclusions. A tragic character starts the story at his height, showing signs of being incapable of change. This causes the character to enter into a downward spiral, failing miserably. Theme becomes the really important message but still needs to be handled carefully.

If you are going to do a morality tale, you need to spoon-feed the bitter medicine with some sugar. At the lowest point, the character may have an epiphany, make a sacrifice, or find redemption. When Oedipus realizes he has slept with his own mother and killed his father, he sacrifices his eyes.

Two Basic Types of Tragedies

- **Pure tragedy.** Steep downhill slide
- **Hollywood tragedy.** Upbeat start, downhill slide with upbeat redemptive ending

Pure tragedies are a steep downhill slide with the lesson to always be in a state of purity and strive for goodness. Neither theme nor plot goals are successfully accomplished. There are no upswings at the end of a pure tragedy, and they are often too depressing for a modern audience to digest. *Requiem for a Dream* is a recent pure tragedy that dealt with the theme of addiction to dreams; by the end, all the main characters are completely destroyed. How do you want the audience to feel at the end of a pure tragedy? Absolutely horrible.

> *"If you can't be a good example, then you'll just have to be a horrible warning."*
> —Catherine Aird

> *"In the darkest hour, the soul is replenished and given strength to continue and endure."*
> —Heart Warrior Chosa

Visual Sacrifices

Most tragedies have shocking visual sacrifices at the end. Tie the visual sacrifice to a metaphor or symbol for your plot and theme goals. In *Requiem for a Dream*, all the characters sacrifice themselves in some huge, symbolic way in Act Three. The lead guy even has his infected, junkie arm cut off in prison, the girlfriend becomes a junkie stripper, and the mom loses her mind and ends up in a mental hospital. What big visual sacrifices could your characters make at the end of a tragedy? Any digital ideas for interesting-looking sacrifices? Keep in mind that it's easy to remove body parts with some simple compositing techniques.

BigGranny once sacrificed two of her fingers to make a potion to help a friend. What types of visual sacrifices could your characters make? What types of original sacrifices could you use some of your digital tools to create?

Visual Sacrifice	Metaphor/Symbolic Meaning
Losing an eye	Losing the ability to see things clearly—loss of logic for right eye, and intuition for left one
Shaving off long hair	Sacrificing beauty or strength
Losing a hand	Loss of creativity
Losing a pet	Loss of companionship or love
Ending up in prison	Loss of freedom

Creating Visual Sacrifices. Think of three possible unique visual sacrifices your character could make if your film were a tragedy. Tie the sacrifice to the theme using symbol or metaphor. Add digitally enhanced effects.

Hollywood tragedies have more upbeat beginnings and happy endings. After a lesson has been learned, it is time for forgiveness with the added possibility of redemption (character turns morally good). Perhaps the prophecy sounds bad at the beginning, but gets twisted into something good at the end.

The main character finds redemption in Act Three, but never achieves perfection.

"We are healed of our suffering only by experiencing it to the full."
—Marcel Proust

"The crisis of today is the joke of tomorrow."
—H.G. Wells

Pure tragedy curve. Notice the way the line goes straight down, representing the characters' steep descents. These tragic protagonists fail to change in their character arcs, which prevents them from accomplishing either plot or theme goals. You can lay this tragic curve over the basic three-act structure or hero journey to add other plot points.

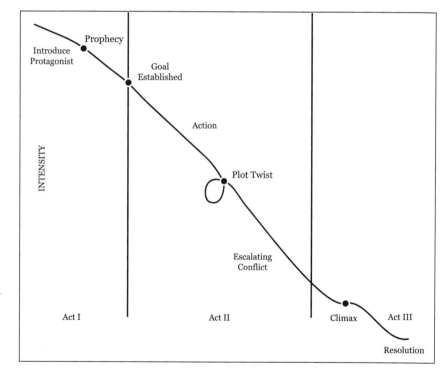

Tragic Truths

How can you play with the truth in your digital short films? The detailed text on the screen that explains what happens to each of the characters in *Transit* makes it feel like a true story. Lots of people feel disappointed when they find out *Transit* is a fictional tale. Why do we like to think stories really happened?

List three ways to make your story seem more like a true one using official-looking subtitles, narration, opening text that says, "This is a true story," or in some new way. In my Bigfoot story, I start with a realistic DV shot of an unmanned, motion-activated, deep-forest surveillance camera. The first shot

shows the camera turning on. Then a shadowy realistic 3D Bigfoot walks by, pauses while hearing the camera, and then checks it out before smashing it to bits. DV works great to simulate real footage and may be used to make your story feel more "true."

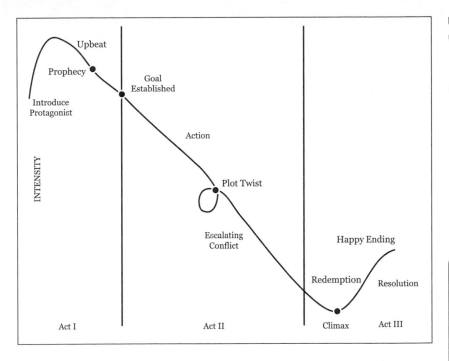

Act I   Act II   Climax   Act III

- Upbeat
- Prophecy
- Introduce Protagonist
- Goal Established
- Action
- Plot Twist
- Escalating Conflict
- Happy Ending
- Redemption
- Resolution

INTENSITY

Hollywood Tragic Curve. Notice the upbeat swing at the top and end.

"What a student calls a tragedy, the master calls a butterfly."
—*Richard Bach*

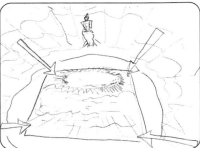

Digitally Enhanced Prophecy. The Bigfoot clan goes to this sacred puddle deep in the caves to ask it oracle-type questions. DV plays future events or metaphoric riddle prophecies across the surface of the water using two layers of video with displacement maps (see Chapter 9). How could you use your software to show a unique genre element prophecy in an interesting way?

project 3.8

Prophecy Riddles. In what new way could you show a prophecy using your digital tools? Maybe you have a talking tree, fortune cookie, crystal ball, freak encounter, telepathic animal, or animated statue to relay important information. Create three digitally enhanced prophecy ideas with at least one twisted metaphoric riddle. Refer to your list of metaphors and symbols from Chapter 2, "Creating Original Characters, Themes, and Visual Metaphors," for ideas about objects to place in your riddles.

Every Tragedy Needs a Prophecy

Tragedies usually have a scene in Act One at a type of crossroads, where the power is amplified, and the witches or seers gather to give a prophecy. The prophecy is usually a statement of theme with an unforeseen twist. It may also be a metaphorical riddle, using the theme to foreshadow future events. Most characters do not listen closely enough to the prophecy or misunderstand it. How could you use your digital tools to relay a prophecy in a fresh way?

Shakespeare creates a clever prophecy riddle in *Macbeth*. The Three Weird Sister Witches say Macbeth will be king until the trees come to his land. There are no trees in his land because they do not grow there, so he thinks he is a sure thing. The trees do come in the form of a rival's army bearing flags with the sign of a tree at the end. If the protagonist ignores the prophecy, defying the will of the gods, he will fail. Usually, protagonists try to outsmart the prophecy and then fail, realizing the riddle too late.

This hand-drawn 2D crystal ball could have DV video layers placed inside to deliver prophecies. What other digitally enhanced prophecies can you create that are original and easy to do?

project
project 3.9

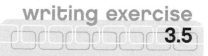

Create a Short Tragedy. Take your short film idea and turn it into a tragedy. How could your protagonist fail at accomplishing both plot and theme goals by refusing to change his or her ways? See how bleak you can make the story. Choose between one of the two types of tragedies for your plot structure. Add an original, digitally enhanced prophecy at the beginning and a visual sacrifice at the end.

superfreak!

Visual Bad Feelings. List three ways we have never seen before to show how bad your tragic characters feel. What is the most interesting thing you have seen a person do when she feels horrible about something she has done? Exaggerate any ideas visually.

"Everything happens for your higher good; the universe works in perfect ways."
—*Sanaya Roman*

writing exercise 3.5

Write a short story based on your short tragedy idea.

Foreshadow Really Bad Things

You must foreshadow super-bad events coming up in film, such as any form of death, defeat, or really tragically shocking circumstances. Audiences will feel like you tricked them, and may not trust you anymore, if you do not warn them in advance. Chapter 4 covers foreshadowing techniques.

Show Us How Bad Your Tragic Characters Feel

Tragedies explore some of the darker realms of vicarious emotions for the audience. We empathize with Macbeth even though he keeps doing horrible things and killing innocent people in his lust for power, because he keeps telling us how bad he *feels* about it. The audience *feels* guilty, too, because we have all done things that we knew were wrong.

In tragedies, make sure you let the audience know how bad your unraveling characters *feel* about doing such horrible things.

Balancing Bad News with Good News

You cannot craft a complete downhill ride without some upswing plateaus that allow the characters and audience to catch their breath. Too many really horrible things in a row will start to seem funny. Two negative events work if the contrast between them is strong enough. Suppose you have a boy crying about his dog running away. The audience thinks that the dog might come back, and that there is hope for a happy ending. Then you show the dog dead from a car accident as the boy rides up on his bicycle. This works emotionally because we have all been in situations that went from bad to worse quickly. If you then were to show the boy getting in a bike accident, it would seem funny, because there were too many negatives in a row. Do not place an equally strong positive right next to a negative either; otherwise they cancel each other out. You could not have the dog run away, then have parents give him a new one that he really enjoys, and then show the old dog dead. It loses its punch. Play with switching from two negative events to a positive then back to two negatives for tragic scene structures.

In any story, there is also the question of what type of emotional makeup the character has to deal with positive and negative events. If the kid is happy-go-lucky, he will recover from the loss of his dog. If he is already really depressed, he may not. Pay attention to how much your characters can take based on their psychological weather and history. The mood of the film will make the emotion specific, too. If it is a happy-looking film with bright colors and a dead dog, we react differently than if it is a moody, dark, and sinister city with a dead dog.

Documentary

The goal of a documentary is to ask a question and answer it. Subjects are treated like characters that evolve through the story. These films are usually about a person, group of people, place, process, or problem. Documentaries are strange, in the sense that they usually reveal themselves more in postproduction. You go out and shoot based on an assumption, message, or question, and then review your footage and see whether the original idea holds. Goals are not as important as relaying large amounts of information, getting to the big truth, exploring questions, or looking in-depth for solutions.

A big part of making a documentary is gaining access or rights to interesting people, places, or subjects. You might want to make a list of who you know, or what types of special access you could get for certain subjects. If your uncle runs a meat packing plant, you will have a better chance of getting inside the place to do a documentary on the subject.

money-saving

Get Permission for Documentaries About Real People. Never do a documentary on an actual person unless you have a contract that says it is okay and a copy of a dollar check as payment exchanged. If you do not, the subject of your documentary can sue you, block the film, and cost you lots of money. In addition, no one will want to play these films unless you have permission.

money-saving

LCV Distribution. Torsten, who made *Liquid Crystal Vision*, pressed his own DVD and self-distributed it online. He passed out flyers around trance parties for a series of free screenings. In less than a month after his DVD started selling online, he had already made his money back. What unique marketing strategies or events can you tie into your website to help sell your own films? This approach works particularly well with targeted subject documentaries where interested communities are easier to access. Color flyers, such as the ones used to promote parties, are cheap to print and work well to pass out at events where your film would be appreciated.

project 3.10

Documentary Idea. Think of an idea for a possible documentary short based on your short film idea. Devise a possible theme that goes with the subject. Decide on a narrative approach to the subject matter. Ask a question and answer it using the basic short film story curve. I could take my Bigfoot story and turn it into a documentary about whether or not they really exist.

Delusions in Modern Primitivism

Delusions in Modern Primitivism is a short film about a heavily tattooed and pierced man looking to take his body art to a new level. The film feels like a real documentary about a new extreme form of body-art manipulation. We meet the main character in an interview-type setting, watching as he drives around Houston talking about his view of society being uptight. Flaws in his thinking are apparent and make him rather endearing. When we find out that this guy is on his way to get a shot to create a scar on his chest, we are shocked at the lengths some people will go for self-expression. The types of guns and equipment used for such a procedure are then explained. In an interview with the shooter, we meet someone who sees himself as an artist pioneering a new field. We get to watch the tattooed guy get shot at the climax and dragged away in an ambulance. Several people in the screening I saw believed it was a real documentary, and seemed disappointed and confused when the director got up and explained it was all fictional and performed by actors.

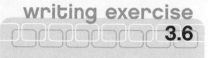
Write a short story based on your documentary idea.

I could take my 3D Bigfoot idea and turn it into a realistic mockumentary about the behavior of the creatures. Official-sounding narration such as, "Bigfoots can often be found tossing huge redwood trees around like toothpicks" could be used to show their enormous strength. A *60 Minutes*-style show could be used to set the tone and mood of the investigative story.

Mockumentary Idea. Create one original mockumentary idea for your favorite subject or combinations of subjects. You may also want to take your short film idea and turn it into a mockumentary as an exercise.

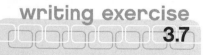
Write a short story based on your mockumentary idea.

Mockumentary

A mockumentary is a fake documentary. They pretend to be revealing truth, but that "truth" is actually all fabricated. Mockumentaries place more of an emphasis on characters as subjects or specific events. Why do characters do what they do? Motivations are explored. The first 15 minutes of *Citizen Kane* is pure mockumentary, exploring the questions who was Kane and what was Rosebud. *This Is Spinal Tap* is another great mockumentary, showing a formally great fictional band going on a downward-spiral rock tour. Less emphasis is placed on theme. How might you include a mockumentary scene in your short film to provide backstory or character history?Digital video looks more real and official than film. Use this to your advantage when creating mockumentaries. Bend the truth in new ways. What types of stories can you think of that take an already far-out idea and stretch it even further? You could even use an aged-film-look filter to make your DV look like archival footage of past events. What types of mockumentaries could you do on old historical characters as if the film had just been found in a lost vault? What types of outlandish characters and situations could you make up? It doesn't matter whether they even had movie cameras back then. You could interview a prehistoric caveman and use lots of film-damage FX just for fun!

Creature Comforts is another classic mockumentary, by Nick Parks, in which he interviews a bunch of claymation zoo animals about their concerns. He originally interviewed people on the street in England about what they were concerned about, and then thought up animals to match their voices. In one clip, we see a Brazilian lion talking about how cold it is in England, matching the voice of someone from Brazil who now lives uncomfortably in the colder climate. This is a great example of taking two separate ideas and putting them together in a fresh way. How could you do something like this with one of your favorite themes combined with digitally enhanced animated characters, subjects, or settings in a new way? You may want to interview a group of people about a question, listen to the footage, and come up with a unique production style to fit the subject and voices.

Faking Believability. What types of visual storytelling devices could you use to make your mockumentary feel more real? You could create news footage, interviews, or composite layers of video. You could also use 3D, have people who seem really official stating things, use fake steadycam TV live-footage styles, incorporate webcams that seem to be picking up what is going on, use text during the opening stating it is a true story, or create Photoshop mock newspaper footage. List five ways to make your idea seem like the truth.

Personal Anthology

A personal anthology is an episodic film with a series of multiple perspectives about a single character. Each episode or segment has its own beginning, middle, and end. The binding logic between the pieces is the theme. These stories will fall apart if you try to weave in more than one theme, because that is the only thread holding the structure together.

A disconnect occurs between cause and effect between sequences. Time and subjects between episodes are often from different points of view (POVs). A character could break her leg in one episode, and then in the next piece not even mention it. These work great as short films, because goals are not as important or time-consuming to develop. As a filmmaker, you can concentrate more on symbolic themes visually. *Memento* does this in a sense, with each segment being 10 minutes, disconnected by the

character's own inability to remember anything after that amount of time.

How do you get a character to achieve his goals if he can feel two different ways about a subject from one scene to the next? You create a map or landscape of the character's psyche with little episodes. Theme starts coming more to the surface as you explore a character by watching what information surfaces each time. You may like the character in one scene, and then hate him in the next as the inner complexity unfolds. The pleasure in a personal anthology is to explore and emphasize contradictions in characters. In *Citizen Kane*, we find out who Mr. Kane was through conversations with the people who knew him. All of them have different perspectives on the man. The audience has to decide which view is more real. There is no one truth about anyone or anything, which gives the audience space to decide for themselves.

What would an original video diary short film look like for your protagonist? Maybe a Bigfoot could find a DV camera and create a series of entries about its life for a short film. Ask yourself what is unique about the way your character would shoot a video diary, hold the camera, choose locations, and what subjects they would discuss.

project 3.12

Personal Anthology Idea. Take the main character in your film and turn him or her into a personal anthology idea. Use the same theme. How could you create a personal anthology-style short film for an extreme character piece, video diary, event, vacation, interview series, video baby book, or as a scene style somewhere in your film to develop character? Where would each episode take place (to work as a metaphor for the inner landscape of the character)? How could you create this type of film with an animated version of the character?

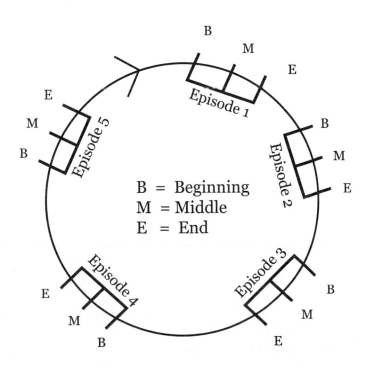

B = Beginning
M = Middle
E = End

Here is a plot structure graph for a personal anthology. Notice how it goes in a circle of beginning, middle, and end episodes, mapping out the character's psyche. Each episode contains its own little three-act structure and should be thought of as a series of minifilms.

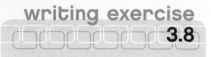

writing exercise 3.8

Write a short story based on your personal anthology idea.

This Bigfoot bar would make a good location for a compound city symphony. Bars are often used to show the nexus of film worlds where different characters meet to interact and exchange information.

project 3.13

Create a City Symphony Idea. Take a location in your short film and turn it into a city symphony. Specify which of the four shapes it would take.

writing exercise 3.9

Write a short story based on your city symphony idea.

superfreak!

Multiple-POV City Symphony Event Idea. Take your short film idea or an event in your film and show it from multiple perspectives using a series of individual characters.

City Symphony

City symphonies are films about a location shown from different perspectives, characters, events, and timeframes. The location becomes a collective character, with the events and characters used to represent a particular place and time. These films have a loose structure, which often defies the common three acts. Linear time structures and cause and effect are not as important. Emphasis is on color and location rather than plot, character, and theme. These are also called *pure concept films*. Audiences will miss having a character be their surrogate to identify with, and may detach a little emotionally.

The Terminal Bar is a short Flash film using old photographs of patrons from a bar in Times Square along with interviews of a bartender. *Magnolia* was about forgiveness in Los Angeles during a specific time. What kinds of places have you been to or could imagine that would be interesting enough to build a city symphony around? What is interesting about your hometown or neighborhood that would show us another world we have not seen before encompassing a strong theme?

Consider the four types of city symphonies:

1. **Environment.** The viewer becomes the protagonist and you let the viewer visit several locations within a specific place to create an impression. *Waking Life* is a good example of a character exploring the world of lucid dreaming.

2. **Event oriented.** Individual characters with individual goals go through a specific place during an event-specific timeframe. Event represents personality of the location. *Best of Show* is a good example, because all the characters are centered around the big dog-show event.

3. **Chronology.** City as character that changes and is defined over a course of time. May be a nonspecific timeframe. *Curse of the Blair Witch* uses this technique with the forest changing at night into a super spooky place.

4. **Compound symphony.** Location becomes a character with other characters living in it and its full of intersecting plot lines. A single theme or concept unifies all the stories. Robert Altman films, such as *Short Cuts*, are good examples.

Multiple-POV City Symphony Event

Films can also be about a specific event told from different, multiple perspectives of the characters. These films deal with the idea that truth is often subjective and there is no one truth about anything. In the 1962 classic film *Rashomon*, we see three completely different perspectives on the same robbery from each character's description. One perspective is from the wife of the murdered man, one is from the thief, and one is from a person hiding in the bushes. These types of films make it hard to empathize with any one character. How might you use this technique for a pivotal event scene in your film where each character remembers things differently or to show different POVs?

Ensemble

Ensembles films are about groups of characters unified by the same theme. All the characters act out different perspectives of the theme, both positive and negative. Common group plot goals such as to survive a plane crash, to overthrow a dictator, to win the game, to get married, to overcome ills of society, or to launch a rocket are often explored. Ensemble films contain several different minifilms about each character. Linear time is observed. The basic personalities of each character are first established. The characters then grow as they all intersect with each other at key plot points to show theme. *Balance* is a short ensemble stop-motion film that calls on all five characters to help keep an abstract floating plane in space balanced. There are three types of ensembles:

1. **Invention.** Ideas start with an *inciting incident* that pulls all the characters together in a *call to action* to do something. Groups of characters all contribute their own special skills to accomplish a single uniform goal. In *Apollo 13*, the characters survive a troubling trip to the moon.

2. **Epiphany.** Ideas start with an inciting incident that pulls a group of characters together showing the same theme. Each character then has an *epiphany* in his or her own separate character arc of discovery. The interactions between characters change the plot and alter each character. *The Big Chill* is about how a group of old friends, after the funeral, deal with the death (inciting incident) of one of their buddies. The theme is the value of friendship.

3. **Disaster.** Ideas start with a little disaster (inciting incident) and move to a bigger version, with a group of characters working to overcome the final disaster. Must clearly establish what is at stake. Leave room for individual achievement. All main characters are developed equally with regard to the amount of screen time. All characters need common goals with different approaches. *Armageddon* starts with little asteroid rocks hitting a city, causing great damage, and then introduces an asteroid the size of Texas hurling toward the planet. This shows how the final disaster will be much bigger if not averted, and clearly establishes the stakes visually. The antagonist is the asteroid. How could you create a disaster or a new form of a disaster with digital tools? You could use a simple DigiEffects earthquake filter to show a new type of disaster.

Science Fiction/Fantasy

Science fiction stories deal with the effect of technology on the human condition, and often digital tools are used to great effect to show us new things. Study *The Twilight Zone* or *Outer Limits* TV series. Rod Serling was perhaps the best short film writer ever. He writes great twists and endings while balancing plot, theme, and character beautifully. Science-fiction films may include the following subjects:

project 3.14

Create an Ensemble Idea. Take your short film idea and turn it into an ensemble. State which of the three types it will resemble. Include any original ideas for using digital FX.

writing exercise 3.10

Write a short story based on your ensemble idea.

"I believe the lasting revolution comes from deep changes in ourselves which influence our collective life."
—*Anais Niün*

1. Stories set in the unknown future. What might happen technologically. Read magazines such as *Popular Science* for new ideas.

2. Stories set in historical past, but which contradict what we know about history today.

3. Stories set on other worlds or planets.

4. Stories on earth before recorded history.

5. Stories that contradict some agreed-upon law of nature. Magic, time travel, psychic phenomenon, invisible-man stories.

Here are some exercises you may want to think about if you want to create a science-fiction film:

1. **Create an original visual motif.** Develop a new culture using combinations of familiar visual elements. If you are designing a fantasy world or alien planet, take two ideas people are familiar with and combine them into a new one. Suppose you are creating a futuristic utopia with the theme of working together in harmony. Maybe the buildings look like huge beehives and the hovercraft ships buzz around like bees inside. The people harvest some sort of sap from the planet that looks like honey and sell it to other species. Combine the beehive visual idea with futuristic new-age hippies. Even if the sets and characters are strange, the audience will relate better to a visual motif of beehive new-age hippies than to a bunch of weird and unfamiliar designs and behaviors that have no context or connection to today's world or theme.

If you designed a race of aliens who were bubble gum pink blobs that floated and gurgled to each other inside silver spaceships shaped like spheres, we would have nothing to hook into and identify with visually or emotionally. Chapter 11 discusses visual motifs in depth.

2. **Design cool gadgets.** Read *Popular Science* and those types of magazines to think up cool devices that would be really helpful to have around today. In *The Jetsons* cartoon, we love to see them put a pill in the microwave and pull out a turkey dinner. What types of gadgets would make your life easier in a science-fiction world and fit nicely into your story?

3. **Create a set of world rules.** It isn't interesting if anything can happen. You need to know the limits of your film world to create believable conflict.

The visual motif of a Yemeni woman helps us get a better sense of the essence of this lizard-looking alien woman.
Illustration by Ann

a. What is the price for using magic or special powers? Maybe you lose a finger each time you cast a spell or need to drink spring water from a special well.

b. How does space travel work in your world? Do they have hyperspace jump gates to traverse dimensions or machines?

c. What are the rules and limits for time travel? Can you make any changes you want and continue to exist, or is it possible to destroy your world? Or can you just watch and not make any changes? Can you travel through time inside your own mind or other people's?

d. What type of energy do the characters in your world use?

4. **Inventing aliens.** Take your film idea and combine it with a strong, alien evolutionary

This alien ostrich-like creature is ideally suited, with his suction-cup feet, to climb around on those pointy rocks.
Illustration by Chris Hatala

foundation. How would an alien creature evolve biologically over a vast timeframe to adopt better to its environment? Do the alien creatures have huge frontal lobes and gills because they are really psychic and can breathe underwater? Make sure their anatomy reflects how they have adapted to life on their planet. How has their communication evolved? What is the history of their world? Base each alien group on separate visual motifs.

5. **Create a new language.** Only use made-up words for those that have no English equivalent. Use subtitles if you want characters to speak in alien tongues. Maybe they click their tongues and sound like birds when they talk. Play with taking the audio tracks through some filters in your sound-editing program or playing the voices at different tones, speeds, or backward to see whether you can create a new way to hear them talking.

6. **Draw a map.** Draw the star system or a map of the globe with geography. Is it a low-gravity planet with lots of tall tress and animals, or a fast-spinning planet with high winds and short night and day cycles? Maybe the planet does not rotate at all and is only livable in a small band. Do your aliens live on an asteroid, neutron star, or space station? Draw a map of the world or city your characters inhabit. Sketch their houses, towns, and natural environments in accordance with your visual motif.

7. **Character histories/ backstory.** Which characters suffer the most in your world? These are usually the ones most likely to act. Make sure they have power and freedom to act. Answer all the character history and backstory questions for your film world. Pay particular attention to things that are very different from our world to make sure you can show these new ideas very clearly.

Short films often do not have too much time to create whole other believable dimensions and still have a plot. Do not always feel like you need to explain everything. Be intentionally vague at times and focus more on the characters. Keep short science-fiction films lean by just picking one or two unique genre elements to showcase.

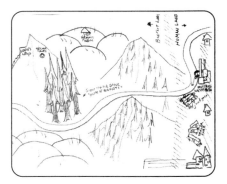

Draw a map of your film world to help orient yourself to the environment.

time-saving

Create a Mad Lib for Plot Point Structures. Below is an example of a hero journey mad lib where a person could replace the underlined words with specific ones and create a new story. How could you create a mad lib for your favorite genre or story style? Write a brief description of a story, and then switch out key nouns, verbs, adjectives, and colors as shown here.

It is a story about a <u>common man/woman hero</u> who works at a <u>boring occupation</u>. He/she is really good at <u>best ability</u> and spends his time <u>verb</u> in a <u>adjective/normal place</u>. One day, the <u>horrible event</u> happens in his land. The hero does not know what to do about the <u>adjective/evil villain</u> causing <u>this big problem</u>. A <u>color/supernatural assistance</u> soon arrives to help the hero by giving him a <u>magical tool</u> and a <u>magical skill</u> to defeat <u>evil villain</u>. The hero leaves home to go find <u>plot goal noun</u>, which happens to be at the <u>most dangerous place</u>. The hero confronts <u>number/greatest fear</u> and almost dies. The hero's <u>new tools and skills</u> save him. The hero returns home with <u>plot goal noun</u> and gets rewarded with <u>reward for journey</u>.

writing exercise  3.11

Write a short story based on your science fiction idea.

project  3.15

Create a Science-Fiction Idea. Take your short film concept and turn it into a science-fiction film using some of the previously discussed techniques.

This 3D Bigfoot idea works well for an original, digitally enhanced production, because you could make the creature look really realistic. They would be fun to animate, too, because they have super-human strength for tossing huge boulders and redwood trees around as part of the unique genre element.

What original visual storytelling shell could you put around your idea to make it more interesting and add layers of depth? Shown here are Ezzie and Big Granny talking about the history of the Bigfoot tribe while sitting in the ancestral cave. As they point to drawings and objects, a match cut to different scenes could happen to show different story segments. Big Granny might point to a lucky bird feather charm and talk about the night she made it for a special battle, which we then see revealed behind the image of the charm sitting on the cave altar as a separate scene in progress. In *Transit*, we fly in and out of stickers on a suitcase. What other original visual objects could you use as a storytelling shell in your film? Would your story be more interesting flying in and out of a photo album, comic book, newspaper clippings, handwritten letters, pictures on the wall, a box of collected objects, a map, or a hand-held computer screen? How could you use this technique for a part of your film?

Short Film Plot Points

If feature films are love affairs, shorts are one-night stands. Shorts tend to have more dramatic climaxes and twists at the end to deliver a final punch to an already high-octane compressed tale.

Ask yourself what is new and different about the way you could tell your story visually?

Start at the End

One of the best ways to start planning for plot points with a film is to craft a surprise ending first and work backward. Take a moment to resist this idea if you do not like to work this way. There is no room in any film to wander—especially a short. Every scene needs to move the story forward to an unpredictable calculated destination. You need a sweet surprise at the end with a twist where you introduce a situation and then turn it all around. If the ending falls flat, it means your plot has disintegrated going into Act Three. Everything needs to move and build to the ending; it is not an isolated, final whammy event. The audience should be able to look back in a flash and see how it was coming all along in a totally unexpected way.

definition

Original Ideas for Shorts New information not seen before, a fresh POV, a familiar plot with innovative film style, a combination of unique genre elements, stunningly original characters, or innovative use of digital storytelling tools.

Adding Surprise Plot Twists

Twists are so wild you might never predict them, which adds to the suspense in your film. If you do a strong enough original twist at the end, you will make an instant classic moment. Think of what stunning turnaround you could include during Act Three, and then see how you could reveal it hidden in the script. Adding twists throughout your script will keep things unpredictable and nonlinear. Twists force radically new turns in the story line. For it to be a good twist, you must not be able to predict it. If the audience suspects you have something up your sleeve, point them to look at the wrong sleeve. You usually need at least two big plot twists in a short and four in a feature.

Twists are wildly unpredictable sets of circumstances that pop up and inalterably change the course of the plot.

Twists can come in many forms, such as unexpected events, unexpected characters appearing, new information, mistakes, misunderstandings, other characters acting in surprising ways, equipment breaking, or characters outsmarting each other. Sometimes big twists involve having the character change plot goals, either by accomplishing the first plot goal and seeing a bigger one to do, or finding out that the plot goal he is working toward is now unnecessary. Plant setup and payoff clues earlier in the story, such as fixing a piece of equipment that sometimes breaks, which will then break later at a key moment.

Twist Brainstorming Ideas

Study your favorite films and add the types of twists they use to the following chart.

"Do not fear mistakes—there are none."

—*Miles Davis*

Accident kills someone.

Lies multiply fast.

Code is finally broken.

Being attacked from several directions at once.

Choice between obtaining goal and love.

Backup never shows up.

Character has sudden epiphany and changes behavior.

Shocking truth revealed.

Secrets revealed or hidden.

Character loses the ability to move, see, or walk.

Incorrect information revealed.

Misunderstanding revealed.

Character switches loyalty.

Lots of little goals need to be done first.

Unforeseen trap.

Characters react in strange ways.

Dead character comes back to life

Unforeseen love triangle exposed.

Clues destroyed.

Key witness killed or disappears.

Innocent people get in the way.

Communication system goes haywire.

Plans are stolen by the enemy.

Character gets caught.

Cover is blown.

Traitor revealed.

Unexpected suspicious opportunity.

Key equipment breaks down.

Worse situation gets even worse during escape route.

Progress toward goal is an illusion.

New information is revealed that changes current situation completely.

Sudden change of plans.

Natural obstacles or unforeseen disasters.

Unexpected event occurs.

No more food, money, air, bullets, or gas.

Shot from an unknown place.

Ticking-clock deadline pressure, such as a bomb about to explode.

Hidden fear or weakness revealed.

Past comes back to bite the character.

Weapon now broken or out of use.

Transportation breakdowns.

Hostages are suddenly gathered.

Someone dies or gets murdered.

Key evidence is misplaced, stolen, or destroyed.

Character thinks he is doing a good thing that turns out to be the worst thing possible.

Unexpected new equipment is installed that messes up plan.

Normal routine is not followed and messes up plan.

Character sneaking around is detected by enemy.

time-saving

Decide Your Ending First. Do you have lots of half-finished story ideas, screenplays, films, or novels laying around? I used to fight this suggestion of knowing the ending before writing the main story. I would then spend far too much time trying to go back and weave the ending in or think up a way to end the story that really didn't fit, because I did not know where it was going. Compare this to taking a road trip. If you have a set destination, you go toward it with that goal. If you have no idea where you are going, you wander around until you find a place to stop or run out of time or money. The energy of the two trips is completely different. The first one builds up to a destined climax, the second one searches for an ending, the whole time feeling lost. Well-planned twist endings, plot points, and treatments are your roadmaps to keep your script on track.

Ezzie accidently falls over into a pool of toxic quicksand during her shamanic journey. She quickly runs out of air and almost dies as she struggles to free herself while sinking deeper and deeper. This twist ends the shamanic journey and takes the story in a new and unexpected direction.

superfreak!

Study Films for Twist Ideas. Think back through some of your favorite films and list the main plot twists. As you watch new films, add twist ideas to this chart.

During her vision quest in the caves, Ezzie finds her trail blocked by a series of thick spider webs. This is a twist since it was unforeseen and forces her to think on her feet. Twists are great places to explore character growth by the way your character reacts to the unexpected situations.

project 3.16

Build Up Your Twists. Create at least four ideas for possible twists in your film. Make the one at the end the most surprising.

writing exercise 3.12

Write a rough short story using as many plot twists as possible.

Using Character Goals to Craft Endings

One way to think up clever endings is to look at what happens to your characters if they accomplish or fail to make their plot and theme goals happen. How could you combine a twist idea with the way your characters resolve their goals at the end of the story? Most Hollywood films have endings in which both the plot and theme goals are successfully accomplished. In tragedies, the protagonist fails at both. Independent and European films often have mixed endings, with one success and one failure. This leaves the audience feeling unsettled and thinking more about the film later.

Character want = Plot goal = Ezzie wants to survive her vision quest and return to the tribe.

Character need = Theme goal = Trust your intuition.

After coming up with as many different scenarios as you can think of, pick the best plot and theme success or failures for your ending.

Plot Goal = Succeeds	Plot Goal = Fails
Ezzie narrowly escapes death and survives her vision quest.	Ezzie finds out vision quest is a trap to kill her, gives up, and dies.
Theme Goal = Succeeds	**Theme Goal = Fails**
Ezzie uses her intuition to discover a secret way out of the quicksand.	Ezzie opts not to use her intuition and gets hurt.

superfreak!

Create an Original POV Twist. List three possibilities to do an original POV twist.

POV Twists

Is your character dead? Some of the best protagonists are dead ones. *Sixth Sense*, *DOA*, *Sunset Strip*, *The Others*, and *American Beauty* all feature deceased main characters communicating their points of view. In what other ways can you play with a character's viewpoint in your story for a new perspective? The character could be dreaming, in an experiment, imagining, daydreaming, on a different reality plane, or having memory problems. These types of specialized POVs can produce great twist endings if you can do them in fresh and unexpected ways.

The point is to see how many different types of endings you can create for both types of goals. It is much easier to work in twists by brainstorming all the possibilities and then flipping these around or combining them in unexpected ways at the end of the story.

Creating High Stakes for Goals
There must be very clear risks for not attaining goals.

Life cannot go back to normal if the character's goals are not met. Make sure the audience understands what is at stake if the character does not accomplish either plot or theme goals. A character's willingness to take a risk is in direct proportion to his desire to achieve a goal. The greater the risk involved, the greater the value of the goal. Death is the ultimate form of risk for a character to take when attempting to accomplish a goal. The very survival of the character should be put at stake while risking some of form of death to accomplish his goals.

Bigfoots who fail to pass their coming-of-age vision quests are banished from the tribe to wander alone forever in the forest as outcasts, or they may choose to beat their heads on rocks until death, as the more honorable choice. Losing one's tribe is a form a death. The rock head-banging choice increases the stakes of what bad things may happen if Ezzie fails to achieve her goals.

Adding Extra Twist Endings
You may want to consider doing a series of endings with an extra twist of gain/loss at the end. Have your characters struggle with making really big decisions, and then turn the situations around on them.

1. Chooses lover over wife, and then lover dies in car crash a month later.
2. Chooses job in Kenya over lover. Finds out job is set up for him to take the fall.
3. Chooses art over lover. Art show flops and character becomes homeless.
4. Chooses job (for money) over lover. Lover strikes it rich suddenly, and finds someone else.

False Endings
You may also want to add a false ending to give your grand finale an extra punch. These occur when the audience thinks the story is over, but it continues. The bad guy is dead, for instance, but he keeps coming back to life. Or you could show a character die, but then wake up alive. Maybe the character gets the quest object and finds out it is a fake. Or the character wins the race, but gets disqualified because another player cheated.

"A man will fight harder for his interests than for his rights."
—Napoleon Bonaparte

project 3.17

Brainstorming Goal Endings. Create a chart to brainstorm possible endings for both the main plot goal and theme goal of your protagonist. Make columns for both success and failure of each goal as shown here. Refer to the previous Twist Brainstorming Chart for ideas on how to add a twist to each possible outcome.

project 3.18

List Stakes for Goals. List three ideas to show what is at stake for your character if they do not achieve their goal.

"If we get everything we want, we will soon want nothing we get."
—Vernon Luchies

project 3.19

Extra Twist Endings. Create two possible extra twist endings for your film idea. How can you make these extra twists visually interesting without dialogue? You could use a split screen and show both choices unfolding at the same time, and then choose one at the end.

project 3.20

False Endings. List three possible false endings for your story.

"The gem cannot be polished without friction, nor man perfected without trials."
—*Confucius*

Creating Three Climaxes

Shorts in general contain three climaxes throughout the story. On a scale of one to three, with one being a miniclimax and three being the most intense, your story climax curve should look like this image.

How do you make a climax? You increase what is at stake, the amount of jeopardy the main character is in, the conflict or the number of obstacles followed by a quick resolution of some sort.

If you put the biggest climax at the beginning, the rest of the film will feel like a downhill slide. If you put the biggest climax in the middle, you will get the same effect. If you have no climaxes until the very end, you may not have an audience left.

The finale climax should be so powerful that it lingers. The best short films have great finales.

Notice the arc of dramatic progression in the intensity of the three climaxes throughout the three acts and how they help define the story curve. Opens with a level-two climax in mid-stride, also called the hook or possibly the inciting incident. Start the film in the middle of a high-intensity mess. At the beginning of Act Two or in the middle of Act Two, you have a level-one climax, usually in the form of a big twist. And almost at the very end, you have your biggest and most intense level-three climax followed by a short resolution. Check to see how big your climaxes are in your story and see what you can do to space them out and keep their intensity in this type of structure.

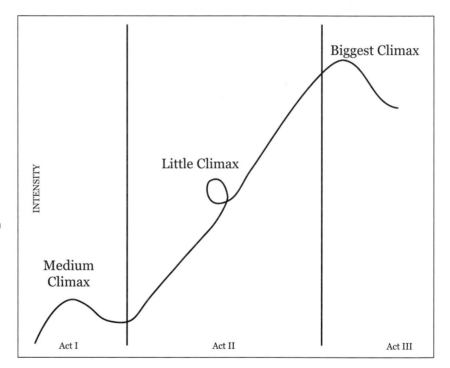

project
3.21

Three Climaxes. List three possibilities for each climax using a chart like the one here.

Medium Climax: Hook Open	Small Climax: Middle as Twist	Big Climax at End
Ezzie gets caught stealing chocolate from some campers.	Ezzie falls into a bottomless pit in the most dangerous cave.	Ezzie discovers that her vision quest is a trap by a mean witchdoctor.

Adding Best/Worst Narrative Flips

Ask what is the worst possible thing that could happen to your protagonist now, which could turn into the best thing later.

Maybe a character says he is leaving his wife, which sounds like the worst thing that could happen to the wife in Act One. Then perhaps the wife goes into Act Two on a personal mission to accomplish something big, and meets someone she likes much better than her previous husband. Or figure out the best thing that could happen but that turns into the worst. Maybe the guy says, "I'll love you forever," but then turns into a jealous maniac who ends up killing her. Try turning situations around like this throughout your story to keep the audience guessing as to what will happen next. Cycle back and forth between this best-to-worst pattern.

Adding Plot Setups/Plants and Payoffs

When you start thinking about plot points, you will want to weave in setups and payoffs to pull your story together.

Setups need to be carefully presented so that the audience does not suspect they are being given key story information. Audiences should flash back to the earlier setups during payoff moments and put the information together in a new way.

In *Lilly and Jim*, Jim tells Lilly that he does not drink coffee after dinner when she invites him back to her place. Later we see the reason he does not drink coffee, watching him have a violent allergic reaction at the climax. This is a classic setup and payoff cycle. Setups and payoffs can occur anywhere, but in shorts, they are usually introduced in Act One or Two and turn the story around in Act Three. Find your climax event, and then ask what object or piece of information could help determine the outcome. Go back through your story structure and plant these objects or information as setups. Study your favorite films to see how many different ways filmmakers use this technique. Well-written feature films with lots of plot twists use some sort of setup or payoff in almost every scene. You can also layer in this technique after you create plot points, by going back through the story and weaving in information that builds toward surprising twists. Some setups may have multiple payoffs, such as an unimportant object that becomes a key tool in several scenes.

definition

Setup/Plant Any information, phrase, event, or object introduced early in the story, that may seem unimportant at the time, but that turns into a key payoff element later.

A possible setup could show this Bigfoot banging on rocks in the background, like a heavy-metal drummer, after acting very angry at the beginning of a film. Later, at the scene of a crime, a clue of strange marks is found on one of the rocks. These marks might match the other ones and link the character to the crime scene. What new ways can you plant information early in the story for a payoff or even multiple payoffs later?

Setups/Plants	Payoffs
Character says something that seems unimportant, such as, "I don't drink coffee."	Character later needs to be rushed to the hospital for an allergic reaction to coffee.
Object given, found, or obtained that seems useless or of small importance at the time.	A useless object becomes a valuable tool or enables the character to accomplish the plot goal in a surprising way.
Seemingly unimportant information is given to the character.	This information becomes the key to accomplishing a plot goal.
Character finds a clue, information, or evidence. We do not see what the character does with this new information.	Character uses the clue in a surprising way that the audience may not see at first. Show the result, such as information being suddenly presented at a meeting. Another character could explain it was sent earlier.
Character states opinion about situation, such as, "The truth shall set you free."	Character ends up in a courtroom, is forced to lie, and then goes to jail for perjury.
An unexpected event causes the character to adjust.	The unexpected event spirals out of control.
Character is drinking soda near a high-tech machine.	System goes down later from someone spilling soda on machine.

Short Film Plot Points

Short films ideally start out fast, windup quick, and end with a surprise twist. Features have a lot more time to develop characters and multiple subplots. Shorts tend to stay more focused on one situation with a series of unexpected problems.

Act One = Beginning = Establishment = 1/6

Act Two = Middle = Development = 2/3

Act Three = End = Resolution = 1/6

Use the following chart to get an idea of how long each act might be for your film. If you are creating a 5-minute film, you know you have about 1 minute to set up your story, 3 minutes for Act Two, and another minute to wrap it up with Act Three. One page of master-scene-formatted script takes about 1 minute of screen time. A 5-minute film contains

about 5 pages of script. If you are doing a really short, short film less than 2 minutes long, you may want to study the plot point structures of TV commercials or other short short films to see how quickly you can tell a story.

Listed here are 9 plot points your short film may include in some form.

1. **Hook.** Transition from real world to film world. This usually starts in the middle of a mess or mid-level climax to get the audience quickly into the story.
2. **Setup.** The lead character is introduced with external wants (plot goals) and internal needs (theme goals). Limits and rules of film world are established.
3. **Inciting incident.** An event happens that changes the status quo (what's normal), forcing protagonist to take action to restore what is normal.
4. **Journey into unknown.** Protagonist sets off to accomplish his goal, leaving what is safe and normal behind and entering the vast unknown (physically, emotionally, or spiritually). A plan is usually established that should not go at all as planned.
5. **Investigation.** Protagonist searches for the goal object or information while encountering a series of obstacles, interactions, or conflict.
6. **Turning point/big twist.** A big plot twist, unexpected surprise, plot goal change, new information, or unforeseen problem occurs to test the new change in the character. The remainder of Act Two up until the climax focuses on the new main crisis. Often the greatest problems occur after we have gotten something that we really wanted.

Page Count and Timing for a Three-Act Structure

Total Film Minutes	Act One: Length	Act Two: Length	Act Three: Length
1	10 seconds	40 seconds	10 seconds
2	20 seconds	80 seconds	20 seconds
3	30 seconds	2 minutes	30 seconds
5	1 minute	3 minutes	1 minutes
10	1.5 minutes	7 minutes	1.5 minutes
15	2 minutes	11 minutes	2 minutes
20	3 minutes	14 minutes	3 minutes
30	5 minutes	20 minutes	5 minutes
45	6.5 minutes	31 minutes	6.5 minutes

project 3.23

Short Film Plot Point Brainstorm Chart. Use two blank pages facing each other in your drawing book to make nine columns. List the earlier plot point headings at the top of each column in order. Brainstorm five possible events, locations, or scene ideas for each plot point. Circle the top choices and write them at the bottom of the page in each column. Keep in mind the plot and theme goal exercises, character history, and arcs you decided on earlier. How could you play with changing the order of the plot points, using some twice, creating new ones, using some plot point structures from other story styles discussed previously or deleting some to tell an original visual story? How could you start your story in the middle?

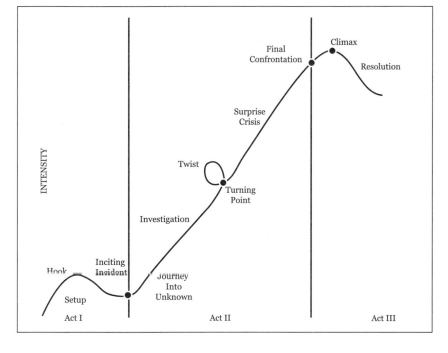

Notice how evenly spaced out each plot point event appears on the story curve.

7. **Final confrontation.** Confrontation between two characters that has been building since the beginning of the story. The protagonist may challenge the antagonist in a battle.

8. **Climax.** The most intense moment of the film. A grand moment full of importance, tension, and epiphanies. Revelation, discovery, or realization for characters or audience that is visual and emotional, not internal. The soul of the story.

9. **Resolution.** Ties up lose ends in the story. Who lives/dies, wins/loses, gets the girl/guy, returns with the treasure, celebrates after a quest, or has a big death scene in a tragedy.

writing exercise 3.14

Write a rough short story of your film idea using the short film plot points you generated in the project. Do not get too attached to this short story and be open to changing it as you learn more techniques.

superfreak!

Short Plot Points. A worksheet to print out for short film plot points is included on the CD (shortfilmplot.pdf). Fill in a different set of plot points each day for possible new story ideas to get a sense of how these work together. It is much faster to think of key events rather than whole stories sometimes.

Plot Points for Feature Films

Even if you are not interested in doing a feature right now, review these plot points to get an idea of what you might be able to add to your short somewhere. Using plot points will make writing treatments and scripts much easier. For a feature treatment, I usually brainstorm a few ideas of what might happen at each of the 40 points, fill in symbolic scene locations, and then play with the order in which they occur. These plot points do not have to occur in this exact order by any means. The film *Memento* opens with the last plot point and goes backward. Lots of films jump around through time, starting after the climax and looking back, or with another character telling someone a story about something that has already happened. You could randomly pick numbers 1 through 40 out of a hat and construct a story using these plot points.

The following 40 plot points are my interpretation of Michael Feit Dougan's 40 plot points.

40 plot points = 3 pages per scene = 120 minutes

40 Plot Points for a Classic Narrative Feature Film

1. **Hook.** Transition from the real world into to the film world.
2. **Setup.** Introduce the protagonist and show what is normal.
3. **Enter antagonist.** Doing what he or she does best.
4. **Supporting characters.** Show us different sides of protagonist and film world.
5. **Plot goal/want.** First plot goal defined when a problem arises.
6. **Theme goal defined/need.** Use metaphor. A character could talk about a fable.
7. **Gauntlet.** Antagonist goals established.
8. **First test.** Protagonist may fail at first test to show his or her weaknesses.
9. **Inciting incident.** An event that changes the status quo (what's normal).
10. **Exile.** The protagonist leaves the familiar world and sets off on goal.
11. **Plot goals restated.** Protagonist is expelled from the comfortable world and thrust into the unknown. Was the choice worth it? Act Two begins.

12. **Theme goal restated.** State goals in relation to theme using metaphors.

13. **McGuffin.** Hitchcock coined this term. A random, freaky, unforeseen event pushes the plot forward, shakes the protagonist out of reverie, and forces action.

14. **Investigation.** The protagonist fumbles around in the dark to answer questions to accomplish the plot goal.

15. **Meet mentor.** A fully realized hero appears who is also a teacher, godlike titan, or supernatural being.

16. **Acquire new tools.** New tools are found or given.

17. **Joke.** Relieves tension and shows the protagonist's Achilles heel. May be in a funny, lighthearted way.

18. **Foreshadow.** Prepares the audience for resolution at the end of the film.

19. **Unique genre color.** Colorful example of unique genre element.

20. **First theme success.** Show character growth with small success related to theme.

21. **Triumph, first plot success.** Protagonist accomplishes the first plot goal.

22. **Betrayal.** Treachery by supporting characters or own weakness.

23. **Big/bad twist.** Unexpected turn of events usually against the protagonist. The plot goal may change.

24. **Torture/escape.** See protagonist suffering. The protagonist will come out stronger and bigger, and is saved by using his or her new skills.

25. **Defeat.** Protagonist loses previous triumph. Added suffering.

26. **Reassess plot goal.** Present situation is reevaluated. New direction for plot goal.

27. **Restate theme goal.** Theme goal restated. Act Three begins.

28. **Mentor disabled.** Protagonist needs to go at it alone; mentor too old to fight or is shackled.

29. **Second joke.** Relieves tension. Something light, playful, or funny happens.

30. **Unique genre color.** Second colorful example of genre element.

31. **Surrender.** Pit protagonist against impossible odds and have the protagonist decide that the goal is unattainable. Protagonist gives up.

32. **McGuffin.** Unexplained freaky and unforeseen plot event forces the protagonist ahead.

33. **New solution.** The protagonist discovers a different plot solution in a wildly unexpected way.

34. **Final confrontation.** The protagonist challenges the antagonist to a fight that has been building since the start of the film.

35. **Death.** The protagonist is defeated and supporting characters are disabled.

36. **Resurrection.** Strength is gathered in preparation for confronting the antagonist.

37. **Sacrifice.** The former perceived plot strength is abandoned in pursuit of the plot goal.

38. **Revelation.** The protagonist has an epiphany of sudden understanding.

39. **Climax.** The protagonist defeats the antagonist in a moment of greatest intensity.

40. **Resolution.** Who lives, who dies, who gets the girl/guy.

In my story, I use a torture/escape plot point to show the character suffering in a death moment in the middle of act two. She is deep into her worst fear and this is where her biggest character change occurs, because she is forced to use her intuition to get out of the mess.

superfreak!

Feature Plot Points. Turn your short film idea into a feature using the 40 Plot Points.

"The way to develop self-confidence is to do the thing you fear, and get a record of successful experiences behind you."
—*William Jennings Bryan*

Attaching Symbolic Settings to Plot Points

What types of symbolic settings are you considering for each scene in your film? Story environments often mirror or contrast character moods or situations in films. Make sure to create a system of location symbols that fit within each scene situation or behavior. If a stuck character lives in a swamp (stuck energy, bogged-down emotions, quicksand) where someone is about to die, a symbolic alligator (one of the most dangerous things in a swamp) may be shown lurking close by to foreshadow the coming death or danger.

When it is time for my character to have a brush with death, she enters The Cavern of the Dead Souls. This sacred Bigfoot burial ground has voices coming from the dead souls that give her wise advice. I could create an auditory sound montaqe of lots of different voices with their words layered together. How can you add originality to your symbolic sets using your digital tools or some simple special effects?

Symbolic Setting	Possible Meaning/Emotion/Mood
Arch	Gateway to new beginning, entrance to heaven or hell (depending on the design)
Attic	Past experiences, hidden things, family patterns
Backyard swimming pool	Suburban life, comfort, similar to others (conformity)
Boathouse	Ungrounded, free, mobile, traveling
Cave	Unconscious, contacting inner self, deeper understanding
Church/temple	Sacred space, sanctuary
Cliff	Danger, decision, risk, unknown, edge
Dark city alley	Danger, underworld, uncertain, violence
Expensive house on a hill	Rich, money, success, power, exclusiveness, above the law
Family dinner table	Family dynamics, seating shows relationships, atmosphere shows emotional mood of family
Freeway	Labyrinth
Foggy pier	Edge of known world, mystery, unclear, things are not what they seem
Inside a bank	Money, power, establishment, control, profit, system
Inside an airport or airplane	Between lives, change, new beginning, entering unknown
Inside an empty old cathedral	Looking back to the traditional past, spiritual, moral authority, sacred space
Inside body of water	Unconscious, sexuality
Inside speeding musclecar	Danger, recklessness, retro, criminal, rebel, youth, cowboy
Island	Isolation, loneliness, retreat

Attach a Symbolic Setting to Each Plot Point. Review your final list of plot points and see which types of settings might work best for each one. Think of at least two possible symbolic locations for each plot point.

Symbolic Setting	Possible Meaning/ Emotion/Mood
Japanese tea garden	Reflective, meditative, Zen, ordered beauty, tradition, harmony
Jungle	Chaos, obstacles, wild, dangerous, hot, steamy, bugs, fever, waterfalls
Ocean	Cosmic total consciousness, emotional weather, expansion
Paradise	Perfection, harmony, inner beauty
Pit	Death of old self, tough situation, darkness
Pyramid	Concentrating power within, ancient wisdom
River	Crossing for change, flowing through things, unconscious flow
Sacred cave	Journey into dark areas of conscious, hidden secrets, going inside
Slum apartment building	Poor, broken, defeated, powerless, poverty, struggle to survive, harsh, dangerous
Stalactite-filled cavern full of bubbling, glowing toxic waste	Hidden danger, dark secrets, unconscious poison, beautiful toxic danger, chemicals
Sunset at beautiful beach	Love, beauty, peace, freedom
Symphony hall	Refined, cultured, snooty, formal, musical world, beauty
Top of hill	Expanded vision, achievement, getting perspective
Top of mountain	Where important things happen, realizations
Train	Wandering, change, on a track returning again and again, always moving
Train or train station	Restlessness, inability to settle down, roaming, new beginnings, endings, passing by

Writing a Short Treatment

"When forced to work within a strict framework, the imagination is taxed to its utmost—and will produce its richest ideas. Given total freedom the work is likely to sprawl."
—T.S. Elliot

project
3.25

Choose Your Plot Points. List your plot points and fill them in with brief descriptions of what happens.

Treatments are plot point roadmaps designed to minimize your suffering. Writing a script from a good solid treatment is a joyful experience. Writing a script without a treatment can easily turn into a big mess. The reason you write a treatment is so that when you start writing Act Two, you do not get lost on where to go next now that you're in the middle. Strong plots are always going somewhere and never feel aimless.

Decide on your plot points and create a scene or major story event list to get you from one plot point to the next.

The first thing to think about when writing your treatment, after you have established the basic plot and characters, is Act Three. Short films rely heavily on surprise endings. Know how your story ends before writing the treatment. How do you want the audience to feel at the end of your film?

Treatment Lengths

You should have some idea going into this process about how long you want your film to be. If this is your first digital film, you should keep it under 5 minutes.

8 pages of script = 8 minutes of film = 1 page of treatment

Treatment Pages	Film Minutes
1/8	1
1/4	2
1/2	4
3/4	5
1	8
1 1/2	12
2	16
2 1/2	20
3 1/2	30
11–14	90–110 (feature)

Pick Your Plot Points

You should have lots of ideas by now. Review the exercises you have completed up to this point. It is time to decide on one set of plot points. If you are not sure which ones to use, fill in the ones for the basic short film idea. If you are doing a mini hero journey, make sure you have some of those essential plot points included. For a tragedy, you need to incorporate those specific to that type of story.

"Unless a capacity for thinking be accomplished by a capacity for action, a superior mind exists in torture."
—Benedetto Croce

Treatment Format

Use Courier 12 font (standard for page-count issues), present tense, single-spaced, with double-spaced no indents between paragraphs in the following format. All caps for each character name the first time the character is mentioned and described. Each new scene location or plot point gets an all-caps heading that briefly describes the place, action, and scene. Do not include any dialogue or any long character or scene descriptions. Treatments for shorts may have more section breaks than a feature. The following page shows an example of how a treatment might look.

Now that you know your plot points and ending, you are sure to keep your story moving and twisting in a good flow of events. Use the exercises in the next chapter to create scenes to fill in the action between these plot points.

superfreak!

Write a Treatment for a Feature. Take out the 40 plot points for the feature exercise. Use one little paragraph for each of the 40 points to write a treatment for a feature-length film. The treatment should be about 12 pages long. You may want to do lots of these in your spare time, just in case you one day have to think up a script idea fast. Sometimes it is easier to brainstorm for plot points and treatments than it is to actually script write (depending on your creative mood).

project 3.26

Write a Treatment. Based on the exercises you have completed in your drawing book, write a treatment for your short film using the previous format.

In these two shots, we see Ezzie get caught while trying to steal chocolate from the campers. This scene serves as the opening hook of the film and has a twist where the campers turn out to be Bigfoot hunters. The witchdoctor Rugaro is able to see what is happening to Ezzie by looking into his sacred vision pool. A match cut on sound and image occurs between the two shots with Ezzie yowling and Rugaro screeching. Start to see the story unfolding visually in your head as you write the treatment.

Example Treatment of a Short Film

Title: The Bigfoot Shamans

BIGFOOT FIELD RESEARCH VIDEO CAMERA. An unmanned video surveillance camera switches on in the forest, capturing the image of a Bigfoot walking by. The creature stops and examines the camera, and then crushes it angrily.

DEEP FOREST CAMPSITE. Two campers sit talking by a fire when they hear a strange sound of wailing in the distance. A huge boulder is tossed into the fire, causing the campers to run away. EZZIE, a teenage Bigfoot girl, approaches the food area of the campsite to steal a big bar of chocolate. Lights go off all around her, along with multiple cameras, as a cage is lowered, revealing a trap as she struggles to get free.

WITCHDOCTOR CAVE. RUGARO, an old Bigfoot witchdoctor, stands screeching and wildly upset, looking into a sacred vision pool. He watches as Ezzie is screaming and trying to get free of the cage.

chapter 4

Writing Scenes, Conflict, and a Short Script

"The idea is like a blueprint; it creates an image of the form, which then magnetizes and guides the physical energy to flow into that form and eventually manifests it on the physical plane."
—Shakti Gawain

All great storytellers have their own distinct personal styles. The more instruments you can play, the less you get stuck playing the same old tune. How can you use some of the storytelling techniques in these chapters to write a script that expresses an original vision of life?

time-saving

Plan Enough Time to Get to Final Storyboards. Keep in mind that most feature films spend *years* in preproduction. The actual shooting usually takes only a few weeks or months. Plan to spend at least half of your total production time getting to the final script and storyboards. Digitally enhanced productions rely heavily on storyboards because many shots are composed of layers from different sources. For the layers to work well together, shot timing and camera angles need to be carefully matched during production.

project
4.1

Preparing To Write a Script. Gather up a stack of 10 3×5- or 5×8-inch index cards for each scene in your film. Use these to write or sketch different approaches for each scene as you go through the rest of the chapters in this book. You may also reserve a few pages in your drawing book if you do not want to use index cards, but you will lose the flexibility of reordering ideas as easily.

Set up a work area where you can spread out index cards, photographs, and sketches across tables, floors, or walls. Arrange the scene index cards in the order they might appear in the film. You may want to color code the individual scene index cards if you have multiple stories going on inside one big one to see how they fit together. Posting pictures from magazines, sketches, or printouts of sets, characters, and shot ideas will help you get into the mood of the story.

Brilliant screenplays are not usually banged out poolside over the course of a week, before the actual production starts on a film. It takes time and lots of rewriting to craft a quality story that thousands or even millions of people will want to see.

Spending the extra time constructing the best script possible is a wise choice for any independent filmmaker. Screenwriting is a area where you can make up points for not having big budgets to shoot your film.

The Joy of Index Cards

After you have a solid idea about your character, plot points, and treatment, it is time to break out the index cards to start generating different approaches for each scene. Do not get attached to any ideas when crafting a story for a film. You will find yourself sacrificing the power of the storytelling just to work in one or two favorite scenes. As you go through the following exercises, try to get at least 10 different approaches for each scene in your treatment to avoid using cliché ideas. Arrange the stacks of scene ideas in chronological order, but be open to switching things around if another way might work better. Spread the stacks of cards out on a wall, table, or floor. You may want to include pictures of characters or sets from magazines or Photoshop printouts in the card piles to help you get a feel for the mood of each scene. Pick or combine the best ideas from each stack when it's time to write your script.

Three-Act Structure for Developing Scenes

Most films use some sort of structure with a beginning, middle, and end. Three-act structure is good to understand and consider when developing visual stories and individual scenes. We are so used to hearing stories with setups, event escalations, and climaxes that we hardly notice it anymore.

Act One: The Setup

Act One sets up the dramatic problem, characters, and film world. Setups in shorts need to happen immediately. **We usually meet the main character, see that what he wants is in conflict with what he needs, and what the obstacles are right away.** In shorts, every word and action must advance the film fast with no time wasted on any incidental information. Main problems are plot goals. Subproblems or subplots raise other questions, either supporting the theme or contrasting it. In *Life Lessons*, Lionel's problem is keeping Paulette from leaving, but he actually needs tension in his relationships to paint for his upcoming show. The subplot is whether or not the art show will be a success.

Your main characters need to make a big entrance in your film. It should take place in the beginning, during the hook, with the protagonist doing what he does best in your film world in a mid-miniclimax. How can you really make the protagonist enter a room visually and emotionally? In *Star Wars*, Darth Vader steps over a dead enemy while getting out of an invading spaceship, whereas Luke drives his hover vehicle around like a reckless teenager.

James Bond does a 5-minute high-spy performance in some exotic locale, usually involving quick entrances and getaways. You know right away that you are watching a spy film and this guy is good at what he does. Force and counterforce are revealed.

You then introduce the supporting characters to reflect the color of the protagonist's world. They allow the protagonist to verbalize what is going on, acting as soundboards for the internal landscape of what the character is thinking. Supporting characters are dramatically different from the protagonist and each other so that we see different sides of the film world through their perspectives. These supporting characters do not always need to be introduced doing what they do best, because they are only there to bring out different sides of the protagonist and the boundaries of the film world. In *Cold Mountain*, the first time we meet Rene Zellewegars's character, she kills a mean rooster with her bare hands that has been terrifying Nicole Kidman's character, which metaphorically sets up their relationship, too.

A visual type of quest is then introduced with some problem to solve. Wants and needs are established. The protagonist goes through a series of tests to show what he or she is made of internally and externally. These scenes define your characters through action. In *Star Wars*, Luke passes out when confronted with the sand people, in a brave but stupid attempt to

One idea I had for introducing my protagonist was to show her doing daredevil motorcycle stunts in a stalactite cavern. I decided not to use the motorcycle idea in the final script. A Bigfoot jumping a Harley-Davidson chopper over a huge cavern full of sharp rocks would be fun to animate (and watch). The first time we see her in the final script is on an unmanned video-surveillance camera in the forest. She is on her way to steal food from campers, which is one of the things she does best.

"I don't wait for moods. You accomplish nothing if you do that. Your mind must know it has got to get down to work."
—*Pearl Buck*

"The meeting of two personalities is ike the contact of two chemical substances: If there is any reaction, both are transformed."
—*C. G. Jung*

In one of my Bigfoot stories, Ezzie tricks her friend Izzy into drinking the toxic-waste cocktail he was trying to get her to drink, for the midpoint twist. This makes Izzy so immobile and dizzy that Ezzie can shave all his prized hair off to teach him a lesson.

"It is the surmounting of difficulties that make heroes."
—Kossuth

"There is the risk you cannot afford to take, and there is the risk you cannot afford not to take."
—Peter Drucker

overcome them. In Act One, we see all the protagonist's weaknesses, which are going to need to be fixed by the end of the story.

Act Two: Obstacles, Interactions, and Conflict

Act Two is about watching the character face obstacles and interact with different characters and situations, while dealing with conflict in a rising arc of intensity and action. This is when life becomes very difficult for your protagonist. Conflicts build in intensity to a breaking point of no return. The risks need to get greater and greater with regard to character choices, actions, and reactions. An escalating curve of dramatic tension through unexpected complications is introduced for the protagonist as the character tries to accomplish his or her goals. What gets your protagonist motivated enough to really fight for what he wants?

This is where you want to lead the audience into identifying with how tough things are getting for the protagonist. Get them to ask themselves questions like, "I wonder if this next character is going to help or hurt?" or "What in the world is going to happen next?" Try to make them understand what is about to happen, and then turn it around to surprise them. The first part of Act Two shows how the character deals with going into the unknown using new skills, while attempting to accomplish his or her goals. Is it worth it? Is the protagonist going to change his mind? What makes the character want to keep going? Throughout any setbacks or defeats, the protagonist is always still planning to achieve his goal. Between the plan for solving the

problem, and what the protagonist thinks will happen, are lots of twists and surprises. Nothing is ever what it seems. Expected results and prior planning do not usually work out.

The midpoint of the story holds a big twist or surprise to shift the main thrust of action into a new direction. A new plot goal may emerge. The first plot goal may be accomplished or become unnecessary. A new plot goal is often presented, causing a new direction for the story and characters to unfold. Really short films do not have time for lots of plot goals, but even a 10-minute film may shift main plot goals in mid-story. The end of Act Two is a good place for the protagonist to give up against unbeatable bleak odds of any success. Pit your protagonist against the impossible, just to watch the character fail and lose all hope.

Act Three: Climax/Resolution

Act Three contains the climax, which is the most intense moment of the film and is hardest to execute. Save the best for last to make Act Three the most powerful and satisfying. The conflict must be solved by dealing with hard choices and unexpected outcomes. This moment sums up the meaning of the film and is usually controlled by the underlying invisible theme. Impulsive characters need to experience some form of death or irrevocable loss. We need to see a protagonist think things through, use her new skills, and learn in mid-action without a plan. This is usually the point the protagonist gives up something dear to escape a dangerous situation—a sacrifice of what has always been comfortable. Luke gives up his sight and uses the force intuitively. Neo in *The Matrix* does the same in a sense.

The resolution ties up loose ends not resolved in the climax. A final insight or revelation into theme is often expressed. If the character experiences a big change during the climax, show them in a new way during the resolution to symbolize the change. Luke comes out in a new Jedi uniform, gets a medal, and then gets a kiss from the princess at the end. List five ways you could show your character as a changed person at the end of your film, in contrast to how we first saw

the character in Act One. Not all lead characters are going to change in a short; if they do, however, really show it.

Twist endings and reversals (explained soon) are where its at in short films. The more twisted, the better. *Planet of the Apes* had a great twist ending with the character riding off into the distance and then seeing the Statue of Liberty in ruin. The pro-human plot and theme got turned on its ear as we realize the humans blew the place up long before the apes took over. Make sure you have a good twist ending for your short film.

writing exercise 4.1

Write a few pages of any story idea using the three-act structure.

Ezzie cuts off all of Izzy's hair as punishment for what he did to her friend. Izzy's biggest fear was losing his hair, and this event shows a nice symbolic visual change for his character arc in the story.

Constructing Individual Scenes

Always try to begin scenes in the middle of the action at the most interesting point. The main crisis or event heats up the action, whereas the individual scenes build to breaking points of emotion.

Every scene ideally furthers plot, while revealing character and exploring theme.

The gap between what happens when a character takes action, and what the character thought was going to happen, is the substance of a great story.

"The true worth of a man is to be measured by the objects he pursues."

—Marcus Aurelius

creativity tip

Writing Is an Improvisational Art Form. Writing a screenplay requires a rather unique way of thinking, acting, improvising, visualizing, and writing at the same time. In each scene, you need to ask yourself, if you were this character in this situation what would you do? Act out the role of each character in your imagination to get to the emotional truth of the scene. Emphasize the actions and reactions of the characters based on how you constructed them in Chapter 2, "Creating Original Characters, Themes, and Visual Metaphors." Keep doing the scene in your head until you feel honest emotion flowing in your blood. If the scene moves you, it will move an audience. Strong emotions are very contagious. Great screenwriters are actors improvising an entire cast and film in their head, while writing the story on the page. If you do not feel the true emotional energy of your characters while creating a film, neither will your audience. These emotionally contagious states are also why directors work so hard to get their actors into the "moment" for each shot.

project 4.2

Create a Scene List with Main Character Goals. Use your treatment to break your film down into a list of individual scenes with character goals. If you are not sure how to group scenes, look for location changes. If you are doing a very short film in one location, break the story down into a list of key events or big emotional changes for the characters. Use this scene checklist to go through your list and identify possible main character goals for each section.

writing exercise 4.2

Write a few pages or a short story based on a possible scene in your script.

"Every time I've done something that doesn't feel right, it's ended up being wrong."
—Mario Cumo

"Out of suffering have emerged the strongest souls, the most massive characters are seared with scars."
—Edwin Chapin

Individual Scene Checklist

1. **Each scene has a specific purpose tied to advancing the plot goal or main story.** Your first scene purpose may be to introduce your main character; the second scene may be to establish the plot goal; the third may be to show theme, develop character, or present the antagonist. Use your plot points to see what types of bridging scenes need to happen between major events.

2. **Scenes link together with cause and effect.** This event happens in one scene, and then this scene happens as a reaction to the last one. Link individual scenes together with a clear cause-and-effect chain reaction.

3. **Each scene has clear goals or objectives for every main character.** Often these goals are in conflict. Characters want different things and try to convince each other to do things that help accomplish their own individual hidden agendas. There is a clear outcome by the end of the scene showing what goals were accomplished. Leave some issues unresolved to linger and make the audience wonder what will happen next.

4. **Decide the best visual way to start and end a scene.** If you are introducing your protagonist, how do you present him or her in the most interesting way? How do you exit the scene during a little climax? Think of each scene as a mini short film with a three-act structure of beginning, middle, and end.

5. **Create strong character identification** for each character in the scene (see Chapter 2).

6. **Each scene should have a clear attitude or emotional arc** where the characters or mood starts out in one emotion and ends up in a different state. Cycle through changing the emotional value charges from positive to negative and back again in unexpected ways. Use things like humor in the middle of great sadness to contrast emotions.

7. **Each scene should contain a surprise, reversal, shock, or twist** that keeps the audience on edge thinking things are never what they seem.

8. **Build up the conflict and complications in unexpected ways.** This will be explained more in this chapter.

9. **Add a layer of subtext to all major scenes.** A scene should never be about what it appears to be about on the surface. Write the dialogue or action straight first, and then go back and cover up characters' hidden emotions and agendas. This concept is explained more later in this chapter.

10. **Use a single location and linear time to contain action.** You may choose to cut another scene into the one you are writing, such as another location, flashback, parallel story, or memory. Each time the location changes, you need to start a new scene heading in your script. Great screenplays often have lots of little 2-inch scenes on the page.

Moving the Story Forward Through Conflict

To be alive is to be in a perpetual state of conflict—unless of course you are a very enlightened being. Something is always lacking in our lives that we are trying to find. If we solve one want, another one pops up immediately to take its place, demanding some sort of action. Most people become bored if they have too much harmony in their lives. It is also painfully boring for an audience to watch a character with nothing lacking, or no desire to do anything or fix anything. How would you tell a story about someone with an absolutely perfect life? How would this look? The first thing you think, is, well, there must be something not quite right. Most of life is about the struggle to find self-worth, love, purpose, and become peaceful in the face of chaos and social inequities.

Building Up Conflict to Show Character

The amount of conflict in a film usually determines the amount of audience interest. Obstacles, complications, reversals, interactions, twists, and crises build up the level of conflict and add complexity to your plots. For conflict to rise, the protagonist and antagonist must be evenly matched, locked together against conflicting goals with no compromise in sight. Your story needs to be full of strong characters willing to fight hard to accomplish their goals.

Different Forms of Conflict

By creating different forms of conflict, you can make your film more surprising. The more you do something the same way, the less impact it will have on the audience. If you always have physical conflicts for your character, it will start to become predictable and boring.

- **Inner.** Different beliefs, desires, voices, or goals inside characters are often in direct conflict with each other. How we talk to ourselves is often an inner argument between negative and positive thoughts. People have inner dialogue chatter going on all the time that often contains conflicting ideas and views about reality and their lives. How would that same type of voice sound in your character's head as he or she faces conflicts? One voice may say, "Take the money and run," whereas the other one says, "Call the police."
- **Personal.** How well does your character deal with other people? What is the character's attitude toward life? Is he charming, shy, violent, or rude? Show the character in conflict with relationships, family, friends, or pets.
- **Social.** Conflicts involving school, work, church, law, political, businesses, justice, or organizations.
- **Environmental.** Conflicts with urban surroundings, nature, diseases, disasters, or geographical locations.
- **Combinations** of the above.

"Difficulties are meant to rouse, not discourage. The human spirit is to grow strong by conflict."
—William Ellery Channing

This Bigfoot is having a personal and environmental conflict with the human joggers in his area of the forest. What unique ways can you show your characters having a variety of conflicts?

project 4.3

List Ideas for Different Forms of Conflict Between Plot Points. Come up with one idea for each of the previously mentioned forms of conflict to use somewhere in your story. You may want to list some ideas for each of these forms of conflict between major plot points in Act Two. Pick the ones that work best to possibly develop into your script and write them on index cards inside your individual scene piles.

This character's scene goal is to find the lost crystal Bigfoot skull to save the tribe from disease. The conflicts and obstacles he has to endure include an inaccurate map, falling boulders, other competing Bigfoots, a ticking bomb, giant spiders, hidden traps, venomous snakes, broken glass, inner fears, and an evil spirit. You may want to sketch a timeline of visual conflicts for some scenes.

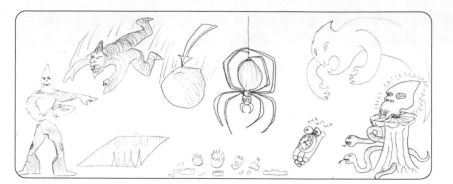

"Life shrinks or expands in proportion to one's courage."
—Anais Niün

"Obstacles are those frightful things you see when you take your eyes off of the goal."
—Hannah More

Play "Let's Make It Worse"

Stories that suffer from the "everything happens too easily" syndrome lack enough conflict. Creating good varied visual forms of conflict is an art form. Aim to develop original types and combinations of conflict we have not seen before onscreen. Use good visual metaphors and symbols for objects and situations whenever possible.

1. **Give the character a righteous cause.** Have the character be on a selfless quest of some sort or have a virtuous motivation to accomplish the scene goal.

2. **Raise the stakes.** What happens if your character fails to achieve the scene goal? In *The Matrix*, if you die in the game world, you die in the real world (unless you get kissed). This is an irrevocable loss that raises the stakes considerably. Personal loss, impact on the greater world, family loss, death of some kind (emotionally, spiritually, physically) all increase the level of conflict. To make it more interesting, you can also raise the stakes for what good things happen if the character succeeds.

3. **Show characters with opposite goals (or antagonists).** Who or what is trying to stop your protagonist from achieving his goals?

4. **Physical obstructions.** River crossings, wars, jungle, mountains, possessed trees, gauntlet, security, lasers, snakes, electrical cords in water, or a glass protective case.

5. **Inner/psychological.** Intellectual or emotional problems, psychological flaws, fears, obsessions, pride, schizophrenia, or jealousy.

6. **Mystical forces.** Strange accidents, games of chance, signs, coincidence, synchronicity, moral choices, ethical codes, supernatural forces, gods, or paranormal world occurrences.

7. **Unexpected event occurs.** Refer to the Plot Twist Chart in Chapter 3, "Developing Plot Points," if you need ideas.

8. **Unexpected character appears** who either helps or hinders protagonist.

9. **A mistake or misunderstanding** further complicates the situation.

10. **New information** or a discovery requires a change of plans.

11. **The character suddenly changes his or her mind** about plan or goal.

12. **Another character acts in a surprising way,** changing the stakes, such as threatening blackmail or changing loyalties.

13. **New information makes a plot goal mute,** forcing a bigger plot goal to be established.

14. **The character accomplishes his or her first goal** but sees a bigger new one now.

15. **The character outsmarts an opponent**, gets tricked, or is captured.

16. **Ticking-clock** factor that adds tension through time pressures. Usually this is a bomb in the corner or a time limit of some kind. A rendezvous occurs, an event begins, a race starts, a deadline is set, a character is due to arrive, stars line up, a meeting takes place, a disaster about to strike, fuel running out, air low, door closing, a window of opportunity gone, or a plot goal mute after a certain time.

17. **Combination of conflict** uses original visual combinations of the above methods.

18. **Arrange new lists of favorite conflicts chronologically to fit the scene.** You would not want your character to have to battle debilitating fear of spiders after new information makes the plot goal unnecessary.

"Calculation never made a hero."
—John Henry Cardinal Newman

Creating Emotional Scene Arcs

Real life forces people to travel through a vast array of emotional states and changes each day. Think of how many moods or emotions you have experienced since you woke up this morning. Pay attention to the speed of emotional changes you go through during intense events. Lots of fast emotional changes in each scene will help keep the audience emotionally involved in your film and make the story seem more real. Each scene should have an emotional arc, where it begins in one emotion and then moves through several different contrasting emotions, triggered by the events and character reactions. Mix and contrast heavy painful moments with lighter happier ones. Audience emotions rise and fall with these changes. Emotions are generally short-term experiences that tend to burn out fast, so you need to keep changing them by introducing new ways of being.

Robert McKee points out in his wonderful book *Story*, that there are two basic states of being: pleasure (+), getting what you want; and pain (−), not getting what you want. At the beginning of your scene, assign a plus or minus value to each main character. Suppose you have a scene in which two people are baking a cake. At the beginning of the scene, they are both in pleasure (+) states, excited about baking the cake together. Then Character A starts to argue that the cake they are baking is the wrong kind (−) for the occasion, while Character B disagrees saying it's the perfect cake (+).

project 4.4

Play Let's Make It Worse. If you have a scene that feels too simple, try increasing the conflict. Suppose your character's goal in the scene is to walk across a room and get a statue. Make a list of all the things that might prevent your hero from getting that statue. The more impossible the feats the characters overcome, the larger than life they become. List 1 idea for each of the preceding 18 ways to create conflict in your film and arrange events chronologically.

While Ezzie is trying to retrieve her lightening bug friend from a snake, she stops, overcome with a sudden flood of compassion for the hungry creature. The snake smiles back up at her in a tender moment, and then she continues to search for the bug by sticking her arm down its throat. The scene would not be as interesting if Ezzie did not pause to reflect on compassion for a moment first. How could you add more emotional changes into your scene to develop character? Think of how many emotions you go through during an intense series of events, and make sure your characters contain similarly rich emotional arcs.

Character A gets angry (–) and throws flour on Character B, who gets upset and starts crying (–). Now they are both negative. Character B hits Character A over the head with a rolling pin, knocking A out. Character B happily continues baking the cake (+), while Character A is knocked out (–). As Character B is pulling the cake out of the oven, Character A wakes up (+) and trips B (–), ruining the cake. Now they are both switched again. At the start of the scene, they were both positive, but then flipped back and forth between negative and positive. This shows multiple emotional changes over the course of several events, and is much more interesting to watch.

Setting the Pace of Your Scenes

You need to keep the audience interest as you move from one scene to the next. All scene types have a different shape and pace. The six listed here start with the fastest pace and go down to the slowest one. Make sure all of your scenes fit into one of these six distinct shapes:

1. **Accelerating** scenes have the fastest pace and place the protagonist closer and closer to his goal. Characters are in the middle of intense action, conflict, or interaction toward obtaining goals, and we get a peak at them at the most interesting points.

2. **Decelerating** scenes move characters further and further away from the goal. The character gives up, fails, or makes a compromise. Obstacles or conflict are greater than character.

3. **Arcing** scenes are when a character grows through a revelation or drastic behavior swing. These scenes reveal character arcs changing throughout the story.

4. **Circular** scenes have a goal but no climax or payoff, and the character ends up back where she started. Used to show fate, cycles, or comedy. Fate meaning no matter what the character does, it just does not work out; tension and frustration build as the character looks for new ways to achieve the goals. Characters are chasing their own tails.

5. **Flat** scenes are missing an obstacle and have the slowest pace with no rise in excitement or drop, providing only exposition. These scenes explain information difficult to understand that builds the foundation of the story. You need to slow down

the pace with scenes like this to deliver lots of new ideas. These types of scenes deal with who, what, when, where, and how packed tightly together. The opening scene of *Mission Impossible 2* shows Tom Cruise rock climbing and getting his next assignment from his spy glasses. It is a flat scene that basically lays out the whole plot of the film in 5 minutes. The sunglasses explode at the end, which is a minor payoff. This flat scene feels exciting because of the swirling 360-degree camera rotation around Tom against a backdrop of stunning natural beauty. How can you make one of your flat scenes look accelerated? Flat scenes must contain information about plot (goal), theme (need), and character (personality).

6. **Transitional** scenes glue two scenes together and close gaps in time between events or places. If you have a character who is in Paris but says he must go to Peru, you do not cut to a shot of him suddenly sitting in some hut in Peru. You might show a map with a line going across the ocean or create a quick series of travel shots to show time, events, and places changing. Here is a list of possible transition scene techniques:

- **Map.** Use a line across a map to indicate movement. How could you use your digital tools to show an animated map? How could you use motion graphics in a fresh way to show gaps in time, events, or places?

"Having a goal is a state of happiness."
—E.J. Bartek

Composing a Good Pace

If you have only accelerating scenes, you will burn the audience out or become too predictable. If you have too many flat scenes, you will put the audience to sleep. Constructing scenes together is like composing a song. You need both fast and slow dynamics to keep it interesting and varied. If you sense a part of your script drags, turn the pace up by using a faster version of the scene or inserting an accelerating scene. If the action is getting too fast and confusing, add a slow flat scene. Be careful of using long slow-paced scenes heading into the climax; otherwise, the climax may fall flat. Scene shapes are great to play with when fine-tuning your script. Pay attention to composing a good pace when writing your first draft. You may want to draw a scene-shape timeline graph of your story to see how it looks, as shown here. You can find a Photoshop file with all the scene shapes on the accompanying CD (sceneshapes.psd).

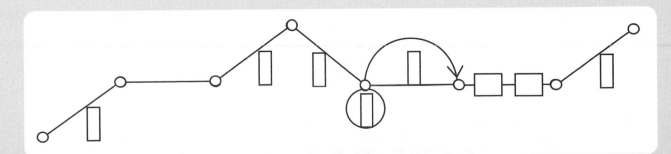

project 4.6

Create Transitional Scene Ideas. Using these techniques, think of two original ideas to bridge each of your major scene changes.

- **Subtitles with an establishing shot.** Use an establishing long shot of a new location or photograph with subtitles. A Photoshop image of a mountain village with the subtitle "Peru" would serve as a visual transition into the new location. It would not work as well to show a character already inside a hut with the subtitle "Peru."

- **Visual match cut.** Place the same objects or shapes into the two scenes, joining them visually. If one shot has a stage play with a painting of a sun behind the actors, match cut the shape of the sun with a real sun in the same spot on-screen in the next scene. Feel free to play with space and time like this if it makes sense.

- **Verbal.** Use the same word, phrase, or slang between scenes. *Austin Powers 2* has a great visual and verbal transition scene where they do a play on the shape of the flying spaceship with words such as *dick, willy, two balls, privates,* all cutting to new scenes of people using these words mid-sentence while cutting to the rocket launch.

A line going across a map is a classic animated shot to show characters going from one place to another. How could you use animation or motion graphics to create new types of transitional shots? On this map, I could have an animated little Bigfoot running across the map with different text lighting up for locations and sound effects. A pan-and-scan technique could be used across the map, creating a quick 2D animation look (see Chapter 9, "Digitally Enhanced Storytelling Techniques").

This logride whirlpool serves as the match cut for two scenes between characters at different ages. They used to go to the pool as little Bigfoots and are both remembering those times, watching the swirling water as adults. Past and present scenes are cut together to show them remembering. The words between the scenes tie together with Izzy saying something as a little Bigfoot that Ezzie answers as a grownup. What new ways can you think of to create a visual match cut for a multiple series of transitions across time?

In these two shots, we have a visual match cut with the Indian carving a Bigfoot statue and a Bigfoot running in the forest. These shots happen at the beginning of the story where I plan to cut back and forth several times to the Bigfoot running and the Indian carving. A match cut on audio will occur as the Bigfoot gets closer to the camp and screeches.

- **Character trait.** Show one character yelling in an office, cut to another yelling on a ball field. Or contrast character traits between two scenes.
- **Sound.** A bell going off in a school room cuts to an alarm going off at a nuclear plant. Or try contrasting sounds between scenes. Cut from something soft to harsh, such as a symphony performance to a noisy factory, to show the change in mood.
- **Lighting.** Cut from a very dark room to another very dark room. Or a glint from the sun to a lens flare coming off of a watch (an easy digital effect). A spotlight at a circus could cut to a desk lamp, matching the same illumination shape over a chair.

Creating Reversals in Scenes

Almost every scene in your film should have a reversal. This technique is one of the most powerful tools you can use when writing scenes for a script to build up suspense. Reversals keep the audience guessing as to what is going to happen next and pulls them into the story, prompting them to search for the new surprise. When you understand reversals, you will see them in every mainstream movie you go to and in almost every scene.

Reversals set up expectations for the audience, and then deliver on them in totally unpredictable and surprising ways.

Here are several ways to create scene reversals:

- Introduce a character with a clear scene goal.

- Create a set of expectations in viewers' minds as to how the goal will be accomplished.
- Introduce complications, conflict, or interactions.
- List several ways the audience expects a character to achieve a goal and have the character fail at each attempt.
- During the character's last attempt to accomplish the goal, have the character do something unexpected and succeed. This usually involves something being in the scene that the audience does not yet know about.

A ski-chase scene in a James Bond film shows the spy trying to get away from the bad guys (goal). 007 tries every trick he can think of, but is still close to getting caught after several encounters with the bad guys. He then skis off a cliff, and a hidden parachute comes out of his backpack. This is an example of a classic scene reversal.

Reversals come in all shapes and sizes. You can think of reversals as little lies in the scenes telling the audience to trust you, this is the way it is, and then Pow! Your perception of the situation changes 180 degrees.

After Emmy shoots the butcher in *Transit*, we see a shot of two policemen running down the street. We start to worry as we think she is going to get caught. Her head pops up over the policeman, and we see that she is standing in front of an outdoor movie screen. This is a great reversal that keeps us off balance wondering what is going to happen next. As an audience, we are led to believe the police are chasing her, but then the situation turns around in a surprising way.

Ezzie throws a big rock at a spider web blocking her trail. The rock bounces off the web and hits her in the head, knocking her out. This a reversal since it is unexpected. I could do a series of these reversals and make a funny scene where she tries various techniques to get through the webs and they all backfire.

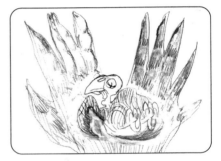

Ezzie battles mountain lions, other Bigfoots, bats, and snakes to save a condor friend. The condor ends up dying of a heart attack in her hands after she rescues it. The scene purpose is to show the death of the bird friend, and Ezzie's scene goal was to save it. If the condor had been supposed to live in the scene, I could have had Ezzie think she killed it by mistake, and then have had the bird come back to life to create a strong scene reversal.

writing exercise 4.4

Take a scene from your film and write a short story of characters experiencing as many reversals as possible. Use the Reversal Chart for ideas if you get stuck.

superfreak!

Watch a Film Just for Reversals. Choose one of your favorite films and watch it for reversals. See how in almost every scene, the character or audience expects one thing to happen, but another thing occurs instead. List the general types of reversal situations you see, as in the chart to the right. Great scene reversals will make your films feel edgy and like anything can happen. You need to really study scene reversals to understand how many ways they can be accomplished.

project 4.7

Create Scene Reversals. Create one surprising reversal idea for each scene in your film.

This hungry Bigfoot eats a live bird, tearing it apart with his hands and teeth in a shocking way. I could use a 2D particle effect for the squirting blood. What digitally enhanced elements of shock can you add to your film?

Reversal Brainstorming Chart

> Character takes action expecting one result and gets an antagonistic reaction instead.
>
> Character sets off to do one thing, but ends up doing something different.
>
> Another character acts in a surprising way.
>
> An event that seems positive at first reveals itself to be negative.
>
> An emergency situation turns out to be a drill.
>
> Two characters are talking about two totally different things without realizing it.
>
> Hero saves a person's life in a daring way, but then the person dies anyway.
>
> A character goes into a place to meet someone and ends up in a fistfight.
>
> A character seems like he is going to get away, but then gets caught in a surprising way.
>
> A normal-looking relationship reveals itself to be very strange.
>
> A character who you once thought was a good guy turns out to be a bad guy.

Adding Elements of Shock

Shocks are unexpected and impossible to predict but do not change everything. This technique is used to startle the audience. Add shocks and surprises to your scenes to maintain suspense, stimulate curiosity, and hold the audience's attention. Good shocks will keep the audience guessing, asking themselves, "What in the world is going to happen next?" **Building up suspense is the second most important thing you do in your film—next to evoking emotion.** Conflict and suspense often go together. As the end of the story approaches, shocks and surprises should increase.

1. **The character behaves in a startling way.** In *Life Lessons*, Lionel complains to his art dealer about having to pick up his assistant, Paulette, at the airport. In the next scene, at the airport, he looks really nervous. Paulette arrives and tells him she didn't want him to pick her up; she acts really angry and disgusted with him. The audience starts to wonder what is going on with these people; nothing is what it seems. Lionel acts very differently around Paulette than he did with his art dealer just moments ago. In nearly every scene in this film, both Lionel and Paulette each do something startling to make the audience reevaluate what is actually going on.

2. **The character does something inexplicable.** Maybe a character does something we think is mean-spirited, but that actually turns out to be a nice thing. Weird things characters do need to relate to their history or theme goal. Do not just make the character act strangely to keep the audience off balance.

Create Two Elements of Surprise. How can you make your characters behave in startling and inexplicable ways during some scenes?

Foreshadowing Techniques

Foreshadowing, or representing possible future events, in your story will help the audience understand where you are taking them in your film. Audiences are trained to expect foreshadowing. You can foreshadow story information in the following ways:

1. **Plot goal object metaphor or symbol.** Use a plot goal object metaphor or symbol early in the film as a practice version for accomplishing plot goals. In *Star Wars*, Luke fights with a spherical droid, not realizing he will later fly off to blow up the big, circular Deathstar.

2. **Character warning.** Have another character give a warning. In *Seven*, Brad Pitt's character's detective buddy, played by Morgan Freeman, tells him in a bar in Act Two that these types of cases do not have happy endings. The audience has been warned, and is a little bit more prepared to have Brad's wife's head show up in a box during the final scene. If we did not get this warning, we would be more upset about the ending catching us off guard.

3. **Prophecy.** These are usually used in tragedies, such as riddles delivered by witches at crossroads, but could be used in any type of film. How many different ways could your main character get some prophetic information early on?

4. **Dialogue or words.** A character could see or hear something that points toward future events—perhaps a sign on the road or a newspaper headline. Maybe a character overhears a conversation, a slip of the tongue, a TV show playing in the background, someone at a gas station saying that a storm is approaching, or an "I have a bad feeling" type of comment.

5. **Dreams/visions.** Place metaphoric activities or symbol objects in dreams or visions to signal the direction the plot is moving. If a character is trapped in a room full of black lions during a dream or vision, the audience will expect that something unavoidable and unlucky is about to happen (trapped with black cats). Metaphoric or symbolic dreams are great places to use digital tools.

6. **Metaphoric or symbolic cutaway image.** Use a metaphoric or symbolic cutaway image, such as an owl hooting in a tree as a symbol for death.

Ezzie suddenly realizes that she can communicate with snakes and spiders when they start talking to her as she is tied up at her lowest point (surprise). The snake on her shoulder symbolically represents her positive higher self voice and the spider on her other shoulder represents her negative fearful inner voice. Assigning the two new characters symbolic functions gives me more to play with in the scene. This creates a good cop/bad cop dynamic between the three characters as they assess her situation.

The animated cave drawings in my film often serve to foreshadow upcoming events. As Ezzie walks toward the Cave Of Dead Souls, the little drawings try to warn her not to go inside. How could you use Photoshop to create custom newspapers, signs, or billboards to foreshadow upcoming events in your story? Can you think of any ideas for using DV or animation to create TV news footage or images playing inside the set to foreshadow events in your film?

project 4.9

Foreshadow the Main Events. List one way to foreshadow the main events in your story using each of the six techniques discussed in this section.

writing exercise 4.5

Write a few pages showing different characters who experience a foreshadow type of event and then have that situation manifest itself almost immediately just for fun.

superfreak!

Create Two Coincidences. Create two coincidences and use them in Act One and Act Two to set up meaningful patterns for later in the story.

Ezzie watches a strange three-headed mutant snail crawl under a rock in the toxic waste-dump cave. When she turns the rock over to see the snail, she finds a newspaper with an important article about the increased number of Bigfoot sightings in the area. How can you use coincidences in an original visual way somewhere in your story?

Visual Metaphors/Symbols to Foreshadow Events

Metaphors and symbols enable you to foreshadow plot points and develop situations visually. For instance, you can use small positive or negative strange occurrences before an actual big event. A character might receive an uplifting telephone call before something good happens, for example, or a troubling telephone call before something negative occurs.

Using Coincidences

Introduce a coincidence at the beginning of your story, and then turn it into a meaningful pattern. Perhaps you could have a character who keeps running into someone, and those chance meetings actually relate to something that occurs later in the film. You may show a vicious attack at the beginning of your film, and this attack (and others) may be part of a pattern of a grand conspiracy. A character could discover a strange object or situation that turns out to be symptom of a bigger problem in Act Two.

Never use coincidences to get out of a story problem, especially during the climax or ending. **Audiences tend not to believe coincidences that help your character out of tight spots, and instead respond better to coincidences that make life more difficult for characters.** Characters could suddenly appear with information. Synchronistic events could happen, such as running into people, finding things, ending up in the right places, having accidents, overhearing some information, being mistaken for someone else, or having a misunderstanding.

Event About to Happen	Metaphoric/Symbolic Image Description in Script
Death	Dead bird on the sidewalk
Loss of important object	Old tombstone getting washed away in a thunderstorm
Someone about to steal	Police cars with sirens racing down the street
Two people about to fall in love	Other couples walking by holding hands and kissing
Someone about to trick someone	Card game on the street
Accident about to happen	Object falling from a window to the sidewalk near where the character is walking
War about to break out	People fighting on the street
Serious illness	Small annoying wound that grows with sickness
Crazy murderer about to strike	Discovering room full of sculptures made out of human bones
Someone about to kill someone	Person blowing out a candle
Bad luck	The character tripping over a symbolic object and falling down by accident
Lover dying in the future	Character has a strange vision looking into symbolic reflective surface

Deus ex machina is Greek for the phrase "god from machine," and many ancient playwrites used the concept behind this phrase to solve story problems in Act Three. A god in a cage was lowered onto the stage to decide the fate of the characters and outcomes of situations. Neo in *The Matrix* is brought back to life at the end with a kiss that breaks the rules of death for the game. Avoid using deus ex machina solutions to get out of plot problems; they are usually a weak approach.

Adding Dramatic Irony

Irony is a method of expression in which the intended meaning is the direct opposite of the usual sense. This may mean that something really good happens, but that it has an equally negative element balancing it out. Here are some ways to add irony to your story:

1. Give the character exactly what she wants, but make it too late for her to enjoy it.
2. Push the character further and further away from his goal, letting him get really down, and then have him land right in the middle of where he needs to be to accomplish his goal in an unexpected way.

> *"The real artist is the one who has learned to recognize and to render what Joyce has called the "radiance" of all things, as an epiphany or showing forth of the truth."*
> **—Joseph Campbell**

3. Have your character throw away the one thing that makes her happy, without realizing it soon enough.
4. Have your character try to destroy something, only to be destroyed by it in the process.

Incorporating Revelations and Epiphanies

Revelations usually involve showing a character having an epiphany in Act Three. Important information about something not previously known is revealed or exposed. Truth is finally forced out into the open, and this usually happens right before the climax (but can occur anywhere in the story). These moments are usually linked to coming full circle on a character arc cycle, as we see the character realize his big change. Revelations must have a direct relationship to the theme, and usually answer the question, "What inner block is keeping the character from achieving their goals?"

Do not use flashbacks to show revelations or dialogue that begins with lines such as, "And then I realized…." Use dramatic actions to express the core emotion of the revelation. In *Life Lessons*, Lionel smears paint all over his face after talking out loud about women being "chippies," while suddenly realizing how he uses turbulent relationships to fuel his painting, making him look like a monster. Don't let the character tell us everything, especially if it's painful. Leave some space for the audience to draw their own conclusions about why Lionel is suddenly smearing paint all over his face and is looking shocked at the thoughts going through his head.

Just as Ezzie is about to give up finding the shamanic journey cave, she slips off of a rock ledge and ends up falling into the cavern right next to the hidden chamber. This adds some dramatic irony to her quest since it seems like she's doomed, but actually ends up in just the right place.

superfreak!

Create Three Ideas for Dramatic Irony. Add any irony ideas that might fit into your scenes.

writing exercise 4.6

Write a few pages showing different characters who experience some extreme form of dramatic irony.

Rugaro the witchdoctor finally reveals to Ezzie that he had a vision, which caused her parents to be banished to the Land of the Yeti's when she was a child. This revelation helps set up the motivation for why Rugaro wants Ezzie to be banished from the tribe or die in the cave.

project 4.10

Create One Revelation. Place the revelation idea on an index card in the corresponding scene pile.

writing exercise 4.7

Take the scene in your film where your main character experiences their biggest realization or epiphany, and write a few pages describing what this event is like for them in detail. Experiment with different visual ways to show the deep inner changes occurring in their reality.

definition

Subtext Feelings, motivations, and thoughts below the surface of dialogue and action in a scene.

Izzy tells Ezzie that he has just the thing to "settle her nerves." He mixes up a toxic-waste cocktail from old oil drums marked with a sleeping Bigfoot warning picture. The audience wonders how much her nerves are going to be "settled" or if he is planning to trick her by knocking her out completely.

Revelations may take many forms, but typically fit into one of the following three categories:

- **Shocking information revealed** that relates to a character's motivations, causing a revelation for the character or the audience.

- **Sudden realization or epiphany** for a character based on experiencing the events and intense conflict in the film.
- **The audience may have a revelation** about a character that the character himself is not yet aware of.

Adding Subtext to Scenes

Scenes that feel too flat, simple, boring, fake, or unreal often lack a layer of emotional subtext to the main action. Subtext in each scene is essential to evoke strong emotional reactions from your audience.

All protagonists have a conscious plot goal in each scene and an underlying unconscious need, fear, block, wound, or hidden agenda. A character often does or says something that has multiple meanings to hide actual thoughts and feelings under the surface. What is not being said is sometimes just as important as what is said. The character may be aware or unaware of hiding these underlying thoughts, emotions, or fears. These strong subconscious emotions lurking below the surface determine a character's speech and behavior.

Viewers like to try and figure out why characters do things. Audiences are skeptical when characters tell them how they really feel. It is more interesting for the audience to watch characters try to avoid difficult situations, while being unable to express their true emotions. Characters who hide their true motivations appear more realistic than those who come right out and say what they want or what they are thinking. All of us run actions and dialogue through an inner filter before we act or speak.

Think about how often you hide your own true feelings or thoughts in certain situations to feel safe, accomplish a secret goal, or follow a hidden agenda.

Emotions motivate characters to act and react in very extreme ways, which may be used to drive subtext ideas. Characters are often unaware or like to pretend that they are not experiencing strong emotions. Pay attention to how you act differently when in the grip of a heavy emotion, both positively and negatively, and use your own experiences to help you create believable characters and situations.

Theme often comes between what a character says and what the character really means. The theme of *Lilly and Jim* is that communication problems exist between the sexes. Everything these two say to each other is basically what they think the other one wants to hear. "Do you want some coffee at my place?," Lilly asks Jim again after he has already told her he does not like coffee; however, he suddenly agrees to coffee. The subtext of the scene is whether these two stand a chance of becoming intimate on this date, not about drinking coffee. How do you notice subtext in your own life? Do people say one thing when they mean another?

Subtext Idea Chart

Character says one thing but means something else. "I'm going to get you out of this mess," rather than "I love you so much, I'm willing to risk my life to save you."

Character does one thing but means something else. Takes a kid to the park to play but meets a connection to sell a stolen item.

Character A makes Character B an offer he cannot refuse. Character B knows he will be punished for refusing, or Character B may see the offer as selling his soul.

Character A pretends Character B is not hurting her feelings during a conversation.

Character pretends that she has everything under control but inside she's coming apart.

Character changes painful subject to avoid getting too emotional over current situation.

Character cracks a joke to keep from crying.

A very calm character suddenly throws an object into a big mirror to show how he hates himself.

Character A orders Character B to do something, causing Character B to do it with a forced smile and lots of underlying tension.

Character A's true emotion changes during scene activity (for instance, arranges flowers happily at first, but then turns very violent).

Character A does something nice for Character B instead of saying how he feels (for instance, Dad fixes a bowl of ice cream for his son and himself to cheer kid up).

Character A forcefully denies doing something that he did do when Character B confronts him.

Two characters fall in love while walking their dogs. Loaded dialogue said with a smile might include such statements as "Be careful, Sparky might bite you."

Character A takes Character B to a romantic spot to break up the relationship. Character A might say, "You know how much you mean to me," right before saying, "I don't think we should see each other again."

Character acts in accordance with his emotion.

Character reflects underlying emotion in her attitude (for instance, she acts angry when she sees another character approach).

Character says he is doing one thing, but is covering up a hidden agenda.

Character talks about something completely different than what she is feeling, but she radiates the underlying emotion.

Character adopts an understated approach to deal with an intense emotional scene (for instance, the character may be told about the death of loved one, but sits silently in a chair after being told the news).

Character uses body language or appearance to show underlying emotions (for instance, slouching if depressed, messy clothes for inner mess, facial expressions, or gestures).

The physical action of the character shows emotional state (for instance, an upset character stabs another one in the hand with a fork).

Use external symbolic atmospheres to mirror inner world of characters (for instance, nature shots, weather, time of day, color of walls, setting, light quality, and sounds).

Wife says with no emotion to husband, "I love you so much, it scares me." Wife actually means, "I need you to pay the bills; please don't leave me."

Character A acts like they do not like Character B, because they are jealous Character B might get between them and Character C.

In this shot, Ezzie is caught on a rope bridge that is unraveling over a deep abyss full of hot lava. Instead of getting all flipped out, she cracks jokes about how they just don't make things the way they used to to cover up her fear. The subtext is that she is scared to death of falling into the lava, but on the surface, she is laughing because she is learning during her vision quest that getting all upset impairs her intuition in dangerous situations and makes things worse.

superfreak!

Watch a Favorite Film for Subtext.
As you view the film, write down what each main scene is about on the surface and what contrasting emotions or hidden agendas lurk beneath the surface.

writing exercise
4.8

Write a few pages using as many subtext ideas as possible for a character in your film in any situation or series of events.

project
4.11

Think of Ways to Develop Subtext in Each Major Scene. Use one index card for each scene idea. Place the card in the appropriate pile. Rewrites are a good place to develop subtext ideas more deeply, but you should be thinking of them during your first draft too. You may want to list the main action or dialogue, and then go through and list the underlying emotions, theme goals, hidden agendas, or masks that each character might be feeling or using during each scene. Ask yourself the following questions to add subtext to scenes:

1. What is the key emotion motivating each character in the scene?
2. What is causing inner conflict or tension?
3. What must be stated with clear dialogue, implied, or not said at all?
4. What physical actions can you use to show underlying emotions? A happy character who just quit his job may skip down the street, for instance.
5. How can you use as little dialogue as possible to express your character's inner state? What types of visual images, sounds, atmospheres, or events can you use to support the emotion?
6. How can you have the characters say what they mean while talking about something else? "It sure is beautiful here today," said while looking straight at another character, might translate with subtext into, "You sure are beautiful today." To use this technique, you may want to write your dialogue straight, then go back over it adding the subtext.
7. Is it appropriate for a character to say or do the exact opposite of what they want or need due to some underlying fear?

"It is the heart always that sees before the head can see."
—Thomas Carlyle

"Too much agreement kills a chat."
—Eldridge Cleaver

11 Ways To Say "I Love You" Using Subtext

Notice how many different ways people tell each other they are in love:

1. "I don't want to go without you."
2. "Do you know how beautiful you look right now?"
3. "I'd walk through fire for you."
4. "You know I'd do anything for you."
5. "Do you know how much you mean to me?"
6. "I don't know what I'd do if I lost you."
7. "Here's an extra set of keys to my apartment."
8. "I've never felt this way before."
9. "You were the only one who ever meant anything."
10. "I am the most fortunate sentient in this quadrant."
11. "Here's looking at you kid."
    —Humphrey Bogart

Many characters may not even be fully aware of being in love as they say these lines. The subtext of what the characters say reveals their subconscious perspectives, and may help the audience see the true emotional situation before the character actually does.

Writing Dialogue

Dialogue is usually the last thing you think about before writing your script. By the time you get to this phase, the characters should be more than ready to start talking to you; they will be if you have prepared the rest of your story well.

Keep the audience hungry for dialogue, using it only when you cannot show something visually. The more dialogue you use in your film, the less impact it will have on the viewer.

The way people talk to themselves and other people defines their own interpretations of reality. Shakespeare has a distinct voice for each character. You should be able to go through your script at the end, strip all the characters' names from the dialogue, and still be able to tell who is talking. To develop a good ear for writing realistic dialogue, listen to the various ways people talk to each other in your own life.

1. **Vocabulary.** Each character should have a different set of words he or she uses, which are unique and distinct from all other characters in all other movies. Gangsters in Oakland talk differently than the ones in New York or Vegas. If you don't know how a gangster in your hometown talks, make it up. When slang makes it hard to understand what is going on, you need to cut back on it or use subtitles. "You lie like a Persian rug" sounds more interesting in a script than "that's a lie." Let the full glory of your character's own individual color come through in his or her vocabulary and word choices.

2. **Grammar.** How does the character put words together in a unique way? Yoda talks backward. George Bush Senior dropped the first word of sentences: "Wouldn't do that." Some characters may like to use tags at the end of their sentences ("Isn't it?" "Oh wow!" "What do you think?" "Okay?" "You hear what I'm saying?") Make up words or use old ones in new ways relevant to your character history or backstory for tags. Try writing the dialogue straight first, and then go back over it and experiment with different grammar structures. Experiment with dropping words, reversing words, and creating new ones. Have your character run off at the mouth, not finish sentences, or add signature tags at the end. Avoid using cliché tags. Ending a sentence with "oh shucks" is much different from "oh dunderdoodle!"

3. **Mindset.** No two characters view the world in the same way. A mathematician sees everything as equations. Stockbrokers relate everything to the market. Football players talk like they are always in a huddle. Priests speak as if they are the voice of God. The Queen refers to herself as "we." Use spoken metaphors that relate to your character's history for his or her dialogue. No two people have the exact

This Bigfoot wants to be a cowboy, even though he is too big to ride most horses. His state of mind causes him to say things such as, "Let's rodeo" rather than "Let's get out of here," and "I feel like a horse that was ridden hard and put up wet" rather than "I'm tired." How can you color every line of dialogue your character speaks with his or her own personal flavor? While writing dialogue, keep a list handy of each character's five traits to see how many traits you can reflect in word choices.

"Your words create what you speak about. Learn to speak positively."
—Sanaya Roman

"Your words are the bricks and mortar of the dreams you want to realize. Your words are the greatest power you have. The words you choose and use establish the life you experience."
—Sonia Choquette

superfreak!

Tracking Speech Patterns. What specific techniques do you notice people use to talk to each other? Keep a page in your notebook to write down speech patterns or good lines you hear that really show us who the character or person is underneath. What types of sayings do the people you know use, and what do these "say" about who they are? Ideas are plentiful until you really need one, so it helps to keep a running list of interesting things people say and track the subtle ways they communicate differently in a variety of situations. It is especially important to track dialogue when you travel, because language and slang tend to be very regional.

past, future, physical attributes, socialization, experiences, or money. What people say to themselves and others defines their reality and shows us who they are in a sense.

The following list identifies some common communication patterns you may want to consider using for some of your characters to create believable dialogue:

1. **Use questions to answer questions.** Character A asks, "How was the party?" Character B replies, "Have you ever fallen through a skylight?"

2. **Character avoids questions.** The character responds with silence, changes the topic, tentatively speaks ("Yeah … I guess …") or indefinitely responds.

3. **Character responds with action instead of speech.** Character A asks, "How do you feel?" Character B punches a hole in the wall.

4. **Character is in own world.** Character A keeps asking Character B about something while Character B just keeps talking about something else, ignoring Character A's question. Or both of them could be in their own world, talking about completely different things.

5. **Character goes off on tangents.** Have your character get distracted by another thought or conversation and start talking about something else. Character A says, "Juno never did like poodles." Character B replies, "I wonder if ghosts dream."

6. **Character doesn't say what he really means.** Avoid using "on the nose" dialogue, which means characters say what they really mean. Decide what your characters really mean to say, and then have them blurt out the opposite or something off the subject completely. Place the feelings of the characters beneath the surface of what they say (subtext).

Ezzie and her half-blind lightening bug cave guide keep having their important survival conversations interrupted by the bug accidentally flying into rock walls, dangerous crevices, and spider webs. These interruptions usually happen right before key information is about to be revealed by the bug, which helps create more suspense. Having the lightening bug bump into things throughout the story also foreshadows his death later, when he flies into the mouth of a hungry snake.

creativity tip

Are You an Actor Looking for Your Big Break? Some actors these days are making original short films that showcase their other talents as storytellers and directors. Billy Bob Thornton wrote and directed *Some Folks Call It a Slingblade* after his acting career failed to take off. The short was so successful he was given a big budget to turn the idea into a feature, and now makes big feature films.

Vin Diesel is another actor who got his break by making a short, *Multifacial*. This interesting short film is good to study for dialogue. Vin plays an actor going around New York City to a series of auditions requiring mindsets from black hood, to rapper, to soul musician, to Puerto Rican family man. What short film ideas would be perfect to showcase your acting abilities?

7. **Characters interrupt each other.** Create sentence fragments, which allow characters to cut each other off mid-sentence or to finish sentences for each other.

8. **Character speaks differently around different people.** Bring out your character traits by revealing different sides when faced with different people. How do you talk to your mother differently than to your best friend?

9. **Character dialogue is interrupted.** Another character walks into the room, a bell goes off, the phone rings, or the door slams.

10. **Characters who know each other really well use chaotic dialogue.** When you talk to someone you know really well, you do not explain things as much. You can jump all over the place in a conversation quickly because the other one knows you well enough to keep up.

11. **Character uses short dialogue bites.** Keep dialogue under two screenplay-formatting lines for each character to avoid talking heads. Beginners tend to write their dialogues too long.

12. **Read dialogue out loud as you write.** If the lines are hard to say or sound awkward, keep rewriting.

13. **The first and last lines of dialogue in a film are very important.** Make sure the first and last lines of dialogue in your script are powerful and original.

"Be still when you have nothing to say; when genuine passion moves you, say what you've got to say and say it hot."
—D.H. Lawrence

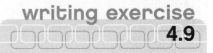

writing exercise 4.9

Write a conversation between two contrasting characters using as many of these dialogue techniques as possible.

project 4.12

Create a Dialogue Profile for Each Speaking Character. Review your five character traits and make sure you develop as many of these traits as possible in each line of dialogue. Use one index card for each character to create ways to construct a unique voice. After you write the first draft, you may want to go through every line of dialogue and see where you might be able to use some of the previously discussed techniques.

Top 10 Overused Cliché Dialogue Lines to Avoid in Your Script

1. Let's get out of here/Come on, let's go. (Just end the scene; don't use this tag!)
2. I'm too old for this _____.
3. I've got a bad feeling about this.
4. Trust me / Don't you trust me?
5. What do you want from me?
6. What do you mean? (Do a monologue.)
7. Why don't you pick on someone your own size?
8. It's nothing personal/This time it's personal.
9. Nothing is as it seems.
10. I've loved you from the first moment I saw you.

definition

Monologue. More than eight lines of uninterrupted verbal communication in a screenplay.

money-saving

Create Great Monologues and Attract Top Talent. A big part of Quentin Tarantino's success relates to his ability to write brilliant monologues that top stars are eager to perform in his films. *Pulp Fiction* has a classic scene with Christopher Walken as a solider telling the Bruce Willis as a little boy character about how much his father's watch has been through to end up in his hands. This monologue was a brilliant way to get us to quickly understand why Bruce Willis's boxer character is about to risk his life to retrieve the watch. The better your monologues, the better the money and people attracted to helping you make great films.

Rugaro the witchdoctor delivers a scathing monolouge to Ezzie after she gets caught on video stealing chocolate from the campers. He outlines all of her past transgressions, including her being related to the famous Bigfoot caught on video back in 1967 by Robert Patterson. Rugaro is worried that many hunters will now come into their area of the forest and cause much trouble for the Bigfoot tribe.

Utilizing Monologues

Monologues are cheap to shoot and can convey large amounts of story information, while showcasing good actors and dialogue when done well. Monologues are often used to compress time or space in a film or to save money.

Monologues are the most personal form of communication, with an audience, to convey a message or theme. *Some Folks Call It a Sling Blade* has a chilling monologue in which we hear Carl tell us why he hacked his mother and her friend up with a sling blade when he was a teenager. This really helps us to understand his character. It is subjective enough for the audience members to make their own decisions about how something this gruesome could occur.

Monologue Checklist

Keep in mind the following guidelines for creating strong monologues:

1. Does it build character, forward plot, and relate to the theme?
2. Is the monologue properly motivated with a good reason to do it?
3. Does it contain a unique voice, dialect, or word choices?
4. Is it around half of a script page and no more than a page and a half in screenplay format?
5. Is the character or plot revealed in ways impossible by any other means?

"If you can talk brilliantly about a problem, it can create the consoling illusion that it has been mastered."
—*Stanley Kubrick*

You have five types of monologues from which to choose:

1. **Soliloquy.** A soliloquy is a direct address in a convincing tone to the audience to convey inner feelings. A good soliloquy occurs at the beginning of *High Fidelity*; the movie beings with the camera on back of a character's head while the character is saying, "Am I miserable because I listen to pop music?" He then rattles off a list of songs to show how depressing they can sound. He is speaking to the audience outside the diegetic film world, breaking what is known as the fourth wall. Crazy people talking to themselves also qualify as soliloquy material.

2. **Expositional (explains).** Expositional refers to information that affects plot. This could be all you need to know about story facts. The opening monologue of *Mission Impossible 2*, when Tom Cruise's character gets his assignment through the exploding glasses, explains the whole plot. You might also have one of these at the end, where a character explains how he feels about everything that has happened.

3. **Metaphoric.** Metaphoric monologues communicate theme while looking inside the landscape of the human heart or brain. You cannot always see desperation, depression, or rage. Sometimes you need to have the character verbalize a feeling to get to the current scene emotion. The *Crying Game* frog and scorpion fable is a good example of using a metaphoric story to convey theme and emotion.

What original ways could you use some of your digital tools to show us how the character feels while he talks? You could fly into the character's eyes, mind, or heart using 3D or 2D animation with a metaphoric monologue voiceover.

4. **Anecdotal.** Anecdotal monologues reveal information about the characters. In *Eyes Wide Shut*, Nicole Kidman tells Tom Cruise about the overwhelming passion (theme) she once felt for this sailor in a hotel lobby. This monologue is the heart of the film and explains what motivates Tom's character's reaction (getting a little wild that night).

5. **Dueling/variations.** This is similar to dialogue, but people speak for a long time. These can be directed at supporting each other or in counterpoint:

   • **Supporting.** One character picks up where another character leaves off, with the same types of conclusions that support the other's views. Each character needs to have his own "voice"—that is, different grammar and vocabulary— but the characters need to tell the same story together. Characters may be in different locations or time.

   • **Counterpoint.** No cause and effect here, just two separate conclusions drawn from each opposing side. Legal movies with two sides exchanging plot are counterpoint, as are presidential debates.

In the movie *Swingers*, an answering machine monologue features a series of nine messages left on a potential girlfriend's answering machine. She comes home and plays all the messages, which get increasingly desperate. This is a monologue in a very original form. She picks up the phone at the end of it, after getting all of them at once, and tells him never to call again. What new way could you create a monologue that doesn't look like one we have already seen in a film? Watch for different approaches in the films you see and record any good ideas in your drawing book for possible future use.

In one of my other Bigfoot stories, Ezzie delivers a monologue to Izzy while cutting off all of his hair. She explains she is torturing him as revenge for her dead friend that she thinks Izzy killed.

"There's no right way of writing. There's only your way."

—Milton Lomask

Monologue Approaches

You may also choose to have a character not in the shot deliver a monologue.

The powers of storytelling are really revealed in monologues. The strongest ones combine techniques doing everything from expositional, presence, absence, OS, VO, and other fresh approaches. *Reservoir Dogs* uses all the previously discussed types of monologue, and they are part of what makes it such an original crime film and a great one to study.

definition

Offscreen (OS) The character is not present in the scene, but we hear her talking, and she can affect events.

Voiceover (VO) A character talks over a scene. We do not see his lips move as he talks over the scene, and he can even be in the scene, but outside of the film world commenting on what is happening. Maybe your character does not want the person in the room to hear what he is really thinking, but does want the audience to know.

"It is not because things are difficult that we do not dare; it is because we do not dare that they are difficult."

—Seneca

Writing a Short Script

Visuals and action must carry your story more than dialogue in a film, adhering to the old "show, don't tell" rule. Great visual storytelling requires you to make each scene as emotionally powerful as an award-winning photograph that moves you. Every frame should be brilliant to look at in some way. Filmmakers are like painters, using images, light, and color to communicate, but they also get to use sound and movement on the screen. You want to fill your script with peak visual metaphorical moments whenever possible. Most of our lives would not look very good onscreen. Occasionally, however, we look around us and notice we are standing in a postcard setting with the perfect light and composition. Your job as a screenwriter is to create powerful images that communicate your story. When writing your script, keep the following in mind:

1. **Describe everything seen and heard on the screen.** Imagine the movie playing in your head, while describing what you see and hear on the screen, using the fewest, most descriptive words possible.

2. **Use present tense.** Screenplays are written in the present tense happening in the visual "now."

3. **Eliminate all forms of the verb "to be."** *Is, are, he is, they are*, and *there is* make your writing sound weak. Do not write sentences such as this: There is a big dog in the car. Instead, write like Hemingway, simple but beautifully visual, causing

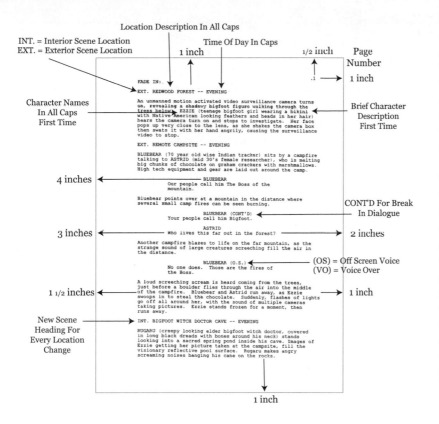

Location Description In All Caps

INT. = Interior Scene Location
EXT. = Exterior Scene Location

Time Of Day In Caps

1 inch   1/2 inch   Page Number

1 inch

Character Names In All Caps First Time

Brief Character Description First Time

4 inches

3 inches   2 inches

CONT'D For Break In Dialogue

(OS) = Off Screen Voice
(VO) = Voice Over

1 1/2 inches   1 inch

New Scene Heading For Every Location Change

1 inch

Master Screenplay Format. Notice the margins and the way different elements are capitalized and spaced on the page. You need to understand screenplay formatting to write one without a computer. Use a screenwriting program, such as Final Draft or Movie Magic, to do the formatting for you, after you understand the structure. Character names are in all caps above dialogue. The first line of each scene location is in all caps with time of day. The first time you introduce a character, type his or her name in all caps and give a brief description of the character in parentheses. Use a CONTINUED at the bottom of the page if the scene is cut off in the middle or when a character's dialogue is interrupted by a scene description. OS stands for offscreen, meaning the character is talking but is not in view. VO stands for voiceover, which means the character is talking over the shot and may not even be present in the scene.

us to *see* the scene easily without any flowery writing. For instance: A big scary Rottweiller guards the beat-up white 57 Cadillac next to the airplane junkyard. Get the color and flavor of the image in as few words as possible.

4. **Eliminate all metaphors that cannot be seen or heard.** Screenwriting is not poetry. Do not write lines like, "as if the sunset were bleeding sadness." How would you communicate that onscreen? You can say, "The door slams like a gunshot," however, because you could replace the sound of the door closing with a gunshot sound to add subconscious tension, which works great in films.

5. **Do not use "we see" or "we hear an explosion."** There is no "we" in a script. Write it straight like you are describing what the audience sees and hears on the screen as you roll the film through your mind. "The haunted house on the hill explodes."

6. **Never include camera shots or editing notes in a script.** They are distracting and not the place for such information. If you want a close-up of a character's eye, try something like "Neil's pupil dilates as the crash occurs." This forces the reader of your script to see Neil's eye up close. You may not be able to concentrate on writing the script if you are too busy planning and directing each shot at the same time.

note

Movie Magic Screenwriter. A Mac and PC version of this software is included on the CD and does all the formatting automatically for scripts up to 40 pages. This is a fully enabled student version of the software that will print out a watermark on each page. A PDF Quickstart guide (moviemagic.doc) is included to help you get started with using the software. As you type your script, you can usually make formatting choices by just pressing the Enter, Tab, a first-letter key for pop up menu choice, and arrow keys. I choose Movie Magic Screenwriter for the CD because it is one of the only companies that offers free versions of its software for short scripts that do not time out or expire.

project 4.14

Read a Script. If you have never read a film script, you will have a much harder time writing one. Read at least the first five pages of an online script to get an idea of how they sound and how the format works. There are also some sample short scripts on the accompanying CD.

"When writing, don't criticize the words coming out. Just let them come."
—Joseph Campbell

Read Some Scripts

How many scripts have you read? You need to be reading other people's screenplays to get a sense of the writing style. You would not try to write a novel or a poem without reading one first. Order scripts that are in the same genre or similar to your project to see how they visually juggle plot, theme, and character. Call Script City at (800) 676-2522 or contact them online at **www.scriptcity.com**. They have a great selection of TV and animation scripts, too, and they cost from $15 to $20 each. Local theater or drama bookstores also sell scripts. A great way to study films is to order the shooting script, and then rent the film and pick apart the choices and changes that the director made.

There are also lots of free screenplays posted on the web. Do a search for your favorite movies and see what comes up. You don't have to read the whole thing; just read enough until you get the hang of the way they sound.

project 4.15

Write Your Script. Begin by comparing the treatment you wrote at the end of Chapter 3 to your new piles of index cards that are full of multiple scene ideas. Go through the other chapter projects and add any ideas you think might work well to an index card and place the card in the pile for that scene. When you sit down to write your first scene, go through all the index cards you have been generating and choose the best ideas. Switch the order of the final plot points around with the index cards after you get a really good feel for what each scene is about. For example, it might be more interesting to have your last scene first, with the character trying to remember something that has happened or some other unique plot approach. If the ideas have shifted dramatically, you may also want to rewrite your treatment at some point to keep your script on track.

Register Your Script

Register all feature-length screenplays with the Writers Guild of America (WGA) West, (323) 782-4540 (**www.wga.org**). You can register online or mail them your script and a check for $20. Then they mail you a script-registration slip.

This legally protects you if your ideas show up in someone else's movie. You should register your short film scripts if you are worried about any problems. Mostly this is necessary if you are sending your scripts out or reading them to other people who might be tempted to borrow. You should also register feature-length treatments and any major script revisions.

Getting Feedback from Others

After you have finished your script, making it the best you possibly can, and have registered it, you will want feedback from others. Screenplays are not meant to be read, but to be read *aloud*. Here are some guidelines to keep things constructive during group readings:

1. Have people tell you what they liked best about your script first, before they mention anything that might need work.

2. When giving feedback on someone else's script, be gentle. Do not use sweeping general statements such as, "This is the worst thing I've ever heard." Try, "I don't quite understand why your character Travis refuses to talk to anyone during his interview for his new job." Gear criticism toward what confuses you, rings false, or seems like something that would bug you if you were watching the film.

3. When presenting a new script, do not start off by listing a long series of disclaimers about why it's not quite there yet. Fake confidence; otherwise people will focus on the negative points you presented earlier.

4. Love hearing your work read out loud by others so that you can learn how to make it better and know your own strengths and weaknesses.

5. Ask what needs to happen to make the script ready to shoot, and make the needed revisions.

6. Ask for any suggestions of scripts of films that are similar to your story that you might be able to read for more ideas.

> *"Artists who seek perfection in everything are those that cannot attain it in anything."*
> —Eugene Delacroix

> *"Nothing you write, if you hope to be any good, will ever come out as you first hoped."*
> —Lillian Hellman

superfreak!

Form a Screenwriting Group. Keep it to fewer than 8 people. Meet once a week, and takes turns reading 10 screenplay pages from each person. Give constructive feedback for each script. This should be around 3 hours total, depending on how many people are in the group. Have someone keep track of the time limits for each person. Plan for each person to come each week with enough copies of his or her pages to hand a set out to readers. For homework, take the scripts home and make comments on each other's pages to hand back at the next session. Practice pitching ideas, too. Make it fun by meeting at a good cafe or at someone's house. Usually people who write in screenwriting groups have less trouble staying motivated than those who write all alone.

project 4.16

Get Some Feedback on Your Script. Read it to someone or have a few people read it out loud playing different parts for narrator and characters. You might also want to read your script into a tape recorder to see how it sounds first.

group project

Get Some Feedback on Your Script from a Group. Choose one person to be the narrator and one person for each character. It is best if the author can just listen, but the author may read a part if not enough people are available.

"Dullness is a misdemeanor."
—*Ethel Wilson*

"You have to be reckless when writing. Be as crazy as your conscience allows."
—*Joseph Campbell*

Save Time for Rewrites. Keep in mind that 90 percent of screenwriting is *rewriting*. Most Hollywood scripts are rewritten from scratch about 20 times before they are ready for production. One way to approach a rewrite is to go through your script focusing on specific techniques discussed in Chapters 1 through 4. You might do a rewrite pass just focusing on using metaphors or developing more sub-text in each scene. After you get a bunch of new ideas, you may want to do a fresh rewrite from top to bottom and see what happens. Keep doing this until it feels ready to shoot and gets good feedback.

project
4.17

Read Your Script Aloud. Do this in a small group of people, into a tape recorder, or just to yourself. See whether you can tell which parts work and which you need to fix.

Scripts Are Written to Be Read Aloud

After writing your script, you will want to read it out loud to see how the dialogue sounds. Ideally, it works best to have other people read your characters while you listen. If you are the only one around for a test run, you may want to record the script into a tape recorder. The first time you do this, you may want to read it straight and flat just to see what holds up. The second time, you may want to put more emotion into each character's lines. You will hear dialogue that works and lines that do not sound true, which will need to be fixed.

Screenwriting Exercises

The following scriptwriting exercises are good to use for practicing the techniques in these first four chapters. All of these situations take place in one location in continuous time (no flashbacks or time jumps). They should be written by hand in screenplay format and be exactly five pages in length. Create full closure for each one, meaning we know at the end who does what to whom. You may want to give yourself 1 hour for each one to see what comes up. These are great in-class exercises to do each week or in a screenwriting group. You write differently under time pressures with lots of limitations. Sample scripts are on the accompanying CD for "The Jumper" and "The Pusher."

1. **The Jumper.** Character A wants to jump from a very high place. Character B wants to stop Character A. We need to know whether Character A jumps by the end. One turn of events in the middle. (jumper.doc)
2. **The Secret.** Character A has a secret. Character B wants to make Character A confess, but the secret is not the one Character B thinks it is. Play with subtext with regard to what Character B thinks and wants to know.
3. **The Pusher.** Character A wants to push Character B in a direction that Character B does not want to go. Character A has a hidden agenda that Character B does not know about. (pusher.doc)
4. **The Package.** Character A gives a package to Character B. Character C is trying to intercept it. Who gets the package and why?
5. **Significant Other.** Character A brings Character B to meet two loved ones. Each character has a hidden agenda (goal) during the meeting. Who gets accepted and why?
6. **The Invitation.** Character A wants to join an exclusive group that Character B is in. There are three judges who approve whether Character A can join. Character B is not one of the judges. Does Character A get into the group? Can be up to 10 pages.

Final Short Script Checklist

1. Have you made your story as visual as possible?
2. Do you have colorful locations, unique situations, and original characters?
3. Do the main characters have clear goals with challenging obstacles in each scene?
4. Is the action (moments without dialogue) unique? Does the action have credible motivations and achieve clear goals?
5. Do twists and surprises in the plot keep the audience guessing as to what will happen next?
6. Are there any nonessential characters? Take them out.
7. Are there any holes in the story?
8. Do any of the characters have false motivations?
9. Has this script received good feedback that says it is ready to go into production?
10. Is the story confusing, or not straightforward enough? Simplify the plot.
11. Does the story lack depth or meaning? Develop your scene subtext and theme more.
12. Is the story uninvolving? If so, develop characters and strengthen relationships between the protagonist and the antagonist.
13. Is the story is too claustrophobic? Add characters.

"It is only when I am doing my work that I feel truly alive."
—Federico Fellini

superfreak!

Write a Script for Each of the Preceding Ideas. Give yourself 45 minutes from start to finish just to see what comes up. Keep them to five pages exactly to see whether you can nail the story in a given amount of time. You can write it out on paper following a rough screenplay format and type it out later if that is easier.

project

4.18

Answer the Script Checklist Questions. Being as honest as possible, answer the preceding 13 questions in your drawing book. Make your script the best you can before going on to Part 2. Make sure to do a final round of feedback from others before going into production.

group project

Write a Script for Each of the Screenwriting Exercises Each Week. Choose one of the exercises in this chapter or make up your own.

Tips for Approaching Screenwriting Exercises

A good way to approach the preceding exercises is to make a list of possibilities for the key elements. For "The Jumper," I first made a list of interesting places for a character to jump off of that would look good cinematically. Then I made a list of possible twists that could happen in this type of situation and a list of possible characters for both Character A and Character B.

I came up with a Bigfoot girl thinking about jumping into a bottomless pit and talking to a spirit of the Bigfoot goddess (jumper.doc). They both jump in the middle and end up falling at the end while still talking.

Places to Jump Off	Midpoint Twist	Possible End Twists	Character A	Character B
Golden Gate Bridge	A beats B up.	Lands in a convertible	Distressed holy man	Another jumper
Sphinx	They both jump.	Jumps by mistake	Teenage Bigfoot girl	Ghost
Lip of bottomless pit	A jumps.	Saves other from jumping	A dog	Goddess spirit
Half dome	B jumps.	Still falling	Sad child	Bird
Spaceship door	B ties up A.	Drags B down, too	Unemployed clown	Statue

Visualizing Your Script

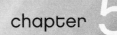

chapter 5

Shot Visualization

"Vision is the art of seeing things invisible."
—Jonathan Swift

Making a great script come to life on the screen is a joyful experience. If you followed the techniques in Part I, you should have a very visual story ready to break into shots. The script you wrote may change quite a bit as you go through the exercises in the rest of this book. You may want to do a complete rewrite, incorporating new ideas for telling your story more visually and digitally, after you finish the book. Complete the exercises as you go through the following chapters based on the script you just wrote in Part I. Feature-film scripts and their final movie versions often differ dramatically based on the visual storytelling decisions made during preproduction and production. Ideally, you would be thinking of all your visual storytelling techniques when you sit down to write an initial script and then you would develop the ideas even further visually on the screen during preproduction and production.

Scary Monster Underwater POV! What new ways could use a camera POV shot to help the audience really get into the emotional mindset of your characters? In this example, a subterranean monster lurks just below the surface of the ocean. The camera shot at water level gives viewers the uneasy feeling that at any moment the monster could swim up from under the water and attack. You could use this POV technique to communicate the theme and emotion of fear. These types of visual shooting styles need to be planned in advance to make your shots work well as a whole. How could you design a new form of scary monster for your stories using your digital tools? Maybe the monster's eyes spit dangerous particle trails, or perhaps the monster can morph into different shapes to hide.

Each script's design process differs depending on the story, the people working on it, and the technology involved. Experiment with the ideas in these next four chapters to see what types of approaches you could take with developing your film.

Producing the Final Storyboards

The steps outlined here are just some suggestions you may want to try while developing your script. These may be done in a different order, or you may develop your own approach to creating final storyboards.

Steps for developing a digital short film include the following:

1. Write a script (Part I).
2. Determine the organizational structure of the film (Chapter 5).
3. Create a line script (Chapter 5).
4. Create a rough shot list (Chapter 5).
5. Design the basic composition of main shots (Chapter 5).
6. Draw rough storyboards, blocking out each shot (Chapter 5).
7. Create a unique visual style for the individual segments and the entire film (Chapter 6).
8. Adjust character posing techniques, actions, and gestures (Chapter 6).
9. Decide on a color palette and color map (Chapter 6).
10. Develop a narrative sound and lighting design strategy (Chapter 7).
11. Consider new narrative approaches for editing scenes and images together (Chapter 8).
12. Incorporate new visual ideas into final color storyboards.
13. Plan digital special effects, animation, and shot layers (Part III).
14. Create an animatic (Chapter 5).

This chapter covers Steps 1 through 5, to break down your script visually and compose a set of rough storyboards for each shot.

Reread the Script

Many times what you thought your script was saying differs from what ends up in the final version. It helps to sit down and read the script a few times to get a solid handle on the story. Recheck your theme to make sure it is the one you started with, or see whether the script has a different one now and make any necessary adjustments.

Creating an Animatic

To produce a slideshow test of your film idea, follow these steps:

1. Scan your final storyboards. Name each shot with its number and a brief description of what happens, such as 001vidcam.psd. This type of naming style will help keep the files in order when you go to drag and drop them into your editing timeline.
2. Create a rough soundtrack of any dialogue or important sound effects. You could just say the lines into your DV camera, and then cut the dialogue up in your editing program to match the storyboard shots.

3. Import the scanned images and soundtrack into your editing program or After Effects. Time each drawing to hold on the screen for the same amount of time as your estimated final shot length.

   This produces a slideshow version of your film and gives you a very good idea of what parts might need more developing.
4. Drop in final shots as you finish them, over the storyboard drawings, to watch the film take shape during production.

project 5.1

Reread Script. Take out your final script from Part I and read it over again a few times (3–5) to get a deeper feel for the story.

Determining the Organizational Structure

All the structural design you just put into writing your script can now be broken down into main events, sections, and emotional changes or arcs. During key moments you will adjust lighting, camera angles, sound, backgrounds, shot length, and anything else that helps the audience really understand the emotional shifts going on in the story.

What ways can you see to break your story up into blocks of shots (sequences) or groups of shots (scenes)? Is there a clear organizational structure to your story? Is the story a set of locations, categories, associations, arguments, or slow series of backward reveals? What main events happen in each sequence? What emotional flavors do each event produce? You need to grasp the logic of the structure, events, and emotions in your film, which should be fairly easy to do if you wrote the script. This enables you to design each scene visually in a unique way, to fit the whole story.

Usually films break down into sequences by locations. My example story can be organized into five sequences, as shown in the images on the right. The first scenes take place in the forest with the unmanned video surveillance camera and at the campsite with the Indian and female Bigfoot researchers. The second sequence takes place in the mean witchdoctor's cave, when Ezzie gets banished from the tribe and sent on an impossible vision quest. The third sequence starts when she enters the dangerous vision quest caves. The fourth part is her Shamanic journey. The fifth

"The thing always happens that you really believe in; and the belief in a thing makes it happen."
—Frank Lloyd Wright

Terms Used to Deconstruct Scripts

Acts. Series of sequences grouped into three acts forming the beginning, middle, and end of the story.

Sequences. Series of two to five scenes that climax in a big shift for the characters. One sequence could be a whole act or even the entire film for a short film.

Scenes. Collection of story events that may be divided by location or time segment. One scene every 2 minutes is the norm.

Events. Meaningful experience that changes a character's life. Universal experiences may change from negative to positive and back again (truth/lie, life/death, loyalty/disloyalty, love/hate, victory/loss, strong/weak, right/wrong, good/bad, hope/despair). An event usually occurs through conflict, not coincidence.

Beats/Moments. Smallest exchanges of behaviors with a action/reaction cycle between the characters. The characters' emotions and motivations often shift slightly from beat to beat.

project 5.2

Find the Structure/Events/Emotional Arc of Your Film. Create a rough list of the main sequences, scenes, events, and emotional changes in your film. Determine the emotional arc of your main character or story.

"I shut my eyes in order to see."
—Paul Gauguin

"Start by doing what's necessary, then what's possible and suddenly you are doing the impossible."
—Saint Francis of Assisi

sequence is the resolution, when she leaves the caves and rejoins the tribe with her new powers.

Usually sequences happen between major plot points with one or two big events. Scenes break when you have a new location, different style change, or an event that breaks the emotions into another space. A sequence usually contains two to five scenes. A scene usually has lots of separate camera shots, depending on the length of the film. Even a short film is a collection of mini-scenes that need to be separated to treat each of them differently visually. If it is a heavy, violent scene, you might make it really dark with red lights and fast cuts. A play-

ful scene may include soft pastel shapes and long, relaxing camera shots.

What is the emotional arc of your film? Each time a big event happens to the characters, the emotions usually shift based on their reactions. List the main events and emotional mood changes for the story to determine the emotional arc. Your character may start out impulsive and oblivious, then move through many different emotions in the story to become grounded and wise at the end. This change would be the main emotional arc of the film, with little emotional changes happening in each scene or sequence.

101 Camera Shots for Storyboarding

This section presents some shot ideas to keep in mind when visualizing your film. You may want to consider where you could use each shot in your film to discover which ones communicate the story best, evoke the most emotion, and create nail-biting suspense. Not all the following terms are "official" camera shots, but you still need to consider them as storyboarding possibilities. The image accompanying each shot shows how to draw it or gives

information about how the camera moves during the shot. The emotions listed for each shot are just my opinions, to give you an idea of how you might think about emotions and shots. I invite you to record your own ideas next to mine in the book (if it's *your* book) or in your drawing book. Add any new camera shots, or ones I've missed, from movies you see, along with the emotional impact you experienced when you saw the shot.

project 5.3

Visualize 101 Possible Shots. As you read through the following list of camera shots, imagine ways to use each one somewhere in your film. Create rough sketches of any shots that you think may work really well to tell your story. Expand your story when necessary to imagine shots that do not fit, such as adding an extra character for a three-character shot if your film only has two characters. This is just an exercise to help you think of ways to use shots you may not have considered before.

superfreak!

Sketch 101 Possible Shots. Go through the following list and make a rough sketch of each shot idea to possibly use somewhere in your film. This is just an exercise. You may want to draw each sketch on a 3×5-inch index card and lay the cards out in order on the floor to see what comes up. Arrange shots in chronological order, and then play with changing the order.

Storyboard	Camera Shot Name	Description	Emotions, Psychology, Ideas
Basic Shots			
	360-degree arc shot	Moving camera circles all the way around the subject at a strange angle.	Under a moving microscope attention. Full awareness of subject. Off-balanced interviews/interrogations.
	*Aerial shot (AS)	Extreme high-angle view. A shot from above, usually very high up. Airplane or helicopter POV.	Expansive, overview, coming into a world/flying out of a story.
	Angle on	Object shot at an angle rather than straight on.	Another view, important; study this image.
	Another angle	Shot from another angle different from the previous angle.	Look at this differently, from another POV. Different sides to the same subject.
	Arc shot	Moving camera circles around subject rather than a straight line. Objects appear more solid and 3D. Adds depth.	Examining. Strange arc creates attention grabbing shot movement.
	Bank shot	Camera moving on a-crane-type motion in a circular orbit.	Great view, Wow! shot. Mechanically perfect movement, expensive.

Note: The asterisk next to a camera shot indicates that the section "Digitally Enhanced Camera Shots" in Chapter 9, "Digitally Enhanced Storytelling Techniques," explains how to create this shot digitally.

continues

continued

Storyboard	Camera Shot Name	Description	Emotions, Psychology, Ideas
	Car mount; Bike mount	Shot from moving car. May also be from bicycle, motorcycle, skateboard, scooter, or 3D flying surfboard.	Scenic traveling through space or world. Heavy conflict if moving through and area full of aggression.
	CGI (computer generated image)	3D or 2D image, may be animated to look like part of the scene.	New thing never seen before, fascination.
	Close-up (CU)	A shot from the neck up of a person or character. May also be a CU of a body part or subject.	Intimate, having access to the mind. Good for suspense (hand picking up a knife).
	Crane shot	Using a crane-type device to travel high above or over different subjects.	Great view, God POV, precarious, high above things, overview, flying, higher world.
	Cross cutting	Intermingling two or more scenes.	Opposites/contrast, parallel stories. to suggest parallel action.
	Cutaway	Shot inserted into a scene that interrupts the flow of action. May show action in another part of a location. Brief. Used to cover breaks or problems in the primary shot or introduce a new important detail.	Another event/subject in the same location. Look over here, break, another thing happening, tension/release, cause and effect.

Storyboard	Camera Shot Name	Description	Emotions, Psychology, Ideas
	Dolly in/out; Camera up/back; Dolly up/back	Horizontal movement along the lens axis of the entire camera with a dolly-type device. Rolls into subjects and back out.	Moving through space. Use wheelchairs, skateboards, wheelbarrows, rollerblades, scooters, bicycles, cars.
	*Double exposure	Two images exposed on top of each other. Easy to do with DV.	Simultaneous, complementary, juxtaposition, artsy, thinking two things at once, daydreams, inner thoughts, abstract.
	*Dream POV	Wavy, dreamy image of subconscious; could be montage.	Dreamy, out of this world, hallucination, stream of consciousness, strange space and time-warping effects.
	Dutch angle; Canted frame	Strange camera angle that is not parallel to the horizon. Weird tilting of the subject in the camera frame.	Strange, disorder, mayhem, off-center, off-balance, funky.
	Dynamic cutting	Fast series of unrelated shots or story tangents (objects, people, details). Form of montage.	Side story, theme metaphors, visual symbols, mini subplots.
	Establishing shot (ES)	Shows overall location, mood of and placement of objects in the scene.	Overview, orientation, wide long shot, place locator. Distinct mood for the scene.
	Extreme close-up (XCU); Detail shot	Just the lips or eyes or any really tight close shot.	Very intimate, claustrophobic, surreal closeness.

continued

Storyboard	Camera Shot Name	Description	Emotions, Psychology, Ideas
	Extreme long shot (ELS)	A subject with some background and lots of far-off scenery.	Small person in big world, expansive, establishing mood of film world.
	Eye-line match cut	First shot is a person looking at an object up and to the left. Cut to the object in the upper-left half of screen.	Looking at subject offscreen.
	Falling POV	Show what a character sees when he falls down or jumps out of an airplane.	Creative falling POV.
	Flash cut	Extremely brief shot that may only be one frame. Subliminal effect. May also be a series of short staccato shots that form a rhythmic effect.	Subliminal. Creates extreme tension by not showing the viewer enough, drawing them into the scene.
	Fly into subject	Camera appears to fly into or inside a subject. Great for fresh POV using digital effects.	Inner thoughts. Fly into the character's eye as if going into the brain to see thoughts. Could also fly into objects such as a rug to search for microscopic clues.
	Flying	Camera appears to be sailing through the air.	Flying, falling, gliding, freedom to move like a bird.

Storyboard	Camera Shot Name	Description	Emotions, Psychology, Ideas
	Follow shot (FS)	Moving shot that follows a subject through a space.	Shows subject's relationship to film world. Journey, chase scenes, investigation, discovery, conflict with world, obstacle courses, battles, one against many, one of many. Dreamy when slowed down.
	*Freeze frame	Single frame repeated or held to imply freezing of-action. Good for funny takes and freeze-frame endings.	Funny frame or moment, important moment, mistake, decision, reaction. Frozen in time memory.
	*Graphic mask (Vignette)	Viewer sees scene through cutout matte layer. Graphical image placed over shot to suggest POV. Binoculars, gun sight target, keyhole, space visor.	Voyeuristic, spying, tension with target, magnified, observer, position of power.
	Group shot (GS)	A group of people or characters in one shot.	Relationships, families, situation illustrated by arrangements, strong individual emotions within group.
	*Handheld, handicam	Handheld camera usually with lots of jarring motions.	Jarring, disorienting, chase POV, amateur shooting style.
	High hat	Very low camera angle, about a hat height off the ground.	Dug's perspective, vulnerable, looking up at the supreme authority subject.
	Intercut	Two scenes occur simultaneously to form one sequence cut together. Shows parallel action or strong contrast.	Contrast between two simultaneous scenes.
	Insert	A close-up shot of an object that implies great importance, such as a lost key under a table.	Important, look at this, key to puzzle, new information, unknown element revealed.

continues

continued

Storyboard	Camera Shot Name	Description	Emotions, Psychology, Ideas
	Into frame	A new subject moves into the frame from offscreen without changing the shot.	Look at the new character or subject. Reveals new information. Who's this? What's this?
	Into view	The camera moves and reveals a new subject.	Revealing things we cannot see offscreen. Surprise.
	Iris in/out (Irising)	Old-fashion technique to show camera lens closing down, shaped like a circle.	Focus on this spot. Old focal-point technique.
	*Jump cut (JC)	Cut in the middle of a shot that seems to jump around the subject. May look like bad editing or be a style choice. Compresses time and action.	Less time onscreen than actually happening. Agitation, unsettling, intense, something's not right, off-balance, unnerving, different sides to the same story.
	Long shot (LS)	A subject with lots of background and some far-off scenery. All flaws in shot visible if not perfect.	Subject's place in the world. Establishing relationship between character and setting.
	Master shot; Cover shot	Shot that covers the whole scene completely. Framed to include all speaking characters and action. Usually a long shot.	Shows space and relationships of subjects placed in space.
	Medium close-up (MCU)	One to three characters from shoulders up.	Coming together of intimacy or solidarity.

Storyboard	Camera Shot Name	Description	Emotions, Psychology, Ideas
	Medium shot (MS)	A shot taken from the waist up on a person or character.	Most common shot for a character.
	*Mind screen	POV from inside a character's mind, thoughts, daydreams, emotions, dreams, inner thoughts, meditations.	Inner thoughts. Fly into eye ECU. Cut to dreamy abstract version of inner thoughts.
	*Mirror/reflection shot	Big, highly reflective area in frame with its own subject and action occurring. Good way to combine shot/reverse shot in a single shot.	Reflecting on a memory or deep thought. Mirrors represent looking into ourselves.
	Montage (MON)	A series of shots used to build moods or provide information. French for "to assemble." Typical ones include passage of time shots with seasons changing around one tree (or calendar pages flipping).	Conflict, moods, metaphors, emotional flashes, realizations, sudden ideas; to reveal place, theme metaphors, time passing, traveling, intensity shattering inside square frame.
	Moving shot	Camera moves to follow a moving subject such as a bouncing ball.	Movement rhythm of subject.
	*Multiple-image shot	DV makes it easy to show multiple shots in one frame. Arrange creatively to suggest relationships.	Relationship between two things. Contrast. Simultaneous time or space. Juxtaposition of ideas.
	Over the shoulder (OTS)	Looking over the shoulder of a character. Used to show where things are in relation to the character.	Space between two people during a conversation. Peeking over someone's shoulder.

continues

continued

Storyboard	Camera Shot Name	Description	Emotions, Psychology, Ideas
	Overhead (OH)/ bird's eye view	View of scene photographed from directly overhead.	Layout of space, depth, voyeuristic, surveillance camera, bird-in-a-tree POV.
	Pan; pan left to right; pan across; pan up	Camera rotates horizontally around its base without any dolly movement.	Good for following actions and lines in space. Scanning space.
	*Pause or beat	Reflective shot to let film breathe. Usually lasts for at least 10 seconds.	Moment to absorb, reflect, contemplate, catch breath.
	Pedestal up/down	Camera going up and down along the vertical axis without tilting.	Slow reveal of a subject or object from feet to head or head to feet. Scanning emotion of body parts up to face.
	Point of view (POV)	What the character is seeing. Usually this character is not in the shot.	View from a character's eyes.
	Profile	Side view of the character.	Conflict, strong silhouette, character facing something on the other side of the screen.

Storyboard	Camera Shot Name	Description	Emotions, Psychology, Ideas
	Projection shot	Video projected on the subject or on a screen behind or beside subject.	Special effects shot, driving shot in still car with moving scenery projected on the screen behind the windows to look like a moving shot.
	Pull-back	Dolly or zoom effect that starts on a CU of an object and then widens to include more of the area around an object.	Object as it relates to surrounding space.
	Reaction shot	Shot of characters reacting emotionally to something that just occurred.	Reaction. *Big*, emotional moment.
	Retracking	Backward movement of a camera, usually on a dolly along the same path that was already covered in the same shot or previous scene.	Backtracking, pulling out, moving away, getting some distance.
	Reverse angle	The reverse of the previous shot angle.	Filling in the whole perspective. Other side of the scene.
	*Reverse motion	Run shot backward in post. (Falling objects reversed appear to be going up; things that break and then go back together.)	Review info. Look at something in a new way. Replay backward to examine how something happened. Turing back time
	Reverse POV (RPOV)	Reverses POV, usually used to show a character's reaction to the POV.	Reaction. Other side of camera perspective. Filling out space.
	Roll	Entire frame rotates around a single point in the frame. An angle change of camera-line sight axis.	Spinning, disorienting.

continues

continued

Storyboard	Camera Shot Name	Description	Emotions, Psychology, Ideas
	Sequence shot	Long traveling shot with carefully choreographed action and camera movement replacing the need for editing smaller shots in between.	Long complicated Wow! shot. Following subject through busy spaces. Continuous real-time feel. Opening shot in *Touch of Evil*, which used a crane.
	*Slideshow	Series of still images. *Run Lola Run* did this with the people she ran into in the street. (In a few photographs, you could tell what happened to them in the future.) Cheaper than creating moving montage images.	Time capsule, specific moments, photographs over time. Juxtaposition ideas between stills. Slideshow subplots or mini stories.
	*Slow motion (slo-mo)	Camera speed increased above the normal frame rate to give the impression of the action being slowed down.	Time slowing/stopping. Suspended state of animation.
	Smash zoom	Very fast zoom.	Crashing into subject, whoosh, traveling into the subject at high speed, impact.
	*Special effects	Added elements in shot. Lens flares, explosions, lightning bolts, disappearing objects, or 3D monsters.	Heightened reality.
	*Split screen	A frame with two or more shots occurring simultaneously, often divided by a line. The screen can be split diagonally, horizontally, vertically, or with an alpha channel shape mask for interesting effects.	Different scenes happening at the same time. Two people talking on the telephone is common for a split screen. Could also show different dimensions occurring at the same time.
	Static shot	Camera is locked down and does not move.	Normal, still and almost eerily slow because most cameras shots are moving now.

Storyboard	Camera Shot Name	Description	Emotions, Psychology, Ideas
	*Star filter (shaped filters)	Creates starburst pattern across the frame. Can be done in post. Any shape may be used.	Bursting into another dimension. Stars work well for perspective long-view traveling road shots.
	Steadicam	Camera suspended on a body harness for very smooth-moving shots.	Following, creeping after silently, gliding through area.
	Stock shot	Footage you buy from stock shops of shots you need but do not want to create or are unable to shoot yourself. Newsreel footage, aerial city scenes, microscopic scientific footage.	Skylines, aerial shots, elephants stampeding, historic events, faraway places, microscopic, time lapse, disasters, newsreel.
	Straight on	Camera looking at the subject from the front or back without any angle.	Flat, direct, mug shot.
	*Strobe	Digital slow-motion effect with action broken into still frames and updated or switched with new images at a rapid rate.	Unreal, broken scan of space, motion trails, dreamy, suspended slow time.
	Stunt cam	DV camera doing dangerous shots such as jumping out of airplanes or off buildings.	Wild POV.
	*Super-slow motion (Extreme)	Exaggerated slow motion that is even slower. Good for drawn-out, dramatic moments such as death scenes.	Time warped, slowed down, occurring out of normal space and time.
	Swish pan (whip pan, flick pan, whish pan, zip pan)	Rapid movement of the camera that blurs the frame to show what the eye sees when a head turns quickly.	Quick head turn POV, danger, alert, rush to see something.

continues

continued

Storyboard	Camera Shot Name	Description	Emotions, Psychology, Ideas
	Symbolic nature theme shot	Shots of animals, plants, subjects in surroundings, to suggest theme or plot.	Visual poetry. Cut to one bug eating another one during a fight scene between two characters.
	Take	Exaggerated animated look in which the character does an extreme reaction shot.	Strong character reaction, exaggerated humor, cartoon look.
	Three shot	Three characters in a scene arranged *symbolically* to show relationship. If it's a love triangle, make sure they form a triangle in the frame with a bed on fire between them or some other symbolic object.	Triangular relationships between three characters with symbolic placement and objects between them to represent the situation.
	Tilt up/down	Vertical rotation of the camera about the lens axis parallel to the scene.	Revealing height of subject. Head-tilt POV.
	*Time lapse	Super-slow or super-fast shot to show passing of time in a new way.	Time passing quickly/slowly. Flowers blooming in real time, clouds moving by at a rapid rate.
	*Titles/subtitiles/ super	Text or images laid over a frame on the screen. Credits, translation, location names, backstory text, animated graphics.	Text information, locations, dates, translation.
	Tracking shot	Shot that follows a character or an object moving through a scene. Can also be used to move away from or toward a stationary subject.	Follows subject.

Storyboard	Camera Shot Name	Description	Emotions, Psychology, Ideas
	*Truck left/right	Horizontal movement of the entire camera with a dolly-type device.	Seeing how a subject moves through the world. Car- or skateboard-following POV.
	Two-T shot	Shot from nipples up on a character.	Medium/close-up shot. More intimate than a medium shot but less intense than a close-up.
	Two shot	Two people or characters in one shot.	Relationship. Put something symbolic between.
	Zolly	Dolly in while zooming out or zoom in while dollying out. Background shifts focus, causing a strange warping zoom effect while foreground stays the same.	Unreal, distortion, something is not what it seems.
	*Zoom	Moving shot where lens moves inside the camera to change the focal length and field of view over time. Used to bridge shots. Usually ends on a CU.	Voyeurism. Picks subjects or objects out of a scene. Scanning scene for important parts.

continues

continued

Storyboard	Camera Shot Name	Description	Emotions, Psychology, Ideas
Transitional Shots			
	*Alpha mask	Many editing or effects programs give you the option of building animated custom transition shapes using alpha channel masks.	Symbolic shapes between two scenes.
	*Blackout/Whiteout	Immediate darkening or lightening of the screen that does not mean the end of the film.	Abrupt stop. Break. B/W color could mean symbolic states such as passing out (black) or dying (white). You could also go to any other color, too, such as blue.
	Bridging shot	Shot to cover jump in time or space. Maps with lines, railroad wheels, calendar pages.	Traveling between places. Jump in time.
	*Crossfade	Slow fade from one scene to another that takes place over a range of frames but always involves at least one black frame between the fades.	Slow transition to another space.
	Cut	Abrupt change from one shot to another in the course of one frame.	Next thing. Most common and best choice in general.
	*Dissolve	Slow fade from one scene to the next without any black frames in between.	Softer connection than cut between two shots. Second most common transition next to cut.

Storyboard	Camera Shot Name	Description	Emotions, Psychology, Ideas
	*Fade-in	Scene appears slowly from a black or colored screen. Most movies begin with a fade-in and end with a fade-out to black in the script.	Beginning of a new story. Soft transition to another place. Waking up.
	*Focus in/out	Incoming shot comes into focus, or outgoing shot goes out of focus.	Gaining or losing perspective. Dreamy shift in what is important to see.
	*Graphic match	Two visual shapes in two different scenes cut together. Lights, background paintings, shapes, color.	Wow! shot, parallel metaphor between scenes, juxtaposition, visual synchronicity.
	Match cut	A cut between two shots that have: 1) The same action in continuous motion, 2) Two shots of different subjects that share the same graphical elements in the same spot, or 3) Two or more shots of the same subject in the same position with continuous motion to show the passage of time.	General Wow! shot if you can work it in. May be used to show passage of time or to point out identity. An example is cutting from the shot of a ring on a girl's finger to the same ring worn around the neck of an old woman to show they are the same person in a different time.
	Match dissolve	Dissolve from one image to another that is similar in composition, shape, shot size, or appearance. Softer and slower than a match cut.	Wow! dissolve.
	*Natural wipe	Transition from one shot to another by having an element in the frame move across it, revealing a new image.	Wow! reveal. A truck driving by in full frame reveals a new UFO space shot underneath it as the truck moves by in the frame.

continues

continued

Storyboard	Camera Shot Name	Description	Emotions, Psychology, Ideas
	Shock cut (Smash cut)	Two scenes cut together that produce a shocking juxtaposition for the audience. Shot of kid's birthday party cut to shot of a slaughterhouse.	Shocking juxtaposition makes you look at something in a different way.
	*Slow Fade/Dissolve	Slower passage of time than normal fade/dissolve.	Time slowing down, reflective, dreamy.
	*Solarization	Scene fills with light.	Light burst, epiphany, awakening, spiritually enlightened moment.
	*Wipe	One scene pushes another scene off the screen either horizontally, vertically, in a spiral, or in any other manner.	Pushy new thing happening that's more important now.

"You can't try to do things; you simply must do them."
—*Ray Bradbury*

"Great things are not done by impulse, but by a series of small things brought together."
—*Vincent van Gogh*

Feel free to combine shots listed in the preceding table into one shot. Close-up and medium shots with several people are often called MED 2 shots or CU 3 shots.

Focal Lengths and Depths of Field to Consider

If you are able to play with any of the following techniques using your digital camera or animation software, you may want to include them when planning your shots now. The ones with stars next to them may be simulated in postproduction using digital tools.

How could you use a fish-eye distortion effect in one of your shots to create a sense of warping reality? Notice how the lines on the edges of the shot bend and bulge on the sides.

In-Camera Techniques	Description	Emotion, Psychology, Ideas
*Deep focus	Short focal length with small apertures to achieve focus in both foreground and background of great depth.	Great depth. Vivid detail.
*Fish-eye	Distorted circular bulge effect. Extreme wide-angle lens. Background warps, middle bulges out in a circle.	Disorientation, warped mental state, strange state of mind, or woozy emotions.
Long lenses	Makes action appear to be confined to smaller space. Things seem closer together. Minimize perspective.	Compresses space of action.
Medium focal length	More flattering to people's faces.	Flattering for portraits.
Microscopic	Small DV cameras that shoot magnified footage.	Microscopic POV.
*Rack focus	Changes focus from one subject to another in one shot.	This subject was important, but now look at this one.
*Shallow focus	Shallow depth of field used to isolate the subject from indistinct foreground or background. Subject is more in focus than the rest of the frame, which appears fuzzy.	Look at this subject, not the rest of the frame. Epiphany moments, isolation, subject feeling separation from film world.
Shutter speeds	Trails image of subject moving with slow shutter speeds.	Disorienting or dreamy quality.
*Split diopter	Allows for two separate areas of focus in frame. CU lens attached to lens-like filter.	Two subjects important. In postproduction, you can use two layers of video, blurring the bottom one and then cutting out masks in the top one for important areas in focus.
Telephoto	Graphical flattening of the image. Eliminates depth while emphasizing scene width.	Flattens and widens. Lateral tracking shots to create tension between subjects standing a few feet apart.
Wide angle	Shooting in tight spaces. Shows characters symbolically in their environments. Gives a deep focus effect when lots of depth in shot.	Depth distortion when used for CU.
*Zoom	See entry in camera shots.	Can also zoom into a still photo scanned at high resolution.

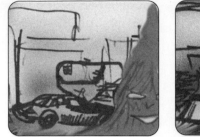

Digitally Enhanced Stunt Shots. Do you have any dangerous stunt shots in your film? This overhead shot has a character getting run over by a truck. You could blue screen the characters for this sort of stunt shot, and then reveal them using separate layers of a truck driving by in postproduction. How could you use some of your digital tools to create exciting stunts while keeping your actors safe?

Combining Camera Shots. A zolly shot is a combination of a dolly out and zoom-in shot, where the camera is moving away from the subject, while the lens is zooming in. This keeps the characters in the foreground the same, but warps the background in a really weird way, causing a "something is not what it seems" feel to the shot. Two characters could be discussing something that is not what it seems. A very slow zolly shot may amplify the emotions of the situation visually by making the objects behind the characters appear to be closing in, while the characters stay in the same position in the foreground. What other shots could you combine to get new ones? Make sure the idea behind your new camera shot fits the story subject of the shot.

---

movie note

Slow Shutter Speed, Blurry, Trailing Look. *The Book of Life* is a great DV film to study for its use of innovative DV shooting techniques. Slow shutter speeds (under 1/25) are used throughout the film, giving it a unique look. A dreamy, lush film world is created to match the scene emotions.

"Only he who can see the invisible can do the impossible."
—*Frank Gaines*

Creating Original Camera Shots

New camera shots are created by people like you. What ways can you tell us a story using the camera to reveal information in a fresh way no one has seen before? The opening shot of *Moulin Rouge* is digital, giving the camera a new type of wings to see a city that is alive as we fly over the different layers of Paris. Digital tools give you lots of opportunities to try new things and to make your films look more like moving paintings.

project
5.4

Create Your Own Camera Shot. Combine several of the previously discussed shots or design a new one to create a unique camera shot for your film. Have this new shot be motivated by a unique way of seeing a story element in your script. If you want to use a shot that is not on the list, it counts as a new one to add. Have fun with this! You could combine a Bungie-cam with a jumping-off-bridge POV. Make up a cool name for each of your signature shots. If it's a really brilliant shot, email it to me with a description, storyboard, and shot name and I'll add it to the website list of expanded camera shots (and credit you).

money-saving

Poor-Man's Steadicam. This tip might work depending on your camera and tripod. Place the camera securely on the tripod and hold it very carefully from the stick in the middle, underneath the camera seat. The weight of the tripod acts as a counterbalance to smooth out the motion of the camera when you move with it. Not perfect, but a good inexpensive technique.

money-saving

Save Your Scary Monster Budget. In the famous classic film *The Cat People*, we never actually see the monsters. All of it is done with shadows and sounds and actors reacting to scary things the audience never even gets to see. This principle is based on the idea that our imaginations can conjure much more frightening monsters than what any Hollywood special effects studio could create. This technique is especially important in low-budget films because it can save you loads of money. *The Blair Witch Project* did the same thing, just suggesting the presence of an evil thing. How can you scare the audience while saving lots of money?

movie note

The Matrix. *The Matrix* movies are good to study for original, digitally enhanced camera shots. In one fight scene, there is a rotating 360-degree pan from the *outside* of a spinning slow-motion character doing a martial-arts move. To create this shot, a circle of rotating cameras were placed around the actor, and then the shots were edited together to look like one continuous shot. Very eerie, because we have not really seen this before. What ways could you use multiple DV cameras to edit together a new type of single shot?

To Frame Tight or Not to Frame Tight?

Keep in mind that the closer you frame a shot, the more you may trap the viewer into watching something. It is usually good to allow space for the audience to choose what to look at and decide how they want to feel about it (or at least think they are choosing).

You also may use tight framing to create the opposite effect, making the audience wonder what is going on outside the frame that they cannot see. This technique can save you lots of time, because you do not have to dress shots for the outside-the-frame area. This technique works especially well when combined with good narrative sound design.

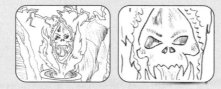

In the first shot, your eyes get to wander around and decide what they want to look at. In the second shot, you must look at the face of the object.

This very tight shot shows a CU of a character in a pit of quicksand, reacting to events and sound effects happening outside the visible frame. This tight framing allows the audience to imagine what is happening, and see the character's facial expressions up close, but doesn't show the actual events. This technique pulls viewers into your story and saves you time because you don't have to create extra shots.

superfreak!

Creative Shooting Style. Choose a shooting style or original way of seeing things, such as viewing the world through reflective surfaces. You could shoot the whole scene through mirrors or reflective surfaces carefully positioned in the scene. For instance: silver platters, glossy windows, different types of mirrors, computer monitor screens, fish bowls, TV screens, shiny metallic surfaces, sheets of office building windows, shiny cars, bus windows, puddles, fountains, ponds, smooth metallic posts, silver escalator siding, aluminum siding, metallic barns. What other types of creative shooting styles can you develop to show us something in a new way?

definition

Line Script Process where you draw lines with numbers on the top of your script pages to mark off individual camera shots.

Character framing shot names. Notice how many ways you can frame different parts of a character. Use the abbreviations listed for your line script. Close-ups (CU) are usually the cheapest and easiest shots to light and set up for DV. A CU in a 3D animation can be a nightmare; you may have to texture map the character again to stand up to that close of a camera shot. 2D animated close-ups tend to look very flat, but might work for big, emotional expressions.

Creating a Line Script

A good way to start planning a rough shot list is to break down the script using graphical lines and numbers.

Feel free to overlap shots and draw over the words. You may have a master shot of two people talking during a scene, with a bunch of cutaways and close-ups marked off inside that one long master shot. Use the abbreviations from the preceding table to conserve space. For instance, CU means close-up, MS medium shot, and LS long shot. Do not try to include every little camera shot at this point; just get the basic ones down. You use this line script as a reference to create a rough shot list next.

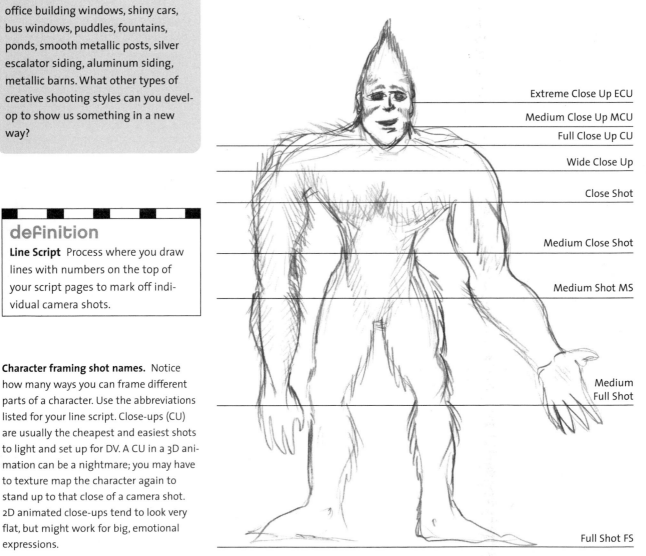

Extreme Close Up ECU

Medium Close Up MCU

Full Close Up CU

Wide Close Up

Close Shot

Medium Close Shot

Medium Shot MS

Medium Full Shot

Full Shot FS

The Character Eye Scan Test

1. Scan your eye very quickly (1 to 2 seconds) over each of the following pictures.
2. Record your impressions of the character in each shot on a separate piece of paper.
3. Turn to "The Character Eye Scan section" on page 232 in Chapter 6 to see how you did.

Using Unique Visual Motif Combinations to Design Sets of Characters

Notice how all of the characters go together using a traveling carnival, pirate, and alien visual motif.

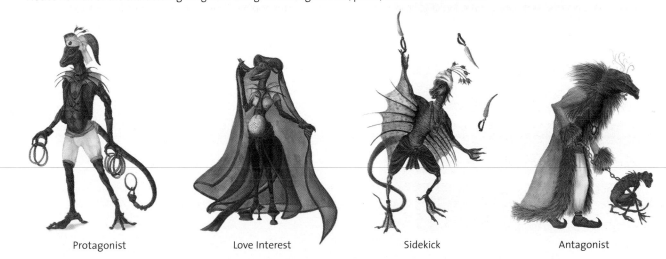

Protagonist   Love Interest   Sidekick   Antagonist

The Color Psychology Chart

Warm Colors

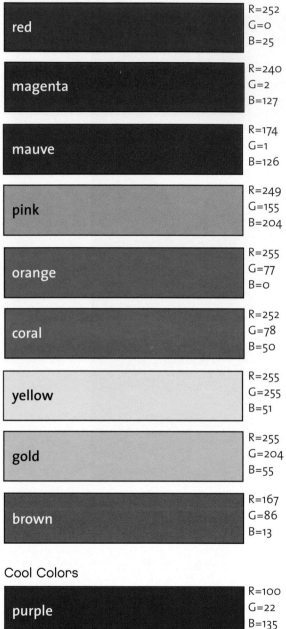

red — R=252, G=0, B=25
Anger, popular, loud, prostitute, debt, warning, vivid, positive, attention grabbing, holidays, passion, violence, sex, aggression, fire, hate, lust, dynamic, dramatic, powerful, heart, seduction, danger, excitement, survival, blood, rage, revenge.

magenta — R=240, G=2, B=127
Sensitive, racy, cheap, hot, plastic, enchanting, optimistic, happy, love.

mauve — R=174, G=1, B=126
Suave, classy, fruity, sophisticated, modern, city, worldly, stylish, impressive, cultured.

pink — R=249, G=155, B=204
Girly, love, soft, romantic, Valentine, young, innocent.

orange — R=255, G=77, B=0
Summer, tempting, fitness, cheerful, heat, bold, vulgar, energetic, harvest, fall, fire, assertive, artificial, clowns, safety, vital, toxic.

coral — R=252, G=78, B=50
Wild, fiery, passionate, sharp, glorious, explosive, spirited.

yellow — R=255, G=255, B=51
Exciting, sour, anxious, sharp, adventure, inspiring, imagination, sun, warmth, daytime, happy, drought, caution, disease, coward, abundance.

gold — R=255, G=204, B=55
Wealth, heat, joyful, lavish, uncertain, rich, mellow, abundant, content, cozy, lion, sun, first place, top honors, ancient, ritual, class, timeless, heavy, greed, idolatry, power, ceremony, corrupt, healing.

brown — R=167, G=86, B=13
Earth, mud, wood, autumn, leather, poverty, dull, reliability, animal, primal, dirty, fertility, organic.

Cool Colors

purple — R=100, G=22, B=135
Grand, regal, leader, superior, majestic, gracious.

violet — R=40, G=19, B=132
Intuition, wisdom, power, royalty, wealth, ritual, old women, loneliness, religion, snob, feminine, isolation, winter solstice.

ultramarine — R=40, G=19, B=132
Calm, peaceful, serene, loyalty, sadness, eternity, intelligence, sky, ocean, water, night, innocence, communication, protection, winter.

Cool Colors (continued)

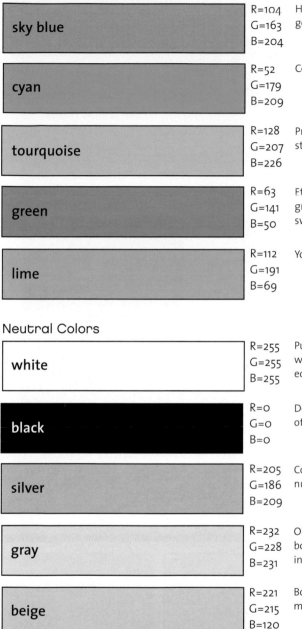

sky blue
R=104
G=163
B=204
Honest, true, good, calm, clean, peaceful, enlightened, tranquility, sky, good will, wisdom.

cyan
R=52
G=179
B=209
Cold, ice, hard, technical, intelligent, analytical, clear, peacock, wind.

tourquoise
R=128
G=207
B=226
Primitive, intuitive, ancient, outdoors, strong, spiritual, free, eagle, stimulating, Native American, sky.

green
R=63
G=141
B=50
Eternal, emeralds, fresh, jealousy, elves, safe, secure, healthy, life, money, growth, fruitfulness, nature, spring, rebirth, creativity, Irish, poison, swamp, evil, envy, snake, youth, sick.

lime
R=112
G=191
B=69
Young, refreshing, sharp, lively, clean, naïve, citrus, desert, sporty.

Neutral Colors

white
R=255
G=255
B=255
Pure, holy, good, clean, ritual, birth, virgin, old, antiseptic, enlightenment, winter, snow, clouds, heaven, bride, weddings, peace, knowledge, light, ecstasy.

black
R=0
G=0
B=0
Death, evil, darkness, blind, cold, mystery, puritan, secret, strength, sober, official, void, abyss, loss, depression, empty, hip, strict, formal.

silver
R=205
G=186
B=209
Cold, moon, alien, second place, technology, futuristic, security, numbness, formal, ice, enigma, dignity, stability, shinny, metals.

gray
R=232
G=228
B=231
Old age, soft, confused, uncertain, unconformity, fog, cloudy, lifeless, boring, in between, vague, drab, ordinary, bleak, mechanical, military, institutional, government, conservative, obedience, decay.

beige
R=221
G=215
B=120
Boring, middle ground, lack of flavor, neutral, normal, uninteresting, medium, classic.

Colors to Avoid in Your Film
Be very careful when using bright or highly saturated colors in your palettes.

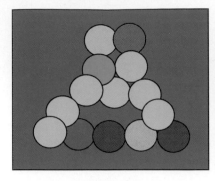

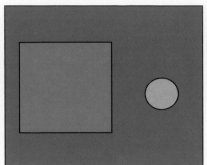

Color Balance Test
Where does your eye go?

Color Balance Composition Test
Which side of the frame is heavier?

Using Color to Show Theme
Blue spiral shapes like this worm are used to show theme.

(See "Developing a Color Palette" on page 244 in Chapter 6)

Creating Palettes from Existing Artwork

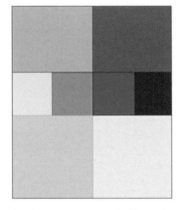

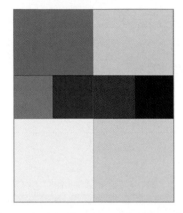

Here is a sample painting to create a palette from.

This bright palette was pulled from the scanned painting after it was opened in Photoshop. Use the Color Picker to select a limited number of warm and cool colors to use for your film.

This cool color palette was taken from the same painting. Notice how all the colors go really well together.

Using Color Maps with Storyboards

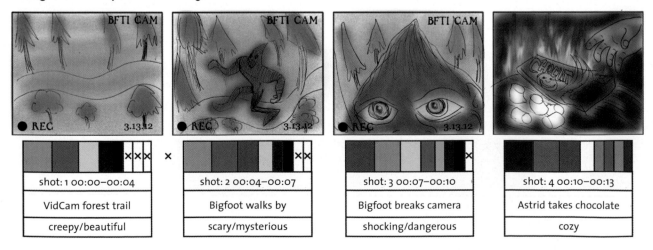

shot: 1 00:00–00:04	shot: 2 00:04–00:07	shot: 3 00:07–00:10	shot: 4 00:10–00:13
VidCam forest trail	Bigfoot walks by	Bigfoot breaks camera	Astrid takes chocolate
creepy/beautiful	scary/mysterious	shocking/dangerous	cozy

Color Palettes from Famous Films

Below are some color palettes created from frame grabs of film scenes. Notice the types of colors that are used and their combinations. These colors are in no way exact replications of the pristine film prints, but they do give you an idea of the types of hues used in films.

The Matrix: Neo is asked to choose between the red pill or the blue pill.

The Matrix: Shootout in the office building lobby with Neo and Trinity.

2001: Opening shot with the apes fighting over the bone.

American Beauty: Opening shot with the mother cutting roses in her garden.

American Beauty: Dinner table scene where daughter storms off angry.

Pulp Fiction: Monologue scene with Christopher Walken explaining the history of the father's watch.

Apocalypse Now: The final scene where protagonist has epiphany while in the water to complete his mission.

Boogie Nights: Opening scene inside the nightclub.

Colors Used Most   Colors Used Least

Color Palettes from Animated Films

Below are some palettes created from frame grabs of animated films. The first few are from *Transit* and show strong color shifts between sequences. You may use these palettes in your own films by doing drop fills from the image files found on the book's CD-ROM.

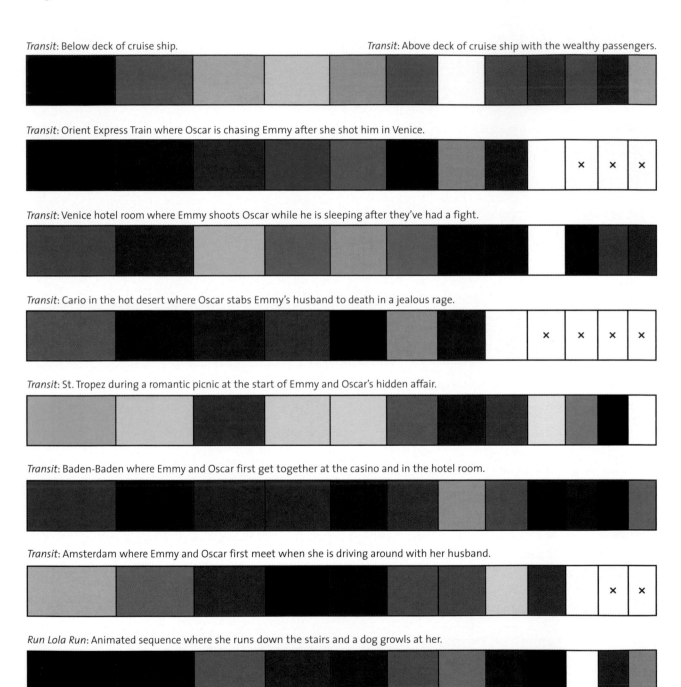

Transit: Below deck of cruise ship.

Transit: Above deck of cruise ship with the wealthy passengers.

Transit: Orient Express Train where Oscar is chasing Emmy after she shot him in Venice.

Transit: Venice hotel room where Emmy shoots Oscar while he is sleeping after they've had a fight.

Transit: Cario in the hot desert where Oscar stabs Emmy's husband to death in a jealous rage.

Transit: St. Tropez during a romantic picnic at the start of Emmy and Oscar's hidden affair.

Transit: Baden-Baden where Emmy and Oscar first get together at the casino and in the hotel room.

Transit: Amsterdam where Emmy and Oscar first meet when she is driving around with her husband.

Run Lola Run: Animated sequence where she runs down the stairs and a dog growls at her.

Colors Used Most

Colors Used Least

Color Palettes from Animated Films (continued)

Waking Life: Scene of character walking over the bridge and discussing philosophy with the poet.

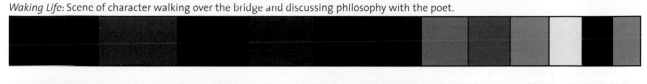

Waking Life: Scene of character in bed with Ethan Hawke and talking about death and the soul.

Colors Used Most   Colors Used Least

The Simpsons: These colors are not in any order from most- to least-used.

Radical Beauty: Nick Philip's 3D animation with a palette that looks great on computers, TV, and film.

Color Palettes from Famous Painters for Use in Film

What favorite artwork with great color palettes could you scan to create original palettes for your film? Make sure the colors in the paintings match specific moods in your story. Use the Eyedropper tool in Photoshop to pull palettes like the ones below. All of the example palettes in this color section are on the CD.

Salvador Dali: "The Hallucinogenic Toreador"

Wassily Kandinsky: "Small Dream in Red"

Georgia O'Keeffe: "Mule's Skull with Pink Poinsettias"

Color Palettes from Famous Painters for Use in Film (continued)

Gustav Klimt: "The Kiss"

Hundertwasser: "Winter Painting"

Brian Froud: "The Mask of Truth"

H.R. Giger: "Humanoid"

Color Palettes from Graphic Illustrations

Bright, whimsical, happy, light hearted, fun, carefree, and funky.

Art deco dark, moody, serious, heavy, intense, urban, and deep.

Retro, hip, funky, classy, and sophisticated.

Pastels, soft, romantic, carefree, gentle, relaxing, and soothing.

Electric pastels, modern, bright, energetic, and loud.

Color Palettes from Graphic Illustrations (continued)

Use the Color Picker in Photoshop to drop-fill your 2D or 3D animated films with the palettes below that are available on the book's CD. Experiment with shifting the hue ranges in Photoshop to create new palettes to fit your story.

Latin earth tones, hot, spicy, multi-cultural, and heavy.

Muted pastel earth tones, retro, classy, understated, soft, businesslike, and compassionate.

Safe bright colors, hot, energetic, fun, and fast.

Dark urban, sophisticated, edgy, and cool.

Hot modern art deco, energetic, brilliant, rich, and retro.

Cool, crisp, sporty tones.

Warm Latin tones, funky, western, and earthy.

Safe, highly-saturated bright colors.

Dark, rich, hot colors, fire, passion, danger, and heat.

Applying Color Palettes to Images

Notice how the mood of the scene changes dramatically as different sample color palettes are applied.

Colors to Avoid

The Simpsons Animated TV Show

Transit: Venice

Transit: St. Tropez

Transit: Baden-Baden

Salvador Dali

Pulp Fiction

Georgia O'Keeffe

Radical Beauty

Waking Life: Bridge

Waking Life: Bed

The Matrix

Creating Simple 2D Animations in Adobe After Effects

Hand-drawn street scene scanned into Photoshop and color filled.

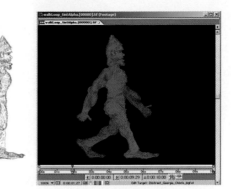

Hand-drawn cutup character.

Hand-drawn truck cut into pieces with separate layers for tires, character, and ramp.

Truck composition is animated across background using position keyframes.

Use the Anchor Point tool to zoom in to specific areas of larger compositions or for pan-and-scan techniques.

Notice the way the frame zoomed in to the previously placed anchor point area.

One character was turned into a gang by duplicating the character composition over and over.

How can you use bluescreen characters or photos with hand-drawn art to create unique visual styles?

Creating Simple Special Effects Using Layers

All of the following techniques are explained in Chapter 9 and are on the book's CD.

Photo of a car opened in Photoshop.

2D animated hotrod with spinning tires, windows that roll down, and characters created with bluescreen dog heads on actor bodies.

Fisheye lens effect created using the Bulge filter.

Subject disappears using two layers of video with an opacity fade.

Shallow focus effect created using two layers of duplicate video with a mask and blur.

Reflection shot created using two layers of video, 3D tilt, rotation, and opacity.

Subject's head explodes by using three layers of DV with an animated mask.

Mindscreen shot created using two layers of video and a Bezier mask with opacity.

Displacement mapping DV actor faces onto other objects.

This statue was brought to life by adding DV lips to the object.

Creating virtual sets using photos.

Adding DV actor faces to animals.

Using light rays to make a bluescreen actor more part of the 3D set.

Using combinations of special effects to create new visual styles.

Making giants using simple bluescreen actors on photo sets.

Creating virtual sets using layers of DV, photos, 2D, and 3D elements.

Case Study: The Deep Step Music Video

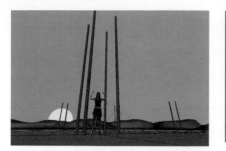

1. A rough 3D animatic was used at the bluescreen shoot to help direct the shots.

2. The DV camera was turned sideways for maximum resolution.

3. A fan was placed next to the singer to make her more part of the final 3D desert scene.

4. A ladder was used to get overhead shots of the full body to create 3D crane shots.

5. Careful storyboards were used to frame each shot so they would all work together later.

6. A light was placed on the bluescreen set to simulate the direction of the sunrise.

7. A grayscale elevation map was created in Bryce using the Terrain Editor.

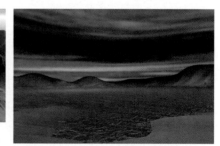

8. A UV texture map was created using Bryce procedural shader tools. A test render was then created in Bryce to use as a reference for texture mapping in Maya.

9. This is the final terrain as it looks rendered in Maya.

10. A DV sunrise was shot over 45 minutes and then time-stretched in After Effects down to 2 minutes.

11. A moving cloth reference was shot to aid in creating the blowing 3D flags in Maya.

12. Flags were created using soft-body particles with wind, gravity, and turbulence dynamics.

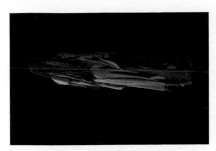

13. Irena was carefully keyed out of each bluescreen shot using After Effects.

14. The keyed DV footage was mapped on planes placed in the 3D desert using Maya.

15. Shown here is a final shot of the bluescreened singer in the 3D desert with the DV sky.

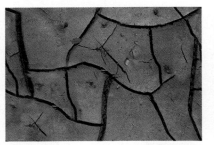

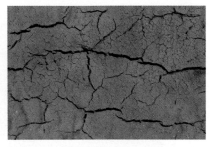

16. Creating a dirt texture map that stretched across such a large surface without tiling was challenging. Three separate texture maps were combined using the Crater procedural shader in Maya.

17. Shown here is a final render of the dirt with the shadow of a flag pole.

18. This is a final shot of all the elements.

19. Long dissolves that looked like double exposures were used as part of a visual style choice.

20. Maya hardware buffer sprite particles were used in this shot.

21. These particles were added in After Effects using Delirium's Fairy Dust and a Knoll Lens Flare.

22. One animation motion path was created for particles and then duplicated 12 times.

Creating Simple Digitally Enhanced Film Looks

No-film look using a DV actor, 3D set, and DV timelapse sky.

No-film look using cut-up photos, DV clouds, and bluescreen actor parts.

Dark-moody-film look using curves, noise (grain), and hue adjustments.

Old-damaged-film look created using DigiEffects Cinelook plug-in.

Bright-retro-future look created using hue adjustments, levels, and curves.

Extreme visual style created using displacement mapping with two clips.

O'Brother-type-film look created using curves and hue adjustments.

The Matrix-type-film look created using curves and hue adjustments.

Create a Line Script. Draw vertical lines down the margins to indicate different shots. Refer to the example line script image to see how this might look. A full-page line script example is on the CD if you need a more extensive visual reference (linescript.psd).

Rough Shot List. Create a rough shot list from your line script. Sketch thumbnails of any complicated shots or Wow! shots you may want to include.

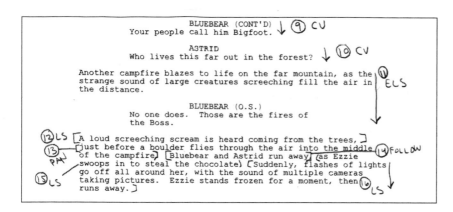

The Line-Script Look. Notice how the lines block off certain sections of the script with brackets, shot names, and numbers. These lines are supposed to overlap to show smaller shots within larger ones for possible editing choices.

Making a Rough Shot List

Creating a rough shot list will help you to see your story visually. Every time the camera needs to be repositioned, it becomes another shot. The lens of the camera serves as the eyes of the audience. The director of a film shows us what is important in each scene by what is framed to attract audience attention in each shot. When creating your rough shot list, think of the following techniques to reveal story information:

1. **What is important** in this scene or shot? Ask who is important too.

2. **What order of story information** creates the most suspense? Make a list for each scene to decide the order of important information that needs to be shown.

3. **How do I want to show this character/subject?** What framing of the character best describes the emotion of the moment or particular character traits in action? Do you need a CU to show an intense facial expression or an LS to show the character doing something with his or her whole body?

This Bigfoot has a drinking problem for his worst character trait. A CU of his hand on a half-empty bottle of moonshine, is the first thing we see when this character is introduced. The most important thing to know about him is that he drinks. What is the most important thing to know about each of your characters? How could you show us this first by using a specific camera shot in an interesting way?

How could you simplify some of your scenes into one long shot to save production time? In this scene, where my Bigfoot character is banished from the tribe, I could arrange the characters so that the action can take place in one long, rolling shot. Placing the characters in a darkly lit cave setting makes my production job easier, too, because dark shadows cover much of the set.

"Every second is of infinite value."
—Johann von Goethe

Rough Timing for Your Shots

What do you think is the average length of a shot these days? Think about this for a moment. You need to get an idea of how many shots you will be storyboarding for each minute of each script page. The average shot length is 3 to 4 seconds long. If you know you want to use longer shots in your film, factor that into your rough shot timing. The following chart will help you determine how many boxes to draw for thumbnails, storyboards, and the number of shots to think up for your final shot list. Long establishing shots to set up a location may be around 10 seconds. You could also do a 10 minute short film in one continuous moving shot. No rules apply to shot length. Find what works best to tell your story. Independent films sometimes tend to have longer shots, because setting up each shot requires so much time with lighting, sound, and staging. MTV-style cutting features 1- to 2-second shot bursts.

For a 5-minute Short Film

	Script Page No.	Total Time	Possible Number of Shots
Act One (1/6)	1	1 minute	12–15
Act Two (2/3)	2 to 4	3 minutes	36–45
Act Three (1/6)	5	1 minute	12–15
Total Number of Shots	Approximately 50–60 shots to design and create if shots average 5–6 seconds each.		

What is a Thumbnail?

Even if you cannot draw, you can draw thumbnails. Drawing thumbnail-sized (very small) shots helps you try out basic shot compositions fast. Usually they are small rectangular boxes with very rough gesture-type shapes. Use stick figures for characters and blocks, squares, lines, or simple shapes to show objects. No details are necessary at this stage. Use arrows to indicate shot or object movement. Some people like to sketch these simple drawings in a larger storyboard size (4×3 inches) and then add the final details over the rough lines later.

Rough Timing of Shots with Possible Number of Shots

Total Film Minutes	Act One Length	Number of Shots	Act Two Length	Number of Shots	Act Three Length	Number of Shots
1	10 secs	1–3	40 secs	8–10	10 secs	1–3
2	20 secs	3–6	80 secs	15–20	20 secs	3–6
3	30 secs	5–8	2 min	25–30	30 secs	5–8
5	1 min	12–15	3 min	36–45	1 min	12–15
10	1.5 min	17–23	7 min	44–55	1.5 min	17–23
15	2 min	25–30	11 min	88–110	2 min	25–30
20	3 min	36–45	14 min	93–118	3 min	36–45
30	5 min	61–75	20 min	160–200	5 min	61–75
45	6.5 min	78–98	31 min	248–310	6.5 min	78–98

time-saving

Short Short Films. Study TV commercials to see how the timing of shots and plot points differ for really short films. You should have enough information about story structure and camera shots to creatively reverse-engineer any film for basic structure. A super-powerful 30-second film will be more successful than a mediocre 30-minute film. You could focus on creating one powerful visual moment or emotion with a strong theme. Many commercials feature a log setup, with a surprise plot twist at the end that is worth studying for timing.

Time the shots of some of your favorite films or shorts to see how the lengths vary to communicate the story in the best way. Fast 1- to 2-second cuts usually occur during intense moments. Lots of these short shots will be CU or cutaways from talking characters. You can see why crating a short 2-minute film will keep your hands full; after all, you may have more than 30 shots to plan out, light, stage, shoot, edit, and sound design. A 30-minute film may require close to 300 separate shots!

project 5.7

Rough Timing. Beside each shot on your rough shot list, add how long the shot is in seconds. Use a stopwatch while acting out each shot in a mirror or count the seconds in your head as you imagine each shot unfolding. You may want to time each shot out three times and take the average length if the estimated time varies much.

Estimating the Length of Each Rough Shot

Act out each shot from your script with a stopwatch or using a clock with a second hand, to get a sense of shot length. For moving camera shots, see them in your head and count 1 Mississippi, 2 Mississippi, to get a real feel for how long a second is if you do not have a stopwatch. A second is a very long time on screen. Make sure and read the dialogue aloud, acting out character actions in each scene, while visualizing transitions and music. This process is called *slugging the boards*.

Designing Camera Shots

> *"The real voyage of discovery consists not in seeking new landscapes, but in having new eyes."*
> —Marcel Proust

Understanding how our eyes naturally work will help you design better shots. Pay attention to where your eyes move around in a film. You can do this by pointing your finger at the screen, and moving it around to follow the motion in the shots that is leading your eyes around the frame. Great films have a very carefully choreographed, visual, ballet-type movement through the images. The viewer's eyes should be dancing or jerked across the images to evoke specific emotions.

What we *look at* is guided by our idea of what to *look for* in the frame.

Previous experiences with films, art, and the world determines what the audience assumes and expects visually. This is one of the reasons original visions are always appreciated, because new perspectives expand the possibilities of our world.

Visual Tempos

The timing of your camera shots often help to determine the visual rhythm, beat, or pulse of your film. Shots tend to get shorter during intense climactic moments. Developing a sense of timing takes practice. Pay attention to the tempo of your shot lengths as related to the movement in the frame. Make your editing more interesting by adding a visual tempo with flashing lights, pulsing sounds, ticking clocks, rocking ships, shaking cars (while driving) or accelerating movements in chase scenes. What other ways can you show time as a tempo on the screen?

In this cave shot, when Ezzie starts banging rocks together during her Shamanic journey drumming, the sounds and motions of the scene mix together to build mood and atmosphere. A series of tempo-building shots could be created with rocks pounding, glowing fungus gurgling up in bubbling globs, bats hanging upside down, flapping their wings to the beat, water dripping on rocks, and rattlesnakes shaking their tails. Editing all of these tempo shots together would add a real pulse to this drumming scene. This visual rhythm idea serves the story well, too, because the sounds are supposed to induce a shamanic trance for Ezzie.

What Moves the Eye

Think back to the last movie you saw. Which moments in the film really held your attention? What were the strongest images? At what point in the film did they occur? We often are so busy watching that we don't take time to think about what captures our attention and why. We know that the human eye is drawn to specific things. Here are the items that will capture the attention of your viewer, listed in order of importance:

- **Movement.** Our eyes naturally go to even the slightest movement in a still frame. If there are several moving objects, our eyes jump between them. If everything is moving, we get a headache fast. A good rule of thumb is to have just one new thing happening at a time to lead the viewer's eye around the frame.

- **Color differences.** One small patch of bright color against a dark background draws the eye into it. In general, warm colors attract the eye more than cool ones. Pay attention to this when lighting subjects in order of importance for each scene. Maybe the main character of the moment gets a yellow light, whereas the rest are all in blue lights. You could also put a bunch of red objects in a line with one hot pink one; the eye will go to the pink. If there are several light areas in a dark frame, our eyes go back and forth. See the color insert section of this book for visual examples.

- **Weight of objects in frame.** Objects with more weight or mass get more attention, but this can be manipulated if done consciously. Big objects in the distance have less weight than smaller objects in the foreground that take up more screen space. (More on balance soon.)

In this shot, I could create a series of movements using the "one thing at a time" rule. First, I could show a huge bullfrog hop across rocks in the glowing fungus pond. Then a bat with glowing red eyes could sweep by. A creature could then surface from below the fungus. Notice how the storyboard sketch is drawn for this series of actions with numbers to show the order. If all of these movements happened simultaneously, the audience would not follow the action because the screen would be too busy and confusing. Notice how your eye is guided across the frame in the direction of each new movement.

This giant glowing yellow lightning bug helps Ezzie find her way through the dark caves and also serves as a symbolic light source for higher guidance. The movement and glow of the lightning bug will help guide the viewer's eye through the shadowy tunnels and caverns.

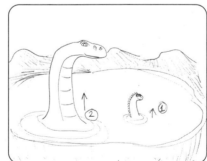

A small creature pops up out of the glowing fungus pond first, and then a large Loch Ness-sized monster head emerges. Notice how your eye is drawn to the bigger head. Objects with more weight draw our visual attention inside a frame. How can you use this idea to guide a viewer's eye through your story?

project 5.8

Moving the Viewer's Eye. Take out your rough shot list and add notes to each shot regarding how you are planning to move the viewer's eye around the frame. You should have already broken each scene into a list of important things to look at. Play with the order of these visual reveals to see how you can make the story more interesting. Make quick notes or draw arrows on thumbnails to show how you might want to present new story information using the previously discussed ideas. If a new character in the background is about to become important, move the character into the foreground of the scene, or plan on changing the character's lighting to a lighter and warmer version just before the character's entrance. Tension is created when we see one character pop out from behind another, or when we see a gun under a table that another character does not know about yet. Most scenes will have an obvious order of story information to reveal, but some may leave room to get really creative.

Show your characters walking into a set and out at the end for clean entrances and exits.

Creating More Interesting Camera Shots

The camera is a roving mechanical eye, revealing the story as it slides across the images. Think of the camera as being in the privileged-spectator position (having the best seat in the house for the story being told). Keep in mind that video is inherently more intense, emotional, aggressive, and vulgar than the lush and beautiful world of film. When planning your camera shots, remember to use these digital qualities to your advantage. Study films you like and add to the following list as you see new techniques:

1. Camera movement should create suspense by slowly revealing story information.

2. Do the arrangements of the shots make us concentrate on one particular story detail at a time.

3. Play some shots over and over again for added impact. What types of shots may work best for this? You could slip in really intense moments that are coming up in the film as flash cuts to foreshadow events, build tension, or ask questions.

4. Moving shots are better when motivated by something in the story. A character moves, and the camera follows. If something in the space needs to be revealed, a moving camera shot shows us.

5. Frame each person for his or her personality. Big, powerful, and bossy people get a low angle looking up at them. (For instance, in a dramatic MS, the person may be pushing buttons on a control panel.) A weak

little girl might get an LS showing her dangling her legs in a pond (showing how frail she is in her environment).

6. Never cut to characters waiting to act. Have them in the middle of doing something or walking into the frame.

7. Have characters walk into the frame for a scene and out at the end into another scene.

8. Have one character pop out from behind another one.

9. Crop half of a character out of the frame to make the shot more interesting if you can make it fit the story in some way.

10. Clip the top of characters' heads or parts of faces off to make more interesting compositions. Do not think you have to put the whole head in the frame.

11. Play with extreme camera angles. DV cameras are so much easier to maneuver in tight spots. 3D animation cameras can do almost anything. Try tilting the camera straight down over someone's face from above for an interesting shot. What other extreme angles could you try on a talking head? Traditional 35mm film cameras are huge, heavy, cumbersome things that you can't move around very easily. Embrace what is easy and new with digital filmmaking to tell stories in fresh ways. What other ways can you think of to do original digital camera shots?

12. Shoot CU body parts of characters to show emotion and to use for cutaway scenes (for instance, hands twisting around inside each other to show tension or knees shaking to show fear). Go

through each of the emotions in a scene and ask what type of universal body movement you could cut to, to illustrate that emotion visually.

13. Have the character scan a location with her eyes (eye-line match discussed soon), and then cut back and forth to reveal space several times.

14. Think of each scene as its own little short film with specific shot patterns, visual styles, lighting, sound, and editing to fit emotions.

15. Be consistent with camera movement patterns in shot sequences. Create a pattern where you go through a series of shots. You could do this by creating a series of left-to-right pan shots following a character on his way to work, all going left to right at the same speed and for the same shot length. You could also go up to down or diagonally or any direction in a series of shots. The first time you break this established visual pattern will have a big impact. Make sure this type of shot series reveals the space in a clear way. Study other films to see how you need to break this up to make it work with the narrative elements.

16. Put posters, photographs, signs, drawings, video monitors, or TVs playing mesmerizing DV footage in the background to convey theme metaphors, plot metaphors, or character traits.

17. Take advantage of atmospheric scene space (especially important in documentary). Collect lots of landscape atmospheric shots, close-up cutaways of interesting objects, characters doing things without any dialogue in between takes, subjects working/playing/resting in the background.

project 5.9

Personality Framing. List in your drawing book the characters in your film. Come up with three ideas about how to frame each of them to show their personalities best.

When the scary witchdoctor of the tribe goes behind a rock to consult his magical stone, I could leave him only half visible, making mumbling conversational sounds. This should cause the viewer to lean over in his chair, to see around the rock. Viewers will feel like they are missing something if they are not quite seeing everything or hearing the dialogue, which will pull them deeper into the story. We do not always see or hear everything clearly in real life.

What is the most interesting and exciting thing in the world to look at? Even if you do not have a huge budget for opulent set dressing, costumes, crane shots, or special effects, you still have the human face. Pay attention to the way characters are framed for their personalities and situations to evoke strong emotions and suspense.

Parts of the vision quest cave are lit by a strange, otherworldly, glowing, greenish blue fungus, to help those special scenes have their own unique look and feel. How can you give each scene its own visual style to develop the story emotions?

Shown here is a follow shot that literally bounces alongside of the Bigfoot character as she runs. This makes the viewer feel like he is running along beside, pulling the viewer into the story and adding an almost documentary feel to the shot. How can you use your digital cameras to follow characters through your story?

How could you use traditional painting techniques when creating your camera shots to show relationships? In Monet's painting *The Boating Party*, there are a series of eye-line looks between subjects. Each character in the painting is looking at a different beloved, exploring the theme of how young people usually don't love the person who loves them, but someone else who loves someone else. The looks end on Monet's favorite love and muse, who is looking sweetly at her lap dog. You could borrow this technique and create a scene with a bunch of characters in trees looking at each other, doing and saying different things to show relationships.

18. Moving camera shots should all start and end on still frames to make editing choices easier. You can always throw out the still frame, but you cannot add one if things are always moving in the shot.

19. Shoot with an eye for editing. Pan and zoom shots work better when you start on a still frame, move around a subject, and then end on a still frame. Show a detail cut. Move the camera to another detail cut. The still frames give you room to edit between shots without having to slam two fast-moving shots together.

20. Get a feel for sensing the action in the shot and following it with smooth camera movements. Incorporate still shots between movements for more editing choices.

21. Use dramatic transitions between shots if it supports the story. Refer to the list you made in Chapter 4, "Writing Scenes, Conflict, and a Short Script," in the section called "Setting the Pace of Your Scenes" under "Transitions." Using techniques such as visual match cuts from scene to scene help make the story feel very tightly woven.

22. Keep in mind that shots usually get closer to the characters as the scene progresses.

23. Plan more types of shots for fast-paced scenes. This will give you ample editing choices for fast cuts.

24. Placement of camera and framing are always determined by what is important to the story at that moment. Don't have gratuitous camera movement if it does not add to the story.

25. When setting up shots, make sure the visuals tell the story without any sound or dialogue. Watch great films with the sound off to see how everything in the frame communicates the story as visually as possible through the placement of characters, gestures, set design, prop placement, lighting, framing, and shots.

26. Create each shot to look like a brilliant painting or photograph that moves.

27. Show character thought through metaphoric and symbolic activities. Characters may be shown contemplating reality by pulling paint off walls, drawing patterns in the dirt with a stick, or torturing bugs. All of these actions tell us something about the character. People spend lots of time in real life just trying to understand reality. This pause in action gives the audience a chance to identify with the character and wonder what they are thinking, which pulls them into the story. Let your film breathe in moments like this.

28. CUs tend to motivate POV shots, so make sure you do an eye-line match and shoot what the character is looking at after the CU. Storyboards really help you plan these. You could just shoot a character after the scene in the same framing doing a series of looks in different directions for more choices when editing eye-line matches.

29. Think of the camera as the character's eyes. What new way can you show what the character sees on a POV shot? A falling-down character could be duplicated with someone holding a mini DV camera falling over or an animated camera simulating a fall POV.

30. Place characters on the edge of the frame when they are desperate, trapped, or out of options. Make them looked boxed in by elements composed in the frame.

31. Moving camera shots should take off soft and land soft. This makes editing easier, too, because it is hard to edit all moving camera shots without still frames on the ends. You must have lots of slower moving static type shots, too, to put air in the film. Too many fast moving shots make viewers dizzy, overwhelmed, and immune to more subtle uses of camera movement.

32. Arrange actors in a shot according to their relationships to each other. Place symbolic objects between them, such as telephone wires in the background for communication problems or scissors on the table for tense emotional conversations.

33. What type of experience do you want to invite the viewer into during each shot or scene? Your goal is to help the audience really get into the film world story with original POVs, camera reveals, and movement.

34. Light characters to reveal story. Traditionally, antagonists get darker lighting in a scene.

35. Conflict scenes should be layered with lots of sharp graphical textures, shapes, and lines to convey conflict. You also can add impact by layering textured sound effects, such as firecrackers going off in the background, or sirens, or lightning.

36. Exclude some object of great importance at the beginning of a scene, and then reveal it with the camera in a startling way later. A character could suddenly turn toward the camera and ask for something, as a hand reaches into the frame from behind the camera space revealing a character who has been sitting there the whole time.

37. Arrange your shots with graphical compositions to create patterns of shapes so that lighting, costume, and figure behavior interact with contrasting colors and movement.

38. Put your camera on the floor or street level to see what types of shots might work. Tilt them up a little for dramatic perspectives.

Animal POV? Some DV cameras are very small and wireless, which means they can be attached to things such as animals or remote-controlled toy airplanes for fresh POVs. What would life look like from the eye level of your rabbit, dog, or cat with a tiny DV camera attached to its head?

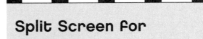

Split Screen for Intimacy

In *Requiem for a Dream*, we see a split screen of two characters falling in love—face to face in two separate shots on the screen simultaneously talking and touching. Sometimes there is a CU of both faces on each side, nose to nose. In another shot, we see the girl talking with an ECU of her fingers touching his skin on the other side of the split screen. These views enable us to see the intimacy developing between two lovers in a very unique and touching way. These shots are much more interesting to watch than two people fumbling around on a couch. What new ways can you frame each of your scenes to show us something new about a familiar situation? Can you use a split screen in a way we have not seen before?

project
5.10

Add 15 of the Preceding Ideas to Your Rough Shot List. Use index cards for new thumbnail drawings or sketches and notes in your drawing book. Add ideas to this shot planning list in your drawing book as you watch films.

Sketching Rough Overheads

Create Scene Overheads. Use a 5×8-inch index card, your drawing book, or your favorite software to design rough overheads for the main scenes in your film.

Sketching some rough overheads of where characters, set pieces, key objects, and your camera might be placed in a scene will help you plan your shots better. Use simple boxes, circles, or shapes for set pieces and

characters, diagonal lines for movement, or any other notation that helps you see the location setup. Programs such as Illustrator work great for creating scene overheads too.

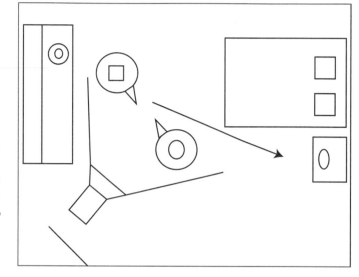

How can you create rough overhead sketches or Illustrator schematics of each scene to show where set objects might be placed? Use arrows with numbers to show camera or character movement. These can get really complicated if you draw multiple camera, lighting, and character setups. You may want to devise a system of symbols to represent different characters from above, such as a circle on the head of Character A and a square on the head of Character B.

Composing Your Shots

Scene Idea Piles. Create a pile of (10–15) 3×5-inch blank index cards for each scene. Draw little thumbnails or sketches on them to illustrate some shot ideas presented in the following section. You could dedicate 1 to 2 pages in your drawing book for sketching each scene if that feels better, but I recommend the index cards so that you can move them around easier later to try different shot combinations.

Composing shots within a frame is a skill you will get better at the more you do it *and* the more you study how other filmmakers create great shots. There are no rules anymore for composing shots, because modern audiences are usually visually sophisticated enough not to get lost in a film. They can still get confused, but are much more flexible than even 10 years ago. Things such as the 180-degree rule used to be the way you did things. Now it is a choice. Use the ideas presented in this section to help make better shot compositions. The first time you go through this process, it might seem like a great deal of work. The more

you think of these things, the more you will naturally compose shots taking into account these compositional approaches intentionally.

Using the 180-Degree Rule

This rule was created to help the viewer not get lost in a space and usually comes into play when two or more people are in a scene having a conversation.

Modern audiences can take lots of strange camera moves in a scene and not get lost. If you choose to break the 180-degree rule, or any fundamental screen direction rule, do it intentionally and with great thought.

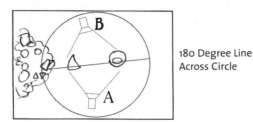

Overhead

180 Degree Line
Across Circle

Notice how if you move the camera over the 180-degree line across the middle of the circle, the shots will get confusing spatially on the screen. All shots from Camera A on the bottom half of the 180-degree line will work fine. If you move the camera over the 180-degree line where Camera B is, however, the placement of the characters on the screen flip and become confusing when edited together.

Camera A

Camera A

Camera B

Camera B

Here are some guidelines for working with the 180-degree rule:

1. Draw a circle (360 degrees) around an overhead sketch of the space where your actors, set pieces, and important objects will be placed. You should already have an overhead sketch from the preceding exercise.

2. Figure out the best place to put your camera.
3. Find the dividing line (180 degrees) to split the circle in half (180 degrees) with your camera on one side of the line and the subjects you are shooting on the line or on the other side of the line.
4. Moving the camera over this line may confuse people, especially during two-shot, conversation-type scenes. Shots obtained from just one side of this line will feel more consistent to viewers.

definition

180-Degree Rule Technique used to help keep viewers from getting lost in film world space, by keeping the camera on one side of a line drawn across the space.

project 5.13

Cutout Magazine Frame. A good exercise to help your eyes learn to see like a camera involves taking a piece of paper, or paperboard, and cutting a small 2-inch-wide rectangle in the middle. Practice sliding your cutout rectangle across the surface of images like a camera. Use big coffee table picture books, or magazines with good photos (*National Geographic*, for example). Notice how the cutout rectangle reveals new information as you move it across the images, much like panning a camera around a location. You may want to cut out two L-shape pieces of paperboard to give your rectangle zoom capabilities so that you can focus in on smaller or larger areas of the image by adjusting the lengths of the sides.

project 5.14

180-Degree Rule. Find a scene in your film in which to apply the 180-degree rule.

definition

Eye-Line Match Cinematic technique where the camera shows us what the subject is looking at offscreen. The first shot shows a character looking in a specific direction, such as up and to the left. The second shot shows us what the character is looking at by placing the subject in the same spot as the previous look, such as a UFO in the upper left of the screen.

Eye-Line Match Cuts

Cameras often follow the eyes of characters in a scene. Eye-line match cuts are used to show us what a character is looking at offscreen. A character looks up and to the right in one shot. In the next shot, the subject the character was watching appears in the upper right of the screen to match the direction of the look.

Plan your eye-line match cuts into the storyboard level to make sure your shots are going to look good together. This will become even more apparent when you do a rough animatic. If a character looks left, your next shot needs to match the direction of that look with a subject on screen to the left. Character looks down, and you then show what the character is looking at

below. If a character suddenly looks up, and the next shot shows us a mouse crawling across the character's toes, the audience will wonder what the character is looking at above and gets confused. Watch films to see how they cut on these looks and where the objects in the next shot are placed.

If your eye-line match cut lines are even a little off, your editing will be a nightmare and the shots will feel like they do not go together. Audiences have been trained to expect these cuts, even though most viewers are not even aware of the concept. At this point, just note with arrows in the thumbnails which direction the character is supposed to look during eye-line match cuts, to make sure you match these look lines when you plan your next shot.

Eye-Line Match Cut. Notice how in the first shot, the Bigfoot is looking up and to the left. Take that look and draw a line in the direction of the look. This line will help you find the spot in the next frame to place your look subject.

project
5.15

Eye-Line Match. For every shot in which you have a character looking at something specific, design a look direction at the end of each shot with a cut to the next shot matching the reverse POV spot. You may want to compose the second shot first, and then plan what direction your character needs to look to match the subject spot in the next shot.

Rule of Thirds

The *rule of thirds* is a compositional technique filmmakers use to help frame shots. The rule of thirds can sometimes enable you to improve the composition of your shots dramatically. The idea behind this rule is to break the screen up into thirds, both horizontally and vertically. You then frame your scene elements and subjects along the lines.

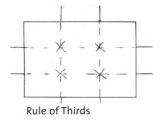

Rule of Thirds

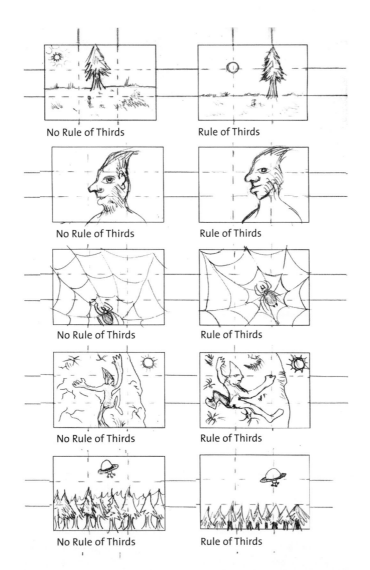

No Rule of Thirds   Rule of Thirds

No Rule of Thirds   Rule of Thirds

No Rule of Thirds   Rule of Thirds

No Rule of Thirds   Rule of Thirds

No Rule of Thirds   Rule of Thirds

Notice how the shots using the rule of thirds look better compositionally.

project
5.16

Rule of Thirds. Divide each of your thumbnails into lightly drawn tic-tac-toe grids as shown here. Move objects or lines in sets to land on these lines or intersections. Adjust character eye levels to match on these lines.

project 5.17

Angle Shots. Go through your shots and thumbnails to see whether any would benefit from using better angles.

Angles

Angle or diagonal shots give a sense of depth, dimension, and interesting perspective lines. Too many flat, straight-on shots start to look boring.

It is good to plan your angles as much as possible during the storyboarding process to make sure they go together in the final shot sequences.

Too Flat

Too Flat

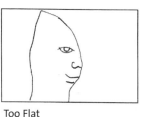

Too Flat

Better at Angle

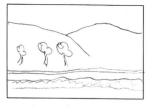

Better at Angle

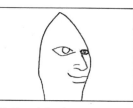

Better at Angle

Notice how the shots at angles look better and have more depth.

Using Camera Angles to Show Relationships

Camera angles can also convey a sense of relationship to subject. By raising or lowering your camera angle, you can influence the way the viewer perceives your subject.

Camera Angle the Same Height as the Subject. *When the camera and the subject are at the same height, the viewer feels equal with the subject.*

Camera Placed Higher Than Subject. *When the camera is placed above the subject looking down, we get the feeling that the subject is less important, inferior, or smaller.*

Camera Placed Below Subject. *When the camera is placed under the subject looking up, we get the feeling the subject is more important, larger, superior.*

Balance

Each shot needs to be balanced properly for the composition to work well. When planning balance for narrative impact, remember that our eyes move to the side of the frame with the most weight. The real size of the objects is not as important as the size they appear in the frame.

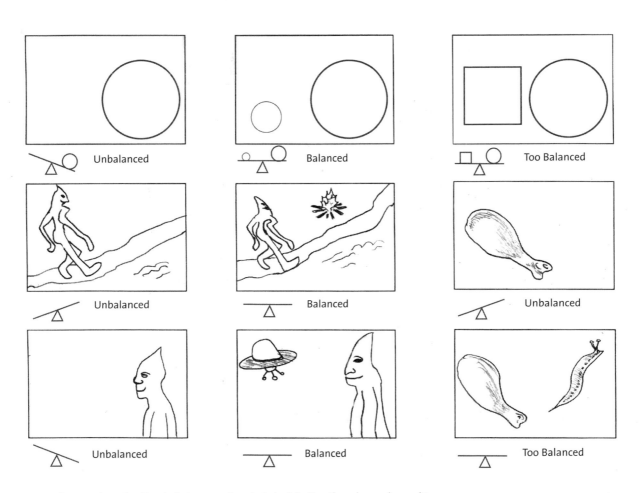

Notice how paying attention to balance makes shots look better. If you have a heavy, big object on one end of the frame, add a smaller object on the other side to balance out the shot. Do not place an equally big object on the other side; otherwise, it will be too balanced and will look static and uninteresting.

Add Room for Leading Looks. Go through your rough thumbnails and adjust the composition for leading looks.

Leading Looks

Another aspect of balance is leading looks, meaning that you have allowed for the compositional weight of the look. If you have a side view of a person looking to the left, put this person on the right half of the frame to allow room for the look to occur. Objects such as TV sets, vehicles in motion, and subjects with slanted compositions also need to have room ahead of them for good balance.

Not Enough Look Space

Room for Leading Look

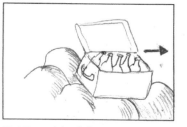

Not Enough Look Space

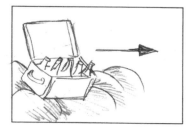

Room for Leading Look

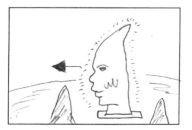

Not Enough Look Space

Room for Leading Look

Notice how the shots with room for leading looks have better composition.

Leading Lines

Designing shots with strong graphical lines will lead the viewer's eyes to specific areas of the frame. Once you know what subjects or objects are important to show in each shot, you will be able to design set elements around them to point at those important areas.

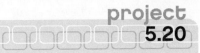

project 5.20

Use Leading Lines. Go through your rough thumbnails and find three places to use a leading line composition.

Eyes Go Here

Subject On Leading Lines

Eyes Go Here

Subject On Leading Lines

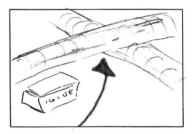

Eyes Go Here

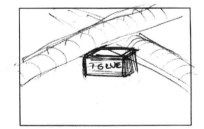

Subject On Leading Lines

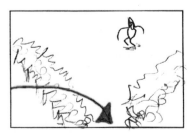

Eyes Go Here

Subject On Leading Lines

Notice where your eye goes as you look at each frame, composed with lines and subjects. Be careful about placing important subjects away from where the lines in frame lead our eyes.

definition

Creating Screen Depth 3D sense of space inside a 2D image playing on a flat screen.

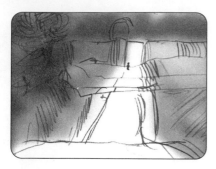

Planes. This shot of a hilly road creates a great sense of depth with multiple layers of space.

Adding Foreground Objects. This shot through a gate looks much deeper and more dynamic than just showing a car driving up to a house. How can you take some of your more ho-hum shots and play with adding foreground objects and camera angles to see through things in new ways? Make lists of foreground objects from films you watch to see what types of things they add. You could also composite foreground objects in postproduction as a layer. If you shoot tree branches against a blue sky for easy color keying, you could add the branches as a foreground object layer later. These extra foreground layers can also be used to block out parts of the frame to remove garbage cans, telephone wires, or advertisements. What other symbolic objects could you shoot to add to your shots as foreground object layers later?

Creating Depth in Your Camera Shots

A movie is a moving 2D image projected on a flat screen. You need to show how this film world is three dimensional and has depth by consciously creating your shots to convey the deep space in each scene. Without depth, your shots will feel flat and boring. Some shots are meant to feel flat to serve the story, but most look better with as much depth as possible.

15 Techniques to Create More Depth in Your Shots

Use as many of the following techniques as possible to add depth to your shots.

1. **Volume.** Rounded-looking objects in scene; big pieces work especially well to show perspective.
2. **Planes.** Layers in space. Slices of action or images going backward into the frame, such as stacked buildings from middle ground to background. Define depth by *overlapping* planes. Light the edges of each stacked layer to add depth. You could also add fog between layers in postproduction, or make the deeper layers blurrier with less saturation to appear further in the distance.
3. **Foreground/background.** Place objects both in the area near the camera and far away to show distance. You may want to composite foreground objects in postproduction, such as tree branches, windows (frame within a frame), flowers, street poles, or any other objects that would make sense. Foreground

objects have sharper outlines, clearer textures, brighter and purer colors, and greater detail. These foreground objects can also be used to hide flaws in the frame, such as billboards, trash cans, copyrighted images, boom microphones, actor mistakes, rendering mishaps, set design problems, or other elements that are not working in the final shot.

4. **Object size.** Things that are far away appear smaller. Play with this when composing your shots. You need to be especially careful of this if you are creating layers in postproduction to add to the background of a shot. You could exaggerate this effect, too. A 3D bug flying around in the background could start out very small, and then fly up to the camera, filling up the frame. A video layer of cars driving by in the distance could be placed behind a character with the cars being much smaller than the actual depth would create.
5. **Shoot on diagonals.** When in doubt, shoot on a diagonal view. This is much more interesting to look at, because we really feel the depth. Draw your storyboards at angles with lots of perspective diagonal lines whenever possible. You will need to match angles when editing or balance them to make them look good next to each other in a series of shots if you use lots of diagonals.

6. **Lines.** Straight lines anywhere in the scene create natural depth by bending with perspective. The stronger the diagonal of the shot, the greater the perspective lines appear. A grid-work row of windows behind an actor walking down a hallway will bend down to a point in the distance if you shoot it at a diagonal.

7. **Color.** Films can achieve depth through changing colors between planes, such as making the ones in the background darker, grayer, and less saturated. Spend time studying how color affects long-view shots. DV people can do this with bluescreen layers of backgrounds or even video layers. The eye easily picks up differences in shading of colors for depth because light changes across spaces.

8. **Frame within a frame.** Shoot through window frames, door frames, keyhole mattes, between two trees or posts, between rocks, through spaces in interesting shapes, or hallways. You may also be able to add frame layers in post if you plan your shots carefully.

No Frame

Frame Within a Frame

No Frame

Frame Within a Frame

No Frame

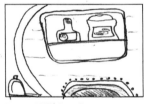
Frame Within a Frame

No Frame

Frame Within a Frame

No Frame

Frame Within a Frame

Lines. This long hallway with open doors spilling light into the hall creates lots of depth in the frame. Each doorway creates a separate layer in space, and the lines of the hallway add perspective.

Frame Within a Frame. Notice how shots using the frame-within-a-frame technique look better and add a sense of depth.

Subject Moving Between Layers. Notice how this shot instantly gets more depth as the sheep travels behind the tree.

9. **Movement.** The subject moves around different objects in the scene to show depth as he travels between the layers.

10. **Cast shadows.** Shadows on walls and objects show us volume and depth across things.

11. **Consider a widescreen aspect ratio 16:9.** You do not have to compose your film in 4:3. Not all DV cameras shoot in true 16:9. Using your digital tools, you can create your own aspect ratios by blocking off parts of the frame with black mask areas for more dramatic compositions. Normal human vision is 180 degrees. A typical big movie screen uses only 20 percent of horizontal vision range, so you can imagine what happens on a TV. By using a wider 16:9 aspect ratio, you immediately open up the frame to more depth and interesting compositional choices. If you show a 16:9 image on a 21-inch TV, things feel quite a bit different than when you see the same film on a big movie screen. Ask yourself, "Where are people most likely going to see your film?" The Internet? TV? On a computer screen? Mobile video phone? PDA? A movie theater?

12. **Shoot the scene from above.** Just one overhead shot can create a sense of depth for your entire scene to establish spatial relationships.

Cast Shadows. You could introduce a group of menacing characters by showing us their shadows first, walking down a dark tunnel. Long cast shadows create a sense of depth in spaces. When planning your shots, consider how could you use shadows to help tell your story.

13. **Move subjects in and out of the frame.** A subject can move in six directions in and out of a frame to add depth. You could have people walking into the frame from each side. Something dropping in from above. A hand reaching out from directly behind the lens. Characters walking off behind items in the distance, popping up from below. Add as many subjects traveling in and out of the frame from all of these directions as you can to create a sense of this film world continuing to exist outside of the frame. This works especially well with a moving camera shot when carefully planned out.

14. **Camera lenses.** Use different depth-of-field techniques to make subjects in the foreground or background appear in or out of focus. Deep-focus techniques can be also be approximated digitally in postproduction by blurring one layer of video and then laying another in-focus copy of the same shot with mattes cut out of, say, a character's face, on top of the blurry one. The face would be in focus while the rest of the frame would appear blurry (see Chapter 9).

15. **Overlap all of the above.** Use as many combinations of the preceding techniques as possible to create depth.

Create Depth. Go through each of your shots and incorporate at least 10 of the depth-creating tips.

Six Directions in and out of the Camera Frame. Make a list of four things that could pop in and out of each scene from each of these six directions to add depth to your shots. This technique makes the viewer feel the film world extends far beyond what the camera chooses to show them on the screen.

Creating Storyboards

Digitally enhanced films often have many layers that benefit greatly from well-thought-out storyboards. Storyboards are the visual blueprints of your film. I think all beginning filmmakers and animators should storyboard every shot of their films before picking up a camera or touching a computer. When you start production on a film, you do not want to be distracted worrying about what camera angle to use all of the time. You may change your mind about some of the shots you storyboard during preproduction, but at least you will have a solid idea of how the visual structure of the film hangs together.

Some people don't use storyboards and still make great films. Some people do not even use scripts and make great films. I learned 3D animation before anything else, and we always storyboard every shot before any production, because it is just too expensive to throw anything away. Hitchcock storyboarded every shot of his films before production and said the film was already made before he touched a camera.

Tips on Drawing Storyboards

When creating your storyboards, keep in mind the following tips:

1. Draw boxes that are the same aspect ratio as your output size. The aspect ratio for video is 4:3; HDTV and film aspect ratios are around 16:9. Do not plan shots in perfect squares.

2. Use arrows to indicate camera movement or motion in the frame.

3. Use arrows along with shot names to convey specific camera movements that may not be understood if you use arrows only.

> *"Trust your hunches. They're usually based on facts filed away just below the conscious level."*
> *—Dr. Joyce Brothers*

4. Use a frame within a frame to indicate zoom areas.

5. Use differently shaped, extra-long, or extra-wide boxes to show pans.

6. Draw multiple pictures for moving objects or characters within a frame if it seems important to the story.

7. Write dialogue beneath storyboard panels so that you can see how the audio track will help tell the story. Try to give the character some activity to do while speaking to make it seem more full. A talking ostrich is not as entertaining as a talking ostrich carving pictures on a tree with his foot.

8. Include shot numbers next to each panel to indicate order. Go from right to left, not up and down.

9. You should not need to explain under each panel what is occurring unless it is confusing, which may mean you need to fix the shot. If you plan to leave your storyboards with someone and will not be available to explain what is occurring in each panel, however, it may be a good idea to provide some textual explanation under each panel.

Drawing Rough Storyboards

Even if your drawing skills are limited to stick characters, you will want to do a set of rough storyboards. The most important thing is that the drawings convey the shot you are visualizing in a clear and easy-to-understand way.

In the next chapters, you will develop a visual look, sound design, and narrative editing style for your film. At the end Chapter 6, "*Mise en Scène* for the Twenty-First Century," you will stylize all the set elements, including colors and specific props. If you have a "gun in a graveyard" shot at this stage, it will turn into a "silver snub-nose revolver in a New Orleans cemetery" in the next chapter, where you get very specific about each visual element.

"Well done is better than well said."
—Benjamin Franklin

project
5.22

Draw Very Light Pencil Thumbnail Gesture-Style Storyboards for Each of Your Final Camera Shots. Use as many of the ideas from the exercises in this chapter as possible. You will need to use your own judgment not to bring too much attention to the camera work and make each shot choice support the emotions of the narrative. Draw these shots on 3×5-inch index cards or in your drawing book. Use rough blocking thumbnail gesture lines and stick figures for characters unless you can draw well fast. Lay the cards out on a table or floor in the order of the story. This will give you more room to switch out ideas and change the order later. You will be fine-tuning each of these shots soon, so keep your pencil lines light and shot blocking rough.

Top 10 Reasons to Storyboard

1. It is cheaper and less time-consuming to make changes at the storyboard level than in the middle of production.

2. To "see" whether your story works. If it does not work at the storyboard level, it will not work as a film—unless you get real lucky, and luck in filmmaking tends to fall on the side of preparation. Pay particular attention to how the continuity between the shots is working. Are there any visual gaps getting from shot to shot?

3. Storyboards provide a visual roadmap for the team. Usually you will work with other people to create a film. Storyboards are the only really effective way to describe a scene so everyone can understand what is going to happen clearly.

4. To get better feedback. With the physical boards in front of everyone, people can point to particular shots and make comments or suggestions much more easily.

5. Storyboards spawn production bibles. Digital filmmaking often requires detailed storyboards, because many shot elements are created using multiple layers from different sources. What layers need to be shot, built, painted, animated, digitally enhanced, or bluescreened to make the whole shot work? Without a good set of storyboards, you may have a hard time planning your production schedule.

6. Storyboards are usually included as part of the client/teacher/investor approval process. You draw up the idea and the client/teacher/investor signs off on each panel. They are visual contracts that protect both you and others from misunderstandings and may prevent the need for major revisions later.

7. To set up your shots. You need to know where to put your camera and what is going to be seen in the shot for set design and preparation. If you know from storyboarding that you are going to see only one corner of a room, you do not prepare the whole room to be shot, just that corner.

8. To previsualize multiple ideas and choose the best ones. You could create several sets of storyboards for one short film and play with the parts that work best. Do not always go with the first idea or shot that pops into your head.

9. To create lots of Wow! shots. Really tight visual filmmaking, especially when incorporating special effects or digitally enhanced scenes, requires storyboards to plan everything very carefully.

10. To create an animatic. Storyboards are scanned into the computer and transformed into a slideshow with rough audio and timing to get a feel for the story. Some animatics have moving 2D or 3D elements. By viewing a rough animatic, you can usually tell right away whether the film will work. It is much better to spot story problems before any production occurs, instead of trying to fix the film in editing.

Experiment with drawing different types of storyboards to plan your film. This sketch shows the entire cave system that Ezzie travels through during the vision quest sequence. By drawing this storyboard map, it is easier to see how the locations connect in the film. This side view will also help us construct the 3D set and explain the environment more when we go to pitch the story to our investors. Many of the preproduction projects you do in this book can be shown at meetings to pitch projects to potential investors, who like to see that you have thought things out carefully.

chapter 6

Mise En Scène for the Twenty-First Century

"True vision is always twofold. It involves the emotional comprehension as well as physical perception."
—Ross Parmenter

Mise en scène (pronounced muse en sen) is French for "placing in the scene." It is a visual style where there is manipulation of staging and action within a shot. It is any visual element within the frame: mood, style, visual tone of the film.

Digital filmmaking is poised to revolutionize the way films look. Powerful software and multiple video-layering techniques greatly expand the palette for modern filmmakers. Most films have a unique visual style that is created to best tell the story in an interesting way. This style may change dramatically from one scene to the next. By using a variety of visual styles, you will help get the viewer into a different frame of mind and emotion for each part of your film. Remember, stories are like roller coaster rides, and each part needs to look and feel quite different for the ride to work right.

In this chapter, you will develop an original visual style, or mise en scène, for each scene or main sequence in your film. The rough storyboards you just planned will get a redesign job in the following areas:

- **Attaching visual styles.** Does your film look like an animated comic book, an old silent movie, or a combination of different existing visual storytelling styles?
- **Planning digital production styles.** Will you be using DV, 2D, or 3D animation to tell your story? Are your actors bluescreened in some scenes and hand-drawn in others?
- **Creating visually expressive characters.** What style of actors or characters are you interested in developing? How will they appear in each scene? What metaphorical activities will they be doing to help develop your story visually?
- **Designing sets.** What visual style will your sets resemble? How will you arrange the staging for characters, set pieces, props, and background elements to help tell the story?
- **Developing a lighting design.** What changing lighting styles will best communicate your story visually?
- **Deciding on a color palette.** What types of color palettes will you be using in each scene or throughout the whole film?

A great film often develops an original visual language or style tied directly to plot, theme, and character. When designing the mise en scene for your film, make sure you have a strong, underlying concept behind each visual decision that fits the story. The lucid dreaming world explored in the film *Waking Life* is developed visually using painted animated layers on top of DV. This visual style gives the film a dreamy quality that helps the viewer get into the alternate reality of the story. If you make design choices based on what you think looks good at the moment, it will not hold together as well, as if the choices are motivated on a deeper level by a clear, conceptual narrative goal.

If you are doing a film with robots, do you want to design a Japanese anime visual style or a classic science fiction one? Notice how much our perception of each character changes dramatically with each of these style choices. To choose the best one, ask yourself which visual style best fits the story and characters.

Using multiple layers of images to make films digitally gives you much more flexibility to design unique visual styles. In this shot idea, the bluescreen actor is turned into a black silhouette, with only his eyes and mouth exposed. You could select live actors out of settings and do similar color or style changes using masks. This silhouette look would work well for a scene in which the character feels like a shadow or dark void.

These stylized 2D hand-drawn characters have a wiggly-line mise en scène to help convey the theme of how nerves affect judgments. How could you create unique textures, graphical styles, or lines that develop your characters or story visually?

"You can't depend on your eyes when your imagination is out of focus."
—Mark Twain

Developing Visual Styles

When creating the mise en scène for a film, it helps to experiment with visually contrasting or exaggerating the moods, emotions, and ideas presented in each part of your story. The first step to developing these styles is to determine what emotions or moods each section of your film is communicating.

Sometimes you will need to adjust your script, and rough storyboards, to fit new visual ideas. In the epic film *Gone With the Wind*, the script line "Atlanta burns" got translated into 20 minutes of screen time, showing different images of Atlanta burning. Stay flexible as to how you may be able to tell your story in new ways as you develop an original look and feel for your film. Add new shots and experiment by changing some of the rough shots you planned in the preceding chapter.

Determining the General Mood of Each Sequence

To develop specific styles, it helps to choose a basic visual mood for each main scene or sequence of your film. If the first scene in your film is supposed to be scary, choose visual design elements to support that mood, such as dark or shadowy lighting, creepy spiders hanging in the foreground, or ominous graveyard images in the background. Some scenes may start out scary but then become funny; you need to address these different moods when planning the look and feel of each shot. When the scene shifts from scary to funny, a new light source may appear, one that shifts the colors from dark tones to dusty pastels to fit the new, lighter mood.

time-saving

Allow Yourself Time to Try Different Visual Approaches. Work back and forth between the ideas in your script and the exercises in this chapter to pick visual styles that best represent your film in an original way. You may have a bit of a struggle as you try different ideas (some of which won't work out) to develop just the right look for each part.

"Trust that still, small voice that says, 'This might work and I'll try it.'"
—*Diane Mariechild*

"You will do foolish things, but do them with enthusiasm."
—*Colette*

movie note

In the film *Waking Life*, one character in a bar tells another one that being around him inspires "holy moments." We then see the inspiring character turn into an animated cloud man. In the next shot, both characters are cloud men, floating in the sky together for a nice moment that fits with the conversation—heaven/sky/cloud visual for the idea of "holy moments." Sometimes when we dream, surreal situations change fast, making this visual style fit well with the mood of the story. How could you use an original visual technique somewhere in your film to help show how the characters feel?

definition

Mise En Scène French for "placing in the scene." Any visual element within the frame. Mood, style, visual tone of a film. Manipulation of staging and action within a shot. These visual areas include camera shots, set design, costumes, lighting, props, behavior of subjects, colors, textures, patterns of shapes, symbolic subject/object composition within the frame, character gestures/posing, and make-up styles. Mise en scène for the twenty-first century includes DV in-camera effects, 2D/3D animation, motion graphics, and digital postproduction special effects and techniques, such as bold color manipulations.

During the shamanic journey sequence in my film, the mood is spiritually surreal. This feel could be achieved by using a visual collage of DV, 2D, and 3D animated layers, to create a dreamy environment. The look and feel of these scenes could be based on the visual style and color palette from Salvador Dali's painting *The Hallucinogenic Toreador*. How could you design a unique look for the scenes in your film to fit the mood based on existing artwork?

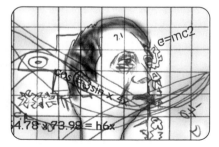

Study highly stylized films you like and see how they work. If you were doing a film about a character obsessed with numbers or math, you might create a mise en scène that shows how this character thinks. Motion graphic numbers and equations could be drifting over the character's face as he or she walks down the street. What other ways can you use motion graphics to design an original mise en scène for your film?

project 6.1

Determine the Visual Mood of Each Scene. Reserve a page or two in your drawing book to write down or sketch mise en scène ideas for each main scene or sequence in your film. List a few adjectives to describe the visual mood at the top of each page. A sequence, as discussed in Chapter 5, "Shot Visualization," may contain a series of scenes. As you go through the following exercises in this chapter, you may want to develop a unique visual style for each of these main sections in your film. If you are doing a really short film, you may need to develop only one visual style. For my film, I would list the following sequence headings with moods across the top of my drawing book pages:

1. **Bigfoot forest surveillance video camera.** Official, real live video footage
2. **Campground.** Cozy campfire to scary wilderness
3. **Witchdoctor cave.** Creepy, dark magic, voodoo
4. **Vision quest cave.** Scary, deadly, beautiful, dangerous, unknown, mysterious
5. **Shamanic journey.** Out of body, surreal, spiritual, floating
6. **Forest.** Beautiful, rebirth, new vision, fresh perspective

Realism Versus Stylistic Film Production Styles

You can choose to show life as it really is in your film or create a unique visual style that is distinctly cinematic. Here are the challenges of realistic and stylized production styles:

- **Realistic.** Depicts real life. Hard to do straight and make it look interesting.
- **Stylized.** Heavily stylized version of real life. If done with too much artifice, may create unreal distance for audience.

Often the best choice is to mix realistic and stylized styles in different parts of your film. Too much style draws attention to itself fast, but it can work well if it helps develop the story in an original way. Everyone has a different line they draw aesthetically between these extremes, and you will need to find your own.

Digital layering techniques open up all sorts of new possibilities for creating heavily stylized films. Each layer of images can have different styles or work together to create a new one. Making things look realistic is usually much more difficult than creating stylized environments when using digital techniques. Keep these things in mind as you design your visual styles in this chapter.

project 6.2

Realistic, Stylized, or Mixed? Decide which approach you are going to take with each section of your film. For my film, I'm going to have the human and Bigfoot world look very realistic, with the shamanic journey parts extremely stylized to show an alternate spiritual dimension.

Realistic/Natural	Stylized/Artificial
Shots occur in linear order.	Nonsequential order of shots or strong editing style
Neutral camera angles, tempo of movement, distance from camera.	Extreme CU, long shots, unusual camera shots
Straight horizontal shots.	Strange angles
Stationary shots or natural motion.	Upside-down shots, Dutch angles, handheld moving shots, dolly, zoom
No distortion of lens or special effects.	Lots of effects, filters, lens changing, compositing
Sound in sync with image onscreen.	Sound designed in post not related to image; distorted, transformed, created
Sharp image.	Soft blurry out of focus
Natural color.	B/W, color correction pass, strange tinting
Regular motion of frames.	Reverse footage, fast/slow motion

"Emulation is a noble and just passion, full of appreciation."
—*J. C. F. von Schiller*

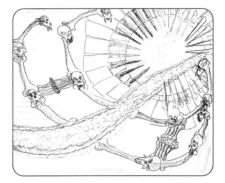

This scary cave was designed with a combination H.R. Giger and Andy Goldsworthy visual style.

Attaching Existing Visual Styles

All great artists develop their own distinct styles. When you know the basic moods and emotions of your film, you are ready to start creating specific visual styles to help communicate the changing story tones. What are some favorite existing visual styles you could you adapt to inspire different looks in your film?

Digital filmmaking allows visual story artists to now create any visual style they can imagine, which is one of the most exciting things about this technology. Twenty years ago, it would have been very difficult to create a realistic Salvador Dali–style film world, full of melting clocks, elephants walking on long toothpick-like stilts, or human figures with surreal body parts. Today, using powerful software, it is possible to re-create or combine *any* visual look you like to create new styles.

List some of your favorite visual styles from painters, photographers, films, animations, comic books, TV shows, music videos, illustrated books, graphic designers, magazines, web sites, video games, illustrators, sculptors, theatrical sets, or other types of art you may want to base film styles around. Decide which of your favorite visual styles may go best with the specific mood in each sequence of your film. Feel free to create new visual styles by combining or altering existing ones, such as a 3D cartoon *Blade Runner* (movie) metropolis visual style for a cold futuristic city scene. You may decide to use only one visual style to carry your entire film, but try to consider creating original looks to apply to special scenes.

I could design a mindscreen shot for my Bigfoot story, using the same technique in the White Stripes music video "7 Nation Army." A constant zoom into triangles from the video could be replaced with a Bigfoot head shape. How could you use existing visual ideas from music videos or other sources for scenes in your film?

"A genius is one who shoots at something no one else can see—and hits it."
—*Anonymous*

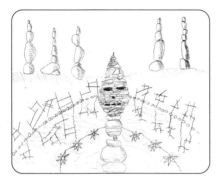

B/W Edward Gory gothic illustrations	Man Ray Rayograph look (cameraless photographs), B/W silhouette of objects
H.R. Giger's haunting, high-tech dreamscapes	2D *Southpark* style
Mystery Science Theatre 3000	Dogme95
M. C. Escher twisted-staircase world	Old silent films
The *Matrix* look (high-tech, organic, cold, futuristic)	*Teletubbies*
Surreal Salvador Dali dreamscape	White Stripes "7 Nation Army" music video look with a constant zoom into graphical triangles to show character's flashing thoughts
Late 60s San Francisco *Oracle Magazine* psychedelic designs	
Blade Runner futuristic metropolis	*What Dreams May Come* (film) painterly, surreal heaven look
Illustrator Robert Williams 2D surreal comic book look	Frida Kahlo's *Nucleus of Creation* painting as an animated comic book world
Veggie Tunes cartoon 3D look	

To show the Bigfoot Native American world flavor, I choose a visual style based on the artist Andy Goldsworthy, who collaborates with nature by using sticks, rocks, and flowers to create art. This shrine has a Bigfoot head constructed of carefully balanced flat quartz crystals, atop a pedestal of balanced rocks. Stick sculptures line the side of the pond, reflecting patterns onto the surface of the water. The documentary of how Andy creates his work, *Rivers And Tides*, inspired this visual style for my film world. What visual styles can you adapt for your film that you have seen in other films or artists' work?

The visual style for my animation *Goth Grrls* was inspired by the gothic illustrations from Charles Adams and Edward Gorey. Who are your favorite artists and how can you adopt their visual styles to create a unique mise en scène for your film?

project 6.3

Attach an Existing Visual Style to Each Scene or Sequence in Your Film. Make sure the visual style fits with or contrasts to the mood of the sequence or scene in some way.

Mise En Scène Design Inspirations for Transit

Each location in *Transit* was inspired by different visual styles. Scenes were designed based on images from famous graphic designers to illustrations on old cocoa boxes. How can you choose a different visual style to match the mood for each location or sequence in your film?

1. **Luxury liner.** Cassandra travel posters.
2. **Orient Express train.** Engraved glass panels on the actual Orient Express Venice Simplon train.
3. **Venice.** Fashion Illustrators such as Charles Martin, L'Hom, and Lucien Vogel, inspired the brittle, angular, violent hard lines.
4. **Egypt.** Design on a cocoa packet.
5. **St. Tropez.** Holiday posters from the 1920s.
6. **Baden-Baden.** Fluid brush and pen lines, color highlights double exposed in camera to show opulence of health spa.
7. **Amsterdam.** Social-realism illustrations and posters of Albert Hahn (Dutch artist), strong black lines and texture to portray working-class life.

Creating Original Visual Styles

Sometimes you know exactly what type of visual style you want to use, based on how you see the film unfolding inside your imagination. These styles often fit with the story flavor you developed while writing your script. If you are doing a meta-physical science fiction animation about life inside a cat's brain, you might combine common physiological brain visuals with specific cat-inspired designs, such as furry frontal lobe cubby holes labeled "mice hunting skill center."

Sometimes visual styles need to change inside a location to fit emotional shifts in the story. In my Bigfoot film, I have a cave that starts out looking like a scary H. R. Geiger stalactite cavern but then turns into a subterranean *Wizard of Oz* yellow brick road feel as the character goes on an inner journey. These specific visual styles are also called *visual motifs*, because they apply a visual look across everything in that part of the film world.

Developing Visual Styles to Match Themes

One way to create unique visual styles is to develop one based on the theme of your film. If your film is exploring how memory changes over time, you might want to list 10 ways to show this idea as a visual storytelling style. You could adopt a pattern of showing the same clip over and over again, throughout the film with slight differences that become more apparent as the film progresses. Maybe there are color shifts, character behaviors that change, dialogue that is cut out or added, lighting shifts, frame tempo changes, different settings,

In this scene, a Native American voodoo mise en scène was created for the creepy witchdoctor's scary cave. How could you take two familiar visual styles and combine them to create a unique one for a scene in your film?

In this scene, an Andy Goldsworthy visual style was applied to the creepy witchdoctor's cave. Notice how the changing style affects your feelings about the character and setting. In the Native American voodoo mise en scène, the witchdoctor feels much more menacing, which helps convey the story emotions for those scenes better than the softer Goldsworthy approach. I decided to combine the Native American voodoo look with the Andy Goldsworthy style, to keep the Goldsworthy visual motif consistent throughout the Bigfoot film world. Choose visual styles that develop the emotions, or contrast them, in an interesting way. Do rough sketches of your ideas in your drawing book, like the ones shown, to get a sense of how the different designs change your feelings about each scene.

project 6.4

Attach an Original Visual Style or Combination of Styles to Each Sequence in Your Film. Start collecting visual examples of styles and paste sample images in your notebook. You may want to scan pictures from books or gather images on the Internet to print out. Find or sketch at least one example image for each visual style to paste into your drawing book. You may also do a quick sketch of specific sets if you know exactly how you want the style to look, or list adjectives and nouns to describe the specific visual elements, such as "grass voodoo doll with little bone needles."

movie note

Bad Animals is a mini DV short featuring actors in silly, full-sized animal costumes riding around on buses and bugging the passengers. The theme has to do with how morose and resigned people have become, which we realize as we watch the bus passengers try to ignore the silly animal characters. Without the animal suits, this film obviously would not work. How could you use costumes from rental stores to tell your story in unique way?

In this sketch, a 2D hand-drawn background is combined with 3D animated characters for a unique-looking mise en scène. A harsh, black-and-white graphical line style with single stokes of etched black ink is used to convey the visual mood of the characters. The theme could be about the dangers of conformity and ostracism, represented well by such striking visual design choices. Each character could be duplicated to be exactly the same, as only 3D can achieve so chillingly, marching in unison. The 2D backgrounds work well to show that the film world these characters live in is a façcade. If the men in suits had flower patterns on their clothes and were all in different poses, we would perceive them to be more of a softer, nature-loving, flower-inspired type of free people. How can you combine graphical design elements, lines, patterns, textures, and production styles to communicate your film theme visually?

project
6.5

Develop a Visual Style to Match Your Theme. What original way can you communicate your theme visually? Create a visual style that shows your theme.

conflicting POVs, different camera angles, or even characters that visually morph or switch before our eyes, from one memory to the next. Some themes are easier to develop visually than others.

How could you have the visual material used to make the film represent the theme? If you were doing a 2D animated film with a theme on class separation, maybe all the workers are animated old blue denim textured cutout figures and the bosses are gold leaf cutout shapes to symbolize class status. This would be a strong visual theme materials choice. If your film takes place in a hot, dusty desert, exploring the theme of decay, you may want to use a smeary, drippy oil paint effects filter over the final film to give it a hot greasy, decaying look. DV, 2D, and 3D animation techniques give you lots of room to play with symbolic textures and materials across surfaces to create unique visual styles.

Developing Digital Production Styles

Digital filmmaking now offers artists a variety of production styles that are much easier to work with than they were in the past. You could shoot your DV film in a traditional style, using real actors and sets, or you could use cut-up 2D animated photographs for the characters, against hand-drawn background sets. If you know 3D, you can create any character or set style combination that you can imagine. One of the biggest advantages when making digital films is that you can manipulate every pixel on the screen and use multiple layers of images on top of each other to create new storytelling styles. These multiple layers may include DV, 2D, and 3D visual elements mixed together. How can you create a unique look for your film using an original, digitally enhanced layering style?

Mise En Scène Choices for the Digital Generation

Creating a visual style for a digital film these days presents an almost overwhelming number of choices. Independent filmmakers have much more freedom to experiment with mixing these new digital styles, to show us things we have never seen before. Make sure each stylistic approach fits the story in some way. Do not worry right now about *how* to do the following digital ideas, just think about what types of unique visual styles will tell your story. When you know what you want to do digitally, it just takes a little research to find the right software or technique (depending on your skill level).

Add to the ideas listed here in your drawing book as you see other digital storytelling techniques you might want to try. Experiment with taking your film idea through some the following production possibilities to create original visual styles that fit specific scene moods. Many of the techniques listed here are described more in Part III.

Digital Character Design Approaches

Real live actors shot on physical sets with a DV camera	Repurposing existing footage from film and TV of characters
Bluescreened actors, puppets, dolls, animals	Real DV actors digitally painted to look like 2D comic book characters
2D photo-cutout characters	Characters shown as symbolic animated objects with bluescreened talking eyes and mouths
3D animated characters	
2D hand-drawn characters	
Using special effects to create new forms of characters, such as glowing orb mentors	Combinations of different production styles for various body parts
	Stop motion/claymation characters

Digital Set Design Approaches

Physical sets shot with DV	Repurposing existing footage from film and TV settings
2D hand-drawn sets	
2D photo collage sets	Traced photos, which are then scanned
3D animated sets	
Miniature physical sets such as a dollhouse shot with DV	DV sets dropped in behind bluescreened characters

DV Shooting Styles

Using slow shutter speeds for trailing, blurry, dreamy images	Handicam shooting style
Using different lenses for image distortions	Using small wireless digital cameras mounted on animals or remote-controlled toys
Using a variety of digital cameras for different looks (DV/HD/video phone/microscopic)	Mixing DV, 16mm, 35mm, and old video footage

Digital Postproduction Effects

Adding film-look filters such as old film damage or reversal film look	Applying easy special effects to layers, such as making subjects disappear, change scale, or float
Manipulating colors of each layer or shot, adding tints, going B/W, shifting colors mid-scene	Using motion graphics to help tell the story
Using fast motion or slow motion for distorted time effects	Applying painterly looking special effects filters to match moods
Creating unusual aspect ratios by blacking out parts of the frame	Adding particle effects, such as fairy dust and spraying liquids
	Scan and pan animations over old photographs

A flat, shaded, 2D animated Bigfoot would have a much lighter feel visually than a realistic, highly detailed 3D animated hairy version. 3D tends to feel more serious than 2D. I'm using 2D, flat, shaded Bigfoots during the animated cave painting shamanic journey scene, to contrast the more serious, dangerous, and realistic 3D visual style of the Bigfoot world. The human world in my film is always shown in DV, with 3D realistic Bigfoots, to have a documentary film style. How could you use combinations of different production styles to better communicate the changing emotions and moods in your story?

Slow Shutter Speed Effects. Using slow shutter speeds as a DV visual style may work well for scenes that are supposed to feel disorienting, soft, or dreamy. Here are some examples of slow shutter speed effects (shutter speed set to 8) using a Sony TRV-900, zooming in and out really fast. Handheld experimental techniques are going to keep evolving as people discover new ways to shoot. Notice how in the rightmost picture, the trails coming off the mixer lights form dancing neon musical notes in the air. How could you develop an interesting shooting style using your DV camera in a creative way?

project
6.6

Creating Digitally Enhanced Visual Styles. Go through each scene or sequence in your film and create a digitally enhanced production style. Explain briefly how each visual style fits your story. In my first scene, I'm using a 3D animated Bigfoot character against a DV forest set, with motion graphic video camera readouts over the top. The color will be adjusted to black and white, with a video-look filter, to make the footage look like an official documentary film. This visual style fits with the story because the scene is supposed to be recorded from the POV of an unmanned video surveillance camera in the forest. Even if you are shooting your whole film traditionally with real actors and sets, see what types of digitally enhanced techniques you *could* use to create more interesting visual styles.

Lightning Bolt in the Heart. This character has an animated lightning bolt striking a tree over his heart as he watches his long-time girlfriend walk out on him. Experiment with finding new ways to use animated elements or pieces of video layers over characters to help develop them emotionally. What places in your film might benefit from a similar approach to create a unique visual style?

Developing Visual Styles to Show Inner Life

Externalizing inner events and character states seems to be a growing trend with modern filmmakers. Our vast array of digital tools are ripe to construct new ways to peek inside our character's hearts, minds, and spirits. How can you show inner realities to create fresh film styles using some of your digital tools?

project
6.7

Show Inner Landscape. List three ways you could show a character's thoughts, moods, emotions, visions, ideas, dreams, daydreams, or abstract inner landscape in your film using some of you digital tools and layering techniques.

Creating Visually Expressive Characters

Taking the characters you created in your script and getting them onto the screen requires careful thought. If you are doing a DV film, you need to cast actors that add genuine charisma and appeal to the characters you created in your script. If you are doing an animated film, you still need to cast voice actors and design costumes, posing, gestures, and actions. Not all the tips in this section apply to animated characters, but most of the exercises have some relevance to designing one. Part III focuses on each production style for character design. Right now, just get a general idea of how people perceive characters on the screen.

"A man can be short and dumpy and getting bald, but if he has fire, women will like him."
—Mae West

project 6.8

List Characters. Make a list of all the main characters in your short film. Try to keep the number of characters in your short to as few as possible. List any background characters that need to be developed visually too.

"Exuberance is beauty."
—William Blake

Casting Styles

What types of actors are going to best tell your story? If you are doing an animation, what types of voice actors will best portray the essence of your characters? Do you want a group of beautiful people or funky-looking freaks with amazingly distorted profiles?

The most important thing when casting actors is to look for screen presence. This is also called sex appeal, charisma, or visual magnetism. When certain actors come onto the screen, you cannot take your eyes off of them. You usually cannot see this screen presence with the naked eye. It is important do a video screen test or bring your digital camera to a meeting and take some stills. People often look completely different on video than they do in real life. Skin tones in particular are very important to test for when using DV, because it will pick up every line and blemish. Some people's skin looks good on video, and some people's doesn't, even though they may look fine in real life. Bring a tape recorder to record voices too, because the same strange distortions may occur. You might love the way a person's voice sounds when you talk to him or her on the phone, but when you record for your film later and play it back, it may sound completely different.

What style of actors or characters best fit your story? Do they look like beautiful people or fascinating freaks?

money-saving

If you are using real actors, you may be able to go over to their houses and dig through their closets with them to create some outfits that fit their characters. Thrift stores and costume rental shops are also great resources for creating original costumes on a budget.

project
6.9

Create a Unique Costume and Makeup Style. Decide on a unique clothing and makeup strategy to fit the main characters in your film. Refer to the Psychological Color Chart in the color section of the book to help pick wardrobe colors. Attach a clothing style, store, or famous designer to each character if this helps you to see them better. These visual clothing styles could include Native American, the Gap, Armani expensive Italian suits, or hard-rock suburban teenager.

Creating Costumes and Makeup Styles

Coming up with clever and inexpensive ideas for designing costumes and makeup styles will contribute to creating a unique-looking film. How can you design costumes for your characters that help the audience understand them better visually? How do you judge people by the clothes they wear or their types of hairstyles? How can you take these socially preconceived perceptions and develop your character history through the wardrobe, makeup, and accessories?

How can you make your film more visually interesting by creating a unique makeup style for each of your characters? How can you develop backstory, character history, traits, and unique qualities using makeup? Maybe the first character is a nature-loving, innocent, hippie girl with symbolic flowers in her hair and red rosy, country girl cheeks. The second one is a futuristic party girl alien, with silver glitter gel all over her skin and striped blue and silver lips and wearing a bright blue wig. The third one could be a futuristic vampire, with costume-shop teeth, a Lone Ranger mask, and a hand-drawn spider mole on her face. Just $10 worth of cheap drugstore makeup and you can give your film a unique look by designing your characters' faces to match the story. You may want to take some rough character sketches into Photoshop and play with designing makeup styles and colors before buying anything. Make sure all the individual character styles look good together on the screen.

Costume Ideas	Makeup Ideas
Halloween costumes	Paper mache masks on actors
Theatrical period-piece wardrobes	Monster makeup
Thrift store color-coded outfits	Futuristic silver garbage bag aliens
Hand-made furry animal outfits	Fake vampire/crooked teeth
2D paper doll clothes superimposed over actors	Big-hair wigs, bright wigs, or hair dyes
Good guys wear purple clothes, bad guys wear red	Heavy, white face powder with deep red lipstick
Ethnic clothing styles to symbolize character states	Bright red or pink wigs on all the main characters
Dirt thrown on clean white shirt to show long journey	Instant tanning cream to make actors look suntanned
Silver dance jumpsuits on characters with 3D long, silver wigs	Adding glue on purple eyelashes to lower right eyes
Old thrift store ball gowns with shaved-head masks	Drawing symbols on faces with an eyeliner pencil
	Mud or dirt smeared over face to simulate living-in-jungle look

Developing Character History and Backstory with Costumes

When you know the general visual style of the costumes you want to use in your film, you may want to think about how you can use specific character wardrobe choices to develop character history, film world, or backstory information.

If you want all the characters in your film to wear long, blue robes and veils, perhaps each robe has an embroidered symbol on it that says something about the role each character plays in the film world. What original ways can you design each character's outfit and style to develop your story better?

Clothing	Possible Symbolic Meaning
Cape with family coat of arms	Comes from royal bloodline
Uniform	Loyal to specific organization
Veil	Likes to stay hidden or must keep face hidden in film world
Sacred feathers	Spiritual character in touch with nature
LCD cloth that shows character moods	High-tech, futuristic world where feelings are easy to see
Team shirt	Character likes sports and is a team player

project 6.10

Design the Main Character's Costumes and Makeup Styles. Take each main character and see how their specific costume and makeup style could help develop their character histories or current emotional states in each scene.

Dressing Characters in Silly T-Shirts

Wrap your character in a T-shirt with a message that tells us who they are in some way. Go to a funky T-shirt shop and get an idea of the types of statements you could create that might help the audience understand your character a little better. What is the funniest T-shirt you have ever seen? What original T-shirt design would best describe each of your main characters? Here's a list of some interesting T-shirt sayings. Imagine your protagonist In each of the following T-shirt messages, and notice how your perception of your character changes dramatically. You could design a visual costume style where all the characters in your film wear different symbolic T-shirts to show changing character states.

- Next Mood Swing in 5 Minutes
- Princess in Training
- I'm Just Visiting This Planet
- Stand Back and Let a Real Psycho Show You How It's Done
- White Trash Princess
- F.B.I. Federal Bureau of Intoxication
- Hello My Name is: King of the Fricken Universe
- Trailer Trash Hick from Hell
- Poison (Underneath a skull and cross bones with a happy woman's face in the place of the skull)
- I Only Do What the Voices Tell Me to Do

Notice how your perception of this character changes dramatically based on the T-shirt design.

LCD panel clothing styles could be created by blue screening characters wearing bright green fabric. You could color key out the clothes separately from the blue background to run mood video layers across. Perhaps when characters are happy, there are sunflowers all over their jumpsuits, but when they get angry, the video changes to fire scenes. This is an example of using a digital technique to design costumes for characters in a unique way, while helping to develop the emotional weather of each scene. The clothing layers in this shot are playing ultrasound video of an unborn child. This visual style might work well for abstract, inner-reality types of scenes. Video stock images by Artbeats.

Adding Accessories to Develop Characters

What accessories could you add to your characters' costumes to help further develop their character history, backstory, or film world? What prized possessions do they always carry with them? What do the things they carry with them say about their character states, histories, or personalities? What do they wear chained to their bodies or hanging around their necks? Refer to the symbols section in Chapter 2, "Creating Original Characters, Themes, and Visual Metaphors," for ideas about how to give accessories deeper meanings. If your character grew up in a religious cult, maybe he or she has a special tattoo on the back of the neck that helps him or her solve the plot goal in a surprising way.

Jewelry	Weapons	Accessories
Royal ring	Mini gun belt buckle	Tattoos with symbolic pictures
Picture pendant	Ornamental sword	Symbolic bindi
Symbolic bracelets	Handmade whip	Laptop computer
Ball and chain around ankle	High-tech utility belt	Military goggles
Big bone stuck through nose	Kung fu weapons	Pet bird/lizard on shoulder
Body piercings	Gun/laser/stun gun	Electronic implants
Gang headband	Handmade dagger	High-tech X-ray visor
Special watch	Explosives on belt	Mask
Crown	Fingernail 3D weapons	Lucky doll or symbolic object
Prayer beads	Magical lasso	Flask for special drink
Religious-looking icons on belt buckle	Poisonous pet snake	Oxygen tanks

This character has a lot more personality with a bone in his nose, a parrot on his shoulder, and a forest utility belt. He seems visually prepared to deal with any situation and looks well traveled. What character traits, history, backstory, or unique qualities can you develop visually by adding accessories?

movie note

Costumes in the *Matrix*. Neo and Trinity wear long black trench coats in the office building lobby shootout scene. The trench coats work well to hide the guns. Most of the characters on Neo's team wear all black all the time. The bad guys in this film wear black-and-white suits. This simple use of color and costumes to build a specific costume style in the film helps viewers to easily identify which side each character is on. How can you contrast your protagonist and antagonist with simple and original costume designs?

project 6.11

Add Accessories to Develop the Backstory. List three items like the ones listed previously to help develop each main character visually.

project 6.12

Sketch Some Rough Ideas for Character Design. Take each main character and draw a rough sketch of how they might look with their new costumes, makeup, and accessories. If you already have pictures of the main characters or actors, you may want to add these costume changes in Photoshop.

writing exercise 6.1

Write a few pages about three different characters who reveal their histories and character traits by their personal styles, clothing, makeup, or accessories.

Acting Styles

What acting style will best represent the characters in your film? Do they act like normal people or exaggerated, overly dramatic characters? Realistic actors act the way people do in real life, which can get pretty crazy. Stylized acting involves overacting, such as Pee Wee Herman cartoon-type characters. Be careful with creating overly stylized characters who are so unrealistic that the audience has trouble relating to their exaggerated behaviors. Some cultures, such as India and Hong Kong, embrace overacting styles in their films. See what fits your story best. In Goddard's *Breathless*, the American girl gave a very subtle, restrained, almost wooden performance. This fits nicely with her mysterious character, which her French boyfriend struggles so hard to understand.

project 6.13

Realized Versus Stylized. Decide on an acting style for your characters and explain how it works with the story.

movie note

City of God. The Brazilian director of this film read a book about a rough housing project on the outskirts of Rio de Janeiro, and then decided to make it into a film. Fernando Meirelles recruited about 200 slum kids from the actual area to play parts in the movie. He chose kids with similar life experiences to the characters in the film, and got some amazing performances. How can you use real people who are similar to the characters in your film to capture more emotionally authentic acting performances?

"Just learn your lines and don't bump into the furniture."
—Spencer Tracy

In this scene, two Bigfoots play chess with large carved rock pieces, while talking about making a deal. The chess game activity serves as a great metaphor for the subtext of the scene in which they are trying to outmaneuver each other. What activities could you give your characters to help develop emotional subtext?

"Just sit there and have them go through the moves. When you see something you don't like, change it."
—Joshua Logan's advice to directors

As these characters walk through a rocky area full of creepy snakes and spiders, one character explains how he plans to blackmail the other one. Each character has to be careful not to step on anything as they navigate through the rocks, which is a good metaphorical activity to fit the scene mood and subject. What gestures, posing, or metaphorical activities could you give your characters to help show the emotions around scene motivations?

Character Posing and Staging Techniques

When deciding how to best to present your characters onscreen, consider the following ideas:

1. **Give characters metaphorical scene activities to make the actions and dialogue seem more natural.** In real life, you often speak while doing other activities. This technique is used in method acting to loosen up nervous actors. Search for a physical action that is somehow related to the emotion you are trying to evoke. If it's a sad, relationship-ending scene, have one of the characters packing up his or her belongings while delivering the dialogue. Characters in scenes could be playing a game, fiddling with a pet, doing a crossword puzzle, fixing some symbolic object, walking down a path, doing needlepoint—all of these activities could be designed to say something about where the character is at emotionally during the scene.

2. **Make sure all the characters' actions are motivated by their stories.** They move to the window to see someone coming, not just to dart around the room to look busy and confuse the audience.

3. **Always give each main character a clear objective or goal to get or an accomplishment in each scene.** "What's my motivation?" to get information, to get money, to trick someone. If character scene motivation is not obvious in the script, make one up that fits the scene. How do you show this motivation through gestures, posing, and metaphorical activities?

Scene Event/Emotion	Metaphorical Character Activity
Character thinking about seeking revenge	Show the character cleaning guns, sharpening knives, checking equipment.
Character hearing news that makes him angry	Show the character cracking walnuts with a hammer, and becoming more violent as the scene progresses.
Character becoming a new person at height of character arc change	Show the character dying his or her hair or shaving it off completely.
Two characters trying to get information out of each other	Show the character playing a game such as chess while talking.
Character about to have a nervous breakdown	Show the character trying to comb knots out of a messy lap dog's fur.
Heading into the unknown	Show the character walking down a dark road into dense fog.

4. **Use character gestures and picturization techniques.** Every emotion is connected to a *universal* physical action that transcends spoken language. Discover ways the characters can communicate what they are feeling or dealing with by using their bodies as visual communication devices.

If your character is trying to make a hard decision, have the character kick a curb repeatedly, pull the petals off a flower, or break sticks. Use as many gestures, poses, glances, shoulder shrugs, head tilts, lip licking, teeth grinding, leg crossing, or meaningful silences as possible to give the audience a chance to absorb emotions visually. Our bodies express what we are thinking and experiencing long before we even realize it sometimes. Build up the motion of the actions with the scene as the emotion peaks. If the character starts out chopping wood with an axe slowly, have the character chop faster and faster as the tension builds in the scene.

This character suddenly becomes overwhelmed with desire for a forbidden lover who just left. To show this emotion, he runs to the treehouse window and opens it, letting the cool air blow over him. He then rubs fresh snow on his hot face to illustrate the cooling of his inner emotions. See how much of your dialogue you can cut out, replacing it with characters showing us *how they feel*. Use universal physical actions to show character feelings in each shot so that viewers can understand, without any soundtrack, everything that's happening.

This Bigfoot kisses a handmade flower prayer boat before kneeling and gently laying it into the sacred spring as a gesture of reverence. What specific ways can you plan the movements of your characters to reveal inner emotions? If she would have just tossed in a premade prayer boat from a pile, we would see that she did not really respect the gesture very much, that she found it to be more of a chore than a sacred act.

How People Communicate When Talking

7% verbal or dialogue

38% volume, tone, pitch, rhythm of voice

55% body movement

? % telepathy

You could also argue that a large percentage of communication is telepathic, which is why it's important while rehearsing scenes to tell your actors what they should be *thinking about*.

These two characters discuss a thorny issue while walking between sharp piles of animal horns. The staging symbolically shows us that they are on opposite sides of the fence. The sharp and dangerous emotions are developed using the pointy shapes, building a visual barrier between the two characters. What objects could you place between your characters to help us understand how they feel about each other? How could you plan to move characters around a set so that they stand between different symbolic objects as scene emotions shift? If the conversation here shifted to a more friendly tone, they could walk into a field of flowers to show the emotional change.

Notice how in this shot, we see the girl standing closer to the older man, smiling at him to show she likes him better. The younger Bigfoot is placed on the far side of the frame to show he is the odd man out. His fists are clenched in an aggressive gesture, and he is leaning toward the couple to show conflict. Hot lava boils between the characters in the background to help develop the scene emotions even further. How can you arrange your characters inside the frame to show relationships? If the girl were in the middle of the frame, she would be in a more neutral position between the other two characters.

5. **For long shots with characters, encourage them to use broad gestures.** Big sweeping movements with arms and legs show up better in the frame against a large background. For close-ups 2 inches from the camera, every facial twitch will show up easily. Keep the scale of your gestures in mind for each shot.

6. **Use staging techniques to show character relationships.** How can you position characters in the frame to help us understand how they feel about each other? If you have three characters in a car, maybe the two who agree more with each other are positioned on the right half of the frame, whereas the other one is on the far left to show isolation. What types of symbolic objects can you place between characters to show relationships?

project 6.14

Add Character Posing and Staging Techniques. Go through each scene in your film and see which of the previous posing and staging techniques you can apply to help develop the emotions, relationships, and story.

superfreak!

Study your favorite films with the sound turned off to see how character actions are used to show inner thoughts and feelings. List each action example and what emotion or thought it is showing.

The Character Eye-Scan Test

Turn to the first page of the color insert section in the middle of this book, and take the Character Eye-Scan Test, as follows:

1. Scan your eyes very quickly (1 to 2 seconds) over each of the 6 images.
2. Record your *impressions* of the character in each shot on a piece of paper. How does he feel in each shot? What is he doing? What kind of character is he? Take a moment to do this now before reading any further.

Review the answers you wrote down. Notice how the character is actually the same in each image (flipped horizontally in some) but that the background changes. The visual area surrounding the character makes him appear more happy in front of the party picture, menacing in front of the fire, crude in front of the raw butchered meat, like a thug in front of the rundown street scene, peaceful in front of the sunset, and hungry in front of the fruit stand. Our minds make the connection between foreground and background images to produce a feeling almost automatically. Keep this technique in mind when designing and composing shots to evoke specific emotions.

Developing Set Designs

Settings are designed to support or contrast the emotions in each scene. The backgrounds and sets behind your characters work to visually cue the audience on how to *feel* each shot.

Virtual Set Design Using Scanned Photographs

Independent filmmakers usually cannot afford to shoot multiple locations, especially in exotic foreign lands, with large casts and crews. Photoshop works great for creating virtual sets, in that it enables you to combine different parts of photographs for bluescreen or animated characters.

Do you have a photography book of images you want to use that you do not have the rights to or that you cannot afford to license? There are some ways to get around this. People do it, so I'm going to just explain how you might want to go about it and leave the moral and legal issues up to you. This is strictly a technique for students who are not making any money off of their films. Suppose, for instance, that you want to have a scene that takes place inside the Great Pyramid in Egypt, and all you have is a coffee table book with some really nice pictures.

1. Scan (at 300 dpi) several photographs that would work well for background sets.
2. Import the images into Photoshop and reduce the dpi to 72 (digital video resolution), with the height and width around 3000 pixels to give you room to pan and zoom across the surface of the image.
3. Cut the images up into groups of objects in Photoshop, such as statues, wall panels, columns, separate pyramids, or whatever else works visually.
4. Move the cut-up pieces around to construct a new set, using Photoshop layers. You may want to try flipping the images horizontally or vertically, if they still look too close to the original photograph. Try scanning images out of several different picture books and collage them together for original-looking sets.
5. Drop in your bluescreen or animated characters on top of the large Photoshop image for a unique virtual set design. Characters could walk behind or between the Photoshop image layers in After Effects.
6. To get a more illustrated look, you could trace the photographs and then scan them as line drawings to use as backgrounds.

After you become a more professional filmmaker with a budget, you will want to purchase any stock photography you use in this way. You could also take pictures of interesting architecture in your town, or on vacation, to use in this way. When you start designing virtual sets using photos, you will develop a better eye for taking pictures that work well together.

How could you plan a scene in your film in which a character is having an emotionally dangerous conversation? One character could be standing in front of a window through which we see a rock climber dangling from a steep overhang (or the character could be standing in front of a picture of this). This would help the audience associate the feeling of dangerously dangling from the rock with the inner character emotional state of danger at that moment. Experiment by having your characters move around a set, standing in front of different background images or objects, or participate in activities to help develop the emotional shifts in each scene. Study some of your favorite films to see how this technique is used. Be very subtle with the background images you choose and how you present the staging. The audience should not really notice the connection, but should feel it on a deeper level. How could you use images and text to create background signs, pictures, or posters in Photoshop? You could also place symbolic sculptures, objects, or metaphorical scene activities in the backgrounds to help develop character emotions.

project
6.15

Place Emotionally Charged Background Images in Scenes. List three ideas about how to use background images to help the audience understand where the characters are at emotionally for each main scene in your film.

Photo collage temple in *Beyond*. This shot for our music video *Beyond* was created by using layers of cut-up vacation temple photos and 3D rendered models from temples all around the world. The staircase the character runs up is two blocks from my house in San Francisco, dropped on top of the photo collage temple, with the sides of the stair shot cut off. This process is explained more in Chapter 9. For now, just know you can re-create almost any setting if you have some good photos. The temple pictures on the side in the first long shot slide back as we zoom into (scale up) the star temple, making it feel like a big traveling shot with the camera moving between layers. You could also add cloud or fog layers between the image layers to get more depth.

project 6.16

Create a Virtual Set Idea. What scene in your film might work using photo collage sets? Draw a sketch of your idea with the different types of layers, such as stairs, columns, towers, roofs, patios, or swimming pools.

Creating Visual Moods Using Textures

Textures applied to characters, clothing, objects, or shapes in the scene work well to develop or contrast emotional moods. If you have a scene that is soft, playful, and romantic, you may choose to fill the set with fluffy pastel pillows, furry soft rugs, candlelight, and a fireplace. A scene with a life-or-death violent conflict occurring may include shiny knives hanging on the walls, harsh lighting, blood-red floor tiles, and sharp-looking metal furniture with hard lines and edges sticking out. Find the cliché idea for emotional scene textures, and then toss that out and think up more original ones. One way to create more original textures is to ask yourself how your particular film world style would approach the design. A romantic Bigfoot scene would have items like fluffy bear skins and torches for candlelight.

Virtual set designers and animators have more flexibility as to how they want to texture map each object. How can you use symbolic textures not seen before, using hand-drawn, photo collage, video collage, or 3D texture mapped sets? 3D enables you to texture map any object with any texture you can imagine. A table covered with fresh, green grass between two characters has a much different emotional feel than a rough stone one crawling with little bugs.

Scene Emotion	Possible Object Textures
Romantic	Soft fabric, fluffy pillows, fur, satin, candle glows/shadows on walls, roses
Tense	Metal, sharp edges, bars, nails, grates, traffic jams, siren lights
Happy	Polka dots, flowers, happy faces, childlike patterns, rainbows, bright colors, plastic toy textures
Sad	Metal, antiseptic, gray industrial, dirty, rain soaked, graffiti, rundown, black fabric, lilies
Angry	Sharp edges, red-hot surfaces, inflexible metal blades
Scary	Old haunted house textures, stuffed dead animals hanging on the walls, twisted metal gates, old and chipped statues, spider webs, thick dust, brittle wooden floors

Designing Conflict in Scenes

Scenes with heavy conflict need to be designed to support that specific tone. Use strong aggressive lines, objects at war with each other visually, sharp textures, and hard shadows or shapes attacking each other in the background.

Designing Conflict. Focus on the areas in your script where the most conflict occurs. What ways can you make the images or textures in those shots represent that conflict in an original way? List three ideas for each major conflict area.

Apply textures to objects and across surfaces in your rough storyboards. Sketch possible texture designs for each main scene in your drawing book first if you have time.

In the first shot, the Bigfoot sits on a rock, banging rocks together, with a rock wall in the background. In the second drawing, he sits on a tree trunk banging wood chunks together, with a forest in the background. Notice how the rock textures make the character and scene feel colder and more harsh emotionally than the softer wood. How could you take this shot and apply different objects and textures to show other scene emotions? If it were a happy scene, the character might be twirling sunflowers rolling around in a flower garden.

Notice how in this heavy conflict scene, all the edges are very sharp. The spiky rocks seem to attacking each other around the characters. How can you design your high-conflict scenes to help convey the emotions more visually?

Conceptual Lighting Design

A big part of your film's visual style will come from the lighting in each shot. Lights tell us where we are in a sense, who is important in a shot, and how we should feel about the events occurring.

Digital Lighting Advantages

DV cameras have an added advantage over film cameras in the way they are much more sensitive to light and usually require much less light to record images. There are some very fast films now that shoot in very low light, but they are usually much more challenging to use than DV cameras on film sets. High definition is sensitive to light, which will make light-sensitive cameras more important in the near future.

Every light source has its own color, which will affect the color of every object in your scene. Light sources seldom seen before in their somewhat "pure state" can now be shown quite easily using DV. Most digital cameras have low-light modes. Locations with low light may work well to evoke certain scene emotions or new lighting styles.

What types of dark nightclubs, caves, closets, nighttime gatherings, candle-lit rooms, dark forests, or campfires could you use to create a unique, low-light style in your film?

Animators need to think about lighting design, too. 3D programs enable you to create any kind of lighting setup imaginable. 2D animation programs enable you to add additional animated or DV light layers and use lighting effects plug-ins. DV footage may have additional light layer effects added in post.

Light tells viewers the following:

- **Where.** Reveals the space to us.
- **What.** Disguises or illuminates subjects.
- **Who.** Reveals who the character is.
- **Mood.** Siren, candle, flashlight, chandelier, desk lamp, campfire, and office fluorescents all have a different feel.
- **Depth.** How far we can see into the frame?
- **Texture.** Patterns the light casts.
- **Source.** Symbolic light sources. A light coming from a burning house has a much different feel than one coming from a cozy fireplace.

project
6.19

Develop a Unique Lighting Style for Each Scene. As you go through this section, think of ways to create a unique lighting style for each scene in your film. Pay close attention to how you can exaggerate or contrast emotions by adjusting the lights during key shots.

Light for Textures Tip

Cast your lights so viewers can really see the interesting textures across objects in your scene. A slight tilt of a light source may suddenly reveal a hidden spider web, wood-grain pattern, metallic reflection of a sharp blade, or the shiny surface of puddle. What interesting textures that symbolically go with the scene emotions can you emphasize on your set with lighting adjustments?

What types of inexpensive and unique lighting styles could you design to take advantage of DV's sensitivity to light? This lighting design uses strings of Christmas lights with symbolic shapes and colors to develop scene emotions. In the first shot, the character stands in front of a string of blue, moon-shaped, blinking lights, which makes her appear more earthy, introspective, mysterious, and intuitive. In the second shot, the two characters stand in front of red chili pepper blinking lights that help evoke the aggressive, overheating emotions of the encounter. Refer to the color section of the book to see how the emotions of these shots change with the added color coming off the lights. As you go through the exercises in this section, import the scans of your rough storyboards into Photoshop and practice applying different lighting designs.

Light Factors

The visual style of your shots will be controlled somewhat by the quality, direction, source, color, and texture of the lighting.

- **Quality.** Intensity, how bright/dark
- **Direction.** Path of light projection from brightest source point to fall off in the distance
- **Source.** Object emitting light
- **Color.** Symbolic color to best tell the story and emotion of the scene and characters (filters, gels, and colored lights, for instance)
- **Texture.** Semitransparent shapes, patterns, or cloth placed between the light source and the subject to soften or cast textured light patterns

Three-Point Lighting

The advantage of three-point lighting setups is that your characters will not look flat against backgrounds, but will have volume that almost pops them right off the screen with an illuminated perfection. The most important characters in the shot should be considered strong three-point lighting candidates. Make background lighting dimmer and softer, or in a cooler color, to help the characters stand out even more.

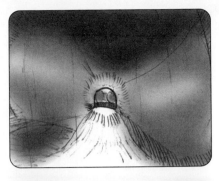

A set lit with a spinning ambulance siren has a much different feel than one lit by an altar of glowing candles. What types of symbolic light sources can you place in each of your scenes to help develop the emotions and story?

This is a typical three-point lighting setup. Notice how the light is hitting the character from all sides, to help separate the character from the background and add depth and volume to the shot. If you cannot afford a professional three-point lighting setup, how can you use other light sources positioned around the character in a similar fashion? A desk light might work for the kicker light, a light box for the fill light, and a ceiling light for the backlight. Hardware stores have all sorts of inexpensive lighting setups that may work for your own unique lighting strategy.

Two Types of Film Lighting

Motivated light comes from within a set and is natural to the scene (such as window, lamp, or car lights).

Unmotivated light is added light for extra dramatic impact, not coming from any obvious place in a scene (a perfectly lit face in a dark room, for instance).

Different Lighting Styles

You can use basic lighting styles to contrast or exaggerate the different moods in your film, as shown in the following table.

project 6.20

Pick Lighting Styles. Go through your film and choose basic lighting styles to contrast or exaggerate the emotions in each shot, scene, or sequence.

Creating Different Lighting Styles for Individual Characters

How can you use specific lighting styles to develop individual characters visually? You might have a really creepy antagonist who is usually backlit to create a dark, frightening silhouette. Maybe your leading lady is always lit with soft and diffuse three-point lighting to make her look and feel even more adorable. In *The Godfather*, Marlon Brando was always lit from above so that his eyes were in shadow (to make him appear more mysterious). Experiment with the following techniques to create original lighting styles for individual characters.

Hard	Soft
Clearly defined, bold, sharp light and shadows	Fuzzy, soft light
Straight rays off light, often from a single source	Bounced light
Harsh midday overhead sun	Diffuse, even light, like an overcast sky
Crisp textures and shadows	Softer textures and shadows
Hard edges to objects in frame	Softer edges

The antagonist witchdoctor Bigfoot could be lit mostly with a backlight to create a mysterious, creepy silhouette. A brighter lighting setup might have the protagonist sitting in light beams cast from holes in the rocks above. In this example, a spotlight layer was created in Photoshop and then placed over the shot. Using similar techniques and software, you can create digitally enhanced lighting designs without even having to plug in a single lightbulb! How can you design lighting around each character to evoke specific emotions?

High Key and Low Key Lighting Styles

- **Low key.** High-contrast lights set up to cast lots of shadows. The main key light is placed in a low position to cast more shadows off of subjects. A good way to remember this is to think of how just before the sun goes down, shadows get really long.
- **High key.** Flatter lighting set up to have low contrast and smaller shadows. The main key light is placed higher on the subject, which flattens out really dramatic shadow casting. Think of how the high-noon angle of the sun flattens shadows during peak afternoon hours.

High Key	Low Key
Fill and backlight	Less-intense key light on the side. May be a single light source for the shot.
Low contrast	Strong, extreme contrasts between dark and light areas in the frame.
Soft, transparent shadows	Sharp shadows, with a dark void around characters.
Comedies, dramas, adventures	Danger, somber, mysterious, horror, noir films such as *Blade Runner*.
Light, fun, happy	Sad, heavy, dark, scary.

Using Shadows to Develop Lighting Styles

You can use two types of shadows to increase depth and volume in your shots:

- **Attached shading.** Shades features across the surface of objects. A person's face with a single candle flame on the right will produce dramatic attached shading effects across facial features.

- **Cast shadows.** Shadows objects cast across walls in the background or on other surfaces (for instance, a person holding a candle casts a silhouette against a wall).

In this image, a character standing in front of a fire casts a shadow against the rock wall.

Utilizing Cast Shadow Patterns

How can you use cast shadows to build up the emotional textures in your film? What types of semitransparent or patterned objects could you place between your light source and subject to add interest or conflict? Venetian blinds filtering sunlight into a room add vertical slits and visual tension across a scene.

Lighting Effects

A variety of transparent items can be placed between light sources and subjects to cast different illumination qualities. Interesting patterns of light and light textures help develop scene emotions. A shot that is supposed to feel sacred may use light patterns cast from stained glass church windows across the character's face. Many of the following lighting effects can also be created in post using 2D and 3D animation software.

How could you use digitally enhanced shadows to help tell your story? You could create different layers of animated cast shadows and place them into your scenes. In this shot, a character bravely fights a monster. The inner emotion of fear the character feels is shown by the way his shadow is running away, not matching the action of the pose. If you shoot the character shadow movement on a bluescreen, or render it out as separate alpha channel layer, you can then use it to create unique shadow layers. Fill the shadow layer with semitransparent gray and feather the edges. Apply a 3D tilt effect to the shadow in a program such as After Effects to arrange in the correct position. This type of visual technique could even become a style in your film, to develop the subtext of each scene. There are also special shadow casting plug-ins that take alpha channel images and create shadows for you.

In this image, a fiery torch illuminates the side of the character's face, creating an attached shading pattern of light and dark areas coming off the features to reveal the surface shape.

These two Bigfoots are about to beat up the one sitting down. To develop the emotions of the scene, long shadows coming off of the aggressive Bigfoots are cast like bars over the one on the ground to show conflict and dominance. How can you use shadows to help develop emotional scene textures?

You must be very careful not start any fires, because most lights get very hot (and, therefore, it's extremely dangerous to drape things over them). Try holding items up in front of lights or hanging them off stands between the lights and the subject to cast patterns. Lighting equipment can get expensive fast, too, so I have added cheaper versions for some of the following ideas.

Here are some ideas for creating lighting effects:

- **Silk.** Thin pieces of silk can be draped over lights to cast a softer light quality. Colored silks can be used in the same way as colored lights or gels (but with a much more subtle quality).
- **Sheer fabrics.** Use sheer fabric or thin fabrics with symbolic designs that cast interesting light patterns

across surfaces. Nylon or fishnet stockings stretched over lights produce textures in various colors. How could you use fabric with symbolic designs to show emotion in your scenes?

- **Lacy fabrics.** Any fabric with holes in it, or see-through parts, may work well to cut the light source up into interesting shapes.
- **Nets.** Placing nets or netted fabric over or in front of lights will generate interesting textures.
- **Flags.** Professional film lights have little black flaps called flags that can be bent to constrain the spread of light coming from the source.
- **Bounce cards.** White silky bounce cards are great to use for fill lights, or to fill out three-point lighting setups. You can also use a large piece of white poster board.
- **Reflector boards.** You can use shiny silver reflector board to bounce light off of. A cheaper version is a piece of cardboard covered with tinfoil. Shine light onto to a

shiny surface and adjust the board to reflect light onto the subject.

- **Black wrap.** Wrap the rim of your light source with this heavy-duty black foil to create interesting shapes for the opening of the light. You could sculpt a tiny hole opening or a symbolic shape. Regular tinfoil may also be used.
- **Light screens.** Metal screens with patterns may be placed over or in front of lights. Cheaper versions could include pieces of iron gates, jewelry draped over light to cast patterns, cheese graters with holes, patterned see-through kitchen utensils, interesting-looking metal objects from the hardware store, or bent wires.
- **Lighting gels.** Colored pieces of semitransparent gels that color lights.
- **Handmade gobos.** Use paperboard or cardboard and cut out interesting shapes, such as a miniature stained glass window, with an Xacto knife.

project
6.22

Character Lighting. Go through your film and make notes on how you may want to light characters differently depending on the story.

Character Lighting Styles

- **Frontal.** Eliminates most shadows, flat looking. May produce shadows depending on height.
- **Sidelight/crosslight.** Sculpts character features (sharp shadows cast on walls by nose, cheekbones, and lips, for instance). A slight triangular shadow off the nose is good to aim for when setting these lights up.

- **Backlighting.** High/low angles create dramatic silhouettes. Good when combined with frontal lighting to create an illuminated contour that helps characters stand out against backgrounds.
- **Underlighting/low key.** Light source coming from below subject. Suggests offscreen fire effect. Great for distorting features. Dramatic and horrific facial effects.

- **Top lighting.** High frontal light brings out cheekbones on face. Can also be very unglamorous (such as a pool hall light above a table).
- **Kicker.** Backlight on side to highlight a character's temple or cheekbones.
- **Eye light.** Frontal light usually placed on top of the camera and aimed at the character's eyes to create extra sparkle.

Lighting Effects. Go through your storyboards and come up with three ideas for things to put between your lights and subjects to add interest and develop the story.

This handmade gobo design was created by cutting paperboard or cardboard into the shape of a church window. The see-through glass areas are covered with different pieces of lighting gels or transparent colored paper from art stores to simulate stained glass panels. When this mini church window is held in front of a light, it will cast these colored patterns across the set, adding a very specific emotional feel to the scene. What other symbolic lighting shapes could you create for your film using this technique? These same handmade gobos can also be easily created as alpha channels layers in Photoshop and used to break up 2D and 3D light sources in software programs.

Choose light colors to go with the emotions for each scene.

- **Glass objects.** You could also use other types of see-through objects placed in front of lights, such as small stained glass windows, pains of glass with colored gels pasted on in interesting shapes, aquariums, colored glass bowls, mirrors to bounce light off, or moving handheld mirrors bouncing light off them to give the light a sense of movement.
- **Other light sources that cast interesting patterns.** Christmas lights, lava lamps, rotating lampshades with cut-out patterns, candles in front of statues casting shadow patterns on walls, and spinning siren lights.

Using Colored Lights
Most film lights are colored using filters. Professional colored lights are often expensive and hard to find. If you are on a tight budget and want to use colored lights, experiment with using colored lightbulbs in your light sources. Animators can color their lights much more easily in software programs. Refer to the Color Psychology Chart in the middle of this book to choose light colors for your scenes. How can you use light colors to cue the audience emotionally? An angry character may be lit with a red light, whereas the calm one gets a cool blue light. You may want to change light colors on a character's face as the scene progresses to show big emotional shifts. Or characters may move from a red-lit area of the scene to a blue one as they go from angry to sad.

Bumping Up Available Light
What places in your shots could you choose to bump up available light, with additional lights for more dramatic effects? DV is so sensitive to light that it easy to blow bright lights out inside the frame, creating an interesting look all its own. If you have a character sitting by a window having an epiphany, you could add a light source behind or by the window, to make the character appear to be floating in a cloud of white light, amplifing the emotion.

Available Light Light sources already on sets, such as lamps, overhead lights, glowing objects, or sunlight through windows.

In this sketch of a miniature set idea, the green light from the aquarium could be bumped up by placing a light behind it, shinning into the scene. The tiny set lamp could also be bumped up using another light source shining down from above.

Bump Up Available Light. Go through each scene and see where you might be able to exaggerate available light sources for more dramatic impact.

The moon illuminates this character's head, casting a glowing halo to symbolize greater intuitive understanding. This light source idea was inspired by Hindu mythology calendars, which often show heads in front of moons or suns to symbolize enlightenment. What existing symbolic lighting setups can you adopt from paintings or photographs for shots in your film? How would this shot feel different if the character was lit from behind by a huge bonfire, flaming scarecrow, or burning house?

Notice how the symbolic shapes of the hanging lights affect our perception of the character and mood.

Light Source as Symbol

What symbolic light sources could you design for your sets to help develop emotions and story?

"We do not remember days, we remember moments."
—*Cesare Pavese*

project 6.26

Light Sources as Symbols. Go through each scene in your film and list at least one possible symbolic light source.

writing exercise 6.2

Write a story that uses as many symbolic light sources as possible.

Symbolic Light Source	Possible Meanings
Big portable stage lights	Big budget, super illumination, professional, movie stars
Birthday cake with candles	Celebration, getting older, fun, making wishes, childlike, annual
20-foot-tall bonfire	Gathering of energy for big event, communal fire
Burning bush	Miracle or fire, holy, guidance, higher communication, pay attention, communication with unseen realms
Burning house	Disintegration of family, broken relationships, destruction of foundations, losing everything
Burning wooden/ straw effigy	Letting go, casting a spell, protest, ritual, riot, summoning the power of the symbolic shape
Campfire	Primitive, survival, outdoors, warmth, light
Candles burning in shapes such as a circle of saints or symbols	Sacred space, altar, intentions, ritual, holy
Car headlights	Temporary, direct, harsh low spotlight, threatening, moving, mysterious, ominous
Christmas lights	Holiday cheer, celebration, sparkles, magical, twinkles
Fire dancers/jugglers	Future, primitive, wild, primal, danger, elemental, ancient
Fireplace	Warm, cozy, romantic, life-sustaining, comfort
Flashlights	Searching through the unknown, examining darkness or fear, unsettling limited scope of vision, guiding light
Funeral pyre	Death, rebirth, memories, ritual, change, endings

Pulsing Moving Lights

What types of dynamic lighting effects can you add to your film? Pulsing neon lights outside a city window at night create an eerie sense of urban breathing. A swinging, overhead, bare lightbulb can feel like a blade slicing through the air.

Even the simple turning off and on of a light switch can add a sense of hyper-disorientation to your shots. Animation programs enable you to do all sorts of fun things with moving, pulsing, blinking, or multiple moving lights.

Symbolic Light Source	Possible Meanings
Glowing character	Enlightened being, radioactive, in love, beaming with joy
Plug-in glowing lawn birds/geese	Holy place, artistic residents, funky, uncommon, protectors
Glowing statue	Illuminated symbol, turned on, active, alive, powerful
Harsh midday sunlight	Hot emotions boiling over, breaking points, melting
Lava lamp	Funky, retro, liberal, youthful, fun, psychedelic
Light box/light table	Working light, examining, study, illuminating the unknown, details, scrutiny, solving a mystery
Light switch turning on/off fast	Disorienting, between worlds, strobe, unsettling, things appearing and disappearing, unseen changes occurring
Lit fountain	Illuminated flow, energy moving, life, source, grounded
Moonlight	Intuitive, romantic, cold blue magic, quiet, peaceful
Swinging overhead lightbulb	Sharp slicing motion in air produces uneasy feel of being cut open, exposed, unsettling, danger, uncertain, shifting emotions, examining, ungrounded, violence
Symbolic lamp shapes such as a 3D talking saint	Mentor, protector, guiding light, supernatural, divine
Torches	Primitive, cavemen, jungle, caves, passing-the-flame ceremony, keeping the torch burning for some reason

project
6.27

Moving Lights. Think up one idea for using moving, pulsing, or blinking lights somewhere in your film.

superfreak!

Add Lights to Overheads. Gather up any ideas that you think might work for lighting your film. Take out the rough scene overheads you drew. Add the light sources to the diagrams with arrows, colors, and light spreads to show what is being lit by each source. It is fine to use Photoshop or Illustrator to add the lights.

Developing a Color Palette

"Each of us makes his own weather, determines the color of the skies in the emotional universe which he inhabits."
—Fulton J. Sheen

"I try to apply colors like words that shape poems, like notes that shape music."
—Joan Miro

Color design is an area that can make or break your film or animation. Review the color palettes used in your favorite visual stories to see the types of color combinations they use and how much color choices affect the emotions for each shot. As you go through this section, experiment with developing one color palette for your whole film or separate ones that go together for key scenes.

How can you use strong color design choices to help tell your story and evoke different sets of scene emotions? In *The Wizard Of Oz*, Dorothy leaves the dark sepia monochromatic world of Kansas for the fully Technicolor land of the yellow brick road. In *Blue Velvet*, the happy American small town scenes are presented in bright primary colors. The first shot in this film is a close-up of three big red roses against a white picket fence with a clear blue sky in the background (red, white, and blue). The darker side of town over

(where Isabella Rossellini's apartment is located) is covered in muted dark wine colors. These extreme color shifts really help the audience understand that there are two very different worlds occurring in these films. The extreme color changes in both examples work well to help shift the audience's emotions fast from scene to scene.

Color Balance

Take the Color Balance Test in the color insert before reading this section on color balance.

Color affects balance and composition in shots because our eyes naturally go toward warm, bright, or white colors in the frame. Notice how your eyes went straight to the yellow circle in the Color Balance Test and how hard it is for your eyes to even leave that spot. Keep this technique in mind as you add colors to your rough storyboards. Experiment with arranging your shots so that the viewer's eye goes to the

Miscellaneous Lighting Tips

1. Start with a single source light per shot, and then add lights only as needed.
2. Remember, our eyes are always drawn to the brightest spot in the frame. The light/dark contrast tells us where to look on the screen. The most important figure or subject in the shot gets the clearest light. Bad guys traditionally get darker lighting, with good guys in bright lighting throughout the story.
3. Underlight your scenes rather then overlight. DV will blow things out quickly with too much light and collapse shadows into darkness without enough light. You want to be able to see details in the shadows and not large areas of flat black (unless this is a style). Most people starting out will use too much light. Aim to underlight your scenes as much as possible.
4. What you see on a set with lights is not necessarily what you will get on tape. Experiment with how your DV camera shoots in different lighting situations or have a monitor on the set to see what you are actually getting with each shot.
5. Be daring, break rules, and do unexpected creative things with your lighting approaches.
6. Use shadows to build suspense at key moments.

brightest area first. How could you use bright or warm colors on an important character or object to make that character or object stand out more in your frame?

Brightness gives an object extra weight in a shot composition. An object with greater mass may be used to balance out one with brighter colors. The small pink circle balances out the large green square to make the frame equal in compositional weight.

Creating a Color Palette for Your Film

If your film has multiple locations, you may want to design a different color palette for each one, or group of locations, to fit the changing moods. Notice how in each part of the movie *Traffic*, a different visual look is used, especially with regard to color. The Mexican world is tinted in grainy, hot yellow sepia tones. The world of the rich girl and politician father is in cool, traditional blues with sharp, expensive-looking, subdued lighting. The San Diego drug dealer world is very beachlike with a full, sunny, warm palette. In *Transit*, the same extreme color shifts occur between each of the seven locations. During the Egyptian pyramid murder scene, the colors become almost monochromatic with hot sand to help us really relate to the overheating emotions.

Pop Color Psychology

Every visual decision you have been making for your film is about to get a symbolic paint job. Deciding what colors to use in your film is similar to the way a painter picks a palette. Each color means something, and they all have to create a strong emotional mood when viewed together. The meaning of different colors is very subjective across different people and cultures. White is worn at weddings in the United States, for instance, whereas in India, it symbolizes death.

Read through the Color Psychology Chart in the color insert to see which ones might work best to express the mood of each location in your film world. Add any of your own color meanings next to the ones listed; after all, this is a very subjective chart.

The most important thing to remember is to use very limited palettes to allow the viewers to make finer distinctions in color changes. Study films such as *The Matrix* to see how little color there is on the screen. Use lots of neutral colors with small amounts of bright ones to lead the eye around the story taking place inside the frame. Monochromatic coloring, in which you tint the whole frame a single color that varies only in lightness and darkness, is a great way to start planning color for scenes. You can then look at where to add certain colors for more emphasis. Import your rough storyboards into Photoshop and apply different color palettes to see what works best. Duplicate the storyboard panel layer, apply Multiply to the top one, and paint or drop fill the lines on the bottom layer to retain the lines of the drawing if your color is too messy.

project 6.28

Find the most important visual spot in each shot of your rough storyboards and plan a color strategy to make that area brighter or warmer. If the important spot moves, how can you apply colored lights or brighter colors on moving objects to lead the viewer's eye? How can use this technique in another way, such as placing unimportant objects in bright spots, to distract the audience for a moment while something else happens in a darker area of the frame?

"Color is directly connected to a particular vibration that, when used properly, will connect the brain almost instantly to that which it seeks to know."
—Joseph Rael

project 6.29

Create Color Palettes for Your Film. Decide how many color palettes you want to use in your film and create four-color RGB palettes. Separate warm and cool colors.

"Creativity is harnessing universality and making it flow through your eyes."
—Peter Koestenbaum

Part of my film's visual style will be showing the way the characters get information by staring at the surface of water. In this shot, when Ezzie's stops to eat her stolen chocolate, the witchdoctor's face appears up out of blue spiraling water (theme color and symbols) and summons her to his cave.

Using Color to Show Theme

When picking a palette, you may want to consider choosing a color to represent your theme. You can then apply this color to certain theme objects, or symbolic shapes, throughout your film. In *Transit*, the color red is used to show the seduction-of-an-innocent theme. Oscar the butcher has bright red hair and is covered in a bloody apron the first time he meets Emmy. The murder weapon is wrapped in a bright red scarf and thrown out of a dark train. Red strawberries are fed or rubbed on characters in various scenes. Blood from the fatal knife wound and gunshot are shown against neutral-colored backgrounds to really stand out. *American Beauty* is another film that uses the color red as a theme symbol worth studying in depth.

For my film, I chose a cyan blue to represent the theme that everyone has a unique life purpose to find and fulfill. I then chose the symbol of a spiral to represent my theme and placed blue-colored spirals in as many scenes as possible. There are blue spiraling ripples in the river when the witchdoctor's face appears on the water, spiral carvings on the cave walls, a glowing fungus blue spiral path the character walks (and which also lights the cave scenes blue), spiral snakes, spiral bone and rock sculptures, and even a glowing blue spiral worm on the character's head as she surfaces from the quicksand and has an epiphany at the end.

Color Tips for Planning Film Palettes

- Stay away from really bright, highly saturated colors. These will not look good on NTSC and generally will give your animation a less-expensive look and feel. If you do need a bright palette, try using one from TV shows such as *The Simpsons*. These colors are proven safe bets. There are some samples of colors to avoid—refer to the color insert in this book.
- Study movies that have color palettes you really like, with similar moods or styles that may work for your film.
- Try using lots of neutral tones, such as browns, grays, golds, blacks, and whites, with small touches of brighter colors to lead the viewer's eyes. Science fiction films such as *Dune*,

Dark City, *Alien*, *The Matrix*, *Lord of the Rings*, and *Blade Runner* use lots of monochromatic color schemes that make significant emotional impacts.
- Scan a painting using a palette you think fits the mood of your animation and has a limited color scheme. Use the eyedropper from Photoshop and pull colors off the painting for cool, warm, and neutral colors. *Gardner's Art Through the Ages* is good reference book in which to look for traditional painting palettes. Refer to the example palette in the color insert.
- You may also want to grab a DV frame from a favorite movie that uses color powerfully and color pick the palette. Try grabbing two or three

frames from different palettes to cover multiple sets in your animation. Pick films with similar styles and moods.
- Pick a four- or five-color palette with colors that go together in the same hue range and use only these as much as possible. Collect color palette combination books used by graphic designers showing four-color swatch RGB value combinations to make sure your colors go together.
- If you are working on different computers or with a team, use the RGB color value numbers with your palettes to make sure everything will be the same color at the end.

Create a Color Map

Color maps were developed by 2D animators at Disney to help plan color palette shifts. This technique works good to make sure all the colors in your film go together, too. By adding additional spaces for RGB values in your color maps, you can make sure that the blue you are using in shot 347 is the same that you used in shot 3, for instance. If you are working in a group, color maps enable you to make sure that each person on your team is using the same colors.

If you are planning your color choices carefully for each shot, you should be able to see the story unfolding and changing by looking at the color maps. Make sure the colors in each scene match, support, contrast, or develop the story or emotions in some way. In the color insert of this book, there is an example color map for the first four shots of my film. Notice how the color changes help tell the story, with the foggy, moonlit forest in the first shot, and then brown suddenly enters the frame in shot two with the appearance of the Bigfoot. In shot three, brown takes up most of the frame as the Bigfoot gets real close. Shot four uses the same brown for the big bar of chocolate at the campsite. A blazing fire in the background creates a big palette shift between film worlds and locations. I later decided to place a B/W filter over the Bigfoot video shots to create an old surveillance camera look, but decided to keep the color because most DV is shot that way now.

Color Map Example

Color Used Most In Shot   Color Used Least In Shot

Shot #	00:00 - 00:00
Shot Description	
Shot Emotion/Mood	

Notice the way the blocks of color on the left are larger than the ones on the right, to show which colors take up the most space in each shot.

RGB Color Map Example

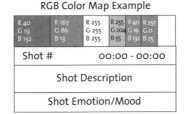

Shot #	00:00 - 00:00
Shot Description	
Shot Emotion/Mood	

If you are creating an animated film, working in a team, or want to be more precise with the colors you are using throughout the film, create an RGB color map. Each time you need a light blue, you plug in the RGB numbers, and all the light blues in your film will match.

project 6.30

Pick a Color and Symbol for Your Theme. What color is your theme? How can you place this color in each scene and use it only to show symbolic theme objects in your film? Create monochromatic background palettes for each scene and then add colored symbols to them. The symbol can be different in each scene to represent the same theme, such as the blood-red strawberries, scarf, and blood in *Transit*.

superfreak!

Create a color map for your favorite film or animation. Fill in one of the color map grids for each main scene or shot to see how color is being used to tell the story. Use colored pencils, markers, or Photoshop to fill in the color squares as you watch the film. Some films with good color palette shifts include *The Lion King*, *The Matrix*, *Traffic*, and *Transit*.

project 6.31

Create a Color Map for Your Film. You can create a separate set of color map boxes for each shot or each main scene. Refer to the example in the color insert to see how one looks.

In the first few shots of my film, I am planning on creating a video surveillance camera look. This extra layer of postprocessing on the final shots will change the visual style and feel of the footage dramatically. We have all seen real video footage from surveillance cameras on the news and automatically associate this particular overhead POV, low-resolution, B/W look to mean the footage is real. What types of existing film or video looks can you use during different scenes of your film to help tell the story?

"It is looking at things for a long time that ripens you and gives you a deeper understanding."
—*Vincent Van Gogh*

Adding Film Looks in Post

In my opinion, almost all DV needs color correction in post (see Chapter 9, "Digitally Enhanced Storytelling Techniques"). You should almost never shoot something and not adjust the colors. Some shots are going to be warmer/cooler or lighter/darker, and you need to even them all out after shooting. You can also add film-look filters in post, to copy 35mm stock looks, such as reversal film, that make the blacks really black and tone down saturated colors. Or use film-look filters to create aged or damage film looks. You may also go in and do an extreme color manipulation pass on certain scenes to create highly stylized looks, such as making everything appear less saturated and dark green for the scary parts. Keep all of these choices in mind as you think about choosing color palettes and creating unique visual styles for your film.

Some 35mm feature films are now digitally scanned and color corrected shot by shot or scene by scene in post. This way, you can get interesting looks, such as the yellow tones in *O Brother Where Art Thou*, which had a very strong color correction pass to give it that warm mustard look. It is obviously much easier to deal with color correction after you shoot or animate, but you need to design any strong post color-correction ideas now if possible. When producing shots for color correction, you want to make sure you have enough information to have flexible color choices. Aim for details inside shadows, wide ranges of colors, nice contrast, and avoid over-exposing and blowing everything out or setting things up so dark that there in no information in the frame to tweak.

Now that you have a better understanding of your film's mise en scène, you can concentrate on applying the same types of decisions to create unique sound and editing styles.

project 6.32

Design a Postproduction Color Correction or Film-Look Visual Style. Are some of your sequences going to be black and white with lots of damage to look like old home movies? Will any sad scenes be tinted blue with a grainy film-look filter for maximum emotional impact? Do you want to make the whole film have a certain limited color range? Maybe you just want to go in and make your blacks really black or everything more midtone. If you know how, you may want to experiment creating post visual styles with some existing footage to see what types of signature looks you can create for your film. This information will help you better understand how to set up and light your shots for the final color-correction pass.

Apply New Visual Styles to Rough Storyboards. Incorporate all the design decisions you made in this chapter into your rough story boards. Use Photoshop or color the shots by hand with markers or colored pencils. Add set design elements, costumes, gestures, activities, color palettes, styles, visual symbols, and anything else you think will communicate your story in the most powerful and original way.

Make the Film You Can Afford Today. Don't get stuck waiting to get funding for your dream feature screenplay or over-the-top budget short film. Make the film you can afford today by being super creative. The more films you make, the better you will get. Some people put off making their films for years, just trying to raise money. The more creative limitations you have, the more interesting your solutions.

Redesign an Existing Scene. Take a scene from your favorite movie and change the mise en scène. Switch genre, characters' social backgrounds, species, cast, ages, colors, styles, set pieces, lighting, and general look and feel. Preserve the actions, dialogue, and essence of the scene. If the set has two characters talking at a kitchen table, redesign it using a different style for the kitchen, table, background, posing, and characters, all in the same position. Do a rough sketch of your new idea in your drawing book. Notice how much changing the mise en scène affects the feel of the shot.

Redesign One Existing Scene. Take the same scene from a film and have each person in the group redesign it independently to see how much it can change. Have each person present his or her ideas when finished with a little sketch.

chapter 7

Narrative Sound Design

*"The evolution of film has led to a new fusion of the audio and the visual.
It's a kind of poetry that abounds in aural metaphors."*
—*Walter Murch*

The golden age of narrative sound design is upon us, with powerful software that can turn a desktop computer into what was once a multimillion-dollar sound effects studio. Digital sound design and manipulation has profoundly affected the ability to shape new auditory styles for films. Being able to use multiple layers of sounds from different sources, manipulated with filters and effects, greatly enhances a filmmaker's ability to craft wholly original soundtracks. In this chapter, you will develop a narrative sound design style for each scene in your film.

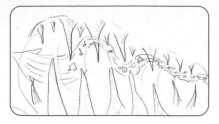

How could you use your digital software to create or combine sounds in new ways? I could record a few minutes of the ocean, and then take it into my sound-editing program and play it in reverse, at half speed with a stadium reverb filter, to create a big, deep, and emotionally powerful new sound. I could then mix the backward ocean, with a howling wind track and whistling flutes, to echo through the dark stalactite caverns. This new combination of sounds would create a unique auditory style and atmosphere, while helping to develop the spiritual mystery mood for those scenes in my film. What sounds could you combine and play with digitally to create original auditory scene atmospheres?

"Animation played a big role in the development of imaginative sound by imposing the perception of one reality on another."
—*Walter Murch*

Soundtracks are fun to create. Most narrative soundtrack ideas involve layering different sounds in the same way we put together layers of images or video to create unique story styles. Digital artists now have the freedom to bend anything you record or pull off sound clip libraries into something completely different—something no one has ever heard before. Sound design ideas in this chapter focus on ways to connect on a deeper emotional level with the audience and how to tell your story more through the soundtrack.

money-saving

How Much is That Mic? The mic on your DV camera is not the best choice. A midrange short shotgun mic (ME66 or AT4063) can be purchased for between $500 and $900. You may want to just rent one for the day of the shoot, depending on your project length, budget, and usage pattern. A professional DAT or minidisk recording system is another way to record good sound. If you are new to digital filmmaking and on a very tight budget that does not include *any* money for extra microphones, you can still grab sounds using the mic on your DV camera, and then mix the audio tracks together in your video-editing program. It will not always sound great, but it will work okay until you can afford to get or rent a better microphone.

project 7.1

Study *Apocalypse Now* for Sound Design. After reading this chapter, watch this film and note how almost every sound design technique discussed in this chapter is used. You can just *listen* to this film and almost get the whole story. In the opening shots, we see Martin Sheen's head superimposed upside down over images of the jungle, helicopters, and war scenes. We are brought back to his hotel room by the sound of whirling helicopter blades, mixing with the whirl of the ceiling fan above him, in a visual and auditory match cut. How could you use a similar technique somewhere in your film to link different locations or shots using sounds?

Technical Sound Information Not Included

Specific technical sound and software information is not part of the enormous scope of this book, because things change so fast and people are using so many different tools. Jay Rose writes some good books on audio for digital video, if you need more practical information on sound. This chapter assumes you know how to record audio, either with your microphone of choice or with your DV camera, and edit basic sound layers together in your favorite DV editing or sound program.

The Importance of Good Sound

The better the sound, the better the image. Most would agree that the sound track of a film is equal to about half of the viewing experience. The action on the screen will become flat without good sound design. Great sound design can sometimes save a bad shot. Bad sound design can kill the best visual shot in the world.

Viewing-Room Speakers

Where are people most likely going to see and hear your film? Speakers color sound more than anything else during viewing experiences. Movie theater sound design can go into greater depth and detail with the space and speaker setup. DVDs enable you to author six-channel surround sound for high-end digital home theater viewing. The tiny speakers on your average TV set will drop out many of the little sounds you would hear in a movie theater experience. If your film is most likely going to be seen on a computer, you need to design based on those speakers. PDAs and video mobile phones have their own speaker projection ranges. Test your soundtrack ideas on the types of speakers they will most likely be heard on if possible.

Sound in the Script

Sound is not a final layer of icing you add to a cake; it needs to be an ingredient soaked throughout the whole dessert like sugar. The best sound design starts in the writing of the script. The more you make films and create soundtracks, the more you will write scripts that encompass sound like another type of character. Sounds influence people in ways they do not fully understand. Hearing is the first sense we develop in the womb before we are able to see, touch, taste, or smell. Remember how moments of complete silence seem eerie? We become so used to hearing certain sounds as we go through our day that we would feel things were very strange if these sounds suddenly changed or disappeared.

Music and sounds are intimately involved in visual storytelling. Sound creates emotional atmospheres. How can you go through your script and make sound more a part of the internal story weave? How can your characters react more to sounds? How could a sound raise a question in your story? How could a sound show character growth throughout the film? How could you use sound in new ways to show some of the other things previously discussed, such as theme?

I could take one of my really scary scenes in the dark cave and keep the lighting really low with just shadows and sounds of the character reacting to things. This would help show emotionally how she can hear things but can barely see, while evoking the fear of the unknown. By using low light and clever sound design, I also save myself the time of having to shoot or animate each shot in this scene as carefully as fully lit versions. How can you use sound design to help viewers understand how the characters are experiencing the events in your story?

project
7.2

Create One New Idea for Sound.
Go through your script and see where you can make sound more a part of the story.

Three Types of Film Sound

- **Diagetic (inside film world).** Coming from inside the film world
- **Production.** Sound effects coming from the film world set such as footsteps, explosions, car radios, and gunshots
- **Nondiagetic.** Sound from outside the film world (for instance, a narrator, background music not on the set, or weird sound effects).

When Ezzie throws the boulder into the campfire, a big sound effect needs to occur. I could record throwing a big rock into a fireplace, with crackling noises, to create part of the sound and then use effects to make the sound bigger. I might also add a unique Bigfoot scream into the crashing rock sound to amplify the emotion of shock. Bigfoots are said to sound like roaring lions in garbage cans, which would be fun to try and re-create in post. As you list each sound effect for your story, think of ways to create the sounds in layers to bump up the emotions.

"Music is your own experience, your thoughts, your wisdom. If you don't live it, it won't come out your horn."
—Charlie Parker

Breaking Down Your Scripts For Sound

It is time to reread your script once more and just listen to how you imagine it might sound. List all obvious sound effects such as door slams, gurgling, gunshots. Take each segment or scene of your film and write down any ideas you have for the voices, sound effects, music bed, or ambient sounds. If a scene takes place in a junkyard, do we hear cars being crushed at key emotional moments, with angry guard dogs barking in the distance, workmen banging on chrome, old car engines revving, or shattering windshields? Think of original ways to create sound combinations for your film as you list the various effects and background noises. You could get an angry guard dog sound by recording a neighbor's noisy barking dog, and then add effects and filters to make it sound scary.

project
7.3

Script Sound Breakdown. Take out your line script or a fresh copy and underline any obvious sounds that need to be created. Answer the following questions for each scene in your film using a 3-by-5 scene card or your drawing book:

1. Mark and list all interior/exterior sounds mentioned in script.
2. Mark and list any shots with music, video, or TV sounds in the background.
3. List all important sound effects.
4. List the emotional changes and mood of each scene.

Bad Sound as an Aesthetic?

In the film *Faces* by Cassavettes, bad sound quality becomes part of the film's style. It has an almost documentary feel of following these characters around. The acoustics in the rooms are terrible. Getting good sound on a set can be challenging if you do not have all the proper equipment and manpower. Create your own sound aesthetic if you cannot afford a good mic or if you do not have an extra person to hold a boom.

Creating a Sound Ambiance for Each Scene

What types of sounds could you combine to create a unique ambiance for each scene? If you have a shot in a jungle, you might want to combine sounds from waterfalls, birds, geckos, wild animals, and water dripping off trees. If you have a scene in a ghetto, you might try people fighting, gunshots, sirens, and loud car radios. A suburban bedroom where a couple is about to have a fight might have rain in the background with thunder and lightning, TV war noise coming from another room, kids fighting, and a whirling fan to show it's a hot temper zone.

In the happy wonderland cave scenes, I could combine sounds of chirping birds, waterfalls, whistling wind chimes, crickets, and soft happy background music to help develop the mood and emotions.

In the shamanic journey part of my film, I could create a unique sound ambience full of driving drumbeats, sitars, Tibetan bowls, heartbeats, ocean sounds, dolphins chirping, and wind chimes. The sound of a constant driving drumbeat would be the foundation for this scene, because shamanic journeys are often accompanied by drumming to shift into other realities.

project 7.4

Scene Sound Ambiance. Take each scene in your script and list at least five possible ambient background sounds. Pay particular attention to how much you can tell us about the emotional state of the characters and story using background sounds.

"No man, however civilized, can listen for very long to African drumming, or Indian chanting, or Welsh hymn singing, and retain intact his critical and self-conscious personality." —Aldous Huxley

Using Background Room Tone

Start developing an ear for how different places sound. You will want to record at least 30 seconds of the background room tone, or scene noise, for each location to use in the following ways when building up the layers of your soundtrack:

- To even out background room tone when editing dialogue or adding cutaway shots
- To lay under any dialogue you may have to redo in post to make it sound as if it was recorded on location
- To cover gaps in the soundtrack when removing unwanted background noises, such as airplanes flying over

Creating Layers of Sound

Assembling layers of sounds in unusual ways helps create an emotional atmosphere within your visual story. One way to start building up layers of sounds is to think of ways to communicate environmental ambiance and symbolic auditory themes.

- **Ambience.** Conceptual layer of sound that conveys the mood of the location or scene. May include background mood music or environmental sound montage.
- **Auditory theme.** Use the same types of metaphors and symbols from the exercises in Chapter 2, "Creating Original Characters, Themes, and Visual Metaphors," *as sounds.* If you are doing the theme of how love can redeem dead souls, you might have sounds that develop that emotional arc in the background. A film may start with sounds that remind one of death, such as sirens or church bells in the distance. As the film switches to more of a love-for-life theme, background sounds might be heard of people laughing. What types of sounds could you use to develop the evolving emotional arc for each scene?

The theme in my film is that everyone has a unique higher purpose to find and fulfill. One way to develop this using sounds is to have the character's name being very softly called inside wind gusts that lead her down the right path to find her purpose.

project 7.5

Create Conceptual Sound Layers for Each Scene. List three ideas for both ambience and auditory theme sound design for each scene in your film.

List Emotion of Sounds. Take out your list of sounds and note the emotions of each one. Add any new ideas about how to make the emotional air stronger by adding or combining sounds to make new ones.

"I believe that music, sound, and auditory vibration make up a critical factor in the graceful path to the next stage of revolution."
—Barbara Marx Hubbard

"By exposing ourselves to more amenable noises—melodious music, the sounds of nature, a running stream, the sea, birds singing, and the like—we can repair at least some of the damage done by unwanted noise."
—Brian and Ester Crowley

Adding Emotional Air

Capturing the emotional air surrounding a scene takes careful conceptual thought. Sound without emotional air has no smell. Ask yourself what the emotion is behind each sound in your film. Is that an angry door slam or a peaceful one? How can you add an emotional charge into a scene by taking a sound that might be in the background and making it into an emotional statement? Two characters could be arguing in a field. We hear the sound of a train coming in the distance that sounds like it is screaming, right before one of the characters crushes the other one with some upsetting information. How can you use sound to clue us into the characters' emotional states?

David Lynch pays careful attention to the sound in his films. The city in *Eraser Head* sounds like a snarling animal, which fits nicely with the emotions in the story. What ways could you mix some organic sounds with production sounds to create a greater emotional impact?

Repurposing Natural Sounds

Take your recording devices on a field trip and gather sounds that will help develop the specific emotions in each scene. If you have a scary and tense sequence, you might make a list of all the places in your area with sounds that make you feel uneasy—places such as a sawmill, traffic jams, loud construction sites, upset animals at the zoo, a neighborhood pit bull with a good growl (behind a secure fence), engines starting from old trucks, jackhammers, leaf blowers, people arguing, boxing matches, dog races, busy city emergency rooms, sirens, or rush hour at the main train station. Sound effects libraries work great for this exercise, too, if you have access to some.

In the cavern of dead souls scene, I'm planning on recording a bunch of older people saying lines that give advice, and then adding lots of effects to make the voices sound like ghosts blending together in the windy drafts. To design the emotional air for this scene, I might use people screaming in slow motion, wolves howling, snakes rattling, and Amazon Indians singing an old hunting song.

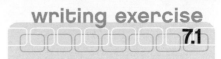

project
7.7

Create an Emotional Sound Chart. List the main mood for each scene. Make a list of 10 sounds that move you in an emotional way to match or contrast that mood as shown in the following table. Use these types of sounds for the following exercises in this chapter. If you have a big emotional change in a scene, list any sounds you think might work well in the background to help develop the changing emotional arc.

writing exercise
7.1

Write a short story that focuses on using sounds to convey emotions.

"See deep enough, and you see musically; the heart of Nature being everywhere music, if you can only reach it."
—*Thomas Carlyle*

Emotional Sound Chart

Happy	Sad	Mad	Tense	Peaceful
Children laughing	Someone crying	Growling pit bull	Dog barking	Seagulls
Cat purring	Wolf howling	Traffic jam horns	Jackhammers	Mountain stream
Light wind chime	Upset wild animals at the zoo	Old, noisy truck engine	Sirens	Frogs in pond
Waterfall	Screams	Snarling man	Fire trucks	Crickets
Surf	Diesel truck horn	Angry crowd	Power saw	Whale songs
Joyful clapping	Baby crying	Sword battle	Construction sight	Dolphins
Happy sigh	Puppy whimpering	Tank	Gunshot	Church choirs
People laughing	Chopping tree down/falling	Lashes from bull whip	Car chase	Horses neighing
Cheering crowd	Plane crash	Demonic laughter	Explosions	Mystic chanting
Canary birds	Crowd in panic	Bear growling	Blizzard	Drum circles
Happy carnival	Ship alarm/under attack	Machine gun/war sounds	Earthquake	Toning
Woman giggling	Wailing animal dying	Car peeling away	Busy signal from telephone	Native American ceremonies
Champagne cork	Dirt thrown on coffin	Lion roaring	Wasp	Someone sleeping
Kissing sounds	21-gun salute	Dishes breaking	Beeper/cell phone	Gentle ocean waves
Sensual groans	People fighting	Punching bag	Dentist drill	Heartbeat
Kids playing	Ambulance	Swarm of bees	Avalanche	Pipe organ music
A child's birthday party	Wailing crowds	Missiles launching	New York City subway	Soft birds singing
Wedding march	Someone getting tortured	Someone getting beat up	Firecrackers	Fountains

"I merely took the energy it takes to pout and wrote some blues."
—Duke Ellington

Contrasting Sounds for Tension

Sometimes it works well to contrast different emotional sounds to build tension in scenes or develop the story. You could have one layer of happy, peaceful sounds and another one with occasional tense firecrackers going off in the distance. This approach works particularly well for scenes with strong underlying conflict.

In *Reservoir Dogs*, upbeat rock music plays during a gruesome scene as a character gets his ear cut off. "I'm so scared, I think I'll fall off my chair" goes the lyrics to "Stuck in the Middle with You." How can you lighten up a really dark scene in your film with an upbeat soundtrack that fits the story?

movie note

Boogie Nights. A great contrasting sound scene occurs when the main character goes to a drug dealer's house to pick up some stuff and another character at the house keeps lighting off really loud firecrackers. The tension created by the loud firecrackers going off is almost unbearable and works well to foreshadow a drug deal about to go horribly wrong. Go through each of your scenes and see what loud activity one of your characters could be doing to add tension, to foreshadow upcoming events, or to contrast emotions.

Foreground	Background
Sad. Characters talking about a sad event and crying	**Happy.** Children's birthday party in full swing
Spiritual. Characters having an epiphany about their spiritual places in the world	**Mad.** Angry fighting between people on TV
Tense. One character blackmailing another one	**Peaceful.** People chanting in a ceremony
Scared. Character in the middle of a challenge making frightened murmuring sounds	**Courageous.** Character in background making whooping war cries

"Music has the capacity to touch the innermost reaches of the soul and music gives flight to the imagination."
—Plato

project 7.8

Create a Contrasting Sound Design Scene. Take one scene in your film and make some notes on different layers of contrasting sounds you could use to evoke two very different and distinction emotions.

Licensing Songs for Soundtracks

Attaching a well-known actor or band to your film will help the project get more exposure and press. The trick is to catch the next big thing before they get too big to want to be in your film. Commercially smaller bands will usually jump at the chance to be in your film if it's a good idea and they like your approach. Contact the Fox Agency in New York for information on licensing famous songs or music for your film at **www.harryfox.com**.

Utilizing Different Sound Sources

A an old car radio plays a song differently than a high-performance surround-sound stereo system, TV, ghetto blaster, computer speaker, Walkman headphones, stack of stadium speakers, intercom, or loudspeaker. Our ears understand these differences. How can you take sounds in your film and play them through another source to create more atmosphere?

In this shot, a Bigfoot watches as a human drives by in a truck blasting music. The sound of the car radio moving by helps contrast how different the Bigfoot forest sound world is from the noisy humans.

Speaker	Emotion/Mood
Old car radio	Nostalgic
Surround-sound, high-tech digital system	Futuristic, cold, expensive, studio
Ghetto blaster cassette player	Urban
Walkman headphones	Enclosed, tuned out of rest of world
50-foot-high stack of stadium speakers	Big sound, rock bands, voice of God, important, omniscient, stadium
Intercom	Formal, informational, sterile
Loudspeaker	Voice of authority, emergency mode
Bullhorn	Authority, race announcer, camp leader, policeman
TV	Free, cheap, commercials, not important, background noise
Computer speaker	Technical, short distance, office space
Mini cassette recorder	Spy device, portable, important hidden sound-recording device
Stereo speakers in backyard 20 feet away	Big sound for atmospheres
10,000-watt party sound system	Loud party, celebration, concert, event
Telephone answering machine	Messages, intimate, important information from people you know
Auditorium microphone	Authority, school, important, pay attention
Helicopter radio	War, air traffic controller, important communication
Ham radio	Independent network, underground, military, worldwide
Old telegraph	Historic, going back in time, nostalgic
Old record player/radio/toy record players	Nostalgic, creepy, out of time
Jukebox/karaoke machine	1950s, retro, wacky, party

project 7.9

Utilize Different Sound Sources. List three ideas for how to use different sound sources in your film. Find one scene in your script where you can record a sound and then play it out of another device.

movie note

In **American Graffiti**, the Wolfman Jack radio show coming out of the car windows as the cars cruise down the street was first recorded as a separate track. It was then played out of stereo speakers rotating 180 degrees in a backyard, and then recorded again with moving microphones to simulate cars driving by. How could you record a soundtrack and then play it out of another set of speakers to create different types of auditory atmospheres?

One idea for using another sound source in my film that fits the story is for the character to find a ghetto blaster on top of a cave shrine. The Bigfoot film world often has items stolen or left behind by campers. When the character presses the Play button, mood music could fill the screen and change the emotions dramatically.

movie note

Apocalypse Now creepy tape.
The plot goal of Martin Sheen's character is to go deep into the jungle and assassinate a renegade army colonel who has lost his mind. When he gets this assignment, his commanding officers play him an audiotape of the crazy guy talking. The shot of the tape rolling forces the viewer to imagine what this guy is like in real life. We do not really see this mysterious character until Act Three, when Martin sees him for the first time too, which adds to the tension. Our imaginations fill in the gap. Hearing his voice on a tape is much more creepy than showing him running around in the jungle cutting people's heads off. This movie uses lots of different sound sources to build up the reality of the film world.

"What we play is life."
—Louis Armstrong

Creating Original Sound Effects

How can you create original sound effects for your film? How can you make that door slam convey an extra emotional punch? A door slamming could be sad, angry, happy, or scary. You could mix a regular door slam with a person screeching, crying, yelling, laughing, or howling. Digital manipulation of sound design opens a treasure chest of new communication techniques. What original ways can you think of to communicate stories with fresh sound design?

Notice the way the character is first drawn in separate pieces for any sections that move. The drawing is then scanned into Photoshop, where each piece becomes a separate layer. This adds greater flexibility to animate using rotation and position keyframes. Some pieces (or layers) are then grouped together in After Effects (or any other animation program) so that they can be moved as one unit—for example, the shoulder, forearm, and hand could move together.

movie note

THX 1138. In this film, the sound of the jet engines was made by having all the women at Zoetrope go into the restroom and scream at the top of their lungs. This produced a high-pitched engine sound we had not heard before, and the sound also triggers a deep instinctive fear reaction based on the underlying screams. People pay more attention to this jet engine sound, more than they would to a normal stock sound of a jet. The boots of the robot soldiers were made by stomping around a museum at night in homemade Frankenstein spring-loaded boots. How could you record sound effects for your film using original techniques such as these?

Sound Sync for Three? Creating sound effects footsteps for characters in post can be time-consuming if viewers can see the characters' feet in the frame. You have to match footsteps precisely for one or two characters walking down a hall. When you have three or more characters walking in a shot, you can just lay in a bunch of footsteps and it will work. Keep this rule of three in mind while planning sound effects.

Create an Original Sound Effect. Look at the list of sound effects in your film. How could you create a new type of sound using some of the previously mentioned techniques?

Sound Needed for Script	Recorded Sound Effects
Footsteps on snow	Person walking on cornstarch.
Lots of arrows shooting through the air	Stick of willow whipped through air repeatedly 24 times at different intervals.
Angry crowd	Record yourself or a few people making angry crowd noises separately, and then layer multiple versions of the tracks. Use an offset time pattern, with each track starting at different intervals to sound like a crowd.
Jet engine	Woman screaming in a bathroom.
Laser gun	Twanging metal with objects or hitting flexible saw blade.
Slimy monster climbing out of hole	Can of dog food being emptied.
Walking through swamp	Fill kids' plastic swimming pool with mud and walk through in rubber boots.
Futuristic city	Gather ambient city sounds and mix with high-tech ambient sounds.

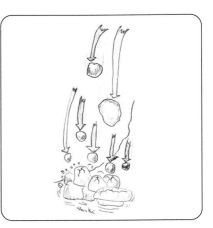

To create a cave rockslide, I could record the sound of one or two rocks falling down a slope and then duplicate those tracks 20 times, raising their volume levels and having them start at different intervals, to sound like a big rockslide. How could you take one sound and make it into something bigger by duplicating it?

Tips on Creating Original Sound Effects Digitally

- Reverse the sound, slow it down to half speed, double the speed.
- Experiment with different sound effects and filters in post.
- Try taking one sound and duplicating it with time offsets to sound big. One rock falling could become a rockslide.

- Blend normal sound effects with primal emotional sounds such as screams, cries, or bear growls—anything to match the emotional quality you are aiming for at that moment.

- Take straight sounds such as a car engine and bump up certain parts of the sound with accents, such as whirling fans or pumping beats for pistons, to develop different spaces inside the sound.

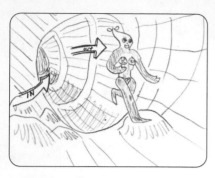

In this shot, Ezzie walks into a cave, we hear her scream, fight off a bear, and see her walk back out. Using sounds to develop the events saves us the time of having to make a 3D bear and animate a whole fight scene. This also pulls the audience into the story, requiring them to imagine what is happening to the character inside the cave. How can you use clever sound design to save yourself production time?

In this shot, Ezzie hears her firefly friend buzz into a hole in the rocks. The sound of bats attacking the firefly is followed by no more buzzing. This tells us we will not see the firefly mentor anymore in the film. The character has already served its purpose in leading Ezzie out of the dark scary cave, and this is an interesting way to get rid of the mentor while creating a strong moment of emotional loss.

project 7.11

Offscreen Sounds. Go through your film and list three ideas for possible offscreen sounds.

Utilizing Offscreen Sound

Sounds that occur offscreen work well to create a sense of the film world continuing outside of the frame and pull the audience into the story by making them feel like they cannot see something important. This forces the audience to re-create what they are hearing in their heads. What ways can you have your characters react to sounds coming from outside the frame?

In the movie *Signs,* we hear the family dog bark as the evil aliens are invading, with Mel Gibson and his family huddled together inside their boarded-up house. One of the kids points out that they forgot to bring the German Shepard inside. We then hear the dog barking louder and louder offscreen as the family just stands listening. The sound of the dog attacking, followed by the sound of it whimpering and then silence, tells us the dog lost. This is much more powerful than showing us the scene, because the more we see of the evil aliens, the less scary they become. It also saves having to set up another scene outside with the dog. What ways can you use offscreen sound to save time and make the scene happen more inside the viewer's head?

"Through vibration, harmony, tone, melody, and meaning, music stimulates within us direct experience of expanded reality."
—*Barbara Marx Hubbard*

Offscreen Sound Ideas

A strange noise coming from another room or place that begs further investigation.	An approaching threat such as a growling dog, oncoming train, madman laughing, menacing voice, clawing fingernails.
A gunshot, scream, laugh, or highly charged emotional sound coming from an unknown place.	A siren, ticking bomb, cuckoo clock, doorbell, or alarm going off.
Strange and highly emotional sound effects, the source of which are difficult to determine (such as baby crying played backward at half speed to build emotion).	Man walking into bank door from street view and then coming back out 10 seconds later. Sounds of gunshots and people screaming while man is in bank.
Another character talking, yelling, or doing something noisy offscreen.	A voice talking against a black screen or landscape scene about an another event.
360-degree atmospheric sounds such as upstairs neighbors arguing or people talking below in the stairs.	Footsteps of unknown origin approaching.

Creating Sound Space for the Audience

Audiences get pulled into a story when they feel they are missing something. Try taking the sound away on certain things or softening it at key moments. The viewer is then forced to imagine what the sound or dialogue might have been. Films are often like puzzles they want to solve, and sound can work great to dangle information. In real life, you do not always hear everything clearly, so this creates a better sense of reality, too. These types of missed sounds create tension and suspense when used well and give the audience space to decide for themselves what is happening.

Cutting Out Sound Completely

Cutting out all sound completely somewhere in your film adds fertile tension. Maybe a character screams over some shocking event taking place, and we see him screaming but hear nothing with the sound removed in editing. This lack of sound would help the audience get inside the character's head and emotions to feel what is happening in a stronger way. The scream could then bursts through the silence after a couple of seconds, bringing us back to the outer-scene reality. This approach would be more interesting than one long scream, depending on the context of the story.

Occasionally when the witchdoctor gets really mad, he picks up a horn and yells into it. This causes his dialogue to get really distorted and pulls the audience into the story as they try to figure out what he is saying.

In this shot, Ezzie steps on a snake and then sees she is in a cave chamber surrounded by snakes as the firefly buzzes in. The scream is cut off into silence to help better pull the audience inside her head and emotions. Just having a long scream would not be as interesting or powerful, depending on how it was done.

Ideas for Creating Sound Space

Muffled loudspeaker.	Mumbled words.
Bad telephone connection.	People arguing in the distance, only hearing parts.
Strange language on a loudspeaker/TV.	Sound cut off completely as if time stops during intense emotional moment or epiphany.
Hearing-going-haywire effect.	
Characters whispering into each other's ears just loud enough to catch parts or miss the whole thing.	Alternate state of mind where sounds change.
Character wearing hearing blocks, such as earplugs or headphones, and then removing them to cut to new ambient sounds in the room.	Person talking softly in the background of someone's mind, so softly you hear only every other word as the character remembers something while looking at an object.
A loud noise covering up important dialogue or sound.	Character thinks he or she hears something like a voice upstairs (and actually does in your sound design) but it turns out to be nothing, foreshadowing an event to come with intruders.
Offscreen sounds not explained, could be another subplot.	

project

7.12

List Three Ideas for Sound Space. Go through your script and think of three possible ways to take sound away or soften it at key points.

writing exercise
7.2

Write a short story that focuses on two characters having a series of misunderstandings from not hearing things correctly.

project 7.13

Cut Out Sound Completely. Find one spot in your film to cut out the sound entirely.

"Rhythmic stimulation, not only from sound but from other factors, influences consciousness."
—Holger Kalweit

In this shot, Ezzie encounters a pack of monster cave wolves. The camera stays on the lead wolf growling, as the other wolves bite her and we hear screaming offscreen. The screen then fades to black with the sound of her yelling and then her giggling with canine licking sounds. Ezzie's ever-present cheerful demeanor and unwavering positivity helps keep these scary scenes light and playful, while adding a nice emotional contrast. How can you incorporate basic character traits or emotional arcs into your sound design?

Moments that might work well with this technique include death scenes, epiphanies, time stopping, big emotional changes, shocking reactions, realizations, accidents, violence, overwhelming emotions, alternate dimensions, changing states of mind, unreal events, slow-motion camera shots, and intense moments. You may see a place in your script where the emotions are very high and the character is supposed to say something (but it's actually much stronger to just have a moment of silence). The audience needs space to breathe and absorb events. Cutting the sound out for a few seconds, especially next to busy loud sounds, can add a great deal of dramatic impact and pull viewers into your story.

In *Run Lola Run*, when Lola gets shot in the heart and is dying in the street, the sound goes almost silent. Time stops. This is in sharp contrast to the yelling police and chase scene that came before. This gives the audience a chance to absorb the impact and choose how to feel, instead of being told this is a sad tragic event full of heavy music, people screaming, Lola moaning, and her boyfriend crying out. We hear nothing. We get to decide for ourselves what she is feeling.

"Sound bypasses the intellect and has the inherent ability to trigger the emotions."
—Joy Gardner-Gordon

Using Sounds to Identify with Characters Physically

Clever sound design can work great to force an audience to identify with a character onscreen in a physical way, while saving you lots of time and money creating complicated camera shots. Suppose, for instance, that you start with a shot of someone frightened in a dentist chair, and then show the dentist drill revving up and approaching the patient's mouth. The screen fades to black, and all we hear is a dentist's drill going through teeth. Everyone in the audience will squirm. Our imaginations do a far better job of filling in the images than we could ever show onscreen. What ways could you save yourself a difficult shot by showing something else with just the sound going?

Go through your script and look for any places you could put one of your characters in extreme discomfort for a moment. Do not show the actual event, but use sound instead. You may want to pan over to another part of the location where we see the result of the sound event, such as fresh blood running into water. You could just fade to black or white for a few moments with the sound running to really let the effect sink in. You might put one of these at the end of your film, as it fades to black, to leave us with the sense that life goes on for your characters.

project 7.14

Create one idea to use sound to identify with a character onscreen in a physical or emotional way.

Shot/Scene/Image Onscreen	Sound Effects
Woman looking up at scary thing offscreen and then screaming. Pan over to a pool of water next to where the woman was standing filling with blood.	Woman screaming, "No, please don't!" Growling bear sounds mixed with crazy monster sound bed, sound of knife slashing a leather couch, screams of a woman dying, drip of blood.
Torture scene with one character strapped to a saw table, getting blindfolded while fading to black.	Sound of chainsaw hitting a soup bone with man screaming.
Long shot of a couple kissing in darkly lit car by a lake at night.	Sound of kissing, tickling, laughing, strangling.
Person walking through the woods, stepping on something. Cut to a shot of trees.	Person walking, sound of foot into watermelon, person screaming, beehive swarming, and running sounds.
Two kids wrestling in a dark tent in silhouette.	Fighting children turning to uncontrollable laughter.

In this shot, Ezzie has given up and is floating through the dark creepy cave on a log. The background sounds go from scary to lighter and happier sounds as she floats into the wonderland part of the vision quest. We hear the sound shift in the distance before we see the new lighter section of the cave, which cues the audience emotionally for the big change.

Using Sound to Cue the Audience Emotionally

Sounds in films are often used to cue audiences on how to feel. Study films for sound cues and you may find that a few seconds before a big emotional shift, a sound will occur to cue the audience. If the emotions are about to go from sad to joyful, with two characters talking about their feelings for one another, the sound of children laughing might be heard right before one of the characters suddenly proclaims undying love for the other.

Using Sound to Foreshadow Events

Audiences have been trained to expect sound cues that foreshadow upcoming events. Be very subtle when using this technique. In *Tender Mercies*, Robert Duvall is having a conversation with his long-lost daughter in the living room of his gas station house. The sounds of screeching truck brakes and horns are heard in the distance, right before big emotionally dangerous moments. These traffic warning sounds also foreshadow the death of the daughter in a car accident.

When Ezzie is sneaking through the forest to steal the chocolate from the campers, the sound of an owl is heard in the background. As discussed in Chapter 2, owls often symbolize death. This foreshadows Ezzie's coming spiritual, emotional, and psychological deaths during her vision quest.

project 7.15

Sound Cues. Go through your script and note sound cues you could introduce before each big emotional change. The trick is not to be too obvious and to come up with unique sound cues that move audiences emotionally. Refer to the Emotional Sound Chart table for ideas.

project 7.16

Using Sounds to Foreshadow Events. Go through your script and note major events that need to be foreshadowed. List three possible sounds to play in the background during other scenes to foreshadow these upcoming events.

Sound as POV

project
7.17

Create a Sound POV Effect. Find a place in your script to use a sound POV effect. How could you tie sound design into your theme?

The way things sound tells us a great deal about their location. Are your sounds moving? Where is a particular sound coming from? Sounds close to us are louder than sounds from far away, which are softer. How could you have sounds moving in and out of the frame? What symbolic objects could you put your sound in or use as a moving sound source on your set? If an actor's head turns while talking, you may want to fade the dialogue down to match the effect our ears would hear. You can change the size and shape of any space by fiddling with some effects in your sound-editing program. Experiment with volume levels to make sounds seem closer or farther away. Adding reverb effects can make a small room sound huge.

In *The Graduate*, Dustin Hoffman's character is forced to demonstrate his new surprise birthday present scuba suit for his parents and their friends. When the camera cuts to Dustin's POV inside the suit during the birthday party, all of the party sounds are silenced except for his breathing through the scuba mask. We *feel*, *hear*, and *see* his alienation from the party, which is a great visual sound metaphor for the theme dealing with the alienation of youth. When he finally jumps into the pool, we hear the water churning up around him. As he tries to surface, we hear the party sounds muffled in the background, as his parents push him back under the water. The family pool becomes a symbol for suburban life.

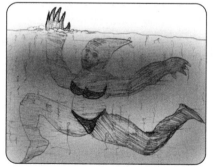

In this shot, Ezzie is drowning in a quicksand pit as the sound switches to gurgling watery mud. This will help the audience identify better emotionally with the character's predicament. A heartbeat sound could be added that speeds up and then stops as she learns not to struggle, adding to the symbolic death feel of the scene.

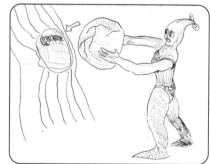

In this shot, Ezzie crawls out of the pit chamber full of rattlesnakes rattling loud and blocks the opening with a boulder, cutting out the snake sounds. This is a good use of sound and visuals to show location and emotional change.

Designing Dialogue Styles

After you have a clean dialogue track recorded, you can experiment with it to get various sound qualities. How can you make your characters sound different using some of your digital tools for added impact? You may want to experiment with using two tracks of dialogue, one on top of the other, with the bottom one slightly distorted. Bring the distorted track up over the regular one, going down at key emotional moments. You might try adding sound effects filters to dialogue tracks to make characters more original. If you have a character who is really scary, you could take each line of his dialogue and add some creepy effect to it, without messing up the lip sync, such as lowering the pitch. Here are some other ideas for creating unique dialogue styles.

To make the witchdoctor's voice even creepier, I could lower the pitch and mix in ominous animal sounds and grunts at key moments. Maybe he hisses like a snake at the end of each sentence, or has an occasional growl between or under words.

Digitally Enhanced Dialogue Effects

Lower the pitch on the voice to make it sound older.

Reverse dialogue for alien-type critters.

Raise the pitch to make the voice sound younger.

Add animal sounds to certain moans, grunts, or emotional outbursts to raise the impact.

Add reverb to the voice to make it sound omnipotent.

Camera moves to match dialogue— character head turns and the sound levels go down.

Add sound effects over the entire voice tracks of characters to make them sound different.

Two dialogue tracks with a distortion on one brought up at key moments.

Play with adjusting or key framing the speed of the dialogue for animated characters to give them funny voices.

Heavily distort the dialogue track and do not worry about matching the lip sync as a style to show a character state, such as feeling disconnected from himself/herself.

project 7.18

Dialogue Effects. Design an original digitally enhanced dialogue sound style for one or all of your characters.

Looping Dialogue Tips

Looping refers to re-creating unusable dialogue tracks in the studio.

Sometimes no matter how much you plan and mic a shot, the dialogue will be unusable and needs to be reproduced in post. Replacing set dialogue with studio dialogue takes practice to make it sound natural in the final soundtrack. Here are some tips to get you started:

1. Get the actor back into the emotion of the scene before recording by reading through lines a few times.

2. Review the shot footage you are going to match for tone and dialogue patterns.

3. Use software with good looping functions, such as ProTools, where you can sync the dialogue easier.

4. The best-case scenario is having an actor in a silent room, or one that matches acoustics of original scene.

5. Let the actor view the film image while recording the new dialogue, with no one else around to make the actor nervous or distract the actor from getting back into the emotions of the scene.

6. Do four or five takes for each line to make sure you get something you can use.

movie note

Apocalypse Now Group Sound. For a battlefield shot, Walter Murch gathered a group of drama students in a big field. He stood in the middle of them moving around him in circles. He would tell them, "You're looking for your friend Sal, who you haven't seen in awhile" and they would move around saying, "Have you seen Sal?" The physical movement of the group around him holding the mic gave the voices a much more real feel than having them standing still in a studio. How could you use a similar technique for a shot in your film?

Moving Group Voice Tracks

One interesting way to produce a nice ambient background track is to record a group of voice actors moving around a microphone. Traditional loop group sessions, where you record groups of voices in a studio, do not give the sounds movement like we hear in real life. The added dynamic of people shifting in relation to the mic as a group is very difficult to reproduce in post. Where in your film might you be able to design a moving group voice track? You may have a character just thinking about their day, hearing all sorts of voices in their head. Or maybe you show a shot of Mardi Gras, with background voices popping in and out, and then add a narrator voice on top talking about the event. You may even want to do a series of vignettes of different characters talking over the crowd, with little stories that happened to each one. This technique can be used to get a great deal of information across in a short amount of time.

How could you set up a microphone and have a group of people move around it while acting out different sound characters in your film? If you have friends who are talented natural sound effects generators, you might try giving them specific sound parts as they move around the microphone. You could get a group of people together and assign each one of them a creepy cave animal voice, and then have them walk around acting out that animal in the specific scene emotion. This track could then be mixed with other ones to provide a unique auditory ambience.

project 7.19

Group Voice Track. Find a place in your film to use a moving group voice track. List the different things you would want the voice actors to say and any other sounds you may mix in later.

"In writing songs I've learned as much from Cezanne as I have learned from Woody Guthrie."
—Bob Dylan

Matching Sound to Camera Shots

What ways can you use sound design to make your camera shots more dramatic? If you are doing a rack focus effect with one part of the frame blurry and another part in focus, you may play with the sounds to match the feel of the shot. The subject in the background could sound farther away, and then become more fuzzy sounding as the focus shifts to the foreground character. A fisheye shot might have a heavy wave distortion filter on the dialogue to exaggerate the warped reality. A split-screen shot might have two different soundtracks playing at the same time to communicate two locations occurring at once on the screen. A fast dolly back shot could have the sound levels go down sharply to amplify the movement away.

project 7.20

Sound Design for Camera Shots. Go through your camera shots and see what types of sound design you could add to enhance the visual power.

Mindspace Sound Design

How could you design sound for the inside of a character's mind in your film? When recording for mindspace sound design, you may want to try putting the mic very close to a voice actor's lips and have the actor whisper their lines. This will sound like voices inside the mind. This whispering technique can also be used to create a sense of intimacy or for narration. We tend to listen differently to whispering. You may want to have one of your characters whisper something important into another one's ear. The tone of voice could be threatening or amorous depending on the emotion of the moment. Voices from six feet away projecting out like normal people often sound very objective in comparison.

In *Apocalypse Now*, we hear the sounds of the jungle as Martin Sheen's character lies on a bed in a Hanoi hotel room. His body may be in the hotel room, but his mind is back in the jungle, to which he dreams of returning. How could you play with switching background sounds from one scene to another to help us understand where your character is at emotionally or mentally?

In *The Limey*, as the father tries to find out what happened to his dead daughter, a guy says something bad about her. The father thinks in a voiceover, "Not my girl"; his lips don't move, but we hear him answer this statement in his mind.

In the short film *How to Draw a Bunny*, we hear what the character is thinking in the background while he talks. This shows us how people think about what they are going to say before speaking. How could you design an original mindspace sound design to help us understand your character's inner life and develop the story better?

During the resolution of my story, my character walks out of the cave transformed by her spiritual experience. I could show a mindscreen layer of the shamanic journey high point on top of her forehead, with the shamanic soundtrack playing over the forest sounds. This would communicate that she is still in that epiphany space, bringing her new transformation back into her old world.

project 7.21

Mindspace Sound Design. Go through your script and find a place where you could pull us into the center of your character's head using a unique sound design approach.

Shooting Without Sound

Some directors prefer to set the camera free to move by shooting without sound. In Fellini's *8 1/2*, he wrote the dialogue *after* he shot the film, and did not even bother with recording any location sound at all. The dialogue is not even synced in many parts. Characters talk while drinking out of glasses. The extreme sound design for this film fits nicely with the dreamy surreal imagery and moods.

El Mariachi did a MOS shoot, which helped produce an almost perfect 1:1 shooting ratio, meaning almost every take made it onto the screen. No retakes needed to be done for actors messing up on a line of dialogue. You may want to study this film just to see how well the shots are set up for MOS.

superfreak!

Create an Extreme Sound Design Strategy in Post. How could you create an extremely unique MOS shooting style and sound design for your film in post?

definition

MOS Shooting Style MOS, German for shooting without sound, refers to creating the entire soundtrack for the film in post.

Sound Problems

You need to learn to really *hear*. Developing a focused sense of hearing happens quickly after you make a few mistakes. Suppose you get back from an all-day shoot at the beach and find that none of the dialogue made it through the white noise of the surf. Learn to recognize any problems with sound recording before you shoot. Pay particular attention to sound recording problems when you do location scouting. Just stand and really listen for a

while in different spots. The following table lists some problematic recording situations that may require post sound fixes or creative solutions.

Sound design gets more fun each day with all the new software possibilities. Now that you know a little bit more about possible ways to use sounds to tell visual stories, and to evoke emotions, your film will hopefully resonate on a deeper level with your audience.

superfreak!

Do a Pure Sound Film. Just as an exercise, take out all visuals. Make a timeline of your film in your drawing book and tell the story just using sounds. Add any ideas you get from this exercise to your final soundtrack plan.

time-saving

Even if you think your location does not have any sound problems, you may want to have the actors run through their lines a few times into the mic on location after the scene is shot. This will give you more choices for editing later. If a word drops out in a take, you can use the dialogue from another track.

note

Wild Line Record actors saying dialogue directly into the microphone on location for each shot. This gives you clean dialogue to edit in post, with location sound tone already in the background. This technique is good for recording sound in problem locations such as beaches, noisy rooms, and city streets. Wild line

dialogue also works well for when actors need to turn their heads or move around away from microphones during a shot. Do several wild line dialogue takes after you record the scene shots for ample editing choices and so that the actors have a better sense of timing and scene emotions.

movie note

Charlie Chaplin's **Modern Times** is another great one to study for sound design. The only character who gets synced sound when talking is the supervisor of the factory, whereas his

subordinates all speak into intercoms and loudspeakers. How can you use how we hear the characters in your film to tell us about their social order?

project 7.22

Eliminate All Dialogue. Just as an exercise, take out all the dialogue in your film and make some notes about how you could tell the story just using your visuals and clever sound design.

You may discover places where you really don't need that extra line of dialogue, which may make your film more powerful.

Sound Recording Problems	Possible Solutions
Traffic noises in background. The rhythm of street noise is hard to edit together and smooth out in post.	Do sound design in post to free up your camera. Record lots of different angles of street tones. Use wild line dialogue. Check mic to see whether it has a "low cut" switch, which helps to drown out low-frequency noises.
Airplanes flying over.	Decide whether you can take sound out in post. If a plane flies by in the middle of the dialogue, it may be easier to just reshoot with DV or use room tone and wild lines.
Wind.	Do sound in post. Avoid if at all possible. If you have a budget, use professional zeppelin and windjammer on the boom, matched to the mic.
Beaches, especially windy ones. Waves create lots of white noise. The rhythm of the ocean is hard to cut together in editing shots.	Try to pick a day without wind or strong background surf sounds if possible. Mic actors as closely as possible and do wild lines.
Creaky houses. Every step of actors, boom person (must wear socks), or crew will produce creak.	Don't shoot in creaky houses; if you do, do the sound in post. Test for this when location scouting.
Dancing people's feet.	Have actors take off their shoes and wear socks if the shot does not include feet. Boom person and crew should wear socks (no shoes) whenever possible.
Voices in scene all sound like they were recorded in different places. Too many different types of mics on the set or room tones.	Have your main actors always speak into boom mics, with secondary characters speaking into other types if you need to switch. Each type of mic sounds different, so plan this into your sound design strategy. Do wild lines if the room tone is all over the place.
Room tone problems. Different areas of the room sound completely different.	Carpets might work. See whether you add an ambient sound design that evens out problem.
Acoustical room tone problems. Sounds seem to echo through room.	Lay down carpets.
Walking shoe sounds on noisy tiles.	If feet are not in shot, have the actors wear socks and no shoes.
Actors mumbling, talking too fast, heavy accents, or hard to understand.	Screen test for voice. If actors are hard to hear or understand in a studio, they are going to be impossible on location.
Camera operational noises.	Add background sounds, such as crickets, to cover noises.
Lots of background sound noises and dialogue that needs to be redone in post.	Could it be raining? Thunderstorms and rain in the background can help smooth out really bad sound that needs to be reassembled in post.
Generator.	Is it raining again? Loud fireplace? Noisy birds in the background? What other background cover-up sounds could you come up with?
Refrigerators, thermostats, ticking clocks, and other soft sounds.	Turn off anything making little noises.

project 7.23

Decide on Your Sound Design. Go over the exercises you did in this chapter and pick out the ideas that work best to create a unique auditory atmosphere for each scene in your film.

movie note

Mr. Hulot's Holiday is an old film by Jacques Tati that takes us on a rollicking auditory experience. This film is great to study for how well sound can tell a story. The camera follows this fish-out-of-water character around on his vacation. The only time he speaks is to say his name occasionally. The sound effects become comical, with the clicking of high heel shoes, leather cushions squeaking on furniture going up and down when people sit on them, wet shoes squashing across a floor, and loudspeakers no one can quite understand.

chapter 8

Preproduction Story-Editing Choices

"How do you want the audience to feel? If they are feeling what you want them to feel all the way through the film, you've done about as much as you can ever do. What they finally remember is not the editing, not the camerawork, not the performances, not even the story—it's how they felt."
—Walter Murch

The way shots and scenes are edited together dramatically affects the telling of a story. Oliver Stone once said that editing is much like the final rewrite of a film. Many editing techniques used in postproduction should also be considered *before* production, to create tighter stories. This chapter does not cover "everything you need to know about editing"; instead, it focuses more on a few techniques you may want to incorporate at the storyboard level to make your film more interesting and unique. A few miscellaneous editing tips for postproduction are also included at the end of this chapter.

The First Edit: 1904. *The Gay Shoe Clerk* by Edward Porter. This short silent film contains one long shot of a woman trying on shoes in a store, flirting with the shoe salesmen as he gets ready to put the shoe on her foot. Cut to a close-up of her foot and leg while seated, as she pulls up her dress to try on the shoe. The emotion building for this cut was lust, and the close-up of her exposed leg, as she pulls up her dress, was the most powerful visual expression of that feeling. This was shocking and racy stuff at the time and shows the power of a good edit. Editing is about choosing cuts that create emotional tension the audience can relate to from their own experiences.

Suppose you decide to cut two scenes together in post, but discover that you do not have the right shots. If you know you are going to be cutting two scenes together before production, you can plan each shot so that they go together much better. You can also test your final storyboard ideas, using an animatic, before going into actual production. If you are an independent digital filmmaker, you need to optimize your time, by not shooting or animating a bunch of shots you may not need. Tight digital filmmaking requires well-planned preproduction, especially if you are using multiple layers of images from different production environments.

Many of the editing ideas in this chapter will force you to rethink your initial storyboards, to communicate in more visually sophisticated ways. Editing is where a film takes shape, and finds a new level of message and storytelling. Twenty different editors will cut the same film 20 different ways, so imagine what you can do with your collection of rough storyboard shots right now. The ideas in this chapter are good to consider *before* you shoot and *after*. You will need to rearrange and add more shots and scenes to complete the projects in this chapter. Incorporate the best ideas into your final storyboards.

Editing Information Is Natural to Storytelling

Films are just expensive stories. People naturally edit when telling a story to a friend by saying *this* happened, then *this* happened, and then *this* did. When telling a story, it is important not to add any information that may be confusing. What details are really important to your

plot and theme? What is the point of each scene, and how can you edit out any extra shots to make your film tighter and more powerful? Keep cracking your film idea open as you consider the following editing techniques. Stay flexible to new possibilities appearing as you try different approaches.

Don't Trash Other People's Films

Even the best Hollywood directors do not always create an Academy Award–winning masterpiece. Almost everyone makes an occasional box office bomb. Find something of value in every film you see. People work so hard on films, and most independent projects are labors of love for all involved.

Juxtaposition as the Core of Editing

Great screenwriting and cinematography alone are not the main ingredients of brilliant filmmaking. The best films with real magic happen when filmmakers use juxtaposition to make the story unfold for the audience in their own heads.

Juxtaposition is the meat and

potatoes of good filmmaking, and is often overlooked by beginners. Audiences learn how to consume stories in films. They like to participate and be drawn into the film world—trying to figure out what is going on for themselves, like solving a puzzle.

Juxtaposition Visual Test

Take the following test before read-ing any further. If you were to see the following two-shot sets, what would you think the Bigfoot is thinking and feeling after each set appears on the screen? Write your answers on a piece of paper.

definition

Juxtaposition By strategically plac ing two visual ideas next to each other, you can create a separate third idea in the viewer's mind.

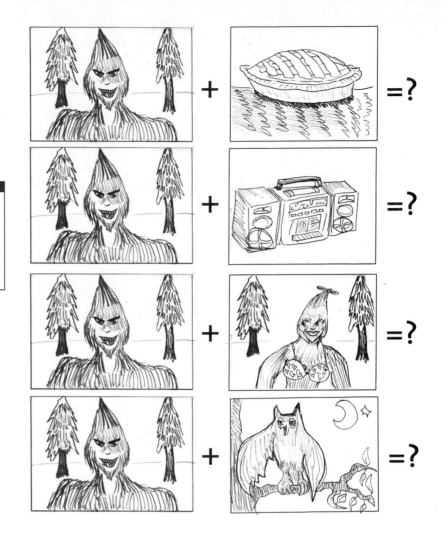

In the first two shots, we might think the Bigfoot is hungry and wants to eat the cherry pie. In the second two shots, we think he likes the ghetto blaster and wants to take it home. In the third set of shots, we think he likes the girl and wants to get to know her better. In the fourth set of shots, we might think he is scared and in a difficult situation. Notice how the Bigfoot is the same in each set of shots. When another shot follows the shot of the Bigfoot, we immediately imagine connections between the Bigfoot and the sub-ject(s) in the second shot, and form a new idea about what is happening.

Juxtaposition new-thought math: 1 idea + 1 idea = 3rd sepa-rate idea generated inside the mind of the viewer, an idea that connects the previous two ideas.

This section covers several ways to use juxtaposition in your film. Some of these exercises are challenging, both creatively and intellectually. Study the way these techniques are used in your favorite films, to get a better sense of how to create original forms of juxtaposition in your own work. When you really understand how to use juxtaposition, your visu-al storytelling skills will rise to a new level of sophistication and depth.

"To me, the perfect film is as though it were unwinding behind your eyes, and your eyes were projecting it them-selves, so that you were seeing what you wished to see. Film is like thought. It is the closest to thought process of any art."
—John Houston

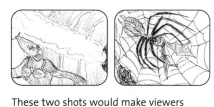

These two shots would make viewers think that Ezzie, inside a cave full of creepy critters, is scared. If the second shot were a beautiful rock sculpture, viewers would think she is enjoying her cave exploration. How can you use well-planned cutaway shots to help develop character thoughts and emotions in each scene?

These two shots help viewers to understand what the Bigfoot thinks about being in a cage. A cutaway gesture of his hand squeezing the bars tells viewers that he is uncomfortably trapped and is thinking of ways to escape.

Juxtaposing Images to Show Thoughts and Emotions

As you just saw in the preceding visual test, if you show a shot of character with a neutral expression, and then cut to a shot of a cherry pie, viewers will think the character is hungry. If you show the same shot of the character, and then cut to a shot of a tombstone, viewers will think the character is sad. Suppose you show the same character with a neutral expression, and then cut to a shot of a growling dog; now viewers will think the character is scared. You may not have thought about juxtaposition much in the past, but now you should. How can you use this technique to help viewers understand what your characters are thinking or feeling in each scene?

Juxtaposition Between Symbolic Shots

By placing one simple symbolic shot next to another, you can create a new idea. Your audience will naturally formulate a connection between the two shots and form a third idea not apparent in any of the individual shots.

"The truth of a thing is the feel of it, not the think of it."
—Stanley Kubrick

Kubrick, in *2001*, managed to cover the history of human evolution in three simple shots. The first shot shows a prehistoric ape throwing a bone into the air; it had been causing problems in the tribe as the new favorite tool. Kubrick then cut to the bone flying up into the sky, turning in slow motion as it starts to fall back down. He then cut to a moving spaceship, shaped like the bone, moving in the same way and in the same spot for a match cut (matched on shape and motion). This is one of the most famous shot sequences in motion-picture history. The thought that resulted in these shots being put together is where brilliance enters into filmmaking; after all, the actual shots standing alone are quite simple to create. Kubrick's opening sequence lacks dialogue and gives viewers plenty of space, allowing viewers to discern the meaning themselves. What ways can you use simple visual techniques such as this symbolic match cut to tell your story or develop theme?

Juxtaposition: First bone tool created (birth of civilization) + Futuristic spaceship floating in space in the same shape as bone (future of civilization) = History of civilization.

writing exercise 8.1

Write a short story that focuses on showing how the characters feel by the way you describe their surroundings between events.

project 8.1

Juxtaposing Images to Show Thoughts and Emotions. Go through each scene in your film and ask yourself what the character is thinking/ feeling at key moments. Juxtapose cutaway shots to help develop these thoughts and emotions. List one or two ideas for each scene.

How can you use your favorite digital production techniques to create original visual juxtapositions? Think of ways to juxtapose different *layers* of symbolic images or styles in the frame, to create things such as animated video collages. In this shot, the character could be riding the Loch Ness Monster through the air during her shamanic journey. The background layers might include aerial cloud stock footage, 3D ocean waves, photo collage temples, 2D animated vector graphics, or hand-drawn sets. A painterly filter could be applied over the entire shot to pull all the different looks together and simulate one unified, peaceful meditation space. Remember, you want to help the viewer understand and identify with your characters. You can do this by juxtaposing different visual style layers, while showing the characters' experiences in original ways.

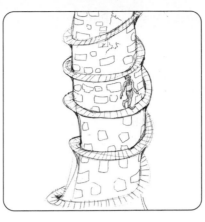

In Ezzie's shamanic journey, she travels into the center of her head during a mind-screen shot, and climbs an endless spinning 3D spiral staircase. Video layers play inside the rock wall shapes, representing her evolution as a soul and showing all of her past lives at once. You can convey this type of abstract theme information best by juxtaposing a series of symbolic shots, which gives the audience space to decide for themselves what is being communicated. I could pick one image from each lifetime, perhaps showing her as different animals, or even people, performing metaphoric life-purpose activities that relate to her current life purpose in some way. The theme of my film is that everyone has a unique life purpose. I could communicate this theme in a subtle and interesting way by juxtaposing all the different life purposes from past lives.

"Attempt to produce the greatest effect in the viewer's mind by the least number of things on the screen. Why? Because you want to do only what is necessary to engage the imagination of the audience— suggestion is always more effective than exposition."
—Walter Murch

creativity tip

If you want to be a really good *visual* storyteller, it helps to sketch any random design ideas you think of as you develop your film story, to combine with other ones later. I got the idea for the spiral staircase shot when looking at different theme sketches (spirals) that Nate had drawn earlier of the film world. The shapes for the rocks looked like weird video screens to me. This spiral staircase was drawn as a set idea to represent the theme. I am using a spiral theme symbol throughout my story. You may want to try sketching a few theme-based film world symbols, settings, or shot ideas to use with the juxtaposition exercises.

When Ezzie gets punished for stealing chocolate from the campers, the witchdoctor tells her she is banished from the tribe to the Cave of Death, from where no Bigfoot has ever returned. She screams, "You can't make me go!" Cut to her tied to a log drifting into the Cave of Death screaming. This is more interesting than showing how the old witchdoctor got her tied up on the log, and saves me the extra time it would take to create those shots. You may be able to use this juxtaposition technique throughout your entire film to save production time and tell a more interesting story. Look for places to cut shots that form a gap in time, to create stronger scene-to-scene juxtapositions.

Juxtaposition Between Two Scenes

Scenes are a series of shots put together to describe an event. Two events placed next to each other produce a third idea. Audiences try to connect the dots between the two scenes to make the events somehow fit together in their heads, while trying to figure out what will happen next in the story. When placing scenes next to each other in your film, use this natural viewing response to your advantage.

Bound, the film-noir lesbian-gangster film, shows two gals talking in a dark car about how they *might* rip off the mob. They discuss trusting each other and the dangers involved. One of the women then says, "I want to see the money." Cut. The next scene starts with a close-up of a bag full of money covered in blood and being carried by one of the gangsters, who is rushing into one of the women's apartment. This tells us that the two gals decided to go ahead with the plan, and that something went terribly wrong. We don't need to see the setup for the heist. It is more interesting to cut straight to the event in mid-action, and watch how the characters react, not really knowing what their full plans are as things get more and more complicated. This technique pulls the audience into the story fast, as they try to figure out what is going on. Notice the strong dialogue/image juxtaposition between the scenes. What ways can you cut out areas of your film and juxtapose scenes like this to make it more interesting, while holding back some important information to create more tension and suspense?

Juxtaposition: "I want to see the money" + Shot of money covered in blood = Something has gone wrong.

project 8.3

Juxtaposition Between Two Scenes. Come up with one idea to use this technique in your film. Cut or add shots if you need to, and write down how the two ideas produce a third one. Look for places where you can cut out bridging actions or scenes. Then find a creative way to juxtapose the end shot of one scene with the first shot of another. You may want to pose a question or create a situational conflict in the first scene, and then show the result in the first shot of the second scene.

writing exercise 8.2

Write a series of brief scene description paragraphs describing several events that connect with big gaps of time in between each one.

Juxtaposition Between Two Stories to Show Theme

Some films jump around through time and tell two different stories simultaneously. These parallel stories usually show the same theme. This technique works well to break up the narrative. Is there a side story, fable, or some event from the character's past that you can cut into your main story at various points? Usually you can place the three-act structure plot points of the side story next to the same plot points in your main story. A character could be remembering something or an event could be taking place in another location at the same time. These two stories run parallel to each other, affecting the way the character reacts emotionally to the main plot situations. It is best to have the two stories tie together at the end in some clever way during the climax to really illustrate the power of the theme.

Mel Gibson's character in the movie *Signs* keeps having flashbacks to a car accident that killed his wife. We see pieces of this flashback through his mind, in chronological order, throughout the film. The theme deals with faith, and he has lost his, along with his preacher collar (a good occupation to illustrate the theme visually). We watch him struggle with the question of his own faith throughout the film. At the end of the film, his wife's last words come back to him at the perfect time, to trigger an idea that saves his son's life. His faith is restored. We find out slowly in the film how his wife died tragically with him there and the effect it has had upon him. His wife's strange last words are the ones that save their son much later. Mel Gibson flashes back to his wife's last words, which we hear for the first time, too, at just the right moment to save the son's life. These two parallel story lines *climaxing at the same time* help tie the ending together and develop the theme.

One way to add another story line to my film would be to develop the campsite scene. The Indian and the woman could be Bigfoot researchers who have captured Ezzie on video in a food trap. As Ezzie goes through her journey, I could occasionally cut back to the researchers making TV appearances. During the climax of the film, and to tie the two stories together, I could have a group of Bigfoot hunters closing in on Ezzie's location.

To add another story line to my film, at key moments I could use cutaway shots of different people giving testimonials about personal Bigfoot encounters. The logger could be saying how Bigfoots are very strong and ferocious, and how he saw one throw a bulldozer over a cliff once. Then I could cut to Ezzie being really sweet and tender during the death of her firefly friend, to juxtapose the logger's statement. I could then have an Indian tell an old Bigfoot legend at another key moment. A forest ranger in a helicopter could cut in somewhere else during the story to add his perspective. This extra story line woven into the narrative could convey lots of backstory information. How can you find ways to insert a second story that juxtaposes ideas presented in the first one?

project 8.4

Juxtaposition Between Two Stories. How could you weave a second story line into your existing one? Explain how the plot points will match during key moments or how the stories will relate.

writing exercise 8.3

Write a short story with two separate story lines that meet up at key plot points.

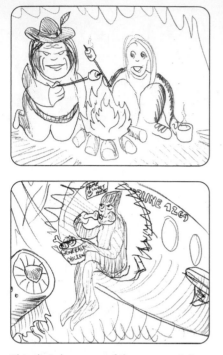

This shot shows one of the campers talking about official Bigfoot research information, which says that Bigfoots are "nocturnal nomadic hunters." The next shot shows a Bigfoot eating a bucket of stolen fried chicken, living comfortably in a crashed airplane, and sitting in a sunbeam. This image contrasts with the camper's statement. If a shot of a Bigfoot hunting at night followed the shot that included the camper's statement, it would be a wasted shot with no power. Look for ways to contrast what characters say in your film with what the visuals on the screen are communicating.

Juxtaposition Between Voice and Image

Dialogue and narration juxtaposed with different images can convey large amounts of information, in a way that gives the audience space to decide for themselves what is going on in your film. Do not *show and tell* the same information; instead, for the juxtaposition to occur, use the two as a contrast.

In *Sex, Lies, and Videotape*, Andie McDowell's character sets up the entire plot while talking to her therapist during the first 5 minutes. As she explains what has been on her mind, such as suspecting her husband might be having an affair, we see cutaways to various aspects of her life unfolding in real time at different locations. Andie is laughing in the therapist's office about her husband's possible affair; this matches with the cut of her husband laughing and taking off his mistress's clothes across town. These scenes could have all occurred separately, but work much better with this type of juxtaposition between what Andie's character thinks is happening and what is really occurring. This also creates an added element of suspense, because the audience now knows more about the situations in the film than does Andie. This is a great way to introduce the characters in the film: a fast economical setup that immediately pulls the viewer into the building conflict.

Juxtaposition: Andie in therapy talking about her life + People in her life doing things she doesn't know about in other places = Things are not going to unfold too well for her.

In *Election*, we hear Matthew Broderick's character talking about his new life, after being fired from the high school Reese Witherspoon's character attended for throwing some of her votes out so that she would lose the school election. Matthew's character talks to the audience like an old friend, over images that contrast sharply to what he is describing. He says he has a great new apartment in New York, but what the audience sees looks more like a closet. The tone of this character's voiceover indicates that life if going grand, but the images on the screen show how his life is much less than it was before he had to move. We laugh at the recognition and dark humor of self-delusion, because we feel pity for his character.

Juxtaposition: Matthew talking about how good his new life is in New York City + Images of how his life is much worse than he describes = His new life is not going well and he is not being honest with himself in this monologue.

project
8.5

Juxtapose Voice and Image. Go through your script and find a place where you can use this technique.

In these final shots of my film idea, Ezzie tells us in a voiceover how much better her life is now that she has passed her difficult vision quest journey through the Cave of Death. She explains how the witchdoctor and her are getting along so much better, as we see her zapping him into submission with her newly found powers. Then she talks about how she has not gotten caught stealing food from campers lately, as we see her use her new telekinetic powers to lift food mentally from campsites while hiding in the trees. She tells us how her rock sculptures are much easier to make now, too, as we see her moving big boulders into place with her mind. Having her say something that sounds normal, but showing her doing something quite extraordinary, creates an interesting juxtaposition with voice and image.

Juxtaposition Between Music and Image

Music that contrasts with what the characters are experiencing can create a powerful juxtaposition. Chapter 7, "Narrative Sound Design," touches on this idea.

During each dinner-table scene in *American Beauty*, Annette Benning's character likes to play happy music from the '50s, such as Frank Sinatra's "I'm Simply Mad About You." This iconic and happy '50s love song is juxtaposed with a tense fight scene at the less-than-perfect modern family dinner table. The husband is talking about blackmailing his boss, and then starts throwing food. This behavior is very far from the ideal 1950s dinner table, and shows how much American family values have devolved into chaos by 1999. The best movies involve you with your own experiences, and dinner tables are popular metaphors to illustrate family dynamics in films. A different American '50s love song is played during each dinner scene until Kevin's character insists on a change. This is an example of using music and juxtaposition to show growth in a character arc.

In *Rushmore*, we see the main character, a weird guy in a modern-day prep school, as the head of all these clubs and activities on campus, acting like he is a huge big thinker. The music in the background is British-invasion pop from the '60s, which brings to mind grandly wild, rebellious, anti-establishment political statements about making the world a better place. Wes Anderson's films are famous for his use of displaced generational pop music, juxtaposed with modern images to show how his characters are not part of this world, (for instance, the use of the Ramones in *The Royal Tenenbaums*).

Juxtaposition: Weird guy shown as head of every school club + British-invasion 60s pop music = Character does not feel part of the modern world.

money-saving

Obtaining the rights to use well-known songs for film soundtracks may be difficult for independent, no-budget filmmakers. SmartSound (www.smartsound.com) makes software called SonicFire Pro that enables you to create original soundtracks for films using their royalty-free music libraries. A Mac demo is included on the CD.

If I could choose any dream song to use in my film, it would be Dusty Springfield's "The Windmills of Your Mind." That song starts with "Round, like a circle in a spiral, like a wheel within a wheel...." I would use this song as Ezzie goes on a violently dangerous log ride through the dark cave full of spiraling whirlpools. The soft tender feel of the song would be a nice juxtaposition for the scary motion ride shot sequence. This song also fits nicely with my spiral image theme. If you could use any song in your film, what would it be? If you are just making films for yourself, your friends, or internal business meetings, and not making any money off of them, you obviously can use whatever music, images, or repurposed footage you want.

"Flaming enthusiasm, backed up by horse sense and persistence, is the quality that most frequently makes for success."
—Dale Carnegie

project 8.6

Juxtaposition Between Music and Image. Come up with one idea in your film to use this technique. Pick your favorite song for the shot even if you know you may not be able to get the rights.

Boogie Nights opens with a black screen and sad circus music playing. Then the music changes to happy '70s disco music featuring "Best of My Love," as we see Burt Reynolds' character, the porn filmmaking king, walk into a nightclub. The theme is self-delusion, mixed with a heady dose of desperation, and the story is full of characters who are happy on the outside and sad on the inside. None of the characters really learn or change during the course of the film. The juxtaposition of sad then happy music fits perfectly with the theme and tone of the story.

> **Juxtaposition:** Sad circus music + Happy '70s disco music = Sadness underneath happiness or things are not what they seem.

The opening shot of *Trainspotting* features the Iggy Pop song "Lust for Life," as we watch the main character running from a crime, with a voiceover of him telling us to "Choose life, color TVs, junk food… not heroin…." The theme has to do with self-destruction and the battle between life and death urges. The energetic fun song is juxtaposed with a guy clearly not choosing life, laughing as he almost gets hit by a car.

Juxtaposition Between Two Ideas

Two ideas appearing in one scene can create depth, tension, and suspense in an otherwise run-of-the-mill story line. How can you save or compress time by presenting two simultaneously?

> **Juxtaposition:** Talking about relationship in a bar + Cutaways of the two of them getting ready to get intimate = They get together after the bar.

Juxtaposition Between Two Ideas. Come up with one idea in your film to use this technique. Try cutting two scenes that are next to each other together in a clever way. Or pose a question in the first scene that is answered somehow in the second one cut into it. It is okay to momentarily confuse the audience; they'll figure out at what time each scene is occurring. At first, it may seem like the characters are daydreaming, but if you plan it well, the audience will get more involved by having to solve the visual timeframe puzzle.

In this shot, two Bigfoots are having drinks at the Bigfoot bar and are talking about rekindling their old relationship. As they talk, a shot of their hands touching over a glass match cuts to a shot of their hands touching each other intimately in a tree house, and then quickly back to the bar for a shot of them looking at each other again, then back to the tree house showing them kissing. This back-and-forth rapid cutting of two ideas takes the emotional question of rekindling old feelings and cuts it together with the result later that night of the encounter. At the end of the bar scene, one character could say, "Let's get out of here," to imply they are heading to the tree house. This is more interesting than showing the two scenes chronologically. I got this idea from the movie *Out of Sight*, in which the same type of scene takes place between Jennifer Lopez and George Clooney at a bar.

Disjointed Editing Style

Another way to pull an audience into a puzzle aspect of your film is to show nonlinear shots (jumping back and forth through time in a confusing way), using memory flashbacks and overlapping ideas. This style tends to focus on the internal state of the character, trying to re-create onscreen how we think as we go through life. The audience will get sucked into the story while trying to figure out what is present time, memory time, dream time, daydream time, or just the character's imagination. They will keep trying to reconstruct in their minds what is happening now in the story, what has already occurred, and what might happen next.

Don't show us everything, don't tell us everything, don't let us hear everything, and mix up space and time to let us come to our own conclusions about what is happening in your film. If you do this too much, you will lose the audience. Disjointed shots need to come together and make sense at key moments. Good films make you think about them later and discuss them with your friends. Modern audiences are getting to be better visual story puzzle solvers, and new filmmakers need to learn how to construct stories with fresh and engaging riddles.

In this series of disjointed editing shots, the character is drumming in the first one. Then she starts to have memory flashes back to key events. These memories and overlapping symbolic idea shots create the feeling of someone reflecting back through her life during a vision-quest type of journey. How could you use a disjointed editing style to show us what someone is thinking?

project 8.8

Disjointed Style Idea. Come up with a way to use this editing style in your film.

"The images in dreams are much more fragmented, intersecting in much stranger and more abrupt ways than the images of waking reality— ways that approximate, at least, the interaction produced by cutting."
—Walter Murch

In *The Limey*, a father comes to Los Angeles to find out what happened to his dead daughter. A series of nonlinear shots occur as he investigates. We see all sorts of out-of-time shots: the daughter as a young girl at the beach, the father in a cab suddenly looking at a grownup picture of his daughter, the father talking to a man at a table, and the father thinking on the airplane. All these shots get tossed together, flashing forward and backward. This editing style really draws us into the mindset of a grieving father remembering his dead daughter and trying to figure out what happened.

Eliminating Exposition in Favor of Juxtaposition

Exposition is boring to watch. This happens when characters talk too much or overexplain things. Bad exposition occurs when nothing is happening and no events are occurring, someone is just talking about events or characters going through

obvious sets of actions. Although all movies need some exposition, strong visual juxtapositions will make your film more interesting. Look for places in your script where characters are just talking heads. Replace those shots with relevant juxtapositions. Hint at things that spark tension in the audience's mind, and let the audience fill in the gaps about what is happening.

At the beginning of *You Can Count on Me*, we see a middle-aged couple driving down a dark road at night. Cut to a big truck driving down the same road at night. Cut to two policemen going to the door of a house at night, looking uncomfortable as they try to tell a young girl something. Cut to a shot of a church steeple. Just the image of the church steeple expresses the conclusion of death in this series of shots. The parents died in a car accident. Watching these simple shots juxtaposed is much more interesting than hearing a character tell us this information.

project 8.9

Eliminate Exposition in Favor of Juxtaposition. Go through your film and see where characters are talking heads or doing obvious actions. Replace these shots/scenes with juxtaposed images to make audiences understand what is going on by connecting the dots in their own minds.

In this series of shots, our character is about to die after slipping on the rocks as she is climbing. She has a memory flash of Big Granny using her telekinetic skills to move rocks. By thinking of this, she is somehow able to activate her own latent telekinetic abilities in this life-or-death situation and reach up and grab the rock as she is falling. These shots would be boring if as she was falling she started talking about the "one time I saw Big Granny do this...." The audience "gets" that she is remembering and understands that she has somehow tapped into this telekinetic ability through the memory.

Editing Action Sequences

The best action scenes have a little story with a clear goal and a path of escalating shot-by-shot events during all the flying bullets, car chases, fight scenes, and daring escapes. Every cut should relay one piece of information or an event in an action sequence.

In *The Matrix*, Neo walks into the office building and goes through the metal detector. He beeps. Cut to one of the guards asking, "Will you please remove all metal items?" Cut to a shot of Neo opening his long black trench coat, revealing a vast array of semiautomatic weapons. He does not say anything. His goal in this scene is to get to the elevator. Every cut shows events that raise the stakes and level of the conflict, much like in a video game. You could easily list each event that happens to Neo on his way to the elevator by looking at each cut. This happens, then this happens, then this happens because that happened (cut, cut, cut).

Juxtaposing to Create Humor

You also can use story-editing techniques to evoke humor by relating a message whose ingenuity, incongruity, absurdity, or play on words has the power to provoke laughter.

Juxtaposition using humor: Getting attacked by bear + Absurd comment by silly Bigfoot: "Did you see the bear?" = Funny laugh because yes, of course, the other Bigfoot most certainly did see the bear throwing them out of cave.

In this action sequence sketch, I would show how an escalating degree of difficulty is apparent in each shot. The first rock she jumps to in order to cross the cavern has a hidden spider nest on top. The second rock is covered with snakes. The third rock crumbles beneath her feet. Simple cuts build tension by not including any extra images that might detract from the specific steps necessary to reach a goal.

project 8.10

List Action Events. Go through any action scenes in your film and list the escalating series of events that need to happen for a character to accomplish the scene goal.

In this scene, two Bigfoots are exploring a cave and run into a bear monster, who violently throws them out. One Bigfoot then looks to the other one and says, "Did you see the bear?" The other Bigfoot pauses for a moment, rubbing his head and looking stunned. This pause allows the audience to absorb the absurdity of the question and laugh. You usually do not stare at someone when he asks you a question. Without the editing pause for this look, we might miss the laugh. This is funny because they both obviously saw the creature as it threw them out of the cave. Notice how there is nothing funny about the shots, but together they form a ridiculous situation of stating the obvious in a tense moment. This is humor created through juxtaposition, which also rings very true to real-life experiences.

project 8.11

Juxtaposition to Create Humor. Come up with a way to use this technique in your film to make something funny.

Applying Dissonance

Another way to create tension and suspense is to use dissonance to manipulate the way the audience feels. This technique simulates real-life situations that get uncomfortable, helping viewers to connect to your story on a personal "been there, felt that" level.

project
8.12

Apply Dissonance. In which part of your film can you use characters picking at each other, strange music, sound effects, weird sets, or tense situations to make the audience feel uneasy?

writing exercise
8.4

Write a short story that focuses on creating as much dissonance as possible.

definition

Dissonance Two things put together to make you feel uncomfortable.

Pacing

How fast do you want to lay out the events in your story during each scene? What pace, rate, or tempo best develops or advances your story in each scene? One way to control pacing is to track the events in your story based on the events per second or minute. A slow section of your film may have 1 big event every 4 minutes. A fast part may have 10 events in 2 minutes. You can play with this timing of events when making editing choices. Refer to the scene-shape exercises in Chapter 4, "Writing Scenes, Conflict, and a Short Script," for more ideas on playing with pacing.

More events = Faster cuts = Faster pace

In the Bigfoot graveyard scene, several different techniques are used to create an uneasy feeling. A sense of color dissonance occurs when everything on the screen goes from bright in the scene before to pitch black inside the dark burned-up crypt. A sense of uncomfortable forward motion or momentum is created, sucking you into the story by causing you to wonder what is going to happen next as the character starts to see the skeletons of those who have come before her impaled on rocks all over the cave. There is a prickly dissonance between her and the other creatures, with snakes hissing at her and hidden growling sounds coming from the dark corners. The soundtrack features irritating water drips over dissonant music with complex-note steps. Another uneasy feeling is created when we start to see some of the skeletons moving but then realize that black vultures (symbolizing death) are actually eating them. One of the vultures then flies up to try and peck out Ezzie's eyes. All of these techniques make the audience feel uneasy and ask, "What in the world is going to happen next?" I got this idea from watching *A Simple Plan*, where the characters first find the money in the crashed airplane. How can you use existing examples of these techniques in popular films to inspire your own ideas?

The first 20 minutes of *Alien* are very slow and boring, showing life aboard a space transport ship. The cuts are long, with slow camera movements, and the events are very slow to unfold. The audience is lulled into a stupor. By the time the evil creature shows up, it is shocking and jars viewers out of their seats, with fast furious sudden cuts for the rest of the film. If you start with the monster and fast cuts, like they do in the latest *Alien* film, the audience gets immune to the effect real fast. You need to contrast boredom with emergency mode, to help the audience identify with the sudden shock of the character's situation.

"I go by instinct...I don't worry about experience."
—Barbara Streisand

Postproduction Editing Tips

If you are the writer, director, and editor of your film, you need a vacation! It is important to take a break between shooting or animating and the actual editing process, to get some distance from evaluating your source footage. Work on the sound without looking at any shots for 3 weeks, work on another project, or better yet, stop thinking about the film completely and go mountain climbing (or whatever you are into). When you sit down to start editing your shots, you need fresh eyes. You want to see without thinking about all the other things that may have been going on before that particular shot or that day, things that may emotionally color your ability to really see the best moments and choices. Sometimes what you thought was a throwaway shot has better emotional charge than the ones you were sure you were going to use.

project 8.13

Determine Your Pacing Strategy. Look at the events in your film. Where can you go slow so that you can shock the audience with a sudden burst of fast cuts later?

writing exercise 8.5

Write two short stories that are each about three pages long. The first one has one big event, and the second one has 20. The stories do not need to relate.

Print Out a Still of Each Shot

Take each final production shot and print out the best representative color still. More complicated shots may require 2 to 3 stills to get the whole shot idea. You can fit 6 to 8 on a page. Develop a system with shot number, tape number, and time code to label under each DV still. Place printouts in a three-ring binder until you are ready to start actually editing. Post these pictures up all around your editing station so that you can see all the choices when you start to edit. When all the stills are up, let your eyes wander until they find the perfect shot each time. This technique also forces you to really look at each shot and understand how it differs from the hundreds of other ones. You'll quickly learn to grab those good, representative stills.

"But the most interesting asset of the photos (representative screen grabs) for me was that they provided the hieroglyphs for a language of emotions. What word expresses the concept of ironic anger tinged with melancholy? There isn't a word for it, in English anyway, but you can see that specific emotion represented in this photograph."
—Walter Murch

Miscellaneous Editing Tips

"Our rate of blinking is somehow geared more to our emotional state and to the nature and frequency of our thoughts than to the atmospheric environment."
—*Walter Murch*

"Detail is electric."
—*Bonnie Goldberg*

This character constructs a huge rock sculpture in bursts of fast-motion action shots. I could increase the speed of the shots as she stacks rocks to convey a sense an intense action. Rock stacking would not be very interesting to watch in real time, and unbearable in slow motion. Occasionally, she sits back down to rest and gaze up at a sculpture in real time. Then she gets back up and stacks rocks in fast motion again, to break up the feel of the shots.

The following tips will help you edit your final film together in a more cohesive way:

1. When you shoot your film, or create it in production, really listen to it to see what it is about. The theme may have shifted or the story may have taken on a different feel during production. If so, you may need to excavate the story.

2. Understanding the story, material, and message in the film is key to being a good editor. Decide "I want to say this," and then try to create it. If it doesn't work, try something else until it does. You need to build a bridge between the ideal of the movie in your head and the real one you are cutting onscreen.

3. Cut expensive shots that don't work. Just because you spent 2 days getting the most time-consuming and expensive shot for your film does not mean you have to use it if is not working on some level. Be brave and cut it if it hurts the film. Come up with a more creative-editing way to tell that part of the story. One bad shot can easily ruin a whole short film. This goes for animators, too.

4. Write your theme on a piece of paper and paste it above your monitor when editing. Any shots that do not communicate theme may be candidates for cutting.

5. Shots that are better emotionally but that have technical flaws are more important than less emotionally charged shots that are technically perfect.

6. Use fast-motion jump cuts for character actions. These can make the most mundane activities fun to watch and compress time in your film.

7. Post colored scene index cards on the wall in chronological order, to track story patterns and make adjustments.

8. Try editing on eye blinks. Watch people when they talk and you will see that they usually blink when they switch thoughts. Walter Murch talks about this theory in his book *In the Blink of an Eye* (Silman-James Press), which is a must-read for people who want to get a deeper sense of the editing mindset. We blink less during fewer events. During a fast and shocking series of events, your eyes blink rapidly, the same way films are cut, to take in all the input. If your actors are really in the true emotion of the scene, you should be able to use their blinks as cues for when to cut. This is why it is also important to videotape voice actors for animated projects, to pull natural gestures and eye-blink cues while the actors go through their lines for editing (which you can use later in your editing).

9. Appreciate the details. You need to develop a relationship between the character and the subject of your film. Use details in your footage to show connections.

10. Editor/director marriage? If you are working in a team and are editing with a director, you need

to be able to translate the director's visions and goals of the film. You also need to know how to fight. This director/editor relationship is much like a marriage, where commitment to the truth of the project must prevail through heated discussions if necessary.

11. Get into a special mindset. You need to immerse yourself in the subject, characters, and theme of your film. Do what works to get you into the emotional state to edit. Play music that fits the mood of the subject you are editing that day or create an editing ritual.

12. Walter Murch recommends standing up while editing footage, because surgeons and other professionals often choose this position for various reasons.

13. Go through the line script and match line script shots with final ones. You may want to try throwing out all the dialogue shots first, just to see what you have without having them holding up the story. Make note of your favorite shots you see from the line script first, to use later.

14. Cut dialogue in problem scenes. Got a scene that does not feel right no matter how you cut it? Try cutting out parts of the dialogue. Often we say too much in the screenwriting process, things that may be communicated better visually in the final footage with less conversation. Use outtakes from other shots in the scene to bridge gaps. To give you more choices later, shoot a few seconds of the emotion at the end of a shot with dialogue.

Just have the character visually express what he or she is feeling for a few seconds, *after* saying an important line. These extra emotionally charged seconds may save your scene later while you are editing out dialogue.

15. Keep telling stories. Write lots of short stories to become a better editor. Keep learning how to describe things and tell stories in new ways.

16. Find visual storytelling patterns. There are patterns everywhere in life: biology, nature, architecture, dance, ritual, and labyrinths. Find these patterns visually in your film footage.

17. Find what connects. What is the thing in your film that connects the character, subject, and audience with the theme?

In my film, I use the symbolic shape of a spiral to connect images back and forth through time and to illustrate theme. During the climax of the film, the character creates a clay symbol with her hands, to brand onto her forehead. As she forms the spiral shape, I match cut to different spiral images in her life, to show how she was always on her path to finding her higher purpose. What shapes or symbols can you connect throughout your story?

"Editing is a kind of surgery—and have you ever seen a surgeon sitting to perform an operation? Editing is also like cooking—and no ones sits down at the stove to cook. But most of all, editing is a kind of dance—the finished film is a kind of crystallized dance—and when have you ever seen a dancer sitting down to dance?"
—Walter Murch

"Nothing great in the world has been accomplished without passion."
—George Hegel

18. Study the language of visual compassion. How can you use a cut of a character with a soft glint in her eyes to convey that she finally acknowledges that she sees something about another character that she hasn't seen before? What little movements do characters make to communicate subtly how they feel? Try mixing up looks from other shots in the film to get the true emotion of the moment, even if you have to use an outtake of an actor taking a break (as long as it's an expression that works).

19. Big screen versus TV? Audiences can sometimes only see things when they are 20 feet high, such as a softening of a look in a character's eye. Make sure you know whether you are editing for TV or for the big screen, and make sure that the viewer can see what you are communicating.

20. Use slow motion to fix shots. Do you have a strong emotional moment that is not working in your film? Try using slow motion. If someone is staring at someone in regular speed and it feels flat, slow it down to half speed, to draw the viewer into the story. Slow motion feels reflective. Voiceover matched with slow motion and a roving camera feels omniscient. Most editing software has a time-stretch function that enables you to adjust for slow- or fast-motion shots.

21. Change speed during big-truth moments. Use slow motion to help moments of truth sink in deeper.

22. Remove your favorite scene. Take your favorite scene out of your film. Sometimes this particular most-loved part keeps the rest of the film from working together. If you take out the best stuff, it is easier to see how to weave together the parts that are not working. Do not get too locked into what works and what does not until you try different approaches. You may be able to put the favorite scene back into the newly woven film that now feels much stronger as a whole.

creativity tip

Develop a Sense of Constant Enthusiasm. Nothing kills a film faster than cynicism. It is your job to create a sense of constant enthusiasm every day for your film and projects. This is especially important when working with a team. Cynicism can easily creep into the editing of your film if you are not careful about the energy you maintain during production. If you are not constantly excited about your film, how can you expect anyone else to be?

23. After your first rough edit, decide which shots you still might need. Progressing to the actual editing stage does not mean that you can't shoot more footage. This may be harder when sets and actors are involved. Be open to shooting more thematic shots or filling in gaps that appear during the editing process.

24. Leave in awkward moments and pregnant pauses. These types of moments reflect on our humanness and give the film room to breathe.

25. Take out sound in shots that are not working. Often a shot does not work when it is time to get the audience into the inner brain of the character or subject. A constant driving soundtrack may detract from this occurring. Try removing all synch sound, and see how the feeling of the shot changes. Leave it silent or add subtle music.

26. Less is more. What shots are not absolutely necessary? Cut them.

27. See with strong opinions that change as you edit. Filmmakers need strong opinions, and editors need to edit with that opinion in mind. Most films work best if the opinion changes by the end. Maybe you show something in the beginning with a strong opinion around it, and then show the same thing at the end with a more evolved opinion, after going through the experience of the film.

28. Recurring visuals. What recurring visuals do you show as metaphors or symbols? These weave patterns for the audience to latch onto. Refer to your metaphor and symbol lists from Chapter 2, "Creating Original Characters, Themes, and Visual Metaphors," to see how you can work more of these shots into your film.

29. Keep technical editing aspects transparent. Your goal in making a film is tell a good story. Do not get carried away with all the digital buttons.

As Ezzie builds this sculpture, she pauses to rest, while stacking huge stumps of redwood trees into a pyramid. This gives the audience a chance to reflect on what she is feeling and thinking at that moment. How can you include pregnant pauses or awkward moments in your film to create a more believable reality?

"An overactive editor, who changes shots too frequently, is like a tour guide who can't stop pointing things out: 'And up here we have the Sistine Ceiling, and over here we have the Mona Lisa, and, by the way, look at these floor tiles....' If you are on a tour, you do want the guide to point things out for you, of course, but some of the time you just want to walk around and see what you see."
—*Walter Murch*

Final Thoughts on Nonlinear Editing

Great editing, as you have seen, is about storytelling, juxtaposition, creating unique visual styles, pacing, emotional impact, connecting with the audience, and finding the truth of your film visually. All the techniques in this chapter are relatively simple to create and edit digitally. The real magic happens when you place the images next to each other and thereby create a new idea in the mind of the viewer.

part III

Creating Digital Short Films for Different Production Styles

chapter 9

Digitally Enhanced Storytelling Techniques

"Think of the computer, not as a tool, but as a medium."
—*Brenda Laurel*

Part I, "Digital Storytelling," of this book showed how important it is to make the audience care about our characters while evoking a series of strong emotional reactions. Part II, "Visualizing Your Script," of this book covered how to tell visual stories using camera techniques, colors, composition, character posing, sound design, and juxtaposition. In Part III, "Creating Digital Short Films for Different Production Styles," of this book you will focus on how to create the shots you have planned, using layers of digital images from your favorite production tools. DV (including HD), special effects, 2D/3D elements, and animation can now be mixed together into an endless array of visual possibilities. Experiment with combining layering ideas that develop a *unique visual production style* and communicate your story in the best way. All the exercises

One of the biggest advantages to making digital films is the ability to combine layers of images and manipulate each one to create special effects, unique visual styles, and innovative storytelling techniques. Shown here are some ideas to get you thinking about what types of characters and sets you may want to use in your film. What favorite production styles could you combine with layers to fit your film idea?

you have done up until this point will help you decide which production look and feel suits the emotions of each sequence, scene, or shot. These last three chapters may be thought of as a digitally enhanced extension to Chapter 6, "Mise En Scène for the Twenty-First Century," to help you develop an innovative and original Mise En Scène.

This chapter will help you think of ways to use layers of images, bluescreened characters, special effects, filters, color manipulation, and motion graphics to tell stories in new ways. Chapter 10, "Using Modern 2D Animation to Expand Our Realities," will push you to think of expanding your film ideas into the surreal and twisted realm of 2D animation. In Chapter 11, "Using 3D Animation to Show Anything You Can Imagine," you will experiment with creating

new worlds, using 3D modeled characters and sets, or layers of 3D animated elements.

The following three chapters are not intended to be a complete software how-to guide, but more of a collection of production techniques presented with narrative slants. More experienced digital filmmakers may be familiar with the techniques discussed, but may have forgotten about how to use them to tell stories. The limited preproduction scope of this book does not leave room to cover step-by-step software techniques for all the different examples and software packages. Many of the images in Part III have their source files included on the CD-ROM in After Effects and Photoshop for you to pick apart. Flash animators can apply many of the After Effects techniques.

Digital Character Design Ideas

Bluescreen Actor

Bluescreen Body Part Combo

Hand-Drawn 2D Character

Rocks with DV Actor Faces

Production-Style Combination Ideas

DV Set

2D Hand-Drawn Set

Photo Set

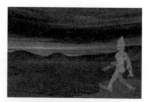

3D Animated Set

Using Digital Video Techniques to Tell Visual Stories

Digital filmmaking is poised to revolutionize the way modern filmmakers tell stories. HD gives digital filmmakers the ability to manipulate *high-resolution frames*. This will open up all sorts of layering and effects possibilities. DV resolution tends to fall apart fast when doing things such as scaling up the image. The mixing of film, IID, DV, 2D, and 3D elements will continue to metamorphosis into innovative visual styles never seen before to communicate in fresh ways. Many things that are hard to show using traditional filmmaking techniques are now possible to create using powerful software. If you know After Effects or Flash, you can put layers of images, animations, and video together in endless ways. If you know 3D, you can build any shot that you can imagine.

Most of the techniques discussed in this chapter can also be applied to 2D and 3D animated stories. I will assume that you know how to use your DV camera, or read the manual, and that you have a basic understanding of nonlinear editing software, such as Premiere or Final Cut Pro. A little experience with effects and animation programs,

such as After Effects or Flash, is also assumed. After Effects is to video what Photoshop is to the still image. If you are serious about making groundbreaking digital films, you need to know how to use After Effects. A few of the compositing techniques in this chapter need to be done in After Effects using the more expensive Production Bundle Version. Special third-party plug-ins are also sometimes necessary for some of the techniques. I did my best to only use techniques that could be accomplished using the standard version of After Effects, and avoided using third-party plug-ins whenever possible for those of you on a budget. Specifically, this chapter covers the following topics:

- Some Advantages of Using DV Tell Stories
- Creating Camera Shots Digitally in Post
- Digitally Enhanced Character Design Techniques
- Creating Virtual Sets
- Fast and Easy Digital Special Effects
- Developing Unique Digitally Enhanced Visual Styles

This flying car was created using a photograph and DV actor body parts for the characters inside. The dogs are my sister's pets, and their bodies are made from a bluescreen shot of the German rock star Xenomorph. The background is a DV shot of the Golden Gate Bridge. What pets, locations, friends, interesting-looking people, or especially scenic shots can you think of using for your film? The car layer with the characters is animated across the DV layer by setting simple position keyframes in After Effects. What simple digital production techniques can you use to show something original? The *Harry Potter* films use flying 3D cars, which look much better, but take more time.

time-saving

Just Getting Started with After Effects? If you are new to After Effects, and are not the kind of person who enjoys reading software manuals, there is a quick start guide on this book's CD-ROM to help you get up and running with the program (AfterFXtutorial.doc). Specific software steps for keying out the blue in bluescreen shots are covered in this file. A demo version of After Effects 5.5 is included on the CD-ROM.

Still Learning After Effects?

A wonderful technical companion book to the ideas described in this chapter is *Creating Motion Graphics with After Effects*, by Trish and Chris Meyer and published by CMP Books. You may want to go through the software techniques in this book and ask yourself how you can use them to tell stories in new ways.

"Guido the plumber and Michelangelo obtained their marble from the same quarry, but what each saw in the marble made the difference between a nobleman's sink and a brilliant sculpture."
—Bob Kall

Incorporate Final Production Environment Choices into the Story. You will come up with new production-oriented story ideas doing the projects in Part III of this book. You might take a character who used to be human and turn him into a talking rock with video lips and eyes. Drastic character design changes may need to be addressed in the script, in places such as dialogue, so that the personality of the character represents more of a rock. Your storyboards might also shift to lower camera angles, to help us see the world from the eyes of this rock living stationary (locked-down camera POV) on the ground. Ideally, you would be thinking of these types of production techniques during the initial writing of the script.

What Are Some Advantages of Using DV to Tell Stories?

"Every artist was first an amateur."
—Ralph Waldo Emerson

Following is a list of some things DV cameras do a little better, cheaper, or easier than most traditional film cameras. Pay attention to how you might use the new functionality being added everyday to the latest versions of DV cameras and software to tell visual stories in original ways.

1. **DV looks real, much like newsreel footage, documentary films, or home videos.** There is a widespread perception among viewers that what is happening on DV is real, and is instantly believable as the unadorned truth. How can you use this DV hard-reality aesthetic to your advantage? You could re-create news footage, do reality shows (that are carefully scripted?), or play with the truth by showing old home-movie footage you created just yesterday.

2. **DV is super sensitive to light.** What kind of dark spaces have we not seen much of before that might work well for your short film? Using slow shutter speeds or low-light modes helps your DV camera record better in darker environments. You could also consider shooting during the daytime, and then add a night-look manipulation effect in post. Even though DV is sensitive to light, it is still important to use professional lighting setups whenever possible, to create more depth and higher-quality shots.

3. **DV footage is cheap to shoot.** It costs only about $4 for a 60-minute DV tape, in contrast to film, which averages about a $100 a minute to shoot and process. How many experimental shots would you try if you had to pay $100 a minute just to see the results much later? What innovative techniques can you pioneer with your DV camera, shooting as much as you want, without spending loads of money? There are many ways to make DV look more like film: using high-quality cameras, 24 fps, slow shutter speeds,

Film Looks Soft and DV Looks Hard?

How can you soften the look of your DV footage? Try using a diffusion filter placed over the lens of your camera with a matte box (if available). You may also want to plan shots in more diffuse lighting environments, such as fog or smoke. What ways could you soften parts of your film and leave other shots or scenes harder, to help convey the changing emotions in your story better? Love scenes might be shot with diffusion filters for a soft, romantic look, whereas fight scenes are shot in hard-lighting setups to help communicate the sharp emotional intensity.

progressive scan mode, manual focus, professional lighting setups, postprocessing, and film-look filters.

4. **It is cheaper to use multiple cameras for one shot.** Film cameras and stock tend to be quite expensive. Rarely do you see independent films with multiple film cameras rolling during a single shot. In the famous factory dance scene in Lars Von Trier's *Dancer in the Dark*, he uses about 100 mini DV cameras, all rolling at the same time, hidden around the set for multiple POV editing choices later. You may want to have three cameras set up around each scene, while the actors run through different approaches to get more fluid performances. With film, you often have to stop actors to set up the next series of shots, perhaps just to read the next line of dialogue. This constant stopping and starting impacts the emotional spontaneity of the scene and makes it hard to keep the actors' energy levels consistent between cuts. You may even want to experiment with throwing your whole script and storyboards out the window and just let the actors improvise at some point. Many directors shoot their storyboards first, and then let the actors loose to experiment with the tape running to see whether anything interesting happens. Music video shoots benefit greatly from multiple cameras during performances. What new shooting styles or shots could you develop that take full advantage of multiple DV cameras rolling at the same time?

5. **Shooting in HD?** If you are thinking about using HD for your next film, ask yourself how you can take what it does best and push it conceptually and emotionally for your film. This hyper-realistic look might work well for a scene where the character is stripped bare emotionally. Long, slow nature shots, sporting events with wide fields, and panoramic, highly detailed shots look great on HD. The high resolution of each frame can be manipulated for zooming in to shots or cutting them up into animated layers. How could you shoot some scenes in HD and some in DV to communicate different looks and feels? How could you cut up different layers of HD footage for scaling, animation, or effects?

6. **Exposure can be controlled while observing and recording the image.** What in-camera exposure effects could you develop while shooting to help viewers understand your character's POV, story emotions, or symbolic visual sequences?

7. **It is easy to vary the shutter speeds.** Some DV cameras enable you to do this in mid-shot to create different looks as scene emotions change. Maybe a character hears some news that makes him really confused, so you switch to a slower shutter speed to get a more blurry effect. You may also have to adjust the exposure, because the image will get brighter with lower shutter speeds. How could you justify blurry trailing images in your story? How could you switch shutter speeds in mid-shot to drive an emotional moment?

In this sketch, three DV cameras are placed around an actor doing Kung Fu moves. You could edit these shots together to give a new jump-cut 360-degree feel. This would be a cheaper version of *The Matrix* "bullet time" special-effect camera shot.

"Become so wrapped up in something that you forget to be afraid."
—*Lady Bird Johnson*

money-saving

Diffusion Filter Alternative. If you do not have a matte box or diffusion filter for your camera, you may want to try placing stretched nylon panty hose over the lens and securing it with a rubber band. Experiment with different shades of hosiery, along with different patterns, such as a delicate fishnet. Other sheer, transparent fabrics may work well too. Zoom into the subject to obtain a softening of the image through the hose, without getting the actual pattern of the weave in your shot. You can also try applying a slight blur effect to the footage in post.

8. **Small and light cameras are easy to maneuver.** What types of moving camera shots can you do that involve handheld or innovative techniques for small and light DV cameras?

9. **Less intrusive cameras enable you to get more natural and intimate-looking shots and performances.** This is in contrast to putting subjects in front of huge and imposing film cameras, under lots of big hot lights, and surrounded by enormous crews. What unique places could you shoot where people do not realize you are filming? You usually do not need a film permit for a one-person monopod shoot.

10. **Small cameras make it easier to shoot in tight spaces.** With a DV camera, you can shoot in places such as closets, cars, narrow tunnels, and crowded spaces. What other tight metaphorical spots could you think up for a scene that has not been seen before in a film?

11. **You can shoot all alone without a crew.** This also enables you to get more intimate footage working with just one actor at a time (or musician, for a music video). How could you take advantage of this intimacy to get more emotionally real footage? What kind of films could you make by yourself?

12. **Everything you need to shoot fits into one little bag.** This means you can travel easier to locations with difficult access, such as rock-climbing vistas, crowded places, museums, historical sites, amusement parks, or even participate in extreme adventure traveling. Some mini DV cameras are about the size of a big bar of soap and can be taken almost anywhere.

13. **You don't have to wait for daily rushes.** You get to review your footage as soon as you shoot. This means you can take more chances right away. What types of experimental shooting styles might you pioneer?

14. **The camera person can see more by holding the camera above or below the eyepiece.** How could you benefit from this advantage? Maybe you could maintain eye contact with your actor and talk the actor through a scene, cutting out your direction dialogue in post.

A handheld shot of someone climbing up the side of a big pyramid would create a unique moving POV shot. A handheld panoramic shot from the top may give a new perspective never before seen with big, bulky film cameras. Various mini DV handicam braces are available for purchase to make your handheld shots less jarring. What new handheld camera shots could you use to help communicate your story better visually?

How can you exaggerate or contrast story emotions using visually tight spaces for sets? A mind screen shot of a character thinking about tunneling through his subconscious might be shot inside an old drainage pipe. Effects could be added in post to create a unique inner-reality visual style.

A roller coaster POV could be created using a DV headcam, or by securely fastening your DV camera to your body during amusement park rides. Filters or special effects could then be applied to create unique, metaphorical traveling shots with a voiceover to communicate emotions or ideas. Be extra careful not to damage your camera or yourself when doing stunt shots.

15. **It is easier to shoot strange angles with a small light-weight camera.** What strange angles could you justify to drive home your story visually? You could stand on a chair behind your actors and shoot the scene from overhead, tilted at extreme angles, for instance.

16. **You can see what you are shooting through the viewfinder flipped up toward you**. What types of one-person films could you shoot? How could you take an idea for your short film and do it with just yourself and a camera?

17. **DV is composed of pixels, all of which can be easily manipulated for postprocessing special effects, bluescreen characters, or color shifts.** Adding animation, multiple layers of images, or motion graphics is much easier these days with the variety of software available. This chapter focuses mostly on these types of DV advantages for you to consider when planning your films.

How could you climb up on trees, ladders, or chairs to get more interesting angles for your shots and add more depth to the scene in the process? Be very careful not to fall off anything trying to get a shot.

How to Combine Layers Using Transparent Areas

Many of the special effects described in this chapter require you to combine different layers of video, Photoshop images, and animation. An alpha channel, mask, matte, and track matte are essentially all the same thing, because they create transparent regions for other layers to play through. Here are six ways to define transparent areas in your layers:

1. **Photoshop alpha channels.**
   Alpha channels can be created in many ways using Photoshop. You can create one by erasing or deleting portions of the image in a layer. After Effects recognizes Photoshop layers with all of their transparencies. You can also create a new alpha channel using an 8-bit grayscale image added to the 24-bit color image to produce a 32-bit image. Most programs that recognize alpha channels interpret the black areas of the image as transparent.

2. **Bluescreening techniques.**
   Keying out the blue background behind a subject creates a transparent area in which other backgrounds can be placed. The various tools used this technique are described later in this chapter.

In this example, a bluescreen character is first separated from the blue background and then placed on a 2D set. Other photos, DV, 2D, or 3D elements and layers can play through the black transparent areas.

3. **Mask tool.** The square, oval, or Bezier pen tool in After Effects can be used to draw shapes on top of DV layers to create transparent regions. To create a mask in After Effects, you need to double-click the source layer in the timeline first. The advantage of using masks is that the points can be animated to match changing motion. This technique is also called rotoscoping. A mask may be inverted or an edge feathered to blend in better with other layers.

4. **Track matte.** The matte layer must be placed in the timeline window in After Effects, right above the layer you want to effect. Click the bottom layer track matte pull-down menu to assign a matte style such as Alpha. (If it is not showing, click the Switches/Modes button.)

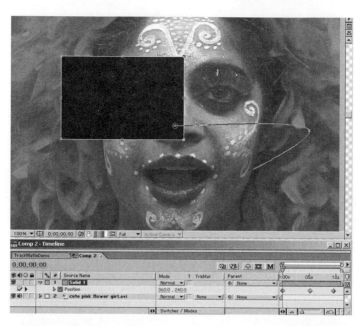

In this shot, the dog is masked out of the background using the Bezier pen masking tool to create a rack focus effect.

An animated rectangle was used as a track matte in this example to reveal the layer beneath. These files are on the CD-ROM for you to explore. How could you use a similar technique to tell us a story in a new way?

5. **Effect>Channel>Set Matte.**
This effect works just like a
track matte but enables you to
place your layers in any order,
and allows you to use one matte
over and over again without
duplicating it.

6. **3D animation software.** All
3D programs create alpha channels for compositing different
layers together.

project
9.2

Think of two original ideas to use with
some of the preceding layering techniques in your film. Explain how the
idea will communicate your story in a
better way. You need to start thinking
in layers and transparencies to fully
grasp the power of digital filmmaking.

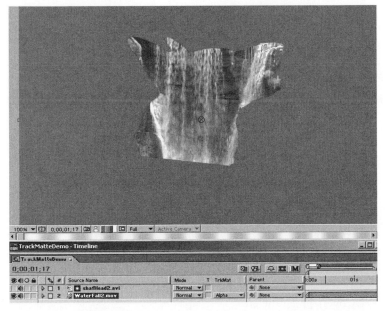

Combining different layers of transparencies. Bluescreen keying techniques were used
first to extract a DV alpha channel of a moving dog head. This alpha channel was then
used as a track matte cookie cutter shape for the waterfall DV footage to play through.
How could you create symbolic track matte shapes to tell your story in a new way?

Creating Camera Shots Digitally in Post

After you shoot something, you may want to spice it up a little in post by transforming it into another type of camera shot entirely, such as taking a regular slow pan and turning it into a swish pan to fit the emotions and ideas emerging in the story during editing.

How can you take your DV footage, or still images, and turn them into new types of camera shots using your digital tools? Following are some ideas to get you started with creating innovative digital camera shots in post:

- **Aerial shot (AS).** Use a pan-and-scan technique across an overhead photograph.
- **Double exposure.** Lay one layer of video on top of another with a 50 percent opacity or transparency. Plan for the composition of the two shots to work well together in advance. For example, the blank sky on the right side of a character's head could be filled with another layer of running horses, located on the right side of the screen. You may want to mask out certain parts of the layers or reduce the scale to get better compositions without a full-screen bleed-through across the entire frame. Multiple exposed video layers are easy to do digitally and can produce interesting results when based on strong narrative concepts.
- **Dream POV.** Fade one layer of video into another one slowly using opacity going from 0 to 100 percent. Try overlapping the end of one shot with the beginning of another one over a few seconds to get a more dreamy feel. You may

want to apply some effects during the fade, such as wave warp or blurs, to make the transition feel more soft and dreamy. A color shift may help the footage stand out as a different dimension inside the character's mind, by tinting the dreamy footage blue or making it black and white. You could duplicate the dreamy video layer and add a feathered blurry mask around the edges to give it a softer frame.

- **Establishing shot.** If you don't have the budget to go to some far-away place to obtain an establishing shot, you may want to use a photograph with some added DV or animated elements to make it look more like a moving video shot.

You may even want to use drawings of fictional locations and then add DV layers to create a unique visual style. How could you combine different pieces of locations that do not go together for an interesting shot?

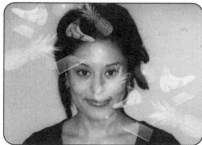

In this shot, Monika is thinking about food. A separate layer of photographs featuring pineapples, bananas, chocolate bars, and mangos was created in Photoshop and then animated across the screen in After Effects. Slight rotations were added to the food objects to make them appear to be floating across the screen as if in a dream. Blending these two layers together creates a unique, animated, digitally enhanced, double-exposure shot. How could you create an innovative double-exposure shot to show viewers what your character is thinking or feeling?

This street scene photograph was scanned into Photoshop, where the sky was cut out. In After Effects, DV cloud footage from another shot is added behind the houses to make the still photograph feel more like a moving shot. How can you make your photographs appear to be live shots by using different layering techniques?

Animating Still Photographs with Video Layers

Still photos can be scanned, broken apart in Photoshop, and animated in software programs such as After Effects or Flash. Use the selection tools to cut out pieces or characters you want to animate and paste into a new layer. Use the Clone tool in Photoshop to fill in cut-out background areas.

Suppose, for instance, that you have an old photograph of someone writing on a chalkboard. First, you cut out the character as a layer and then cut his arm into a separate piece to animate. Each piece could be rotated using keyframes to make the arm look like it is moving. The writing on the chalkboard could be replaced with a different message, as another layer in Photoshop. This message could be slowly revealed, with an animated mask, as his arm appears to move up and down across the now blank chalkboard. In the final shot, the character would appear to be writing on the chalkboard from the photograph. Add drop shadows between layer elements in After Effects to add depth. How could you use multiple photographs animated over each other using this technique for a look in your film? How could you add video elements to the animated photograph layers to make them more dynamic?

- **Fly into subject.** Start with a zoom shot into an object area such as an eye, belly button, mouth, forehead, or other subject. Match cut the next shot with the same shape of the object. A round eye would fit with the shape of a round tube. You could also use your DV camera to zoom into the opening of a pipe, tube, or cave to get the same traveling-into effect. Some DV cameras work better at zooming into small openings.

This photograph of Monika drumming was imported into Photoshop, where her arm was cut out and pasted into a separate layer. The Clone tool was used to fill in the background area where her arm used to be in the second image. The layered Photoshop file was then imported into After Effects, where her arm was animated to strike the drum using simple rotation and position keyframes.

What Is Pan and Scan?

Pan-and-scan techniques involve animating a still photo, or large composition layer, inside of a 720×480-pixel standard-sized DV screen to give the impression of a camera panning across a large area. This technique is often used to add some motion to still images, making them appear more dynamic. Be sure the camera is revealing important information to the narrative as it slides across the large image or composition. Historical documentaries often use pan-and-scan techniques with old photographs, sound design, and narration to create moving camera shots. Where could you use this technique in your film for a photograph, map, family photo album, overhead location shot, or a pedestal character shot?

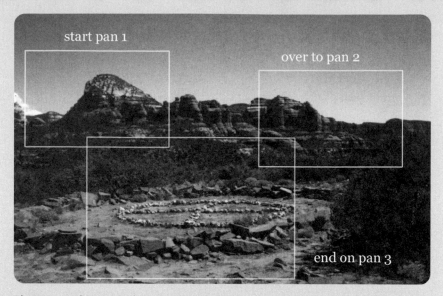

Photo Pan and Scans. *In this example, a photo of the desert was scanned at a high resolution and then imported into After Effects as a 3000-pixel-wide composition. Another 720×480 standard-sized DV composition was created as a viewing frame. The large photo was moved around inside the smaller composition window by setting simple position and scale keyframes. On the third part of the pan, a smaller-scale keyframe was set on the photo layer to make the camera appear to zoom out a little.*

Scene Composition Pan and Scans. *In this example, a large 2D animated composition was created for a scene. A smaller DV-sized composition was then used to pan up the giant woman character, creating a pedestal-type shot. A third pan-and-scan shot for this example could be to scale the whole background down to 720×480 for a zoom-out effect that reveals the whole set. Creating large scene compositions in After Effects with 3000-pixel-wide aspect ratios will give you more flexibility to do these types of digitally enhanced camera moves.*

In this shot, the camera pans into the middle of the scene activity, shown by the black circle guide around the highlighted anchor point.

In the final pan-and-scan shot, this image will appear on the screen, creating a zoom-in effect. A motion blur effect was added to make the zoom feel faster.

The best way to pan and scan around a large image in After Effects is to use the Pan Behind tool, also called the Anchor Point tool. Click this icon, and then move the circle with the X in the comp window to the middle of the spot you want to pan to. This same tool is used to set rotation center points for cut-up layers during character animation, which is explained more in Chapter 10.

#	Source Name	🔲🔲🔲	Parent		0:00s	01s	02s	03s	04s
1	2dstreet_Geo...		◎ None ▼						
	Anchor Point	1497.5 , 1824.0							
▷	Position	326.0 , 350.0			◆				◆
▷	Scale	20.0 %			◆				◆

In the timeline, you would set keyframes for position and scale, after moving the anchor point into position. For those of you new to digital filmmaking, a keyframe is a value (number for position, scale, rotation, and effects) set on a timeline. If you set your scale keyframe on a layer to 100 percent at 0 seconds, and then set another scale keyframe for 20 percent at 4 seconds, the image will appear to shrink (or zoom out) from 0 to 4 seconds.

project
9.3

Pan-and-Scan Idea. Find one place in your digital film where you could use a pan-and-scan technique across a photograph, drawing, map, or photo or video collage.

Pan and scan across animated video collages. Combining different layers of video, photos, drawings, or animated elements can produce some interesting highly stylized looks. How could you create an animated pan-and-scan shot over a video or animation collage for a unique camera shot? Start by creating a sketch of the animated pan-and-scan idea for your film. In this example, a photo, DV, 2D, and 3D animated collage was designed as one big abstract layer that the camera could then pan across to reveal events happening in different locations.

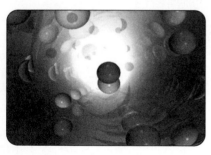

- **Fly-into-the-eye shot.** Glen Grillo created this fly-into-the-eye shot by placing the animated frames of the next tube shot inside the girl's eye. An animated opening circular mask was placed over the second tube shot as the camera zooms into her round iris, to make the tube shot match the camera shot in one smooth zooming motion.
- **Follow shot (FS).** Follow shots when done in unique ways are carefully choreographed Wow! shots that follow a character through a world without any editing. By using digital tools, compositing techniques, and bluescreen characters, you can control all aspects of a follow shot, to show us original approaches. You may want to try doing a follow shot with a bluescreen or animated character walking through different video layers, animated elements, cut-up photographs, 3D environments, or combinations of visual styles.
- **Freeze frame.** Export a still frame of the one you want to freeze from your movie clip into your digital editing program. Interlaced video must be processed through either de-interlacing or field-blending when freeze frames are extracted. Otherwise, they will flicker. You won't see this on your computer monitor, only on an NTSC or PAL monitor. Stretch the amount of time the shot holds on the screen in the timeline. How could you add pieces of video layers, or animated elements over the freeze frame to help exaggerate the feeling? Flames laid across the face of an angry character, with an oval mask and 50 percent opacity, would give the impression of the character's face being on fire.

project 9.4

Follow Shot Idea. Plan a follow shot for your film using digital techniques that fit your story. Draw a sketch showing the visual changes that the character experiences. This example illustrates the life span of a Bigfoot from infancy to old age. The shot starts with a 3D animated, crawling Bigfoot baby against a DV background of a pasture. The baby Bigfoot then morphs into a teenager walking by a stream, where he encounters a UFO. This Bigfoot then changes into an adult having a mystical experience in the forest. The shot ends with the Bigfoot changing into an elderly creature moving so slowly that birds are perched on his body.

superfreak!

Follow Shot Film. How could you take the idea for your short film and turn it into one long follow shot using bluescreen or animated characters?

- **Graphic mask (vignette).** Create a Photoshop shape to simulate a POV looking through binoculars, a gun sight, a keyhole, a scuba mask, a telescope, a microscope, high-tech military infrared glasses, or a space visor that can be laid over video footage. Make sure to plan your final shot composition to take place inside the viewable area or scale the footage down to fit inside the opening. You might want to animate the DV layer beneath the mask for optimal composition and effects. Play with matching these shots to the POV of your character, such as panning back and forth, to simulate the way you would look through a pair of binoculars. You may want to use your digital tools to create high-tech binocular functions, such as X-ray vision, where you see a group of dressed-up people as 2D hand-drawn skeletons. How could you add animated elements to the mask shape, such as blinking lights or digital readout motion graphics? Maybe these special POV glasses could be a quest object in your story that helps the characters achieve their goals while learning to use them in a clever way.

In this shot, a binocular graphic mask was created in Photoshop and then imported into After Effects. DV footage of the Golden Gate Bridge is placed underneath the graphic mask shape to convey the POV of a person looking through binoculars.

project
9.5

Digitally Enhanced Graphic Masks. Shown here are several shapes you could draw or make in Photoshop to lay over your DV footage as a graphic mask. Binocular, keyhole, TV screen, and gunsights are some of the more obvious choices. What other graphical shapes could you think of to show viewers a fresh POV for a character in your film? What ways could you add animated elements to your graphic mask, such as blinking lights or motion graphics?

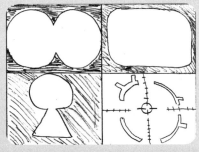

Using a Bluescreen in Follow Shots

One of the more challenging aspects of creating a digitally enhanced follow shot is having a long enough bluescreen actor walk cycle. A bluescreen actor on a treadmill is often used for these types of shots. Or you may want to have objects fall in the foreground, to cut to another bluescreen walk cycle shot, if you do not have a treadmill. Plan out the timing of the events in the follow shot so that the characters react to the elements that will be composited around them in post, such as shielding their faces when an asteroid is supposed to fall at their feet. What types of symbolic objects could your character encounter during a digitally enhanced follow shot?

You may want to incorporate death-defying bluescreen character stunts in your follow shots, such as narrowly missing a bunch of falling rocks. Chase scene follow shots could involve bluescreen characters leaping across building tops and going through impossible-looking obstacle courses made of cut-up photographs. Try slowing down a follow shot to feel more like a dream. Some short films are based on being one long follow shot with a strong concept. How could you follow a bluescreen character flying, falling, or floating through different environments?

In this shot, a separate, masked video layer is placed over a character's forehead to show what the character is thinking. How can you use symbolic mind screen shots to exaggerate or contrast inner character emotions or thoughts?

- **Jump Cut (JC).** This shot is one of the easiest to do in your digital editing program using a razor blade type of tool, cutting out pieces of the clip in the timeline. You could also take the clip and make multiple versions of it, with different in/out points, where chunks of footage are missing inside longer shots. How could you repeat footage, add effects to the same repeating footage, play it backward, fast forward to upcoming events, or do subliminal cuts of other shots to create a unique jump-cut sequence?

- **Mind screen.** There are as many ways to show what a character is thinking as there are stories. Here are some ideas to get you started: 1) Fly into the forehead or eye of the character using the fly-into shot; 2) Composite a masked layer of video over the character's forehead like a screen; 3) Superimpose another video layer of a mask over the face of a character to show what the character is thinking about; 4) Use animated thought bubbles over a character's head with video playing inside; 5) Build a 3D set of a head with movie screens in its eyes; or 6) Shot of character thinking intensely, and then fade to dreamy image of thoughts.

- **Mirror/reflection shot.** Wow! reflection shots are often difficult to capture on actual set locations. Digital tools enable modern filmmakers to create reflection layers in post while controlling every aspect of the shot. How could you add a DV video reflection layer to surfaces such as mirrors, water, shiny metal objects, glass tables, silver goblets, crystal balls, or magical objects to tell us something about your character or film world? Maybe you could develop a unique visual style for your story, where a character keeps

Shoot footage of a character looking into a reflective surface, such as a pond. Add another layer of DV that shows the reflection on top of the water. You may need to match the angle of the pond ground plane to the masked reflection layer using Layer>3D Layer in After Effects. If a good reflective surface is hard to find, create a pond in post using a water layer playing inside of a pond-shaped mask.

remembering past events (or having visions about the future) while staring into reflecting surfaces. The character could see events happening in other locations, see a loved one sending a message, or a symbolic nature shot that sums up the character state at that point in the story. Shoot the scene straight with a character looking into a mirror and then add the DV reflection as a masked layer over the glass using the Add mode.

- **Video collage.** Create a video collage using several layers of clips with masked-out areas that fit together as a single composition using feathered edges, opacity adjustments, transfer layers, roto-scoping, or alpha mattes. You might want to experiment with having different layers of video play through each other. This technique may work best for communicating surreal imagery such as dreams, or to show the inner landscape of a character's mind. How could you create a unique visual style for a scene in your film using a video collage?

- **Projection shot.** Buy or rent a video projector, old film projector, or slide projector. Create or gather footage that fits with your story to project onto subjects or objects on the set, while shooting with your DV camera. How could you symbolically show what is happening in the narrative by projecting video onto your actors during a scene? Perhaps your character is telling a scary story as viewers see frightening images projected onto his face and the background. How could you control more of what the audience is thinking or feeling during each scene by using projectors in a clever way? Digital video projectors are getting cheaper and better every day, and you may want to consider buying one to create unique visual styles for your film. Video mixers, which take two separate streams of video and mix them into one, may also be used for more abstract real-time graphics during projection shots and performances.

- **Reverse motion.** Most digital editing programs have time-remapping functions that enable you to enter in (–100) type settings to play footage in reverse. In After Effects, you select the layer you want to play backward in the timeline and choose Layer>Time Stretch and then enter –100 percent. You also can press Command+Option+R for the clip to revolve "in place," so you will not have to reposition the clip in the timeline. How could use reverse motion to show what a character is thinking?

project 9.6

Create a Video Collage Idea. Find a place in your film to use a video collage. Use at least four separate layers. Explain how the visual concept relates to developing your narrative.

superfreak!

Digital Projection Shot Theater. If your film were a play, how could you use video projectors to create the sets or develop the story? White sheets or layers of screens can be hung to project different layers of DV, 3D, or 2D footage. White-painted blocks or shaped surfaces may be used to project shots. If you shoot a house at an angle, and then project the footage on a large, white cube at the same angle, the house will appear to be more dimensional. An immersive environment could be created using multiple video projectors aimed at each wall, floor, or ceiling. You might consider building a white box type to set around your stage with multiple video projectors aimed at each panel. DV cloud footage could be projected onto all the panels to make it look as if the actors were walking through clouds. This footage could change as the story progresses to fit the narrative. How could you use some of these techniques to create an original look for your film?

Projection Shot Mind Screen. These dancers were shot with projected video of a huge eye playing across their bodies and the background. This technique could be used to show what a character is thinking or to develop the emotional subtext of a scene. How could you have the actors interact with the projected footage? Perhaps the projected eye could be a character in the story, telling the dancers what to do.

- **Sequence shot.** This Wow! type of shot can be created in post using the same techniques discussed for the follow shot, only you do not have to stay with one character; however, you do need to keep the shot moving through a scene without any edits. Expensive cranes are often used for sequence shots in traditional filmmaking. You can create a sequence shot digitally using video collage pan-and-scan techniques. Start with a large background image, to use as a map to keep all the layers straight. Use masked video layers for moving elements, zooming in and out of locations, or areas with characters doing small scenes that set up a film world. To do a good sequence shot requires very careful planning in traditional filmmaking, because you cannot edit out any mishaps in post, cutting to other shots that work better. Digital sequence shots can control every element, because you can break them down into layers, which still requires lots of planning. The trick is to have a good reason to do one, and enough planning and originality to make it feel like the viewer is drifting through a world with an omniscient perspective, while not drawing too much attention to the actual shot itself. How can you combine several of the digital camera shots in this list into one long sequence shot without edits? These types of Wow! shots are often used at the beginning of stories, or new scenes, to establish the film-world look and feel while introducing characters and situations.

- **Slide show.** Shoot a series of high-resolution stills and lay them into the video timeline. Play with the timing of each still to get a rhythm that fits the story's pace or soundtrack at that moment.

- **Slow motion (slo-mo)/super slow motion.** Most digital editing programs have time-remapping functions that enable you to enter a number to play at a percentage of the regular speed. In After Effects, you select the layer you want to adjust in the timeline, and choose Layer>Time Stretch, and then enter 60 percent, or whatever speed communicates the *feel* of the clip best. If there is an audio layer, it will also be slowed down, which might be a nice extra sound effect, or could mess up your dialogue completely. Depending on your story, you may want to create a separate audio file, to clarify any dialogue that gets too hard to understand. Effects can be applied to a separate audio file to add distortion that matches the slow-motion time feel, yet retains comprehension of voices. Frame-blending may be needed to restore persistence of vision, if you want to go below 50 percent, which may also seriously degrade image quality. For professional slow-motion shots, many digital filmmakers opt to shoot on a high-speed film camera and transfer to video if they have the budget.

- **Split screen.** For a simple split-screen shot of two people talking on the phone in different locations, draw a rectangular mask across the top layer of video that stretches halfway across the frame. Adjust the videos playing inside each layer for the best composition. Screens

can also be split into symbolic shapes, using alpha channel types of mattes to play video layers through each other, like cookie-cutter windows. Choose hard edges between the different screens in the frame, or add a feathering of 10 pixels between layers to make the effect softer with a more blended look.

How could you use animated split screens? You could animate a line (or lines) of 10 video screens across the frame horizontally or vertically. By using multiple, small video windows, playing against a full-screen video layer, you may be able to achieve a new, visual narrative idea. This technique might work well for a shot in which you have something like the side view of a house with little video square windows showing scenes of what the people inside each window are doing. These video windows could be animated to expand and contract, based on the importance of the events occurring in the story. How would different split-screen configurations make the feel of your shot change?

- **Swish pan.** Take a normal pan shot, increase the speed using a time-stretch function, and add a motion-blur swish effect.

- **Time lapse.** Some DV cameras have a time-lapse mode that enables you to set the intervals and walk away, letting the camera do the work. If yours does not, set your camera up on tripod and shoot an hour-long sunset, and then speed it up to play it in 10 seconds using a time-stretch type function in your digital editing program. You may also want to take a single-frame video grab or

35mm still at timed intervals, depending on the subject, and put them together as a sequence in post. Suppose, for instance, that you are doing shot of a rose blooming over the course of a week. You could mark where your tripod is (or leave it outside), set framing markers in the background, and then grab one shot a day at the same time and put them together in your digital editing program. How could you do match cut time lapses of subjects changing over the years to show backstory or character history?

• **Titles/subtitles.** Do your typography in a program such as Illustrator, and then copy and paste the text into After Effects or your favorite digital editing program to animate. Experiment with copying simple layout and animation techniques you see used during credit sequences at the beginning of feature films that fit with the style of your film. Having very slick and professional-looking title sequences for your short film is very important to keep it from looking too amateur.

superfreak!

One Long Digital Sequence Shot Short Film. How could you take your film idea and turn it into one long, digitally controlled sequence shot without any cuts or edits? Create a rough diagram of the camera path through the scene(s), paying particular attention to how you move between locations in an original way that fits with your story style.

Split-Screen Composition Ideas

Split-Screen Ideas. Keep in mind the endless possibilities for using split-screen compositions and multiple layers of video in your digital films. Shown here are some configurations to help you think of new ways to divide your screen. How could you use masks, such as circles, around certain layers of video, instead of having all rectangles? What new ways could you break up the frame and have the different symbolic shapes playing DV inside that interact with each other? How could you use a split screen in your film to show how two or more events or characters relate?

When composing shots for a split screen, you need to develop the juxtapositions between the screens as much as possible. These shots also need to be carefully composed to feel visually balanced on one screen. Will you have events happening in your split-screen shot that are occurring at the same time or different times? How could you develop character relationships by using staging techniques across multiple screens, such as placing superior characters on

the top half? How can you create a connection or theme between the different split-screen shots? On the top half, a woman could be looking over the side of a building at dusk, while on the bottom half, we see a man sitting on top of a similar building during the day. Both rooftops could have similar visual elements that pull the two compositions together, such as twisted metal shapes. We might then see both of them walking down hallways in the same split-screen setup. Maybe the characters are always carefully placed on opposite sides of the split screen to show separation. At the end, they may finally meet in a park, as the split-screen match cuts to a full screen of them together, to symbolize visually the start of a relationship. By splitting the screen in half horizontally, it also makes a nice letter-box-looking double frame for more elegant compositions. What original ways can you use split screens to show what two characters are doing, feeling, or thinking, and how they relate to each other visually as the story unfolds?

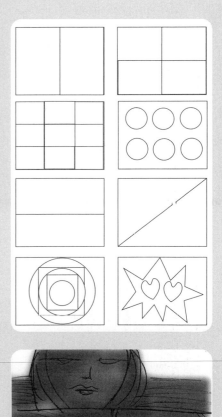

In this sketch, the painting on the wall matches the first shot of the next scene, for a zoom into match cut transition. Leave space above characters to place match cut objects to make your post compositing job easier. What new ways could you create a digitally enhanced match cut in your film? How could you cut out objects in the second shot and add them to the last frame of the first shot?

project 9.7

Create a Graphic Match Cut in Post. Explain the narrative concept behind the match cut element. What symbolic objects could you add in post to create a graphic match between two scenes? The candle flame burning in the first shot could symbolize a new truth opening up during an encounter. The match cut on flames to the next shot of a house burning down could show the effect of the new truth on the characters.

Transitional Shots

Most nonlinear editing programs have lots of choices for applying ready-to-go shot transitions. Sometimes you may want to build your own unique transitions in a program such as After Effects to have more precise control over the timing, look, and feel.

- **Fade in/out.** Most digital editing programs have a fade in/out opacity effect going from 0 to 100 percent (in) and 100 percent to 0 (out).
- **Focus in/out.** For focus in, you want your image to go from blurry to sharp. For focus out, you want your image to go from sharp to blurry. You can create these focal effects digitally by keyframing blur parameters. Experiment with creating a focus in effect by setting a dramatic blur keyframe at the beginning of the clip. After a few seconds, set another keyframe with the blur at 0, to make it appear that your footage is coming into focus.
- **Alpha mask.** You can build any shape of transition you desire between two clips by making a grayscale clip and using it as an alpha channel between two clips.
- **Blackout/whiteout.** Opacity goes from 100 percent to 0 with a black screen underneath. White-out does the same to a white frame.
- **Graphic match cut.** Build your own match cuts in post using still video frames from the second shot composited onto set elements in the first shot. For example, two characters could be talking at a table with a painting above them containing an image that match cuts with the next shot. Zoom into

the painting, or fade into the next shot, with the image in the painting exactly matching the first shot in the next scene. Export the first frame of the second clip into Photoshop (Composition>Save Frame As) and make it look like a painting by adding a frame or painterly-looking filters. Obviously this technique works best if the painting is facing the camera, but may also work with slight angles. Plan for these shots ahead of time by leaving a blank space on the wall above the actors that you can place match cut set objects into later. This technique could become part of a visual style in your film to get in and out of each sequence. You may also want to place an image in one layer of video that will match position in the next shot, such as a burning candle flame on the table dissolving into a burning house on a hill in the next shot. The burning candle could be added as a separate layer of masked video in the first shot to match the fire of the house in the second shot added in post to build a match cut around later.

- **Natural wipe.** You could build a natural wipe by animating a mask layer selection across the frame following a moving subject. If you have a character walking across the screen, you would create an animated mask that follows the character's backside as the character moves across the frame, revealing the next shot underneath. This type of visual technique would work well to show a character leaving a situation behind. What other moving objects in your storyboards could be used as an animated mask wipe?

- **Solarization.** You can create some interesting solarization effects by zooming your DV camera into a bright light source and using the footage as a transition. To build one in post, use a filter such as Final Effects Light Burst or combine with several light effects from packages such as the Knoll Light Factory. By combining smaller spinning twinkle lights, or lens flares, you can create unique solarization shot transitions. How could you add match cut light effects, such as a glint coming off of a metal object in one scene, that match a light in the next shot?

Digitally Enhanced Camera Lens Effects

Creating digitally enhanced camera effects in post gives you added flexibility to communicate the feel of your story. These post-camera effects will not look exactly the same way they would with an actual optical lens distortion, but the overall visual effects can be similar. Refer to books such as *American Cinematographer* to calculate specific numeric values to simulate proper optical lens distortion. Following are some simple

Light Burst Epiphanies. This effect was created using a combination of lighting effects from third-party plug-ins, such as Delirium and Knoll Light Factory. These types of effects can be carefully keyframed into digitally enhanced solarization transitions between shots.

techniques you may want to try to simulate a few traditional camera lens effects:

- **Fisheye.** Shoot with as wide an angle as possible and then apply Effect>Distort>Bulge.
- **Rack focus.** Duplicate the source footage layer (Command+D) and apply a slight blur to the bottom layer to look out of focus. Create a mask around the subject you want to be in focus on the top layer, such as a character. This will make the character look in focus, with the rest of the frame blurry and out of focus. You could really exaggerate this by making the background really blurred. Apply a 20-pixel-wide feather to the mask to smooth out the edges around the in-focus object and background

Fisheye Lens in Post. This shot was distorted using a bulge effect. What innovative types of animated fisheye looks could you develop using some of your digital tools to simulate a distorted mood?

This example shows the same layer of video duplicated three times. The bottom one is then blurred to appear out of focus. The top two layers have masks around each dog that can then appear in or out of focus, depending on the story.

project 9.8

Go through your camera shots and find at least three places to use this digitally enhanced rack focus effect. Explain how the in-focus areas relate to the story.

project 9.9

Shallow Focus Effect. Think up a place in your film to use a digitally enhanced shallow-focus technique to drive emotions and develop the story. Explain how the concept of the effect fits the narrative.

superfreak!

Animate Rack Focus Effect. How could you animate your in-focus areas in new ways? Perhaps a character starts out in focus and then slowly, the mask contracts around the character making him appear more and more out of focus as a troubling situation unfolds in the scene. Or you could have the mask get bigger until the whole frame is in focus, revealing symbolic background images, if the conversation reveals new information that makes the character see things in a more expanded way. Find a place in your film to create an animated rack focus effect and explain how it fits the narrative.

so that the layers blend together better. To switch the focus to another character in the shot, duplicate the top layer again and mask out the second subject to be in focus. Fade between the two masked in-focus layers, and the final shot will appear to change focal areas. How could you use this technique to guide the viewer's eye around the frame?

- **Shallow focus.** This uses the same technique as rack focus to achieve a blurry background with an area in the foreground in focus. Or you may want to have the foreground object out of focus, and the background in focus, by blurring the foreground masked

layer rather than the bottom one, depending on the shot. How could you switch back and forth between the foreground and background, being in or out of focus, to fit with your story? Maybe one character is talking in the background in focus, while another listens in the foreground out of focus, and then it switches as the foreground character starts to speak. Bluescreen characters could easily be in focus, because they are already a separate layer with the backgrounds out of focus. Or you could create a bluescreen character who is always out of focus as a metaphor for deep, inner confusion or shyness.

In this shot, the subject is masked out of the background in the duplicated layer to appear in focus. The bottom layer is blurred to appear out of focus.

- **Shutter speeds.** Shutter speeds are so easy to do with most DV cameras that it makes more sense to do these in-camera. If you forget or want to add one after a shoot, try exporting the grabbed clip at a reduced frame rate, such as 10 fps, to create the jumpy motion feel. Apply Effect>RE: Vision Plugins>ReelSmart (separate plug-in) Motion Blur for a smeary look. A regular motion blur filter will not work as well.

- **Split diopter.** To have two separate areas of the frame in focus at the same time, with the background blurry, use the rack focus technique. Keep both of the top mask layers in focus above the blurry background layer.

Shooting DV Underwater

Many DV cameras have waterproof casings you can buy that enable you to shoot underwater. These start at about $1000, depending on the make and model. What types of new POVs could you shoot while surfing, scuba diving, swimming, jumping into water, white-water rafting, submerged in murky lakes, getting knocked over by ocean waves, water skiing, or shooting in the rain or thunderstorms? You may want to place your set and actors on the bottom of the family swimming pool to create a unique visual style. Use colored transparent light gels or drape colored scarves over the submerged pool lights to get different lighting effects. Or you could shoot at night with lights shining into the pool. You must be extremely careful to make sure that your lights are securely locked down with weights or sandbags so that they do not fall into the water. You may also want to hang a blue or green sheet or screen across the sides of the pool to create bluescreen underwater shots.

This setup might work well to portray an otherworldly ghostly dimension where characters float around with long, wavy hair. All the bubbles from their noses and mouths could be painted out in post so that it does not look like they are underwater. Dark lighting, or color correction, could be applied in post to create unique visual styles. Clean audio can obviously be dropped in later. What parts of your film, or types of stories, might work well to shoot with actors submerged in different watery environments?

This cute, little character was created by taking an actor's head and placing it on a 2D animated body. Using a real person for the head will preserve lip sync and facial expressions. The hand-drawn body could change shapes as the character goes through the story. She could turn into a symbolic butterfly, pirate, moon, heart, star, or flower depending on the situation to create a unique visual storytelling style. You would mask out or bluescreen the subject's head to separate it from the DV body.

DV Character Design Ideas

Creating digitally enhanced characters opens up a vast array of visual styles using DV, 2D, or 3D animated elements. How could you mix a variety of production styles in different scenes to communicate changing character states? A 2D animated body with a bluescreened actor's head might work great for a whimsical part of your film.

Using Bluescreened Characters

Bluescreened characters are shot against a blue background, which is then made transparent in post. Other layers of video, animation, or still images are dropped in behind and around the characters to create new environments. Actors are the most common subjects placed on bluescreens, but these same techniques could be used for stop-motion sets or anytime you want to isolate a subject from a background as a layer. After Effects is usually the preferred software for keying bluescreen characters. The more-expensive production bundle version has more features that make keying bluescreen characters much easier, along with several third-party plug-ins. You can also use simple color difference techniques to pull a character off of a background, if that is all you have available. What new narrative approaches could you invent to utilize bluescreen ideas for plot, character, or theme?

Digitally Enhanced Character Design Ideas

- Real actors on traditional sets
- 2D/3D animated characters
- Bluescreened actors
- Bluescreened actor body parts on 2D or 3D animated characters
- Bluescreened actor body part collages
- Bluescreened animals or animal parts
- Stop-motion characters (claymation, toys, dolls)
- Digitally distorted or semitransparent characters
- Characters created using special effects or filters
- Adding DV/animated lips, eyes, or mouths to inanimate objects
- Combinations of any the preceding ideas

money-saving

Cheap Bluescreen Ideas. Depending on your budget and resources, bluescreen shoots can be challenging to put together. In this example, a roll of thin bluescreen foam material purchased from a photography store is draped over a couch. A bright blue or green sheet hung in the background, duct taped to another one on the floor to reduce corners, may work fine. Blue butcher paper will work in a tight fix but tends to reflect lights. Painting a wall blue or green works well for medium or close-up shots. You may want to scout for long, evenly colored walls in your neighborhood. The backgrounds just need to be a solid color to pull the subject off, but cannot contain any similar colors of skin tone, hair, eyes, or clothing. Shooting characters atop a hill or planning shots against a clear blue sky might also work, depending on the shot. Miniature sets are often built with bluescreen backgrounds to drop video layers in during post, such as moving clouds or sky scenes.

Animal Bluescreening Tips. I found it very difficult to get my dog talent to stand still for my shots. Asking them to sit reduced head movement dramatically. Chicken McNuggets were used as treats to direct eye-line match cuts and move their jaws for dialogue loops. What ways can you use available pets as original characters in your film?

Blue Removal Technique

Create a mask around your subject against the bluescreen. It is easier to suck out the blue color right around the character than it is to do the whole background, because the lighting may be darker or lighter in the corners of the frame. Set the background to a bright color to really see the edges.

Adjust the levels to increase the contrast between the subject and the blue screen. Then use Color Difference to pull a clean, black-and-white alpha channel. The character should appear all white, and the blue background areas solid black with grayscale tones around the edges. Spill suppressor may then be applied to suck out any extra blue around the edges of the subject.

Color-correct the image to fit with the background, such as warming up a bluish-tinted character from the bluescreen shoot, to fit inside a warm sunset scene. Step-by-step instructions for keying a bluescreen shot are included on the accompanying CD-ROM (afterFXtutorial.doc).

200 Narrative Bluescreen Ideas

Below is a list of ways to tell stories using bluescreen characters. Many of these ideas can also be accomplished by rotoscoping characters out of DV footage using masking techniques.

Bluescreen Layer	Composited Elements	Background Layer	Final Image

Subject Walking on Virtual Set—With DV, 2D, or 3D backgrounds; good for saving money on live shots. To create stylized or abstract worlds, add depth with character walking over or behind objects in final shot, create shadows using alpha channel.

Subject Flying—Through air, space, clouds, explosions or other stunts, or abstract reality film world. Paint set table blue to key out. Add things such as cut-up butterfly wing photos or use fans to simulate wind direction in final shot.

Subject Floating—Through clouds, in space, in a dream, levitating, through thoughts, sudden loss of gravity, down a river, in a zero-gravity set, skydiving, jumping off of high places, superhero ability, floating through memories.

Subject's Body Part Exploding—Head blowing up; tummy bursting from a bomb inside; gunshot blast taking off limb; brain exploding from headache, stress, lasers, emotional overload, a new weapon, or a disease.

Glow Around Subject—For a radiant aura, superhero ability, radioactive effect, animated glow outline; glow layer for a ghost, alien, epiphany, angel; to show a supernatural occurrence or religious experience.

Human Face on Animal Body—Aesop-type symbolic characters, dogs that look like their owners, genetic experiments, surreal worlds.

Big Head on Regular-Sized Body—As stylistic choice, to make a character seem strange or cartoon-like, animating larger as the film progresses to symbolically show big-headed theme.

Subject Turns into Another Subject—Actor turning into a flock of birds, glass statue breaking into a ghost, slightly transparent character scattering into particle blast, human morphing into superhero form, man turning into big bug, dog changing into girl.

Subject with Extra Appendages/Body Parts—Eight-armed goddess, Pinocchio's long nose, three-headed dog, eight-legged horse, Siamese twins, third eyeball with special powers, magic trick that makes neck grow, new surgery technique that adds extra nose as symbol.

Animal Parts Collage—Genetic research, symbolic characters, freaky pets, surreal zoo animals, alien critters, magic spells, unique character designs, dream imagery.

Subtracting Body Parts—Losing feet or legs to show crippling mindset, losing top of head during surgery, losing portions of stomach to show weight loss, hole in body wound, losing hands to show tragic sacrifice, losing an eye, character cutting off ear, torture scenes, chainsaw slasher films.

Subject as Silhouette—Subject filled with other video layers or turned into alpha mattes for layer effects, shadow people wandering around without bodies, character's personality doing something different than the character's body, shadow of the character.

Playing with Scale: Giants—Big character in a little world, attack of the giant thing, character stumbling on miniature world, animated spirit 700 feet tall, mythological being, symbolic dream image, aliens, monsters, big people, symbolic characters.

Playing with Scale: Mini Creatures—Tiny characters in a big world, midgets, inner voice, mini me, fairies, dollhouse characters, actors as windup toys, race of mini creatures, spiritual guide, insect/human combos.

Bluescreen Layer	Composited Elements	Background Layer	Final Image

Subject Leaping Over Objects—Superhero ability to leap over buildings, leaping over cars in a busy street while in a hurry, leaping over the moon in a fairytale, leaping over houses like a track star running hurdles, leaping over dangerous animals to rescue someone, leaping over physical dangers.

Subject Doing Dangerous Stunt—Getting hit by car, avoiding explosions, falling out of plane, jumping off train or truck, walking a tight rope, walking through fire, walking through room full of snakes, going through a gauntlet.

Subject Riding an Object—3D dragon, exotic animal, motorcycle, DV insect, stock film horse, toy, inside car, futuristic machines, fantasy creatures, 3D roller coasters, 2D-animated bobsled, jet ski, scooter, skateboard, windsurfing, surfboard.

Subject Falling—In a dream, down a tunnel, down stairs, with a parachute, from a building, down a pit, through a photo collage set, out of a car, from a large rock, off a bridge, from a window, off an animal.

Duplicate Characters/Subjects—Twins, split personalities, genetic cloning, character breaking up into multiple parts, armies, crowds made from a few characters, sub-personalities, symbolic shots.

Subject with Animal Face/Body Part—Symbolic characters, mythical creatures, genetic research, freaky pets, oracles, talking zoo animals, aliens, animated dolls, magic spells, unique character designs, new species.

Actor Face Applied to Object—To show oracle, talking rocks, faces on plant leaves or flowers, ghostly faces on a wall, face on the hood of a talking car, face on a house that tells stories about the people who live inside, face on mountain like the spirit of the mountain.

Bluescreen Layer	Composited Elements	Background Layer	Final Image

project
9.10

Think Of Ten Narrative Bluescreen Ideas. Go down the preceding list and think of some new narrative approaches for using bluescreen techniques in your film. Draw sketches next to the ideas of how you would set up each shot in layers as shown previously. This is just an exercise to get you thinking about new ways to use bluescreen ideas. Can you think of any other bluescreen narrative ideas that are not on the list?

Bluescreen Shooting Tips

Shooting subjects on a bluescreen requires careful thought. The following tips are good to consider:

1. Carefully storyboard and time out each shot, to know which angle the character needs to be positioned, and for how long, to fit with the background footage layers.

2. Have the character pretend to react to things that will be composited later, such as screaming at approaching 3D monsters or holding his or her hands up right before a car is supposed to run them over in the final composited shot. If possible, use monitors on the set to key out the blue behind the actors and drop in background layers or digital set pieces. This will help you to see how well the actors are fitting in to your virtual sets as you shoot. Making bluescreen characters appear to really be in the final environment is an evolving art form.

3. For compositing one bluescreen character, actor, or pet onto another, try matching simple head-turn motions for shots. If you are putting a human face on a cat, shoot the cat first. If the cat turns his head to the right after 3 seconds, have your bluescreen actor turn his or her head to the right after 3 seconds. In post, you would place the face of the actor over the cat's face. Ideally, the heads would not be moving at all, but simple motions can be matched with a little planning.

4. Light so that there are no shadows or hotspots from lights cast against your bluescreen. Your goal is to create a flat, solid blue background behind the subject that makes pulling a flat color key easy.

5. Avoid see-through fabrics or reflective surfaces that will pick up the color blue and be hard to key out.

6. Avoid shiny objects on characters, such as mirrored sunglasses or chrome guitars, that will pick up reflections of lights and the blue floor.

7. Try to give yourself plenty of framing room between the bluescreen character and the edge of the frame. If the character's hands or feet are out of the frame, it will limit your ability to composite the character anywhere inside the frame as a full character. You can always take a fully framed bluescreen character and move him or her out of the frame a little.

8. For good-looking resolution, you never want to scale any bluescreen footage up past 100 percent. If you need a close-up of a bluescreen character, make sure to shoot for that size.

9. Turn your DV camera sideways for a maximum resolution when shooting full-body bluescreened actors. If you shoot in regular landscape 4:3 mode, your bluescreen actor will be much smaller and you'll have lower resolution.

10. Create a 2D or 3D animatic for the film to use as a shot-by-shot guide on where to place the camera and subjects for each bluescreen shot. This will also help the talent better understand the story and get into the proper emotional states.

Xenomorph was asked to imagine that he was a giant stepping on big buildings and cars as he walked through a city. It is very important to get your bluescreen actors into the mood of each shot and help them to visualize the elements added in post. This shot was created around him thinking about stepping on things from the bluescreen shot.

Notice how the bluescreen background is a flat color with no lighting hotspots or shadows. A fan is used to make the actor fit better in the blowing desert final scene. A ladder was used to get this shot so that a 3D overhead panning shot could be created. Notice how much space is around the edges of the frame for easier compositing. If you cut off the actor's feet or arm, you cannot move the character around in your layers as easily.

The shadows for these bluescreen characters were created by duplicating each character layer and filling it with black. These layers were then tilted to match a shadow ground plane perspective. The opacity was brought down to 70 percent with a 10-pixel edge feather to look more like a shadow. This technique also works for animated characters that are already separate alpha channel layers.

Creating Shadows for Bluescreen Characters

When you key out the blue areas around your character and place the character in your background, duplicate the character layer and fill it with black. Use a 3D tilt effect to place the black silhouette at a shadow perspective angle that fits the lighting in the scene. Add a 10-pixel feather around the edges of the shadow and take the opacity down to 70 percent or so, depending on how hard you want the shadow to look. The shadow will then appear to be walking with the character because it's the same alpha channel image, just slanted and filled with black. How could you have the shadows doing different activities and then the characters casting them? Perhaps one character is walking peacefully behind another, with shadows that are fighting to develop visually how they *feel* about each other. You would do separate bluescreen shots for the animated shadows to use this idea.

Rotoscoping Characters Out of DV Footage

If doing a bluescreen shoot does not appeal to you, many of the preceding effects can be accomplished by using multiple layers of video and rotoscoping characters out of shots.

A series of masks is drawn around the character to separate it from the background. Five separate masks are used for each moving piece that crosses over. Notice how few points are used to keep the technique smooth and simple. A feathered blur can be applied to make the edges blend in better with the new background images.

> **definition**
>
> **Rotoscoping** Rotoscoping is the process by which you create an animated mask around a subject that generates an alpha channel by removing the background. It may also involve other frame-by-frame techniques, such as matching character-animation keyframes to moving DV footage guides in the background (more on this in Chapter 10).

Integrating Real Physical Sets with Bluescreen Characters

One way to make your bluescreen actors look more a part of your physical sets, match lighting better, and interact with set objects is to drape areas in bright blue or green sheets to key out set backgrounds in post. For example, you may want to have a character sitting on a chair draped in blue sheets. This would work well in a story where a character starts to levitate or float out of his or her chair. Shoot the actor in the location, draping areas of the set with the blue fabric, and then shoot the same camera shot of just the set and place the two together in post. You could use bright yellow tennis balls in the corners of frames as markers, to motion match simple moving camera shots together in post. Keep this technique in mind whenever you want to separate a character from the set background for postprocessing special effects.

Often this technique works better when placing the subject inside the scene to match the lighting. This is a very time-consuming process, even when using dedicated software such as Commotion. Imagine drawing an Illustrator-style Bezier spline tool path around a moving subject, with keyframe points that you manually set to move with the character. The rule of thumb is to use as few points as possible and as few keyframes as necessary and let the computer calculate the in betweens. Use a separate layer mask for each limb that crosses over the main body, such as walking legs or moving arms. The masks drawn around the character function much like the results of a keyed bluescreen, separating the subject from the background. All the previously discussed bluescreening effects can also be accomplished without a bluescreen by using roto-scoping techniques.

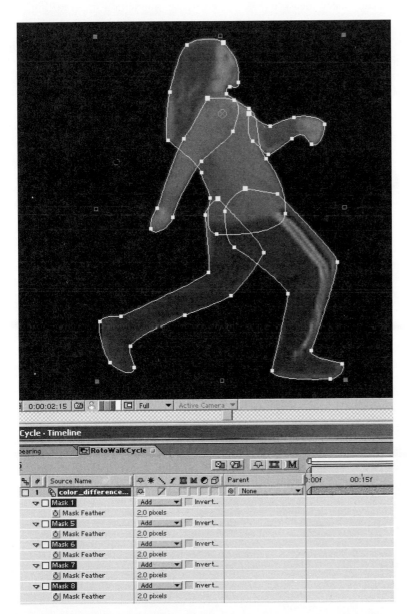

Digitally Enhanced Character Design Techniques

Desktop software has greatly expanded the character design palette for modern filmmakers. The following techniques will help you think of new ways to take the existing characters in your script and turn them into unique creations. Look for ways to combine and incorporate the symbols you developed in earlier chapters with the following new character design ideas.

Distorting and Warping Characters

How could you add some distortion to your DV characters to help viewers understand them in new ways? Maybe you only flash the distorted characters as subliminal cuts during emotionally charged moments. Think about ways to add twisting waves, wiggles, warps, bulging, or pinching to body parts or facial expressions. These effects are easy to do and may help show what your character is about or how the character is feeling in a new and exaggerated way. A subtle warping may give your character a slight feeling of uneasiness, whereas a drastically distorted face could show more extreme emotional states. Use After Effects distortion tools such as FE Flo Motion and Wave Warp together to achieve these effects.

A Warped Monk. The first image is a still shot of a monk. The second one has a slight wave warp distortion over the face with FE Flo Motion distortion knots placed over each eye. How could you distort your characters at key moments to influence what the audience is thinking and feeling? How could you have one character always distorting on the screen to fit your narrative, such as an evil, shape-shifting monster or a person who cannot make up his mind?

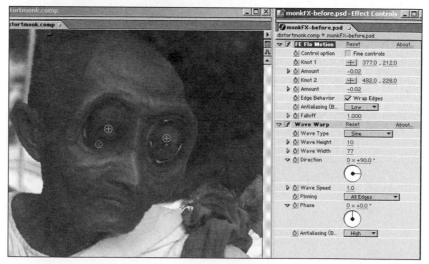

Adding DV Lips, Eyes, and Mouths to Inanimate Objects

How could you place actors' faces on other objects to create characters with unique POVs? Suppose you are doing a film that has a talking character that is rather humdrum. You could make your film much more interesting by turning a secondary character into an object, such as a rock. Shoot a rock in the scene setting and add an actor's face, lips, or eyes to the object in post. To add a whole face to a rock, you would create a circular mask over a close-up of an actor's face talking and then place it over the rock. Adjust the colors on the actor's face to match the inanimate object. To help make a face look more rocklike, you might want to add a noise filter to match the grain in the rock or an alpha channel displacement, textured stone layer. Keep your camera locked down during these types of shots. A little extra planning and you could film an actor turning his head with the same motion you move a camera around a rock to composite the two together.

Actor Face on an Animal Body. For this shot, I took the face of the pink flower girl and placed it on a moving baby cheetah, courtesy of Artbeats. The girl was scaled down to 74 percent to fit on the face of the cat. A zigzag, furry mask shape was created to blend better with the fur, using the Bezier mask pen tool. A slight hue/saturation shift toward the golden color of the cheetah's fur took away the bluish-red tinge on the pink flower girl to match better.

This statue was brought to life by adding a layer of DV actor lips, which were scaled down to fit. The color of the lips was adjusted to match the gold statue. A mesh warp was applied to the chin when her mouth opens to make the face move along with eyebrow lifts at key moments.

project 9.11

Adding Video Lips to Inanimate Objects. Think of three places you could add video lips to set objects in your film. These talking inanimate objects could be commenting about the state of your character or providing important backstory information.

If you have an old doll, statue, or object that you want to be a character in your film, you can add real video lips in post to sync with dialogue. Shoot a close-up of your lips saying the lines. Add bright lipstick, lip liner, and heavy, color contrast make-up, such as white face powder around the lips, to make it easier to mask out or color keyout later. Use the view screen flip up on your camera to compose the shot if you are doing it yourself. Key out the white area around the DV lips and add the lip layer to your object by scaling them down to fit the size of the

object's mouth. If you have a doll that already has lips, replace them with still shots of the DV lips to match when they start moving. What types of symbolic, inanimate objects could you have talking in your film?

In the French film *Amelie*, talking bedside lamps and paintings help the viewer understand more about the character in a unique and whimsical way. What types of everyday objects in your film world might communicate with your characters or the audience?

Ideas for Talking Inanimate Objects

Lamps	Symbolic candles	Sculptures
Paintings	Clouds	Photographs
Statues	Flowers	Food
Toys	Computer screens/TVs	Furniture
Dolls	Book covers	Cars
Wall or wall carvings	Plants/trees	Garbage cans
Rocks	Mannequins	Coffee cups
Kitchen appliances		

12 Digitally Enhanced Set Design Ideas

- Physical sets with digitally composited layers added in post
- Photograph or photo-collage sets
- DV footage dropped in behind bluescreen or animated characters
- 2D hand-drawn sets
- 3D modeled and animated sets
- Miniature stop-motion sets
- Abstract environments created with motion graphics
- Highly stylized, multiple layers of masked DV footage
- Using 3D planes mapped with photos, DV, drawings, or 3D
- Theatrical sets using video-projected backgrounds
- Hyper-surreal environments created with special effects
- Any combination of multiple layers from the preceding ideas

Creating Virtual Sets

What advantages does using digital techniques give you for creating original, metaphorical sets in your films? If you are using BS characters, you can place them in any background set you build from toothpicks to photo collages to fully animated 3D worlds. How could you play with switching sets out from under bluescreened, or rotoscoped, characters in the middle of scenes to show the passing of time, set changes, different dimensions, or other narrative ideas? Many of the effects previously covered for digital

character design can also be applied to set designs. How can you create a variety of set-design production styles for different scenes in your film to develop story and emotions?

You could create an old haunted house that grew rooms, had disappearing hallways, had floating staircases, shrunk into miniature dollhouse scale, or distorted its shape occasionally to match scene emotions. How could you combine DV, 2D, 3D, photographs, stop motion, and special effects to create original sets? How could you make your set pieces come alive using some of the simple digital animation techniques already explored?

Building a Miniature Physical Set

You may want to consider shooting a DV film with BS actors or animated characters living inside a small, physical set. To place the actors into a dollhouse, you need to carefully plan out your storyboards to match the bluescreen camera angles with the dollhouse layout. You may want to consider building a miniature physical set in your garage on something like a large table. Consider draping the surface with fabric, paper mache hills, dirt, rocks, pebble streets, painted-shoebox buildings, sponges on wires for trees, cut-glass rivers, or spray-painted, old Barbie pool furniture. Using bluescreen walls around your miniature sets will enable you to drop in moving DV cloud footage, sunsets, or changing weather patterns. Pay particular attention to using symbolic textures on your miniature sets to develop story and emotions.

group project

Weekend Set Location. Independent DV films, such as *The Anniversary Party*, are sometimes shot in one location, such as a house, to save time and money. Could you rent an interesting-looking place that fits your story and have your actors stay there to do a weekend or two of shooting? What interesting houses or locations do your friends or family have access to that might work great in your film? Rehearse the script ahead of time and plan your costumes. What types of mini vacations could you and your friends take with a few DV cameras and a script or rough improv idea? You could go camping to an old burial ground to do a *Blair Witch Project*–style story with a unique angle.

This set was created using several photos from different angles around Jim Morrison's grave. The actual grave did not work as a set and needed to be reconstructed in Photoshop to better fit the story. What photographs do you have laying around that could be combined in Photoshop to create unique virtual sets?

project
9.12

DV Set Design. Go through each location in your film and list three different, digitally enhanced set design techniques that fit the narrative. For example, you could create a miniature set of a city built with toothpicks for a film about logging rights. Bluescreen actors could inhabit this toothpick city as a metaphor for how important wood is in the film world. What other symbolic materials could you use to construct original sets to fit your story?

Shown here is an idea for creating a film world miniature set on a Ping-Pong type of garage table. Notice how the screens between the individual sets could be painted bluescreen blue or green to drop in DV atmospheres in post. What types of miniature sets could you build to add bluescreened or animated characters?

project
9.13

Miniature Set Idea. What interesting material could you use to build a unique, miniature physical environment for your DV film? Explain how the building materials relate conceptually to the story, such as a drippy DV sandcastle world for a surfer film or animated crabs.

Building a Photo-Collage Set

How can you use animated photographs with DV footage to create an original set idea? It is easy to cut up photographs and move them around to create the illusion of moving camera shots.

In the film *Oh My Father and Some Roads I've Known*, Andrew Gura talks about his childhood in a voiceover while showing freeway maps of Southern California using pan-and-scan animation techniques. The distances between himself and his father grow farther and farther apart as the film progresses. Maps serve as visual metaphor for the distancing of their relationship. All we see in this film are maps and shots of cars on freeways, with a voiceover telling us

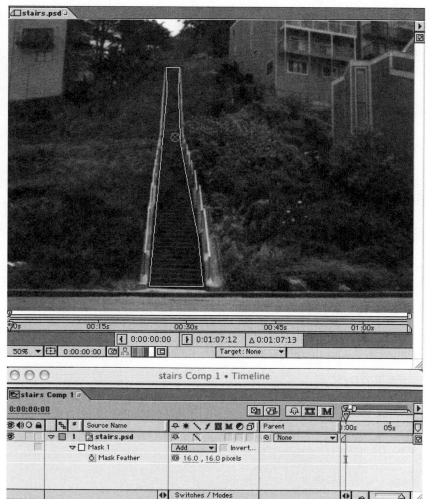

In this series of shots from our music video *Beyond*, the temple was created using pieces of photographs, a 3D star spaceship, 3D sky, and DV stairs. As the camera appears to zoom up to the temple door, the photo layers in the foreground animate up and to the side to create a moving zoom-in shot. The star on the top of the temple is a 3D model that turns into a spaceship and blasts off later on in the story. The stairs that Yap is climbing are a few blocks from my house. I imported them into After Effects and masked out the sides and then laid them over the photo collage.

To create a mask around the stairs, double-click the layer in the timeline. Use the Pen tool on the image that pops up, while pressing the Option key to create a polygonal lasso selection tool. Add a feather around the edges by pressing the F key and entering a number to make the stairs blend with the background photo collage set better.

why the routes change due to family circumstances, and how the visits to his father became increasingly infrequent. What unique visual metaphor could you use as a set to tell a story?

In *Terminal Bar*, Stephan Nadelman creates a short city symphony film based on 2,500 photos taken by his father, who was a bartender at the Terminal Bar in Times Square for 10 years. Interview sections with his father are added as we hear about the crazy drag queens, junkies, winos, and regulars who frequented the bar. Patron photos, newspaper clippings, and video footage of the actual bar and surrounding areas give viewers a sense of history about the place. What old photos and stories do the people you know have laying around that could be put together into a short film?

This was a quick and easy set that involved scanning a picture of the earth at a high resolution to rotate in the corner. A Knoll lens flare was added to the side to look like the sun, with a glow around the edges of the planet. The 3D spinning spaceship star flies up out of the clouds, out of the frame, to appear to be zooming by the camera. The stars were created using white dots on a large black background in Photoshop. Outer space shots can be really quick to make using these types of techniques. They use this type of shot in lots of science fiction films, including *Star Trek* episodes.

project
9.14

Photo and DV Set Collage Ideas. Think of three photo-collage set ideas to use somewhere in your film. Explain whether the characters are bluescreen or animated actors, and how each idea fits conceptually with the narrative.

Using Text and Motion Graphics to Tell a Story

Motion graphics software has turned animating text and lines on the screen into an art form. What new ways can you add animated text or graphics to tell us a visual story? Programs such as After Effects and Flash give you an almost-unlimited ability to move text, shapes, lines, and vector-based illustrations around the frame on top of your footage.

In the *History of Gaming*, Johnny Hardstaff uses animated collage-style motion graphic images, scrolling sideways continuously from left to right, to show us the history of games in a timeline. What ways could you reinterpret your film visually as one long, continuous scroll of overlapping motion graphics and images moving horizontally or vertically?

How could you make a book for your story in Photoshop and have your characters take us on a journey through the pages in a unusual way, using DV for the pictures? You could also film a hand-drawn book you make with rectangles to drop in video or animated footage for the pictures. Or you could do a 3D pop-up book with bluescreened characters. You may even decide to make parts of your film look like a retro multimedia CD-ROM interactive story. If your film had to be in an animated book style, what would it look like? What will animated books look like 100 years from now?

Ideas for Using Motion Graphics to Tell Stories

Subtitles: foreign languages, hard-to-understand accents or slang. Could also be used for gibberish or alien languages.

Thoughts in character's mind: These motion graphics could be animating out of their heads, or across their faces, using displacement maps.

Thought bubbles above characters with animated text and/or video of what they are thinking.

Location names including dates, places, countries, planets, buildings, and areas.

Poetry animating across the screen that helps us understand what the character is thinking or feeling.

Inside a character's head using swirling lines of garbled text superimposed over the forehead to show thoughts.

Text coming out of objects such as mailboxes, tombstones, computers, doors, radios, magic boxes, or answering machines.

A ticker tape text line at the bottom of your screen announcing story events happening in other parts of your film world, or that help to develop the images on the screen.

Text over signs: superimposed over existing store signs, product labels, book covers, newspapers, license plates, real estate signs, traffic signs, or billboards that relate metaphorically or help develop the story.

Creating animated books or letters. Video windows could be placed on the paper to show events, 3D world pop-up books, 2D pop-up books, or an animated bouncing ball over text to help people learn to read.

Using a letterbox-type screen with animated text or motion graphics over or under blank parts of screen. Graphical word plays, single words, or phrases that relate to the narrative. Do not use for wide-screen formatted films or you will cut off text.

Animated graphical words such as the POW! Batman type of comic book text for action or emotions.

One layer of video playing through a thick layer of text on the screen against a background layer of video.

Using text as characters and sets for an animation style. Could be laid over video.

Illustrated image, animation, or text over video, to show situation or concept important to story.

2D animated or bluescreen character walking across the pages of a book, map, pictures, or drawings to tell us a story.

Simple motion graphics to help tell the story, such as timelines, charts, or emotional character gauges.

Emotional graphical readouts of how the characters are feeling on the side of the image.

Characters designed using motion graphics, or animated words in the shape of a human body.

Karaoke-style sing-a-long graphics for musical numbers.

Animated pop-up screens or buttons for interactive DVD-style stories.

project
9.15

Motion Graphic Narrative Ideas. Think up five ways to use animated text or graphics over shots in your film. Add three new general ways to the preceding list for adding text or graphics to your film.

Creating Simple Narrative Digital Effects

You can create many simple special effects using your digital tools to tell stories in new ways. Many of these effects involve duplicating layers of source footage and masking out or applying effects to different areas.

Making Something Disappear

A simple way to make something disappear is to shoot two layers of video, one without the subject and one with the subject. If you want to have a character disappear while walking over a bridge, place your camera on a tripod and shoot just the bridge for 10 seconds. Without moving the camera, shoot the person walking over the bridge. It is very important for this technique that you do not move the camera between the two shots, so that the shots match perfectly when composited over each other. In post, start with shot of the person walking over the bridge, and then fade to the shot of just the bridge to make it look like the person is disappearing.

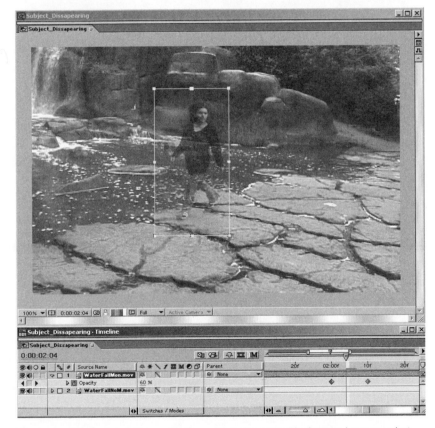

Two layers of DV were used to make the subject disappear. The bottom layer was shot without the subject. The camera must not move and must be placed on a tripod for this technique to work.

Making Something Explode

To make an object explode, use the same technique described previously to make something disappear. If you want to show someone's head exploding, first shoot the background without the person. Then shoot the person with the camera in the same position. In post, start with the footage of the person in the background. When the explosion begins, add a layer of explosion stock footage over the person's head, or create your own explosion using other footage or particle effects. During the explosion, create an animated mask that cuts the person's head off in the top layer of video, revealing the bottom layer of the background without the person. This will make it look as if the person's head blew up.

Two layers of video were used with an animated mask around the character that was pulled down to chop off the head during the explosion. What other ways can you use this type of technique to create simple special effects?

Using Particle Effects

Particle plug-ins can add interesting and easy-to-do special effects to your DV footage. Most particle plug-ins have emitter points that you place on top of your footage, which generate streams of objects, or particle shapes, based on parameters you can adjust. There are many third-party plug-in sets from companies such as Final Effects, DigiEffects, and VizFX. Following is a list of narrative ideas for you to consider. How could you use particle effects to create a new metaphor for how your characters experience life or feel about situations? Maybe flames could shoot out their ears when they get really mad and tears can stream down their faces in an animated hand-drawn style when they are sad. 3D particle systems usually look better and are easier to control if you have the option.

Particle Effects. These particle effects for the *Deep Step* music video were created using Knoll Light Factory and Delirium, which are both third-party plug-ins for After Effects.

Narrative Ideas For Particle Effects

Water fountains	Falling stars	Starlight
Fairy sparkles	Magical moments	Flames coming out of a character's ears
Swarms of insects (add blur)	Unseen realms	Magic jar that opens and spews particles
Dust pouring out of a container	Animated wonder	Character made of particles
Explosions	Rain, drizzle	Background sky full of fiery particles to show a new weapon
Dirt blowing	Visual smells	
Fireworks	Jet engine exhaust	
Blood spurting	Bubbles	Gun blast
Drippy liquid puddles	Smoke, bonfire	
	Spinning vortex	

I could use particle effects to show snakes in the cave spitting at my character.

project 9.16

Think of One Use for Particle Effects. Go through your shots and see where you could use animated particle effects. How you could tie your new particle effect idea into a narrative element that helps drive the story visually? Maybe one character has magical powers shown with sparkles whenever the character is casting spells.

project
9.17

Replace a Sign. Find one place in your film to replace a sign or label to better develop your backstory or characters.

In this shot, a slow-motion effect is applied as the character's hand loses its grip while rock climbing. By slowing the footage down, the audience gets a chance to climb into the character's situation and thoughts. Often, during accidents or intense events, people report that time seems to slow down. How can you use these types of time-distortion effects to pull the audience into your story?

Removing/Replacing Signs or Labels

Often you will need to remove signs or labels in your DV footage to avoid rights issues. You may also want to replace the signs with messages that better fit your plot, theme, or character. A creepy, establishing shot of an old haunted house with a street sign that reads "Maple Drive" in the foreground could be replaced with the words "Ravens Way." This new street sign would better fit the mood of the shot, or could be used to foreshadow some upcoming form of death. Go through your script and see where you could plan shots to replace signs with more symbolic messages on banners, billboards, posters, street signs, advertisements, T-shirts, address plates, product labels, building logos, TV screens, license plates, traffic signs, or bus ads. Use Photoshop or Illustrator to create the new text for the sign, matching the font as closely as possible. Import the text file into After Effects and lay it over the sign region. Use motion tracking to replace the text on signs for moving camera shots. You do this by selecting the region to track around the sign, and then set individual tracking points around the corners of the sign. This effect grows more complicated depending on the amount of camera movement. It may make more sense to print out small, colored labels and paste them onto set objects, such as signs or bottles, before you shoot if possible.

Playing with the Speed of Time

How could you use different speeds in your film to help us understand how time is passing differently for the characters? Maybe you run some scenes a fraction of a bit slower with synced regular-time dialogue. Perhaps you choose to leave in the audio-stretch distortion for added atmospheric effect. You could plan conversations where the characters talk extra fast about exciting things, but then talk in super slow motion about boring things.

project
9.18

Speed-of-Time Ideas. Come up with an original way to use two of the preceding time distortions in your film. Explain how each idea relates to how the character is experiencing time differently.

Time-Distortion Idea Chart

Freeze Frame	Super Slow Motion	Slow Motion	Fast Motion	Combinations
Exaggerated look, key moment in accident, extreme emotional expression, shocking incident, threat, moment frozen in memory	Death scene, special effects shot, stunts, accident, magical tricks, marital arts, different dimensions, space walk, intense emotional moment	Character falling, shocking moment, strong reaction, scream, accident, daydream, peak experience, epiphany, realization, death	Work, tedious activity, exercising, boring chore, chase, superhuman ability, memory flashes, rushing activity	Bluescreen characters running in slow motion with background running at double speed, slow motion and then fast motion to show rhythm of work flow

Defining a Visual Style for Your Film

Digital tools give modern filmmakers an unlimited palette to create new visual styles by adjusting every pixel to communicate in unique and innovative ways.

Using Video Filters for Narrative Impact

Some video filters can be applied to create interesting visual styles. In the movie *What Dreams May Come,* a painterly effect was applied to some of the scenes in heaven for a unique visual feel. Many special effects filters are too extreme to use for visual styles. Experiment with duplicating your source footage and applying effects to the top layer with a 50% opacity to get more subtle effects or use the transfer modes. Most digital artists have their own favorite combinations of special effects filters that they enjoy using. What are your favorite special effects filters and how can you use them to create a new visual style for your film?

project 9.19

List Your Favorite Filters. Go through the filters you have for your video software and list your five favorites. Come up with a few narrative uses for each one in your film and explain how they fit the story visually.

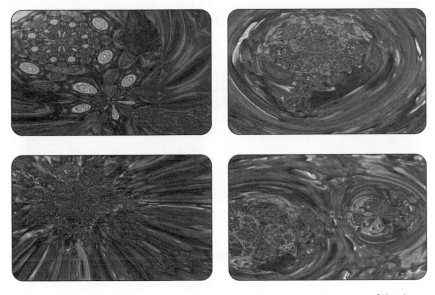

Where could you use extreme filtered effects in your film? You need to use careful judgment with these types of eye candy. These animated filter shots might work as a dreamscape surreal environment for bluescreen characters to be wandering around in or as POV hallucinations.

Using Displacement Map Filters

Displacement maps move pixels left or right based on the luminance of the modifying layer placed on top of the layer where the effect is being applied. This filter technique works great for adding DV faces to inanimate objects. It may also be used before applying drastic distortion filters to preserve lines.

These talking rocks were created by applying DV actor faces to the surface using a displacement effect. The faces were stretched to match the shapes of the rocks and turned grayscale to create shadows on the rocks rather than colored faces.

The first two shots were combined using a displacement map effect to create the third one. Notice how the sparkling water affects the image of the monk, yet you can still see the monk, even though the effect is pretty extreme. You could use this type of effect to create a surreal energy world visual style with symbolic displacement map textures blended into shots.

Using Film-Look Filters

Making your video look more like film starts long before the postprocessing techniques are applied. Often, footage looks more like film simply because the production values were higher to start with, using professional techniques such as careful exposures, high-quality equipment, and three-point lighting setups. Many of the techniques discussed in Chapters 5 and 6 will help make your DV footage look more cinematic, such as creating depth and paying attention to careful composition. Consider using diffusion or neutral-density filters on your DV camera if possible to make the footage more reminiscent of film. Autofocus on most digital cameras will kill the film look effect fast, so make sure you are set to manual focus.

A heavy color-manipulation pass will help, too. Film has darker darks that are more saturated, with highlights that are brighter and more pastel. Try adjusting the gamma color on your camera or in post using curves. Do your best to match the film colors in movies you see, because so many techniques are used to achieve specific looks. *Buffalo 66* was shot on reversal film, creating really dark darks and interesting color tones. To make your video look like old film, you would add effects such as heavy grain (noise), dust layers, scratches, hair, and frame jittering. Changing the frame rate to 24 fps to look more like film is a headache that usually does not really look right in the end. Most people making digital short films are not planning on transferring to actual film, so I'm not even going to address those issues. There are lots of third-party, film-look filter packages available, but they tend to be expensive. If you are on a budget, you can make your own film looks with a little tinkering.

See the "Film Look Filters" section in the color section to get a sense of how to create a variety of unique visual styles that match scene emotions. All of these files are on the CD-ROM for you to explore. Most of the examples have extreme color adjustments using curves and hue/saturation with an animated noise filter and fast blur effects to show you how extreme these looks can get.

project
9.20

Using Displacement Maps. How can you use a displacement map filter to add emotional textures to your film or help tell your story in a new way? How could you use displacement-mapped faces coming out of objects?

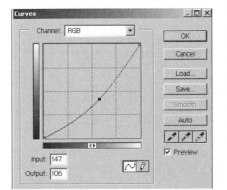

To make your DV look more like film, you may want to play with making the footage darker to get rid of that milky-white look. Effects>Adjust>Curves will give you this dialog box in After Effects, where you can then pull the center point down a little bit. Often footage from cheaper, one-chip DV cameras can be made to look like it was shot with much more expensive cameras using this simple color-adjustment technique. All the DV source files on the CD have this color effect applied.

This *Matrix* film look was created by adjusting the hue to match the sample palette and adding blur and a layer of animated noise. Later, I realized *The Matrix* does not have that much noise or grain, but I liked adding the extra noise layer to this shot to make the 2D set look less flat.

project 9.21

Create a Film-Look Strategy. Pick a feature film you think looks the way you want your film to look and match it using film-look techniques, filters, and color manipulation on some DV footage. How can you create completely different film looks for each scene in your film?

superfreak!

Design an Original 2D Animated Style. If you have access to 3D programs with 2D shaders, or special 2D animated-look software, how could you take your film and develop a unique 2D animated style to help tell the story? Do some colored sketches or test frames of line weight, cell shading, and styles to see what works best for each scene.

Adding a 2D Animated Look to DV Footage

You can choose many approaches and different software to give your DV footage a 2D animated look. DV can be run through 3D programs by applying footage to flat planes, and then rendering with special 2D shaders in Maya or 3ds max. If you are just doing a small number of frames, you may be able to use Effect>Paint>Vector Paint in After Effects to hand draw over areas of your DV footage. Films such as *Waking Life* used specially developed software that was able to take advantage of handheld frame jitters for traditional artists to paint over. How can you use other filters or digital techniques to give your footage a unique hand-drawn feel?

Using Color Manipulation to Develop Narrative Ideas

By having your film in a digital format, you open up endless opportunities to color correct every pixel. Animated films require just as much thought regarding color choices as DV. Color correction for broadcast viewing is not included in the scope of this preproduction book and is not addressed in this section. The following ideas focus more on ways to digitally manipulate colors to better tell stories, develop emotions, and create unique visual styles. There are example shots using the following techniques in the color section and on the CD-ROM. Here are some color manipulation ideas to get you started:

1. **Apply a strong color tone to create a unique visual style.** You may want to take the final edit of the film through a color style pass to give it a signature look and feel. The movie *Oh Brother, Where Art Thou* created a unique, heavy mustard tone to make it feel more like an old film. How could you apply a similar color tone to your film, or individual scenes, to help create a unique visual style? A tragic story might work well with an overall bluish tone. A scene showing the theme of good versus evil may benefit from a high-contrast black-and-white look. Refer to the Color Psychology Chart in the book's color section to pick tones that match the emotions and mood of your story. In the example Film Look color pages, *The Matrix* film look was applied to a shot by shifting the hue to match the sample color palette pulled off of a frame grab.

2. **Adjust colors in each scene to match emotions.** You may want to go through each segment or scene and adjust the colors to bump up the emotional changes, such as adding more red to an angry moment, or bringing down the saturation when a character feels drained.

3. **Adjust warm/cool color shifts between shots in the film.** Not all of your shots are going to have the same color temperatures, depending on the light. If you are shooting a scene outside over the course of a few hours, the light will change. If you change the direction of the shot (away from the sun, for instance), the next shot will be noticeably darker or cooler. These jumps in color can make scenes edited together feel very rough and look like they were shot at different times. Find the clip that has the color you like best and color correct the shots around it to match. This may be as simple as adjusting the levels, or curves, to brighten or darken the surrounding shots. You may also want to shift colors between shots intentionally. If you are shooting something like two characters having a conversation, you may want one character always in a slightly cooler or warmer color range to show emotional contrast.

4. **Change colors during scene to add narrative impact.** How could you subtly shift the colors during a scene in your film to communicate the story in a new way? Maybe you have a scene in which the character starts off happy in bright, saturated colors, but then experiences a sad event where the colors on the screen slowly turn into shades of blue. Most color-correction filters can be keyframed to give you infinite flexibility on how the color changes occur within each frame. What new ways could you keyframe color changes to match emotions?

5. **Adjust color to match film looks.** Directors use different film stock to create a variety of looks. For example, shooting on reversal film (*Buffalo 66*) gives you very black blacks with a harsh intensity around the colors. Try matching other film looks you see in movies to the colors in your DV footage. Remember to have strong narrative concepts behind any color manipulations. *Buffalo 66* dealt with raw emotions and edgy characters that were communicated better using the harsh look of reversal film.

The color palette in the *Deep Step* music video includes warm, golden-sunrise earth tones. The bluescreen singer Irena needed to be warmed up colorwise to fit into the magic hour lighting.

project
9.22

Color Manipulation for Narrative Impact. Think of one original way to use each of the preceding ideas in your film.

6. **Masking out certain areas of the frame for different color treatments.** How could you apply color manipulation to masked areas of the frame or animated masks to help develop emotions? Maybe one character with a sick emotional state is always slightly green, done by masking out the area around the character's body and applying a light color tint with a wide feathered edge to blend with the rest of the frame. If you have a good and an evil character in a shot together, you could mask out parts of the frame to divide the characters using color shifts. An evil character's side of the screen might always be tinted slightly red, whereas a good character gets more of a gold tone.

7. **Adjust colors in each layer differently.** Sometimes it might make sense to adjust the colors on each layer separately to better develop the mood or situations in your story. If you are already using BS characters, rotoscoping, masks, or multiple layers of images, it is easy to adjust colors to separate the visual ideas and add depth. How could you make the characters completely different colors than their backgrounds to show emotional qualities, mental states, or situations? Maybe a character turns black and white when he gets tired, or green when he is jealous. Perhaps the background turns blood red when the character hears a chilling tale about the location, while the actor stays in normal color ranges. Villains could be adjusted to appear very dark even in brightly lit spaces. You might choose to have your backgrounds in black and white, with your character in color, to show that the character is separated from his or her environment. Maybe your character is a colorful artist who works in a gray factory.

Film Festivals for Digital Shorts

Here is a list of film festivals you may want to check out. Submission deadlines are often up to four months before the festival begins, and you may want to note these on your calendar to give yourself a deadline.

Digital film festivals:
    RESFEST **www.resfest.com**
    Transmediale **www.transmediale.de**
    Onedotzero **www.onedotzero.com**

Short film festivals:
    Aspen **www.aspenfilm.org**
Big, big festivals:
    Sundance **www.sundance.org**
    Toronto **www.e.bell.ca/filmfest**
    New York **www.filmline.com**
    Cannes **www.festival-cannes.fr**
    Berlin **www.berlinale.de**
    Rotterdam
    www.filmfestivalrotterdam.com

Semi big festivals:
    Montreal **www.ffm-montreal.org**
    Edinburgh **www.edfilmfest.org.uk**
    LA **www.lafilmfest.com**

Animated film festival:
    Spike and Mike's
    www.spikeandmike.com

Other Digital Techniques

You can use many other digital techniques to make your DV footage look unique and tell stories in new ways. The ones described in this chapter are just a few to get you started. Depending on how long you have been playing in the digital realm, you probably have developed your own favorite layering techniques, filter combinations, or special effects. Every time you learn a new software package, get an upgrade, or get a new filter set, you expand your possibilities for visual storytelling. Continue to create brainstorming lists for new ways to use cutting-edge techniques to tell stories as your digital filmmaking palette expands.

"No one keeps up his enthusiasm automatically. Enthusiasm must be nourished with new actions, new aspirations, new efforts, new vision."
—Papyrus

project 9.23

Digitally Enhanced Cinematography? How could you take some of the traditional cinematic techniques discussed in other chapters and push them in a new way using digital tools? For example, take the 15 ways for creating depth in Chapter 5, "Shot Visualization," and list one idea for doing each of them digitally.

project 9.24

Favorite Personal Digital Techniques. Make a list of your top 10 favorite digital techniques. Figure out how you can use each one somewhere in your film and explain the narrative concept behind the visual design.

chapter 10

Using Modern 2D Animation to Expand Our Realities

"Animation can explain whatever the mind of man can conceive."
—Walt Disney

Modern digital 2D animation styles make it easier to create a short film by yourself with a unique production mix to fit your script. Most of the techniques discussed in the DV chapter can also be applied to 2D and 3D animated films. Traditional 2D animation techniques require animators to hand draw literally thousands of frames for 24-frames-per-second Disney-style productions. "2D animation" can mean many things these days. You can now create modern 2D animated films using techniques involving hand-drawn pictures, cut-up photographs, Photoshop layers, DV, special effects, dedicated 2D software, motion graphics, stop motion, and 3D software. This chapter does not deal much with traditional

time-saving

Keep in mind that 2D animation, even using modern digitally enhanced forms, can still be a very time-consuming process for things such as character animation. Drawing, digitally illustrating, and animating your own 2D films is an almost Zenlike art form that requires much patience.

2D animation techniques, but focuses more on faster, one-person digital 2D production styles. *Southpark* was a groundbreaking TV show for popular 2D animation because it proved audiences will accept and enjoy simple, crude animation techniques with a good script and visual ideas backing up the less-than-spectacular animation style.

If you are just learning to make digital films and animations, you need to decide what you want to do in the future so you know where to focus your efforts. If you want to be a feature-film director and creator, concentrate more on telling good stories with clever production styles

that make compelling and original films. If you want to make a living creating other people's digital films, focus on making sure your production style is professional and flawless.

After Effects- and Flash-style software techniques are presented in this chapter along with some modern stop-motion ideas. Even if you do not think you can draw really well, see whether some of the simple 2D styles, such as animating cut-up photos, might work somewhere in your film. If you know you want to use 2D animation, do all the project bulbs. If you are not sure about using 2D in your film, do the exercises that sound fun.

Our bluescreen dog characters were masked to fit inside this photo car. The windows roll down and the wheels spin. Modern 2D animation can be done with things such as photos and bluescreen actors to save time drawing and animating.

In this shot, it is literally raining cats and dogs. What types of surreal or symbolic visual realities could you create in your film using 2D animated techniques?

Advantages of Visual Storytelling with 2D Animation

You'll quickly notice that working in 2D gives you storytelling freedom you won't find in our three-dimensional world. Here are some of the primary advantages of working in 2D animation:

- **Surreal visual realities.** Anything can happen in 2D and usually does, which is an important idea to develop in 2D stories. Trains can roll over a character's head, the sky literally rains cats and dogs, cars float into outer space and then turn into flying saucers, 300-foot-tall creatures

walk over buildings, heads morph into other shapes, and sets can be as simple as solid white backgrounds.

- **Characters appear not to get hurt or die.** 2D animation has a history of funny violence and characters with more than nine lives. Shows such as the *Roadrunner* make seeing a coyote's head get blown up with TNT seem like a minor nuisance. Kenny gets killed each episode in *Southpark*, but then is back next week like nothing happened. A character's head falls off and the character can still sing. How could one of your characters die visually (and metaphorically), and then come back to life? How could the character get visually hurt and then be fine in the next shot?

- **Suspension of disbelief.** People will stretch more to get into abstract realities, impossible character movements, abilities, or situations. A stick figure with an elephant head photo attached could start floating through the air and the audience will buy it faster than a bluescreened actor or 3D character using the same technique. How could you make the film world in your story more abstract and visually interesting? Review your lists of metaphors and symbols to see how you might find a new abstract style to communicate your narrative concept.

- **More forgiving production environment.** 2D is a much more forgiving production environment, where simple, crude animation techniques are celebrated if the story holds together. 2D animated worlds are often so abstract that viewers have no expectations about how things should look. A sloppy or crude 3D animated character will not play as well. One animator took photographs of dead fish at a market, animated their mouths up and down, and created a whole cast of characters. What types of simple animation techniques have you seen that might work great for your film? What original 2D animated style could you create that is fast to do and works great metaphorically for your story?

- **One-person productions.** 2D animated characters work for free, are always available, are never late, don't need to be fed, and do what you want them to do without complaining. Actors and crew can take up lots of time organizing. If you draw your characters, or use animated photographs or dolls, you can work on your film anytime you feel like doing a shot. Some feature-film directors such as David Lynch and Tim Burton started out doing simple, 2D animated films. How can you start developing your own filmmaking style in the 2D realm without having to worry about organizing large casts and crews?

- **Multiple production environments and materials.** Modern 2D is a mixed production environment bag, encompassing hand drawings, stop motion, animated photographs, digital art, vector-based Flash-style animations, DV elements, special effects, motion graphics, 3D, and claymation. What unique combination of animation materials and production environments could you use to develop a fresh visual style?

These characters are huge eyeballs that bounce when they travel. This design might work well for a film dealing with the theme of seeing things in new ways. What animated body parts or animal parts could you turn into 2D characters that viewers have not seen before to show theme or story?

The characters in this film play sword games where they cut each other up for fun. Particle effects could be used for the blood spurting from the severed body. Notice the simplicity of the drawings and how the background is solid white. How could you simplify your film look down to a solid white background with easy-to-create characters?

These Bigfoots like to hit each other on the head with redwood trees for fun, making their bodies collapse into accordion shapes that then spring back to life. If you tried to do this shot with realistic 3D Bigfoots, it would feel much more disturbing.

These three characters were designed with heads to fit their character traits. The first one has a very sunny disposition. The owl head character is a very wise scholar who has supernatural powers. The eyeball-headed character can see through objects and into the future, with DV footage that plays inside his iris. How could you remove (or change) body parts as metaphors for the human condition in your animated character designs? How could you combine animated elements from 2D, 3D, and DV to create a new look for your film?

project 10.1

Push Your 2D Reality. Find at least 10 things that happen in your 2D film to push reality in new ways visually. Pick ideas actors and sets cannot do as easily. Go through your script and make a list of each ordinary object, activity, or event. List three ways to do each thing more extreme, exaggerated, or surreal. If you have a shot of a cat scratching on a sofa to show a problem pet, take that activity and push it to the extreme. Instead of just scratching the sofa really hard, the cat could strip the whole outer layer, cotton insides, and frame, in a fast series of shots. How could each object have personality, and animated abilities, that are extreme versions of regular ones we see every day?

project 10.2

2D Animation Advantages. Come up with 10 new ideas about how to make your film into more of a visually surreal 2D animated story. Try answering some of the questions posed above if you get stuck.

The Principles of Animation

The "Disney 12" principles of animation are good things to keep in mind when storyboarding and planning your shots. Using these techniques will add more personality and soul to your animated stories. How can you take each of the following and create the principle in an easy way using some of your digital tools?

1. **Squash and stretch.** Fill a sack with flour and drop it on the floor. The bottom stretches out, while the top squashes. Take this same sack of flour and hurl it through the air in slow motion, watching as the flour inside changes shape depending on the velocity and impact. A bouncing rubber ball changes shape in much the same way. When it hits the floor hard, it flattens out. The most important thing is to maintain the same mass. If one part gets bigger by being stretched, another part gets smaller by being squashed. Some places you may want to consider using squash and stretch: for limbs that bend with muscles attached, facial expressions, cheek movements when a character chews, or a stomach that bounces when a character walks.

Bouncing rubber balls, or elastic objects.	Muscles on arms and legs that contract and expand with movement.	Facial expressions where different muscles in the face squash and stretch to fit changing emotions.
Cheek movements on face when a character chews, eats, talks, or screams.	Expansion and contraction of chest and belly when a character breathes.	Eyes squinting at sun, getting narrow when character is angry, getting wider when character is surprised.

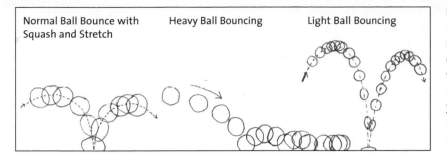

Normal Ball Bounce with Squash and Stretch

Heavy Ball Bouncing

Light Ball Bouncing

Bouncing Balls. Notice how the inside mass of each ball stays the same as the squash and stretch occurs. Think of each object as holding a specific amount of water that must stay the same no matter how much the shape changes. How could you use digital distortion tools, points, or regions to achieve similar effects without having to hand-draw deformations?

project 10.3

Digital Squash-and-Stretch Ideas. Come up with three places in your film to use a squash-and-stretch technique, either hand-drawn or using digital distortion tools.

2. **Anticipation.** Proceed each major character action with a gesture or action that introduces it to the audience so that they do not become confused or wonder what the character is doing. Before your character eats something, have him first reach out his arm and wiggle his fingers while looking at the critter, while licking his lips for a moment.

Character looks at something he is about to grab.	Character changes facial expression to match emotion of action.	Character crouches before running, jumping, or leaping.
Character reaches arm out (in good silhouette) towards object.	Character draws leg back to kick something or run.	Character aims hand at object while looking at it.
A windup or a backswing before throwing something, or hitting something with a club or bat.	Character takes a deep breath, causing chest to swell before blowing out something.	Character aims object before firing.
Character touches another character's cheek, then looks at lips, and licks lips before kissing.	Character looks at seat before sitting, then adjusts long skirt or clothing before sitting down.	Character picks up food with fingers or fork and looks at it (in good silhouette) before eating.

project 10.4

Anticipating. What unusual anticipating actions could you add to your characters to develop traits, history, backstory, or theme? Come up with one idea for each scene.

Before this character starts to drum, she raises her arms, wiggles her fingers, stares at the drum, and loosens up her body by flexing her spine. All of these gestures help introduce the exaggerated drumming actions about to occur. If she just starts drumming right away, the art of animation is reduced.

In the first shot, it is difficult to see what the Bigfoot is doing, especially when you turn the image into a silhouette. The posing of the action in the second shot is much easier to see and better communicates the emotion and attitude of the character smelling the flower.

project 10.5

Using Staging Techniques for Visual Storytelling. Go through each shot in your film and see how you could improve the staging to better communicate the mood of the story and the emotions and attitudes of each character. Make sure the posing of the characters read clearly in silhouette in each of your storyboards.

Great Traditional 2D Animation Books.

The Illusion of Life, by Frank Thomas and Ollie Johnson (Hyperion); *The Animator's Workbook*, by Tony White (Watson Guptill); and *Cartoon Animations* and *Film Cartoons*, by Preston Blair (Walter Foster).

3. **Staging.** Every visual detail in the frame needs to help convey the story line and emotion. If you are creating a haunted house, you would use dark colors, shadowy rooms, black cats, howling sounds, creepy statues, spider webs, medieval weapons hanging on the wall, and other scary things. A collection of brightly colored balloons floating around the haunted house would feel out of place. First determine the feel, emotion, or mood of each shot, and then list visual items and symbols that communicate that specific mood.

The same goes with staging character actions, because you need to direct the audience's attention by showing them precise camera shots that best show the action. If a character is crying, a close-up would best communicate the shot. If the character is really happy, dancing wildly, a long shot would best show this full-body action. Break your actions down into steps where this happens, then this happens, and so on. Only show the audience one action at a time, because they may miss actions that are happening at the same time, or have problems understanding what the character is doing.

Draw rough thumbnails of each character action that reads well as a silhouette. Do your best to capture the emotion and attitude of the character in each pose. Practice acting out your actions in a mirror to get more

natural-looking silhouettes, because most characters do not naturally move in good silhouettes. Avoid hands that cross over the face or the body, because this will be harder for the audience to see. Render out an alpha channel movie of each scene where there is lots of character animation with just the character. If you cannot tell what the character is doing and what the attitude is of the shot as a silhouette, you need to improve your staging. Study Charlie Chaplin films. He believed that if an actor really knew his emotion, he could show it in silhouette.

4. **Slow in, slow out.** This is the same as ease in, ease out, where the timing of the motion between shots changes to give more of a realistic movement and spirited result. Imagine someone lifting a coffee cup to her lips. She would lift it slowly at first, but would accelerate slightly after it was off of the table. Yet, as it neared her lips she would slow it down to prevent spilling. This idea holds true for most character movements. The opposite is true of the bouncing ball principle, where there are fewer frames in the middle of the action when the ball is at the apex of its bounce, causing it to slow preceding its ascent. In After Effects, select all the position and rotation keyframes, and then experiment with applying Animation>Keyframe Interpolation>Bezier to smooth out the motion.

5. **Arcs.** Avoid mechanical precision in your character's movement. Most creatures' movements follow circular paths and move in arcs between positions rather than straight lines. Think of how your arm is constructed in a socket, which causes it to move in arcs. Keep this principle in mind when setting up keyframes for characters. Straight in-betweens run the risk of killing the essence of the action. In good animation, *everything* moves in arcs, however slight (even a rocket launch). This arcing principle is dying along with traditional 2D animation and is often why computer animation looks dead.

6. **Secondary action.** An action that accompanies the main action for added impact. If your character is going to cry, have the character first form a tear in his eye. Then have his hand come up and wipe away the tear, while his face gets sad and his lips start to quiver, making his whole body shake with sobs. If the character were to just sit there with tears streaming down his face, it would not be as emotional. You may want to try animating the main action first, and then add the secondary actions. Find the emotion for the main action, and then add secondary actions to make it stronger.

7. **Timing.** This term in regards to the principles refers to the number of in-betweens to time action with character animation drawn frame by frame. The fewer in-betweens, the faster and more abrupt the action.

Digital Arcing with Rotation. Most animation programs have rotation parameters you can keyframe to create nice arcing movements. This hand-drawn character was broken into pieces in Photoshop using layers, and then imported into After Effects as a composition. Natural joints, such as shoulders, necks, waists, elbows, knees, ankles, and wrists, are good flexible places to place rotation center points for digital character animation. In After Effects, this center point tool is called the Pan Behind tool, shown as a box with four arrows inside. After setting these center points on each body part layer, you can then rotate arm and leg pieces to mimic the way the human body is constructed to move.

Emotion	Main Action	Secondary Action
Happy	Smiling	Uncontrollably starts clapping his hands, laughing, and jumping up and down
Angry	Kicking a shoe as he walks away	Clenching his fist and then punching a hole in the wall
Disoriented	Walking in a drunken manner	Adjusting glasses to see better
Confused	Shaking head back and forth	Scratching head

project
10.6

Secondary Character Actions. Go through each scene in your film and find at least two secondary actions to accompany each main character action. Explain how each secondary action helps develop character, history, traits, backstory, or theme, using symbolic accessories or design elements.

In this exaggerated drumming shot, the character's body sways in extreme movements to match the beat of the music. Her eyes pop out occasionally to look at things around the cave. The ponytail on the top of her head whips back and forth very quickly, almost in a blur, to help visually show the frenzied emotional drumming state.

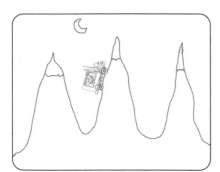

A truck driving over a mountain range could be exaggerated to look much bigger in scale than the terrain, driving straight up and down a long row of steep snowy peaks. A normal truck driving over mountains would wind around them in a much-less-dramatic fashion.

project 10.7

Exaggerate Every Scene in Your Film. Go through your storyboards and see how you could improve your 2D animation ideas using some extreme exaggeration.

8. **Exaggeration.** Take a normal set of actions and make them extreme, such as eyes that pop out of a character's head when he sees something shocking. How could you push each character action into a hyper-exaggerated form? How could you take every event or movement in your shots and exaggerate them to the extreme visually?

9. **Solid drawing.** Does every frame in your animation have weight, depth, and balance? Avoid "twins" where the hands or legs are parallel and in the same position. Make sure each pose has the feeling of potential activity. Avoid symmetrical shapes. Add contrast in form and shape to achieve an active type of balance. Solid drawing principles are extremely important to keep in mind when doing digital 2D animation

techniques, because "twins" usually occur when body parts are duplicated, such as drawing one arm and flipping it horizontally to create another arm. When preparing characters for animation, draw several different positions for each body part. This will give you more choices to avoid "twins" when animating.

10. **Appeal.** Live actors have a screen presence full of magnetic charisma. When a great actor walks onto the screen, you cannot take your eyes off of him. Animated characters need to have the same presence, which is often referred to as "appeal." This does not mean cuddly and cute. This refers to anything that is visually fascinating to watch, such as charming qualities or exceptional character design. All villains should have their own type of appeal, or you will not want to watch what they are doing.

Ideas for Adding Exaggeration

Character riding on a bicycle, horse, or car bouncing up and down wildly.

Angry character has smoke and flames coming out of ears.

Dancing character has spine that whips back and forth at extreme angles.

Character's emotion/expression shown visually with animated symbols.

Character runs so fast it starts a flaming trail behind him.

Character's body parts morph into other shapes, such as arms turning into tools.

Character orders and receives special kit or tool right away.

Character's lips get really big when kissing, then swallow other person's head.

Character eats a bunch of food as we watch his belly get bigger and bigger and then explode.

11. **Follow through and overlapping action.** When a character is moving and comes to a stop, not all things stop moving at the same time. When a character such a Jar Jar Binks in *The Phantom Menace* comes to a stop, his long, flapping ears continue to sway into place. If Jar Jar had short, stiff ears, his lack of overlapping action would have made him less fun to watch.

12. **Straight-ahead action and pose to pose.** In computer animation, pose to pose involves keyframing each main pose and then letting the computer do the in-betweens, which is great for keeping a shot within a set amount of time. Straight ahead means starting with frame one, then keyframing frame two, and so on. This may sound confusing if you have not done much animation, but will become clearer when you start setting up lots of keyframes for your animated characters.

project 10.8

Add Follow Through and Overlapping Actions. Come up with five ideas to use this principle in your animation. How could you incorporate this technique into your character design?

Ideas for Adding Follow Through and Overlapping Actions

Dangling appendages: long ears, tails, ponytails, trunks, soft horns, tentacles, tubes.	Other body parts: arms in movement, hands, tapping feet, long hair or dreads, flapping tongues, wings.	Loose flesh: sagging bellies, rolls of flesh, hanging wrinkles on face, jiggling body parts.
Personality-ending action that helps develop character: ballerina does a twirl and either comes to a graceful stop, or falls over clumsily. Refer to character traits for ideas.	Moving clothing: coat tails, scarves, long skirts or dresses, capes, veils, feathers.	Accessories: dangling jewelry, long belts, weapons hanging from a belt, swinging bags, flimsy hats, chains.

In the first drawing, the Bigfoot's arms and legs are in the same position on both sides, making him look rather boring. In the second drawing, the character has much more personality and appeal, with contrasting arm and leg positions. The shape of the torso in the second image has much more weight and movement than in the first drawing.

This character was designed with lots of overlapping action in mind. Jiggling rolls of flesh, dreadlocks, a flowing scarf, a flapping tongue, and objects hung from the belt make this walk cycle much more fun to watch. Many of these secondary actions could be done using rotation keyframes by setting the center points where the objects connect to the body.

Digitally Enhanced Overlapping Action. To add some simple overlapping action to your character, such as a swinging ponytail, draw one in Photoshop, and then attach it with the rotation point at the base and have it rotate up and down as the character walks.

Modern 2D Animated Design Ideas

"We are all apprentices in a craft where no one ever becomes a master."
—Ernest Hemingway

Digitally animated 2D characters have an almost limitless realm of design possibilities. Following are some ideas to get you started.

1. **Hand-drawn characters** are usually drawn as separate, easy-to-animate body parts, which are then scanned and reassembled in Photoshop as individual layers.

2. **DV body parts** mixed with hand-drawn elements are often used for modern 2D animation. Using DV actors for faces and movement will save you time animating facial expressions, lip sync, or actions. What photographs, drawings, doll parts, or pieces of DV characters could you put together to create a fresh animation look for your characters?

3. **Unusual character trait combinations** often work great for creating original 2D animated characters. How can you take two traits that are opposites and combine them to create a unique visual character?

4. **Superhuman abilities.** Create a 2D character that can do unusual things you always wanted to do. What superhuman abilities would be fun to animate and develop in a character? What ways can you create original characters that personify a part of yourself visually and metaphorically? What would you look like as an original 2D character, and what would you want to do if you could do anything? Maybe as a kid you always wanted to be

This 2D-animated Bigfoot was first drawn as a collection of body parts, and then scanned. The character was then reassembled in Photoshop using layers with body part names. After Effects easily imports Photoshop layers as ready-to-animate compositions.

This character's best trait is that he's the top gangster in his Bigfoot boy tribe. His worst trait is his bad temper, which prevents him from accomplishing his plot goal of being elected chief. His other secondary traits are bratty, little boy, and hip. How can you combine unusual character traits to create visually interesting and fresh characters that are fun to animate?

invisible and have the ability to fly so you could travel to places that were off limits. You could create a character around this idea that could become invisible in an interesting way and travel to far-off destinations. This idea would be fun to animate and would appeal to other people who dreamed of the same abilities.

5. **Play with reality, scale, or physics.** 2D animation enables you to create almost anything you can imagine. How could you design characters that are 300 feet tall, could walk upside down, or stop time? See how far you can push your existing

film idea into a more extreme reality version. How would your story change if your characters were 2 inches tall, or lived in an alternate reality where our rules did not apply?

6. **Surreal environments.** 2D animated environments can be as simple as solid white backgrounds or show us something we have never seen before, such as a whole new world living on a speck of dust. Experiment with creating symbolic or miniature-scale worlds, such as life inside a shag rug, a strange planet in a far-off galaxy, life inside a beehive, or a red blood cell swimming through a body.

Design an Original Cast of 2D Characters. Take your script and sketch some interesting 2D animated character ideas, paying particular attention to visual styles and production techniques. Keep in mind all the things you have learned about character design in the previous chapters.

creativity tip

Don't Knock Yourself Out Trying to Make Your 2D Short Look Like a Walt Disney Film. The 2D animated visual production styles presented in this chapter will look closer to *Southpark* than *The Lion King*. If you are a one-person animation team, you need to think smart and develop a signature digital animation style that best presents the ideas in your story. Traditional 2D animated films require literally hundreds of artists to create that particular frame-by-frame beautiful style.

These Bigfoots are 600 feet tall and only come out during certain planetary alignments. Their favorite thing to do is to squash cars with their feet. 2D excels at creating worlds and characters where anything is possible. If your film was done all in 2D, how could you exaggerate reality to the extreme and still stay true to your story? How could you incorporate extreme metaphors or symbols to show theme? These giant Bigfoots might be used to represent the theme of how genetic engineering could get out of hand.

What surreal or highly stylized worlds could you design for your 2D animated environments? How could you use symbolic objects in your surreal settings to help develop theme?

"Before you begin a thing, remind yourself that difficulties and delays quite impossible to foresee are ahead... You can only see one thing clearly, and that is your goal. Form a mental vision of that and cling to it through thick and thin."
—Kathleen Norris

"We can do anything we want to do if we stick to it long enough."
—Helen Keller

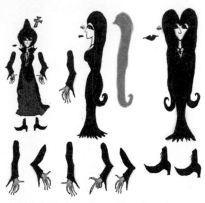

2D Character Drawings. Drawing characters for 2D animation looks similar to paper dolls. You may want to do the line drawings on a piece of paper with a pencil until they look right, and then go over the lines with a black pen. Make sure you connect all the lines so that you can drop fill the colors in Photoshop later. Scan the drawings and import them into Photoshop. Reconstruct the body parts in layers. Carefully name each layer, such as Right Foot, to import into After Effects as ready-to-animate compositions. Then all you have to do is set the rotation points at each moving joint and create the keyframes for movement.

Simple 2D Digital Animation Techniques

Modern 2D animated films are made in a variety of ways. The following techniques are designed for beginning animators who do not have a lot of time. If you have never thought of doing 2D animation before, some of these techniques may inspire you to give it a try.

Preparing Drawn Characters for 2D Animations

Moving parts for 2D animated characters are usually drawn as separate layers, or cut-up into layers in Photoshop. You may want to draw your characters first with a pencil, and then go over them with a black pen, being careful to create shapes that are easy to select in Photoshop. If you draw the body parts in blocks of shapes, it is much easier to select them and drop fill them with colors digitally. Erase your pencil lines after carefully drawing over them with a pen.

Designing Easy-to-Animate 2D Characters

One way to make your animation job easier is to design characters without knees or other troubling joints. Depending on how much time you have to spend animating, you may want to opt for simple design styles.

project
10.10

Draw 2D Animated Parts of the Main Character. Sketch a series of body parts to animate for the main character in your story. Include any outfit changes, props, or side views. Make sure the designs have strong silhouettes and avoid twin arms and legs.

Designing 2D Characters That Are Easier to Animate

Characters in long dresses or clothing that covers the knees. This will allow you to animate just the feet using rotation keyframes.	Characters who often ride skateboards, wear roller skates, ride scooters, or are attached to other floating or rolling objects. This will allow you to animate position key frames and slide characters around on the screen instead of doing complicated walk cycles.	Carefully planned camera shots where walking character's legs or feet are cropped. This will allow you to animate the body up and down in a bouncing motion to simulate a walk cycle without having to keyframe leg and feet movements.
Characters designed with simply shaped bodies, such as circles with feet on the bottom. This will allow you to just animate the feet.	Using bluescreen character silhouettes with hand-drawn details on top. This technique will preserve motion while allowing you to add unique design elements as separate layers.	Design stick figures or extremely simple characters, such as a talking rock that rolls when traveling.

Three Ways to Do a
2D Animated Walk Cycle

Characters need walk cycles that reflect their personalities, weights, and specific designs. A fat character might walk slower with a signature waddle. A nervous tall character may have a long, fast gait. The techniques described here will need to be adjusted to fit your character. A quadruped walk cycle guide is included in the next section (in case your character has four legs). Be advised that walk cycles can be very challenging depending on your character and visual style. Plan to spend at least eight hours to create a really good walk cycle loop for your character, depending on your skill level. All the following files are included on the accompanying CD-ROM.

1. Hand-draw nine separate walk positions that loop. Use the pictures below as a guide.
2. Hand-draw your 2D character in separate moving body part pieces. Scan the drawings and put them together in Photoshop as described earlier, and then import into After Effects as a composition. Use the nine basic walk cycle keyframe drawings as animation guides (walkguide.psd on the CD-ROM), to place behind your character in After Effects. Move the pieces to match the pose-to-pose frames. Your goal at this point is to first get the character walking in place smoothly as a loop.
3. Using the hand-drawn body pieces technique, match the position of each part to a moving DV actor as an animation guide.

In this example, a character was drawn once in pieces that were then placed over the animation guides. This is a pose-to-pose technique where keyframes are set for position and rotation, letting the computer do the in-between frames. Rotation center points are placed where natural joints, such as hips, knees, and ankles, are located on the character.

"As long as you can start, you are all right. The juice will come."
—Ernest Hemingway

Notice how the arms swing opposite the legs. This is just a basic walk cycle. You will need to add personality to it for your character. An old man might limp along stiffly, whereas a young girl bounces up and down with a spring in her step.

This character has a walk cycle full of personality, because Nate the actor was asked to walk like a Bigfoot. The DV footage was imported into After Effects as an animation guide. You could shoot your whole animated film using actors and then rotoscope the movements using this technique to get nice animated movements full of personality. Sketching careful storyboards to match shot angles would be very important when using this technique. Your animation may still need a little fine-tuning to fit your hand-drawn characters. These walk cycle files are on the CD-ROM.

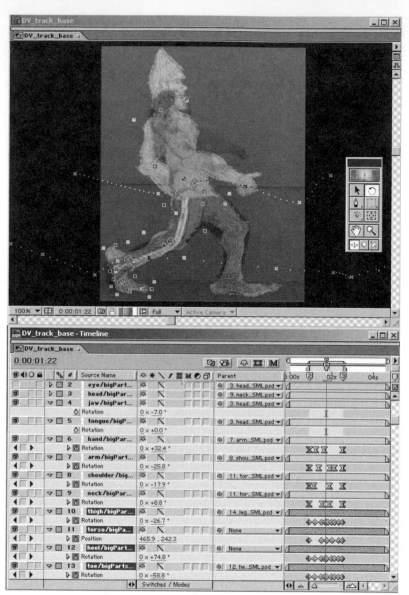

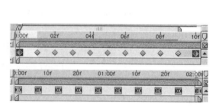

To create a looping walk cycle, you need to duplicate the first keyframe and place it a frame after the last one. If you place the first keyframe in the last frame, your final loop will stick on the double frame.

Getting the Most Out of Your Walk Cycle

After you get a character walking really well in place, there are many techniques to reuse the walk cycle in different ways. The first thing you want to do is to loop the walk cycle into something like a 10-second composition. This will give you flexibility to have your character walk for long periods of time. You can then do a horizontal flip to have the character walk the other direction across the screen. A 3D perspective tilt, along with scaling, may also be applied to make the character appear to be walking toward us at an angle. You could also duplicate your walking character a hundred times and create a whole army. Scale and timing offsets can be applied so all the characters do not appear to be walking the same way. You may also want to use multiple walking silhouettes in the background for crowd scenes. What other ways could you maximize the use of your 2D animated walk cycle? Maybe you are doing a journey story where the character just walks through a series of cut-up photograph sets.

Animating a Simple City Scene

Using 2D animation to create environments is usually much easier than animating characters. Most objects just need to be chopped up into layers and animated using simple position, scale, and rotation keyframes. Following is a simple city scene to give you an idea of how you may want to approach creating 2D animated sets. Once again, it is very important to design objects that are easy to animate.

Lip Sync

Animating the lips of your 2D characters can be very time-consuming. How can you make it easier using your digital tools? In the past, traditional animators have had to draw separate faces for each vowel and consonant. I'm going to suggest some faster ways to make your 2D characters talk that may not look quite as good, but will save you lots of time.

1. **Try animating the mouth layer of your character using horizontal and vertical scaling keyframes.** Squash and stretch the mouth by making keyframes with different scaling values, whenever the audio waveform shows that the dialogue starts. Return to the still mouth image scale when the waveform line goes flat. Experiment with applying Keyframe Interpolation>Bezier to all position and scale keyframes to reduce jerky movements.

2. **Import your 2D drawings into a 3D program and map them onto planes to animate.** If you know 3D, this may work great for your film. Most 3D programs known for character animating have better animation controls than 2D programs. Use deformations on a hand-drawn lips files or hand-drawn mouth shape series to sync lip movement to speech patterns. What other ways could you do this with your favorite 2D/3D software combination?

3. **Shoot CU DV lips of an actor saying the lines of your character.** Use the actual voice track for the dialogue, and then composite the masked video lips over your 2D character's face. Experiment with different filters and looks to make the real DV lips blend better into the animation style you are using, if you do not like the way the real lips look. For example, you could color-correct the DV lips black to better fit a black-and-white character.

4. **Plan smart camera shots** that are looking at other subjects when someone is talking, have characters turned away from the camera when speaking, or plan shots so viewers cannot quite see the characters' mouths when they talk. You will need to show your characters talking sometimes, using the other techniques. Smart camera work can really cut down on having to create lots of lip sync keyframes.

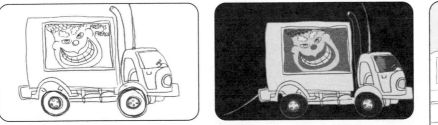

To create this animated truck, a drawing was first done with a pencil and then scanned into Photoshop and drop filled with colors. The wheels were cut out and made into different layers so that they could rotate separately. The window was also cut out with a slight transparency added, so that it could roll down by animating the position keyframes. A character layer was placed behind the window. When the tires were rotating in place, a moving truck composition was created by grouping all the moving layers together. This rolling-in-place truck composition could then be slid across the frame as one piece, by setting two motion keyframes, one at the starting point and one at the end.

This drawing of a city street was scanned into Photoshop and drop filled with different colors. The truck above rolls along the street.

Notice how the lip scaling keyframes start as the bumps in the dialogue waveform begin. Always record your dialogue as a separate track to see where the characters begin and end their lines. The face and lips need to be in separate layers for this technique to work. Use both horizontal and vertical scaling keyframes to make the lips look like they are moving. You will have to play with finding just the right amount of lip movement (number of scale keyframes to set each second) to match dialogue.

Vowels

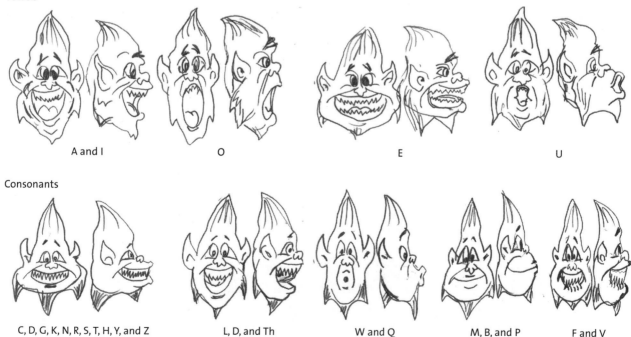

A and I   O   E   U

Consonants

C, D, G, K, N, R, S, T, H, Y, and Z   L, D, and Th   W and Q   M, B, and P   F and V

This chart will help you think of different mouth shapes to use when setting lip sync keyframes. You do not need to match every word or syllable, and it will probably look strange if you do. You may want to videotape your own lips saying the dialogue and use the footage as a guide for creating general mouth shapes.

project
10.11

Lip Sync Strategy. Come up with an efficient strategy to lip sync the characters in your film using your favorite software abilities. Explain why it fits with the narrative concept, such as huge, pink actor lips on funny characters or tight, black line shapes on uptight stick-figure people. Always ask yourself how your design decisions will affect the way the audience thinks and feels about the characters in each shot. What symbolic animated objects could you use for lips in a stop motion, DV montage, or photo-collage style? Maybe you put different voice actor lips on different characters to suit their personality.

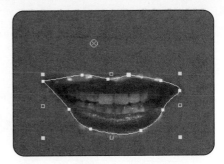

These masked DV lips could be scaled to fit your 2D character and color manipulated to match the design. Each set of lips has a distinct personality, so be sure to cast them accordingly.

project
10.12

Shoot Voice Actors for 2D Animated Scripts. If you are using voice actors for your 2D animated film, you will want to videotape them when speaking to get ideas for any gestures or interesting expressions. How can you exaggerate these later when animating? Try to film them at the same size and angle as your character in the shot, so you can use their faces as video layer guides above the animated-face layer with an opacity of 50 percent. Or if the voice actors move around a lot while standing up, you may want to shoot their whole bodies to inspire animated-character movements later.

"A man would do nothing if he waited until he could do it so well that no one could find fault."
—John Henry Cardinal Newman

Animating Facial Expressions

You may want to do a little acting yourself to help find the right emotional expressions for each shot. Videotape yourself acting like your character or saying your character's lines to use as a facial expression guide. It is very important that you first get into the proper emotional state for this technique to work. If your character has a really sad moment, think of something really sad that happened to you, and *really feel it,* and then act out the character's lines or facial expressions using your DV camera. Take the footage into your animation program and use as a background layer guide.

You may also use a mirror placed next to your computer, but using a camera may help you get the feel and timing of the whole shot better, while helping you to see how the changing facial emotions bridge together.

Stop Motion

Digital technology makes stop motion a bit less time-consuming, because you can now grab still frames directly into your editing software if your camera is hooked up to your computer. This enables you to preview your footage immediately and make adjustments. Almost anything can be used to make stop-motion sets and characters. Clay figures with wire armatures inside to help hold the poses are the most popular. Dolls, toys, paper doll cutouts, painted wooden characters, Super Sculpti, mud, refrigerator magnets, rocks, sticks, flowers, trash, statues, puppets, cut-up photos, robots, and mannequins are all possibilities for stop-motion types of animation. Doing 24 frames per second will probably be too much work for most individual animators or small productions. Experiment with 10 fps or less to find an animation style that works for your production schedule and subject matter.

"We only do well the things we like doing."
—*Colette*

Got Kids? How could you make an animation with your child? You could adopt a favorite bedtime story using the techniques discussed in Chapter 1, "Generating Ideas for Digital Short Films," or create an original character and story idea. If it turns out well, send it to HBO's *Kidflicks* (**www.hbo.com**), which features animations done by young people. The next generation of filmmakers are getting a big head start on their visual storytelling education by using digital moviemaking tools at a young age.

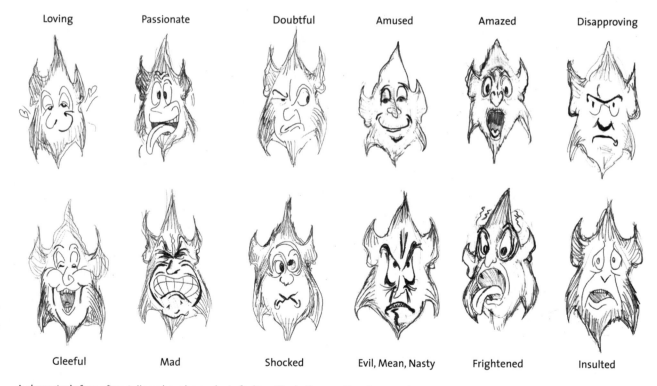

| Loving | Passionate | Doubtful | Amused | Amazed | Disapproving |
| Gleeful | Mad | Shocked | Evil, Mean, Nasty | Frightened | Insulted |

A character's face often tells us how he or she is feeling. Study the emotional expressions above to see how much your perception of the character changes. Even a slight raising of the eyebrows, or tilt of the mouth, can help the audience identify more emotionally with your animated characters.

Got Parents? How could you get your parents or friends to help you make a movie? Maybe your dad could build a miniature physical set with you in the garage. If your mom sews, she could make the costumes. Make a list of your parents' skills and see where you could put them to work as part of your team.

What types of toys or cardboard sets could you use to create a unique style for segments in your film? How could you use remote-controlled cars, boats, planes, or trains in your film? How could you attach small wireless DV cameras to moving toys for unique POVs?

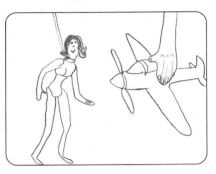

Dolls or toys swinging on a string or moved with your hands out of frame against a blue- or green-screen background may work great for a unique animation style. DV actor lips could be attached for talking parts.

Original Set Pieces and Props. Do you have a special laser gun or important statue in mind for your film? How could you utilize found objects or junkyard parts to glue together, spray paint, and form a new prop? You may want to create original objects using an easy-to-work-with clay, such as Super Sculpti. This material is very inexpensive, nonmessy, baked in the oven to harden, and then painted. Design one original prop or set piece

for your film.

The digital short film *Max* by AWOL features *GI Joe* dolls battling it out in the forest. The sound effects and explosions round out the look and feel of the story. Toy rafts carrying soldiers float down creeks. How could you use toys to make a film? Be careful when using trademark toys for obvious legal reasons. See whether you can paint them or add hair or fabric to make the toys look like original designs.

Stop-Motion Ideas. How could you develop some innovative ways to move stop-motion characters? You might want to do stop-motion mannequins against a blue screen, duct taped to spray-painted blue skateboards with wires pulling body parts

around as they move. Or you could move old Barbie dolls with blue wires against a blue background and drop in DV or photo collage sets. What unique materials could you use to make characters that fit conceptually with your story?

"We would accomplish many more things if we did not think of them as impossible."
—C. Malesherbez

Defining Your Own 2D Style of Animation

It certainly is an exciting time to be a 2D animator using digital tools. Modern 2D animators now have the ability to create longer independent films in a much shorter amount of time than their traditional 2D animating counterparts. In the past, most 2D animators would spend their lives doing one little thing or character in each film. Now you get to write, direct, animate, edit, be the voice actor, do the sound design, and blend your favorite software into a completely original creation. There will be a new wave of 2D

animated feature films done by independents in the next decade as the software and hardware make it easier to create innovative digital films. If you survey the techniques discussed in this chapter and the DV one, you will see there are all sorts of ways to create fun and modern 2D animations. Plan to spend some time developing your own unique mix and style of simple animation techniques. You could spend your whole life making digital films you like and never even leave your studio!

chapter 11

Using 3D Animation to Show Anything You Can Imagine

"What we need are more people who specialize in the impossible."
—Theodore Roethke

3D software can now create *anything* you can imagine. This

chapter was written for digital artists who are familiar with 3D

animation and want to use it to tell stories in new ways. A basic

knowledge of 3D software and terms is assumed, but even those

of you new to 3D will find the ideas in this section useful if you are

designing 3D stories for other animators to create.

Be Patient with Yourself When Learning 3D. If you are just learning to use 3D programs, be patient with yourself; they take awhile to figure out. Plan to spend at least six months to two years getting comfortable with using a 3D program. It helps to team up with a seasoned 3D animator to do those parts of your film if you're new to the realm. If you are serious about being a digital filmmaker, learning how to use 3D software will greatly expand your creative tool palette.

3D elements are often used with DV or film footage, such as realistic aliens in a familiar environment or bluescreened actors in 3D environments. Many of the ideas in this chapter can also be applied to 2D animated or DV stories. 3D animated films are still in their creative and technological infancies, evolving as the software and hardware capabilities improve. The use of 3D in films has increased dramatically in the past decade. One day, the majority of feature films may be made completely in 3D, using virtual actors and sets. This chapter focuses on what 3D does best and how to create characters, worlds, and stories that audiences can relate to emotionally. You will be encouraged to create your own 3D visual style along the way, because photorealism is one of the most difficult aesthetical looks for an independent 3D animator to choose. This chapter explores the following areas:

- Some good narrative uses for 3D animation
- 3D character design
- Using visual motifs to create 3D worlds

Some Good Narrative Uses for 3D

How could you take your basic humans and redesign them as original 3D characters? This gal can plug into computers and generate emotions visually in real-time graphics. What unique abilities could you give the characters in your script to make them more 3D?

3D animation software is rapidly changing the way modern filmmakers stretch their imaginations to tell stories in unique and innovative ways. Where 2D animation often feels more fun and whimsical, 3D animation feels more realistic and serious by its very nature. 3D animation is also very time-consuming and requires lots of digital production experience and super-fast computers, all of which makes this production style rather expensive to create. It is therefore important to *make sure* you have a very good story reason for using the 3D platform. If you can do your film, or shot, in DV, or even simple 2D animated styles, you may not want to even consider using the time-consuming realm of 3D. Make sure you are using this production style to do what it does best, and have a very good reason, such as the shot or style being almost impossible to create using anything else. Following are some good ideas to think about when developing 3D animated stories or elements for your film.

Original 3D Characters. You can create any character you can imagine in 3D. This is the biggest selling point of this very time-consuming animation style. People want to see things they have not seen before, or in drastically new ways in 3D animated films. *Men in Black* shows us an assortment of realistic aliens that all have unique movements and abilities. *A Bug's Life* let us see things from the perspective of insects. *Jurassic Park* has realistic dinosaurs that come alive. *Toy Story* takes us through the world of talking toys with human emotions, goals, and needs. *Lord of the Rings* shows us walking trees and armies of sinister orcs. What 3D added visual elements can you develop in your characters to justify using the production environment?

3D Character Design Ideas

Aliens—any form from any planet. Refer to science fiction films and TV shows for ideas.	Inanimate animated objects, such as dancing knives, food, liquids, walking rocks, or talking toys.	Nature as character, such as talking trees, tornados with faces, sea gods coming out of tidal waves, or fire spirits.
Magical characters such as the ones found in the *Harry Potter* stories.	Metaphorical or symbolic characters, such as a realistic humanoid body with a lightbulb head.	Spirits such as ghosts, demons, metaphysical creatures, or other deities.
Animated animals, bugs, plants, birds, and fish.	Realistic human actors with visual 3D super-hero capabilities such as tools that morph out of body parts. The X-Men stories do a lot with this one.	Mythological characters, such as 12-armed goddesses with elephant heads.
Animated set pieces such as lamps, paintings, or statues.	Characters that change shape.	Exaggerated character designs, such as huge heads with tiny bodies for a visual metaphor.

Original 3D Sets. Any location that you can imagine, you can build in 3D. *Dark City* showed us animated buildings that grew out the ground. *Antz* gave us a peak into life inside an insect colony. *Toy Story* let us see the world through the eyes of plastic dolls. *Final Fantasy* created a completely 3D, futuristic film world populated with realistic humanoid 3D actors, which gives us a peek into the future of filmmaking. *Finding Nemo* shows us what life might be like living in a coral reef or swimming through the ocean. *Lord of the Rings* gave us fantasy worlds full of magical and dangerous places.

Traveling 3D Shots. 3D cameras can go *anywhere*. They are particularly good at moving through never-before-seen environments, unencumbered by needing dollies or tracks for movement. How can you create original traveling camera shots using the inherent flexibility of 3D animated cameras? How could you include unique traveling shots through 3D environments or POVs audiences have never experienced before? What traveling POV shot ideas could you come up with using roller coasters, trains, moving characters, death-defying stunt moves, space shots, or flying into objects?

3D Set Design Ideas

Lost civilizations	Microscopic views, such as life inside a spec of dust or human blood vessel, or flying into a thin wire	Water worlds
Futuristic cities		Surreal, dreamlike realities
Animated buildings	Metaphorical or symbolic locations such as the center of a person's head or a world made out of 3D numbers in the shapes of buildings	Animal environments such as life inside a beehive, anthill, coral reef, or bird nest city in treetops
Alien worlds		
Abstract realities		Alternate dimensions such as psychic realms, heaven, dream planes, and meditations
Magical places such as the *Harry Potter* wizard world and school	Fantasy worlds	
	3D comic-book looks	Metaphorical or symbolic worlds

What types of original 3D makeup could you create for your DV characters?

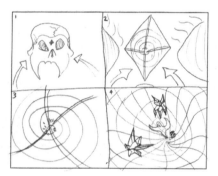

In this sketch, the camera flies into the crystal Bigfoot skull and enters another abstract dimension. What new places can your 3D cameras go?

3D stunt shots can add some big-budget wow to your short film. How could you use bluescreen actors with 3D objects to create original stunts? Use photos or DV backgrounds if possible to save time.

Image/Camera Mapping. Most 3D programs do a good job of mapping photos or DV to simple planes or objects, which can then appear as highly detailed 3D elements.

Adding Digital Makeup/Extra Body Parts. 3D may be used as digital makeup on actors, or BS characters, to add limbs, cut them half, or have something like a worm crawl out of holes in their faces. First you would shoot a carefully storyboarded scene in DV, and then add these types of 3D effects as another layer on top of the source footage. If you want a big worm to crawl out of a character's face, shoot the actor as if it were happening, at the correct angle, and then lay the 3D animated worm face area on top. Sometimes it helps to build part of the character's face in 3D, at the same angle as the camera shot, and animate the worm crawling out for a more realistic look. You can use motion-tracking software in After Effects or 3D programs to help keep the 3D element attached to the DV footage as the character moves. Often bluescreened actors are used so that every layer of the final image can be tweaked for color correction, blending, and additional special effects. What ways could you use digital makeup for a character design, story idea, or as a visual effect?

3D Camera Movement. Cameras in 3D software programs can do almost anything. They are especially good at mathematically controlled motion paths, original POVs, and flying through unusual spaces. The opening shot of *Moulin Rouge* going over Paris is a great example of how 3D, 2D, and film-type footage are being combined to show us camera shots in new ways.

3D cameras work great for flying into tight spaces, such as tubes, wires, holes, trash heaps, eardrums, microscopic realities, or other dimensions. What innovative camera shots could you invent, utilizing all the flexibility of 3D camera movements? How could you use multiple 3D cameras in one shot and edit them together in a unique way? Many beginning 3D animators tend to move their 3D cameras too much. Make sure you have a good reason to move your 3D camera before planning a bunch of rotating, twirling, spinning, or fast fly-throughs that leave the audience confused and overwhelmed as to what is happening in the story.

Realistic 3D Stunt Moves. 3D stunt actors never get hurt, and it's much cheaper to blow up 3D models than it is to destroy expensive cars or buildings. How could you create a 3D enhanced Wow! stunt shot for your film that is too dangerous to do in real life? You could use BS actors against 3D backgrounds or build low-resolution models of the stunt characters in your shots. In the film *Mission Impossible*, there is a 3D sequence in which Tom Cruise leaps from a helicopter onto the top of a fast-moving train going through a tunnel. These types of super-dangerous stunts are now done mostly in 3D. What is the most death-defying dangerous stunt you could think of for a character in your story? How could you do the shot in 3D?

2D Characters on 3D Planes for Better Animation Controls. The 2D animated show *Southpark* was done in Maya by mapping pictures onto flat planes in the shape of the images. This allows the character animators to take advantage of the powerful animation capabilities in the 3D software to move the parts around more easily than using a 2D package. Character animator programs such as Maya and 3ds max have very advanced animation controls where walk cycles can become as easy as pushing a button. The initial setup of characters is time-consuming, but once done, can be used over and over again like an actor who is ready to go at any time and do anything you want. What ways could you build your 2D animation in a 3D program to have a whole cast and set ready to make new movies at any time?

2D Cell Shading for Video and 3D Footage. Some filmmakers are shooting on DV and then importing the footage into 3ds max or Maya to take advantage of the 2D shader capabilities. A shader is like a filter that renders adjustable visual styles. These types of shaders will evolve, along with "waking life" types of effects, to add unique looks to digital films. Many 3D animators also opt for a final 2D shader effect. This enables them to use the 3D program's animation capabilities without having to hand draw frames, and enables them to avoid the time-consuming task of making their 3D film look photorealistic. What part of your film might benefit from a 2D shader look to create a unique visual style?

Distorting Actors. Many traditional 2D animated distortion or morphing effects can be created with an added dimension in 3D. In *The Mask*, Jim Carrey's hands morph into giant comic book–looking machine guns that fire bullets. *Inspector Gadget* has helicopter blades that pop out of the top of his head so he can fly

around with unique POVs and use tools whenever he needs one. What original ways could you have your characters distort or morph body parts into other shapes? How could you apply some surreal 2D animated distortion techniques to your 3D characters? Some good 2D films to study for 3D distortion ideas are ones by Bill Plympton, the master of morphing heads and surreal-looking traditionally animated 2D worlds (**www.awn.com/plympton**).

Using Different 3D Programs for Different Looks. Some 3D animations are rendered in different programs for what they do best and then composited into final layers. What ways could you mix different 3D render styles, 2D, or DV to create a unique look and feel for your film? Maybe the working characters live in simple wireframe worlds, whereas the ruling ones have high geometry to show a theme. The ghosts in this imaginary world could be created using DV shadows. It may make more sense to take an easy-to-create 3D Poser character off the web and bring it into programs such as Maya than it does to model them from scratch. Bryce works great for generating terrain texture maps that can then be imported into any 3D program and mapped onto planes to create mountains. How could you combine what each of your 3D packages do best as layers in a film?

Creating Fantasy Worlds. If you avoid photorealism, it is much easier to create stylized environments based on what your software does best, fast and easy. You could use a program such as Bryce 3D to generate quick fantasy 3D sets, planets, worlds, or space shots to place other 3D, 2D, or DV characters into.

What types of 3D-enhanced body parts could you create to make your character more original?

3D global village theme. In *Liquid Crystal Vision*, a 3D village is shown stretching across several continents between DV footage shot around the world. This is an easy shot, because it involves a spinning sphere globe (low geometry) and a simple village hut model that is duplicated across the surface. What ways can you show your theme or an abstract concept in 3D?

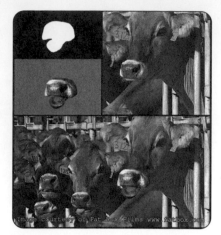

These images show how Nate created a talking cow for Fatbox Films (**www. fatbox.com**). The jaw of the cow was rebuilt in 3D using Maya, complete with buck teeth and a silly moving tongue. Afterward, After Effects and Maya were used to match the elements together into the final shot.

After an object such as this 3D spaceship has been modeled and texture-mapped, it can be duplicated into a fleet.

Some 3D software enables you to do very complicated flocking behaviors. In this sketch, birds do some skywriting with a heart-shaped symbol in the clouds. What innovative flocking techniques can you use to tell your story?

What dream fantasy world have you always wanted to see that you could build in 3D as a set for your film?

Animated Animals or Objects. Working with real animals to get them to do what you need for a shot can be really frustrating. Films such as *Babe* show us talking pigs, with rebuilt 3D faces and mouths for the talking parts. How could you use 3D animals to do things regular animals would not? In *Amelie*, there are floating clouds in the shape of bunny rabbits and talking bedside animated pig lamps commenting on the character's state by talking to animated paintings on the wall. What animals or inanimate objects could you bring to life in your film using 3D? Think of ways to help us get into the talking animal's or object's world to give us a fresh perspective on the story. Find three places in your film where 3D objects could talk about the characters or comment on the story.

Duplication. After you model, texture map, and animate one object or character, it is easy to make copies. How could you use this to your advantage when developing 3D stories? You could make robot armies, twins, gangs, fleets of objects, or factories full of workers. How could you make simple variations of one character to form a group of individuals by modifying parameters such as scale, visibility, color, rotation, and position on individual body parts?

Flocking Systems. Flocking is the ability to animate large groups of objects or characters in a natural-looking way without having to move them individually, and also so that they don't move into or through

each other, which can be a big problem in 3D. After you build one 3D character, it is usually easy to make variations and turn them into a large group on the screen. Some 3D programs have built-in flocking capabilities. Much of the best flocking technology is still proprietary to the effects houses building the code. The *Lord of the Rings* team has pioneered a software called Massive to create realistic fields of clashing 3D opponents, where one large group of characters go out and fight other groups. These types of developing technologies tend to trickle down to desktop software versions a little later. How could you use a flocking technique in your film? What ways could you have a group of objects, such as 3D birds, move in symbolic patterns to help develop your story? What other types of group movement could you develop visually to help us understand your 3D world?

Physics. Many 3D programs enable you to assign properties to objects such as weight, material, velocity, and friction. These objects then assume those properties during animations while interacting with other objects. You can then build a 3D city and flood it with water, after assigning physics to each object, such as cars parked on the street next to glass windows on the buildings. Click Render and the animation happens realistically, almost automatically as the different objects collide with the assigned physical properties built in. Bouncing ball animations using squash and stretch are simplified into creating a sphere and a ground plane, then assigning material properties, such as plastic or steel to the ball, which will then bounce accordingly. How could you add metaphorical weight to some character's walk cycle such as lead, and make other ones lighter as a contrast? Where else could you use physics in a 3D shot to make your job easier?

Hair and Cloth. What kind of hairy-looking characters or designer clothes could help give your film a signature look? You could design a symbolic hairy set, such as a furry breathing organic city. Dressing 3D characters has now become more of a designer's game, with endless clothing choices. What does high fashion look like in your 3D world?

Motion Ride Animation Paths. What kind of POV ride could you take your audience on as part of your film? 3D works great for traveling through spaces in a way DV and 2D animation cannot do. IMAX theaters in Vegas exploit this 3D advantage with amusement park–type immersive motion rides. What original motion path POVs could you use that we have never seen before? How does this idea help us understand your story better?

Interactive 3D Worlds and Games. Many of the techniques discussed in this book apply to interactive worlds and games. When designing an interactive story or game, you still need to create original characters, worlds, game plots, cut scene short films, metaphoric game play symbols, original POVs, good cinematography, and clever sound design that engage players emotionally. How could you turn your film into an interactive 3D game idea?

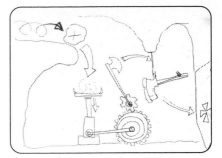

By assigning each object the proper physics, this contraption would be self-animating. How can you design sets that take advantage of this technique to save yourself time animating? This technique works well for background-looping animations, too.

money-saving

Partner with a Clothing Company. Depending on the originality and quality of your reel and script, you may be able to approach clothing designers in your area to help fund your next 3D animated short film. You will need a good pitch, storyboards, and a clever idea to get them interested. Propose that they design the character's costumes, based on their clothing lines, and explain how their particular styles fit with your narrative concept. Credits will appear at the end of the film for the design house. You may be able to swing a deal in which they can play your animation in their stores, on their web sites, or as TV commercials. Clothing companies, such as Diesel, have been known to dress 3D characters in video games.

What other products can you think of incorporating into your short film to fund development budgets? These ideas work particularly well with web-based clickable interactive stories funded with product placement.

group project

Form a 3D Production Group. If you are in school or know other 3D animators in your area, you may want to team up and create a project together, emphasizing each other's strengths. The best modelers model, the best character animators animate, and the compositor shoots any extra DV footage, makes texture maps, and puts it all together. 3D projects can take a long time if you are doing it all by yourself. It helps to work in a group to keep each other motivated and problem solve together when learning new things. Your 3D production group may become so successful that you will have to start your own company!

For our music video *Beyond*, an island with more than 300 blowing 3D palm trees was created using a tree plug-in.

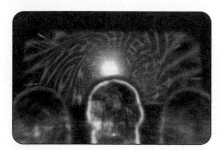

This frame-within-a-frame shot was used inside our 3D *Beyond* spaceship as the view screen when the characters went through a worm hole.

money-saving

Free 3D Models. Do a search for "free 3D models" on your favorite Internet search engine and see whether you can find one that is prebuilt to use in your film. After you know how to import objects, set simple keyframes, and render, you can build all sorts of 3D effects, worlds, and creatures. 3D is where filmmaking is heading, so it's a good investment of your time to learn a 3D program, to give you more visual choices as an independent filmmaker. One day soon, we will be able to go online and download prebuilt 3D sets and actors to make our films.

Realistic 3D Actors. Any person dead or alive can now be re-created in a 3D photo realistically (if we know how they looked). How could you do an animation with a historic dead character we have not seen much of before using a 3D historical set or old 2D photo collage techniques?

Mixing Animation Styles. Real actors can be inserted into 3D worlds. *Tron* was the first film to do this in a really interesting way and is worth studying for its wonderful production design. The story takes place inside a computer and is a great film to study for how simple effects can look great. If you storyboard and plan your bluescreen actor shots carefully, you could create a unique animation style with simple 3D sets. How could you place a hand-drawn 2D character into a 3D set, or a 3D character into a DV or 2D set?

3D Water, Fire, Smoke, Weather, Plants, and Trees. 3D is getting good at doing natural elements and plants. How could you create a wild 3D garden with symbolically shaped water fountains as a set for one of your scenes? You can now easily design your own plants and trees using vast branch and leaf libraries in dedicated 3D plant software. How would the plants and weather look different in your world where you control everything? Where could you add storms, tornados, tidal waves, or lightning to drive the emotions in your film? Maybe it rains blood in your scary world with miniature tornados that buzz around characters' feet, tripping them occasionally, while man-eating plants spring out of the sewers. How

can all of these atmospheric details help us understand your film world better visually? The film *What Dreams May Come* created a unique, digitally enhanced environment that audiences had never seen before.

Outer Space Shots. Outer space has low geometry (lots of space with round planets), which makes it easy to do in 3D. Modeling a simple flying saucer and setting a few motion keyframes against a starry backdrop plane is relatively simple (and can be done quickly). Taking that spaceship and duplicating it a hundred times gives you a fleet of UFOs. Flying rocks with particle tails look like comets. How can you have your 3D story take place in outer space? How can you create unique versions of other planets or alien critters?

Unusual Texture Maps. After you have a 3D model, you can place any type of texture map across the surface, which opens up a bunch of metaphorical possibilities for your stories. How would the perception of humanoid-looking characters change if their ordinary skin texture maps were switched with grass, electrical circuits, stones, fire, long blue fuzzy hair, water, smoke, porcupine needles, fish scales, plastic, wet oil paint, chrome, black lace, or feathers? How could you create theme 3D worlds by using unusual texture maps on buildings, streets, objects, or landscapes? You need to relate each of these choices to the narrative conceptually, such as the grass people being hippies and the stone ones tiered working people.

3D Scanning. Desktop 3D scanners are getting better and cheaper as the technology develops. Almost any object can be 3D scanned. Little statues can be placed on desktop 3D scanners and then inserted into shots with their textures maps in place. On the higher end, there are military-type handheld 3D scanners that can scan big buildings or detect underground cities and then produce exact 3D modeled environments. After an object has been scanned, it can be imported into your 3D program and placed as a set piece or animated using bones, joints, and deformations. What objects could you 3D scan for your film if you have access to the technology?

"You must do the things you
think you cannot do."
—Eleanor Roosevelt

Motion Capture. If character animating is not a thrilling way to spend your time, you could choose to use an actor in a motion-capture suit to generate keyframes. Many schools and digital film and game companies have their own motion-capture systems. If you have access to this technology, how could you use it to save yourself some time animating? You may be able to take the motion-capture frames off of something like a horse and apply them to a your quadruped alien to get a quick walk cycle. There are also lots of motion-capture files available on the web to plug into your 3D characters.

The first Bigfoot is mapped in huge snake scales. The second one is mapped with steel porcupine-sharp quills. Notice how much our impressions of the characters shift dramatically with textures.

This shot was created by scanning a silver 3D Buddha statue and then rotating it inside a flower.

money-saving

Cheap Motion-Capture System. A good trick is to put together a cheap motion-capture system by using two DV cameras recording you from different angles. Act out your scene, map the video on image planes around your 3D character to the correct scale, and use the motion as keyframe guides. This will help you get the hang of character animation and learn more about timing for keyframing.

project **11.1**

3D Advantage Ideas. Come up with at least one way to use each of the preceding ideas in your 3D film. This is just an exercise. Add any 3D advantages I may have missed that you want to use or have seen that interest you. Keep adding to this list as the software capabilities continue to increase.

Things 3D Does, but Not Easily, Fast, or Well

Highly detailed photorealistic (or surrealistic) characters and environments take a long time to build and animate in 3D. Choose a simple visual style for your 3D animated film if you are not working with a big team. Hundreds of artists usually work on highly detailed 3D photorealistic animations. Plastic toys and simple stylized flat-shaded characters are easiest to do. Concentrate on creating original simple 3D characters with a good solid original story.

Brainstorming for 3D Story Ideas

The big *must* for developing 3D characters and sets is that you must have a very good reason to do them in 3D. If you can shoot it with DV, you will save yourself a great deal of time. People want to see 3D things they could not see otherwise. Keep this in mind as you go through all the projects in this book. For ideas, refer to the preceding list of what 3D does well.

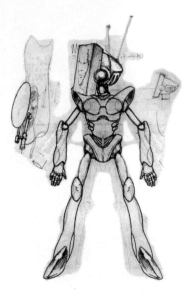

This is a rough sketch of a 3D character. A TV takes the place of his head to display animations and DV based on the character's thoughts and emotions. How can you mix 3D, 2D, and DV in your film?

 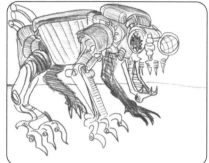

If you want to have a 3D animated character in your film, be very specific about the character's visual motif when doing the brainstorming exercises in Part I. A regular dog would be easier to shoot with a DV camera. A simple "robot dog" is too generic. Use descriptive adjectives such as a sassy, punk, or pit bull made of junkyard parts to really see the essence of the character.

Designing Original 3D Characters

What types of original adventures could these 3D critters get mixed up in? Notice how the design works well for 3D.

A good main character is essential to any successful 3D narrative story. As the computers get faster, the complexity of 3D characters and the audience's viewing expectations continue to rise. The big challenge now is coming up with original characters who are alive with personality and have amazing 3D visual appeal.

Conceptual 3D character designers work in many different ways to come up with their ideas. The more you know your character, the better you can develop it for the most believability and emotional impact. Go through your character history and backstory exercises to choose designs that match the essence of your 3D character.

Remain true to the essence and desires of the types of characters you design or they will ring false and contrived. When bringing an inanimate object to life through the wonders of 3D animation, show us its unique perspective on things. If you are doing a dancing blender, make sure the audience believes that that character is really a blender and has blender wants and needs, not those of a typical housewife or baseball coach, even though that personality may be part of your dancing blender character.

Create a series of columns with different body part types to mix and match for your 3D character. By using columns, you can then choose one from each section and create a truly original creature. This type of exercise is good for modern mythical characters or anytime you need something fresh and unusual.

This character looks fun to animate. He has an interesting trunk and an alien zoo creature type of feel. What unique features could you add to your character to make it more fun to animate?
Illustration by Sam Miceli

Character Types to Mix and Match Randomly

Body Type	Head	Legs/Feet	Arms/Hands	Unique Features
alien	humanoid	biped	human	tail
humanoid	alien head	quadruped	monkey	trunk
sea creature	feline	fins	claws	horn
demon	reptilian	webbed feet	feline	huge warts
animal	borg	triped	hooves	tentacles
mythical	dragon	octoped	lady	big hair
spirit	elephant	bird	vampiric	mohawk
object	dog	objects	boney	brain helmet
light	goat	ape	gloved	plates
hybrid	bloated	bugs	hairy	tubes
plant	shrunken	stilty	beefy	parasites
dinosaur	mutant	obese	long fingers	ball and chain
toy	voodoo	wooden	alien	implants
bacterium	Draconian	peg leg	dismembered	beard
subatomic	insectoid	amputated	glowing	skull plates
element	arachnid	cyborg	cut up	spots
food	bull	elephant	fingernails	holes
symbol	devilish	mermaid	metal	drawers
robot	troll	cowboy	scaly	TV screens
liquid	bird	sumo	child's	hooks
spaceship	grassy	mechanical	ancient	widgets
vehicle	squid	elf	mummy	organic
bird	fish	chicken	robot	weapons
superheroes	TV	huge feet	tentacles	ghost
shape-shifters	frog	wheels	ape	rolls of flesh
prehistoric	crystal ball	hoof	monster	extreme muscles
insect	eyeball	smokey trail	feathers	huge wrinkles
reptile	cow	dog	bone	scales

project 11.2

Different Types of Characters. Try redesigning the initial idea of your main character as a another type. Do four rough sketches with different combinations using ideas from the preceding chart. You may have first thought that the character would be a biped, but now see something more original, such as a winged creature, that fits your theme better.

"I don't have a lot of respect for talent. Talent is genetic. It's what you do with it that counts."
—Martin Ritt

Draw multiple thumbnails of each body part to examine all the possibilities. Keep a visual library in a sketchbook of different body part types. Use pictures of real animals, insects, fish, plants, or people for a variety of ideas.
Illustration by Maia Sanders

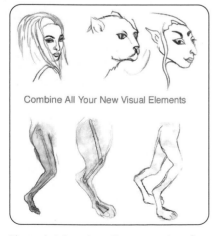

Combine All Your New Visual Elements

These sketches show the progression of incorporating two ideas for a character into one design.
Illustration by Maia Sanders

Start with a Rough Sketch

You should have a good idea of your story by now, which will help you create some rough sketches for your character designs. This is where being able to draw fast and accurately comes in handy. Even if you cannot draw really well, try to get the basic concept or energy of the character down on paper. If you have already designed your 3D character, use the following project exercises to fine-tune the visual concept.

project 11.3

Designing Your Main 3D Character. Using a pencil, draw at least 10 different gesture-type versions of your protagonist in your drawing book. Spend about a minute or two on each sketch. Experiment with proportions of body parts, head shapes, clothing, and postures. This will help get your imagination away from being stuck on one idea at this point. Try not to fall in love with any of your ideas during the conceptual development stages of any project, because it will limit your ability to try new things that may work better than the initial concept.

Maia Sanders came up with the idea of using the alphabet to design character head shapes. Try numbers, symbols, foreign alphabets, or other shapes to help you design beyond the basic ideas.

Create Strong Silhouettes

Strong silhouettes make for good character design. The design must read clearly as a solid black shape to ensure the audience can pick the character out of backgrounds and easily read whatever motion the character is doing. Pay particular attention to strong silhouettes at this stage.

superfreak!

Create a Real Model of Your 3D Character. Use anything you like to work with such as Super Sculpti, clay, or carved wax. This will help you check out the different viewing angles. Here are some pictures of a wax model photographed from several different angles. This scary character has a strong silhouette from some directions but gets a little confusing from the sides due to the low chin.

project 11.4

Draw Your Rough 3D Character Design as a Silhouette. Make one drawing for the front and one for the side. Fill the shape in with solid black and see whether it is interesting, easy to read visually, and original.

Here are some pictures of a wax model photographed from several different angles to check the silhouette. What ways could you create a physical model to help design your 3D character?
Wax model and character created by Ryan Nishimura

Utilizing Visual Motifs

A visual motif consists of any group of people or things that have specific styles with regard to body shape, architecture, clothing, skin type, jewelry, music, transportation, weapons, demeanor/attitude, colors, time periods, or cultural history. You can tell whether a visual motif is a strong one by seeing whether you can come up with specific ideas for your motif in many of these categories. You can also create your own original visual motifs by combining familiar ones.

When you know your character history, it is easier to find a unique visual style or motif to communicate the character's screen presence. Design your 3D characters and sets with strong visual motifs to give them some immediate history and personality. The audience will subconsciously relate to the character better if there is something they are already familiar with in the design. Abstract 3D characters and worlds without strong visual motifs can come off as contrived and flat to audiences, because they have nothing visually or emotionally to latch on to, to help the audience understand the world orientation.

The visual motif here is a forest Bacchae rave, and the design is based on the actress Gwenyth Paltrow. This character also looks fun to animate. Try to draw your character designs so you can see them move, with energy and tension in poses like this one.
Illustration by Jeff Vacanti

Using Familiar Visual Motifs for Your 3D Worlds

A visual motif is a design thread that has some familiar attributes running through everything you create in your animation. You do not want to create 3D characters who look disconnected from their environments or other characters in the story. Often you are creating your own visual reality in a 3D animation; it will look more professional if you pick a visual motif or familiar touchstone to design all the elements around for each particular set of characters or locations. This motif helps the audience relate to your characters.

If you were to pick the visual motif of New York City for a giant 3D beehive, you would incorporate design aspects of traditional beehives with New York City buildings, taxis,

subways, endless layers of life, urban characters, and clothing. If you were to choose a New Age, hippie, utopian visual motif for a 3D beehive, it would look quite different from the New York City one. In general, you would design half of your world as a 3D beehive and half with the common New York City elements we all know.

Visual motifs, when designed consciously, tell the audience what is important to the characters in this world you create, and how they look at life on a symbolic level. Think of how you feel you know a person better after spending some time observing that person, finding out where they come from, seeing where they live, what kind of pictures are on the walls, and their furniture choices.

These two characters would be good for a semihistorical story with lots of culture and background. Create your own history of a made-up culture based on a real one with a fresh 3D dimension. The character on the left looks Asian but has funny ears. The leaping animal head character looks Egyptian but has a very original flair. Both of these characters would work well in 3D and have the added advantage of looking somewhat culturally historic.
Illustration by Donnie Bruce

This character uses the visual theme of a pirate to give it a well-traveled exotic look.

Another pirate motif creature that easily relates to the previous one, because the visual motif is executed so strongly.
Illustration by Maia Sanders.

Resources for Gathering Visual Motifs

National Geographic magazines are one of the best resources for thinking up visual motifs. The pictures and stories they do in each issue are literal gold mines for conceptual designers. You can now purchase the last 100 years of *National Geographic* on CD-ROM or DVD for around $140, which includes a search engine to help you find particular motifs.

For example, you can type in the word "Mayan" and all the issues with stories about the Mayan people come up. You can then use the pictures to make a collage in Photoshop and print color versions of the collage to have beside you while you design your characters. Due to copyright restrictions, I can't show you the collages we have created from our personal favorites in the visual motif arena.

Group your visual motif pictures into categories such as clothing, bodies/faces, architecture, art, jewelry, transportation, religion, landscape, and any other areas that seem relevant. Create collages for each of these sections. Place all the faces on one page so that you can refer to it while designing your character's face. This way, you won't have to go through page after page of collages with only one or two faces on a page. Visual patterns will be easier to spot when the pictures are grouped in specific categories.

Perhaps all the Mayan people have a strange crook on their noses or strangely shaped ears you can exaggerate in some way on your 3D character. Maybe you notice on the clothing pages that they wear a very specific shade of cobalt blue made from the dye of some local plant or something. All these details that you spot as a cultural detective will weave a history for your 3D character—even if it's an alien from another planet who walks on four feet and has a nose like an elephant.

This a wonderful character that uses the motif of a Yemen woman. A visual motif collage was first made from a *National Geographic* article and then the character went through several versions to arrive at this soulful interpretation of an ancient alien-type Yemen wise woman. Illustration by Ann Mikulka Beckman

Developing Your Own Strong Visual Motifs

What types of visual motifs are you most interested in developing for your films? Examine the following visual motif list to get a feel for the vast range of what constitutes strong visual motifs.

What are your 30 favorite visual motifs?

How can you list your favorite visual motifs and then combine them in new ways to create original visual styles for your film world?

Visual Motifs

Mayan	rave scene	Day of the Dead
Egyptian	surreal Dali	SPCA kennel
French Court 1600	Haitian voodoo	racial stereotypes
Hell's Angels	American Old West	pirate ship 1650
modern Gothic	Eskimo 1800	LA rockabilly scene
New Age hippie	tacky cruise ship	tribal African
coral reef	beehive	transvestite carnival
'80s metal bands	kiddy play school	Viking sailors
rainforest tribal	Arabian Nights	Atlantis
Viva Las Vegas	disco Detroit 1980	vampire
Hawaiian luau	Mafia 1960 NYC	Hell
psycho ward	Catholic school	Ancient Greece
medieval prison	southern hog farm	1950 beauty parlor world
Swan Lake	Hopi 1600	trashy Texas trailer park
Frank Lloyd Wright	World War II	Hare Krishna village
Australian outback	Aztec Empire	Chinese Ming dynasty
Quaker	Rasta Jamaica	Planet of the (animals)
Hasidic Jews	Charleston flappers	Disneyland
punk rock	blue-collar factory	Nazi Germany 1940
Italian Renaissance	circus freak show	genetic lab 2050
primeval forest	Florida swamp	Druid village
organic high-tech	Mardi Gras	Robert Williams paintings
futuristic NYC 3012	Texas rodeo	Japanese animation
hyper surrealistic	Utopian Nirvana	futuristic Bombay slum
comic-book style	crop circle world	1950s LA beach postcard
Kandinsky painting	blown-glass city	old painting visual style

Notice the progression of designs with the visual motif of "scary virus" throughout these drawings. This particular motif did not have much culture associated with it, but the idea of creepy, infectious, diseased, organic tissue is woven into the character design. The tentacles were voted down for being too time-consuming to animate. Illustrations by Donnie Bruce and Sam Miceli

List Your Favorite Visual Motifs. Make a list of around 20 visual motifs you would like to work on as possibilities for your film. Add a few key descriptive words to help you define the motif. You may want to keep a separate drawing book just for favorite visual motifs to refer to when designing characters. Pick motifs you are familiar with so that you can provide a deeper level of details for animation ideas. Choose a few ideas from the list that might work best for your film.

Separate Styles Within Visual Motifs

Some visual motifs have several different distinct styles, moods, time frames, groups, or locations associated with them that are important to recognize and define. Make sure you are very specific about these details surrounding your chosen motif to avoid muddling the essence. Suppose you were going to use the visual motif of a motorcycle gang for a group of 3D chickens you are animating. You already have the juxtaposition of chickens being perceived as lacking courage, so this could be interesting if you are going to make your chickens a very tough biker poultry gang. How many different types of motorcycle gangs could you list? The chickens could be a tight-knit Hell's Angels click, a violent gang of renegade ex-cock fighters, an acid rock band on bikes, or a softer group of rich urban bikers who love motorcycles but do not like to fight. Each subgroup has a very different style associated with it, which will determine your design path. Many times, just getting very specific about your visual motif avoids any confusion. You may also want to use different styles within a more general one to design contrasting groups of characters. For this example, you could have several different chicken biker groups meet up at a chicken biker bar to build conflict and play with the contrast.

Biker chickens. Notice the different visual motif subgroups of these two biker chicken designs. Even though they have the same motorcycle gang visual motif, one is very macho, whereas the other one is softer. How can you define your favorite visual motifs to be very specific with regard to subgroups? Illustrations by Maia Sanders and Sam Miceli

Get Specific About Your Visual Motifs. How can you add dates, descriptive adjectives, or group names to help clarify the particular area within a larger visual motif you want to develop? How could you use several different subgroups, within one motif, to show contrast between the 3D characters in your world?

This is a powerful and beautiful-looking 3D character that runs around in cool boots and can fly. Audiences like to see characters do things they cannot, such as fly (which could also result in some interesting camera POVs).
Illustration by Sam Miceli

Attaching an Actor to Your 3D Character

This character uses the idea of a macho-type Robert DeNiro as a ballerina with shotgun barrels for legs. What familiar ideas could you put together in a fresh way to create an original 3D character? Illustration by Sam Miceli

Most 3D characters should have a movie star type of persona attached to them in some way to help viewers understand their essence more clearly. Even if you are suffering from fear of lip sync, and have opted not to have your character speak, you still need to attach an actor's voice to play your character. Pick well-known voices from famous films if possible. Try to stay away from the more obscure TV and foreign film actors unless it is just for your own information. Refer to the Essence of the Actor list in Chapter 1, "Generating Ideas for Digital Short Films."

Design Around an Actor

You may want to design your character's facial features or body type to somehow resemble the actor you have chosen for the voice essence. This will enable the audience to more easily identify the character. Choose actors that would fit the history, visual motif, and mood of your animation.

When you hire voice actors to play the characters, they will appreciate being told that this futuristic valley girl ape is played by a Courtney Love type of voice rather than being told she sounds "cute but rebellious," which is hard to latch on to quickly from an attitude perspective.

The Barbara Walters 3D Character Interview Test

Pretend your 3D character has become so successful that Barbara Walters has requested a 20-minute interview as if it were a real creature. Use questions that will help you define the essence of your character. Listen to the types of questions journalists such as Barbara Walters ask people they interview to try and get the highest emotional response.

How would you animate your character during this interview to show what

it is about visually? Pretend your character is famous in some way that is connected with your animation idea and see what happens. You may come up with unusual questions and interview behaviors that you had not thought of when writing a straight character history, answering questions on paper. All great 3D characters should be able to hold their own in Barbara Walters's interview for 20 minutes on prime time.

If you think your character is not interesting enough, change it until it is. Study good TV interviews to see what makes a character or person fascinating enough to watch for this long in an interview format. Pay particular attention to the setting in which the interview takes place, because it should be one familiar to character's everyday life.

Attach Actor Essences to All 3D Characters. Use the actor list chart in Chapter 1 if you have problems thinking of specific people. If you have already attached an actor, make sure that actor still fits with your new ideas and design.

money-saving

Fashion 3D. The fashion industry is really into 3D clothing using programs such as Maya right now. Make friends with an up-and-coming clothing designer to dress your cast of 3D actors. We will see more of this synergy very soon in the 3D industry, much the same way designers compete to dress the stars for the Academy Awards each year. What types of deals can you swing in this area to fund your next animation project?

This character was designed around Sigourney Weaver. It is made of flesh and bone but moves like an organic motorcycle across a terrain of skin. What unusual textures could you apply to familiar objects to make us think of them in new ways? Illustration by Sam Miceli

Jeremy Irons was the voice model for this creature. How would your perception of this character change if the voice were played by Arnold Schwarzenegger? You would probably have to do some redesign to make a voice like Arnold's work. Illustration by Donnie Bruce

Write a 5-Minute Interview Script. Create a brief script of Barbara Walters interviewing your character to see what would make the best questions and answers for a TV interview. Imagine how the character would act and react to the loaded questions. What is the most difficult question your character would have to answer from their history or backstory? Try to make the interview relate to important events in your film.

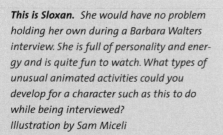

This is Sloxan. *She would have no problem holding her own during a Barbara Walters interview. She is full of personality and energy and is quite fun to watch. What types of unusual animated activities could you develop for a character such as this to do while being interviewed?*
Illustration by Sam Miceli

This solider has a very stylish-looking uniform. And that cape would be fun to animate using Maya cloth. How can you add fashionable elements to your 3D characters for more visual appeal?
Illustration by Donnie Bruce

This pirate motif 3D lady was based on Angela Lansbury. Great clothes make the woman.
Illustration by Maia Sanders

Here is a more final version of our 3D trance DJ. Notice how much he has changed from the initial sketches after more of an essence has been added. His face is still a TV screen only, but now it looks more organic to help us relate better to the character emotionally.

Designing Original 3D Sets

These bats eat hanging upside down at a typical bat dinner table scene. We all relate to dinner tables. Audiences want to see how bats behave differently during mealtimes in 3D.

All of that work you just put into designing an original 3D character will now help you design the set. When creating your 3D sets, show the audience something they have not seen before. A bedroom made of organic breathing furniture is more interesting to look at than one made from a clip-art set of the basic wooden designs we have all seen a thousand times before. If you are using premade models to save time, what ways can you switch the texture maps to make the ideas more interesting? How would basic wooden furniture feel if you upholstered it with a raw bloody-meat texture?

If you are doing a 3D biker rat story, do not put your rats in a human biker bar. Put them in a sewer rat hole with settings that feel authentic to what rats would use to decorate a biker bar, such as bottle cap stools and used tin can tables. Have them talk about what rats are concerned about, like some new sticky foot trap or poison pellets that look like cheese.

Study movies such as *Antz*, *A Bug's Life*, and *Finding Nemo*. These excellent examples show how the animals use things as props and sets that people find familiar. The bug and fish characters in these movies did not eat hamburgers and drive Ford pick-up trucks.

Anatomy Considerations for Animating

One design pitfall for 3D is creating characters that look great on paper, but may be anatomically difficult or impossible to animate well. Obvious problems such as short legs with really big feet are going to make that walk cycle a very challenging set of keyframes. Study anatomy books on animals and humans to see how they are built to move. Take an anatomy class for artists to get a good solid understanding of muscle and bone structure to apply to your 3D characters.

project
11.9

Original Set Ideas. Go through each location in your film and make sure it has a good reason to be done in 3D and is something no one has seen before. How can you use the 3D Advantage list to create better animated sets?

This prehistoric setting would make sense to do in 3D. You couldn't take a camera crew out to shoot this and it is something people have not seen much of before, which will make it more interesting. The 3D characters also fit nicely into the environment.
Illustration by Donnie Bruce

This character looks great on paper but may be challenging to animate due to the knees joined at the spoke.
Illustration by Sam Miceli

Design 3D characters using pictures of real creatures for reference. All of these bug ideas were taken from actual photographs of real bugs zoomed way up. By designing off of real creatures you also run less of a risk in having anatomy problems when animating.

This pirate motif character was designed around Samuel Jackson, as evident in the facial features. When animating this one, you may want to include some little visual tick Samuel does with his nostrils or something to make the character come alive. Illustration by Maia Sanders

Study Actors for Animation Acting Tips

Actors spend a long time developing their screen presences. One of the more challenging aspects of animating 3D characters is getting them to the point where they hold a screen as well as Elizabeth Taylor. When people say that an actor has a great screen presence, they mean that when Liz walks into the picture frame, you cannot take your eyes off of her. How can you make your 3D animated characters do this better?

Start to study actors in films and see what makes some more interesting to watch than others. A great deal of screen presence has to do with the energy of the actor. How do you translate this magical energy to your 3D character? Great animation and design are a good start, but you also need to be studying the little nuances that an actor such as Jack

Nicholson exhibits onscreen with his eyes, eyebrows, mouth, and swaggering walk that make him so electric. Pick one favorite actor a month and rent their top four films. List visual gestures as you watch each film to make note of little ticks they give to their characters to make them so appealing and original.

Acting for Animators

You should be able to act out a walk cycle for your character and may want to act out the motion for each shot. Your goal is to get something original that looks good and is going to move really nice. Most animators work with a long floor-length mirror near their station, a close-up mirror for facial animations next to their computer, and a stopwatch to time out the movements of each sequence.

Fear of Dialogue

The phrase "lip sync" can send some 3D animators into a panic attack. Use dialogue in your stories when appropriate. People glean a great deal of information about characters from their voices and how they talk. Back in the old days (just a few years ago), it was much harder to do character animation of any kind and you did not see many talking 3D characters. With new software, you can now realistically do dialogue and enrich your story lines in the process. Audiences in general respond better and identify more with characters who talk. You do want to have your characters talk all the time, because you are doing an animation, but a little dialogue goes a long way in making your story stronger.

How would you act out a walk cycle for this particular character? Get up and try to simulate the motion across the room you are sitting in. It's great to have big floor-to-ceiling mirrors in your animation studio to test out motion ideas.

Creating Your Own 3D Animation Style

The most expensive and time-consuming stylistic 3D choice is photorealism. Every detail that does not look real will scream out imperfection. What approaches could you take with your 3D animated elements to stylize them in original ways?

Hopefully, you have gathered enough ideas doing the projects in this book to inspire you to make your own digital short film. Keep in mind that a good story will be much more exciting to create, and make every step of the process as fun as possible.

project
11.10

Define Your Unique Animation Style. Use the exercises you have already done in this book to come up with a unique look that fits your story and visual motif.

"If you are not happy every morning when you get up, leave for work, or start to work at home—if you're not enthusiastic about doing that, you're not going to be successful."
—Donald M. Kendall

"Having the world's best idea will do you no good unless you act on it. People who want milk shouldn't sit on a stool in the middle of a field in hopes that a cow will back up to them."
—Curtis Grant

Index

If you like this book, you will love the workshops!

◆ Expanded brainstorming lists from many sections in the book presented in a 300+ page handout.

◆ Examples from famous films and animations exploring how the techniques in the book are used by other filmmakers.

◆ Material that did not make it into the book, from over 1,700 pages of digital story concept ideas.

◆ In-class demonstrations of production techniques from the book, and many new ones that are not found in *Developing Digital Short Films*.

◆ Go through the entire step-by-step preproduction process in one weekend using a binder with easy-to-follow questions for developing original film ideas fast.

◆ Over 100 techniques for adding humor, gags, and funny moments in your films.

◆ Over 100 techniques for adding depth to scenes.

◆ Expand your ability to think creatively through in-class exercises designed to remove blocks.

◆ Many innovative techniques for creating ideas for video games, mobile phones, and interactive media.

◆ Learn how to make money creating digital films and how to use effective marketing strategies.

◆ DVDs full of high-resolution source files from exercises in the workshops, including lots of new tutorials and clip media for digital-storytelling production techniques not found in this book.

◆ Custom-tailored workshops for your school, company, or organization.

See mindseyemedia.com for workshop topics, dates, locations, and information.

www.informit.com

YOUR GUIDE TO IT REFERENCE

New Riders has partnered with **InformIT.com** to bring technical information to your desktop. Drawing from New Riders authors and reviewers to provide additional information on topics of interest to you, **InformIT.com** provides free, in-depth information you won't find anywhere else.

Articles

Keep your edge with thousands of free articles, in-depth features, interviews, and IT reference recommendations—all written by experts you know and trust.

Online Books

Answers in an instant from **InformIT Online Books'** 600+ fully searchable online books.

POWERED BY
Safari

Catalog

Review online sample chapters, author biographies, and customer rankings and choose exactly the right book from a selection of more than 5,000 titles.

New Riders

www.newriders.com